"*The Maker's Diet* is a refreshing change in a world ful... push unsubstantiated programs, each conflicting with the other. Jordan Rubin derives his health program from the most ancient of public health texts, the Bible. Many of his recommendations have been gleaned from epidemiological studies on some of the world's healthiest people and thus are based on history and proven by modern science. I have taught these principles to patients and students for the last twenty-five years, as well as applying them in my own life. *The Maker's Diet* can serve as an important guide to those seeking to restore or preserve their health."

—PAUL A. GOLDBERG, M.P.H, D.C, D.A.C.B.N
DISTINGUISHED ADJUNCT PROFESSOR OF
GASTROENTEROLOGY, LIFE UNIVERSITY
DIRECTOR, THE GOLDBERG CLINIC

"As a race, man becomes progressively more ill despite the steady growth of the healthcare profession to a multibillion-dollar-per-year industry. And we keep searching for new things to instill health. What about going back to a time when man did truly live healthy, with recorded longevity way beyond that of modern times, and applying those tenets? This, through astounding personal experience and a wealth of knowledge, is exactly what Jordan Rubin has done and now explicitly shares with you in *The Maker's Diet*, a must-read for anyone desiring to live a healthy life!"

—MARTY GOLDSTEIN, D.V.M.
DIRECTOR, SMITH RIDGE VETERINARY CENTER
AUTHOR, *THE NATURE OF ANIMAL HEALING*

"Jordan's faith-based journey from near death to vital health bears witness to the power of pure food prepared in simple, traditional ways that reveal the true spirit of culinary and cooking experiences. Chefs everywhere, heal thyself with *The Maker's Diet!*"

—CHARLES H. HALLIDAY, PRESIDENT
FLORIDA CULINARY INSTITUTE

"*The Maker's Diet* is the answer to the many questions surrounding weight loss and health. This ancient but relevant formula for healthy living and nutritional science is just what Jordan Rubin has recommended for thousands of patients with unbelievable results. Diets come and go, but this cutting-edge program is a must for anyone who is serious about optimal weight management with a practical approach to overall health."

—TERRY LYLES, PH.D.
PERFORMANCE PSYCHOLOGIST
AUTHOR, *THE SECRET TO NAVIGATING LIFE'S STORMS*

"Jordan Rubin is a true teacher who brings to us health and nutrition wisdom uncovered from the ages. Read his books and put his wisdom into action for your own life, and you will be healthier."

—DAVID STEINMAN
PUBLISHER & EDITOR, *HEALTHY LIVING* MAGAZINE
AUTHOR, *DIET FOR A POISONED PLANET* AND *THE SAFE SHOPPER'S BIBLE*

"As a coach and trainer, I realize the importance of proper nutrition in the quest for optimum performance. Jordan Rubin's commonsense yet science-based approach to health and nutrition is clearly illustrated in *The Maker's Diet*. However, I believe the best illustration of the power of the Maker's Diet is his own triumph over a life-threatening illness. The Institute of Human Performance is proud to recommend *The Maker's Diet* to everyone from professional athletes to rehab patients."

—JUAN CARLOS SANTANA, M.ED, CSCS
STRENGTH AND CONDITIONING COACH
DIRECTOR, INSTITUTE OF HUMAN PERFORMANCE
AUTHOR, *FUNCTIONAL TRAINING, BREAKING THE BONDS OF TRADITIONALISM*

"Jordan is a man of great integrity with a real passion to help people. Not only is Jordan's story remarkable, but also his health program is absolutely outstanding and has been proven with the test of time. The Maker's Diet has helped transform my life as well as the lives of my family and many in our congregation."

—THOMAS D. MULLINS, D.MIN.
SENIOR PASTOR, PALM BEACH GARDENS CHRIST FELLOWSHIP

"Quite simply put, the Maker's Diet has transformed my family's health. The results of being on this journey with Jordan Rubin have been nothing short of amazing. If your desire is to be healthy and have optimum power in achieving a full and successful life, the Maker's Diet is for you!"

—MICHAEL NEALE
CONTEMPORARY CHRISTIAN RECORDING ARTIST

"In *The Maker's Diet*, Jordan Rubin brilliantly combines biblical wisdom, scientific knowledge, practical solutions, and his own personal life experience to guide us on a path that leads to good health. This book is fascinating and easy to read. It is a must-read for anyone who desires to live longer and healthier."

—RABBI DR. CHARLES IAN KLUGE
PRESIDENT, MESSIANIC JEWISH ALLIANCE OF AMERICA

"In a world of overprocessed, bioengineered, "convenience" foods and fad diets fraught with myths and hype, the modern American diet has proven to be headed down the wrong path. Jordan Rubin's 40-day health experience brilliantly leads us back to the original diet intended for us by our Creator. I will get this timeless and powerfully life-changing book into the hands of everyone I know."

—GINGER LEA SOUTHALL, D.C.
CHIROPRACTIC PHYSICIAN
JOURNALIST, HEALTH & MEDICAL TV CORRESPONDENT

"I want to know as much as possible to be healthier and perform optimally as a person and as a professional. With all of the diets on the market, all of the opinions, it gets really confusing. Jordan Rubin's diet makes sense! His book contains practical information on diet, exercise, and all aspects of health. *The Maker's Diet* is very user friendly and written by someone who practices what he preaches. I plan on giving copies of *The Maker's Diet* to everyone I know!"

—SCOTT SHARPE
PROFESSIONAL INDY CAR DRIVER

THE MAKER'S DIET

JORDAN S. RUBIN

SILOAM

A STRANG COMPANY

Most STRANG COMMUNICATIONS/CHARISMA HOUSE/SILOAM products are available at special quantity discounts for bulk purchase for sales promotions, premiums, fundraising, and educational needs. For details, write Strang Communications/Charisma House/Siloam, 600 Rinehart Road, Lake Mary, Florida 32746, or telephone (407) 333-0600.

THE MAKER'S DIET by Jordan S. Rubin
Published by Siloam
A Strang Company
600 Rinehart Road
Lake Mary, Florida 32746
www.siloam.com

Unless otherwise noted, all Scripture quotations are from the New King James Version of the Bible. Copyright © 1979, 1980, 1982 by Thomas Nelson, Inc., publishers. Used by permission.

Scripture quotations marked KJV are from the King James Version of the Bible.

Scripture quotations marked NIV are from the Holy Bible, New International Version. Copyright © 1973, 1978, 1984, International Bible Society. Used by permission.

Scripture quotations marked NLT are from the Holy Bible, New Living Translation, copyright © 1996. Used by permission of Tyndale House Publishers, Inc., Wheaton, IL 60189. All rights reserved.

Cover design by Koechel Peterson & Associates, Minneapolis, MN
Interior design by Terry Clifton; Author photo by Lucien Capehart

Library of Congress Cataloging-in-Publication Data
Rubin, Jordan.
   The Maker's Diet / Jordan S. Rubin.
      p.   cm.
Includes bibliographical references.
   ISBN 0-88419-948-7 (hardback); 1-59185-714-7 (paperback)   1. Nutrition—Religious aspects—Christianity. 2. Food in the Bible. I. Title.
BR115.N87R83 2004
613.2--dc22   2003022711

Neither the publisher nor the author is engaged in rendering professional advice or services to the individual reader. The ideas, procedures, and suggestions in this book are not intended as a substitute for consulting with your physician. All matters regarding your health require medical supervision. Neither the author nor the publisher shall be liable or responsible for any loss or damage allegedly arising from any information or suggestion in this book.

The recipes in this book are to be followed exactly as written. The publisher is not responsible for your specific health or allergy needs that may require medical supervision. The publisher is not responsible for any adverse reactions to the recipes contained in this book.

While the author has made every effort to provide accurate telephone numbers and Internet addresses at the time of publication, neither the publisher nor the author assumes any responsibility for errors or for changes that occur after publication.

05 06 07 08 09 — 9 8 7 6 5 4 3 2 1
PRINTED IN THE UNITED STATES OF AMERICA

I DEDICATE THIS BOOK TO THE LORD MY GOD WHO
IS MY DEFENSE, MY STRONG TOWER, MY ROCK, MY
DELIVERER, AND THE GOD THAT HEALS. I WILL
SPEND THE REST OF MY DAYS HELPING YOUR
CREATION EXPERIENCE ABUNDANT HEALTH.

M ANY PEOPLE SAY THAT WRITING A BOOK IS MUCH LIKE
having and raising a baby. It starts as a concept, then it becomes
a dream, and then it begins to feel like a chore. Later you wonder how you could ever have been entrusted with something so great,
so important. Soon you question what it will be when it is finished.
You ask yourself, "How in the world will I ever get this right? How did
I get myself into this in the first place?" No matter what goes through
your mind during the process, whenever you think about it, you feel joy,
excitement, wonder, and a huge sense of awe and responsibility.

At the writing of this book, my wife and I are expecting our first
child. Once again, I am asking some of the same questions. One thing I
know for sure, when God births something in you, an idea, a dream, or
even a child, He will take full responsibility to make it everything He
wants it to be if you will just let Him.

Many people have helped me birth and raise this book. I would first
like to thank my beautiful wife, Nicki, who made me believe that I could
do anything with God's help. I also want to thank the following:

- My mother and father, who taught me the principles of natural health and led me to a relationship
  with God
- My grandmother, who thinks everything I do is
  worthy of a Nobel prize
- My sister, Jenna, who witnessed firsthand my journey from sickness to health and prayed for me all
  the while

- Larry Walker, who helped turn this idea into a reality
- Leslie Caren, who helped craft a wonderful resource section (Appendix B)
- The team at Strang Communications, especially Stephen Strang, Dave Welday, Tom Marin, and Barbara Dycus, who believe so strongly in this project
- My Maker's Diet support team, who I believe is called by God to help make the dream of changing the world's health a reality: Robert Craven, Dana Burger, Kerry Jacobson, Jason Kombrinck, Sherry Dewberry, Scott Mawdesley, Dr. Terry Lyles, and so many more
- Two of my best friends and colleagues, Jason Dewberry and Kenny Duke, who told me seven years ago when I was just coming out of illness and living in an RV by the beach in San Diego that they wanted to be a part of my ministry—and they are
- Mike and Meredith Berkich, who have constantly encouraged me to be all that God wants me to be
- Dr. Charles Stanley, who told me that God has big plans for my life and that this message of health and hope will change the lives of millions
- Michael Neale, who helped me turn some words on a page into a great song
- Sally Fallon, whose pioneering work will change the lives of millions and whose recipes help make this a better book
- Dr. Peter Rothschild, who has taught me many things about health and gave me the name of this book
- William "Bud" Keith, who pointed me to the greatest health book of all time, the Bible

Most importantly, I want to give thanks to a loving and compassionate God who looked down from heaven, found a 100-pound, 6-foot-tall lump of clay, and fashioned me into His handiwork. May I serve You all the rest of my days.

Contents

Faith Is a Place

A song of faith and hope
by Michael Neale and Jordan Rubin

VERSE 1

This shell that I've been livin' in
Is only temporary skin
There is so much more here
Than meets the eye
Through my body's prison bars
And out beyond the painful scars
I see a light, shining where you are
In my heart I run away
Break the chains of earthly fate
I know that I'll be whole again
  someday.

CHORUS

Faith is a place that I can go
In my heart and in my soul
I believe
Faith is the rock on which I stand
When I cannot see Your hand
I still believe.

VERSE 2

Outside broken down to dust
Inside I know who to trust
I know You will meet me when I
  run to You
Life is in Your grand design
I know You're not done with mine

So I will keep on running toward
  the light
Though I do not understand
The many facets of Your plan
I realize I'm safe inside Your hand.

CHORUS

Faith is a place that I can go
In my heart and in my soul
I believe
Faith is the rock on which I stand
When I cannot see Your hand
I still believe.

BRIDGE

I know You won't leave me here
You're acquainted with my tears
Somehow I just know a brighter
  day is near.

CHORUS

Faith is a place that I can go
In my heart and in my soul
I believe
Faith is the rock on which I stand
When I cannot see Your hand
I still believe
In faith.

Foreword

JORDAN RUBIN IS ON A MISSION FROM GOD TO CHANGE THE health of this nation. When I was first presented with the manuscript for this book, I couldn't put it down. I had been praying for more than a year that God would lead me to a health plan that was based on the Bible and tested by science. *The Maker's Diet* is just that.

Jordan's journey from sickness to health is a true testament to the handiwork of a loving and compassionate God. God took Jordan through the valley, delivered him, and positioned him to impact lives across the nation. His one and only focus is to help deliver people from the bondage of sickness and disease into the promised land of health.

Our nation's health is at an all-time low. I am constantly asked to pray for people who are suffering terribly from cancer, heart disease, diabetes, arthritis, and so many other diseases. People that I love have lost their lives and many productive years to debilitating illnesses. Perhaps by following the principles outlined in this book these conditions would have been different.

I have personally been following the Maker's Diet and have noticed an immediate improvement in my own health. I have never felt better in my life. To my surprise, the food is absolutely wonderful. In fact, Jordan, his wife, Nicki, and I have shared many meals together that were both healthy and delicious. I believe that making my health a priority will allow me to fulfill my mission to preach the gospel to all the ends of the earth.

One thing that separates the Maker's Diet from all the other health programs I've read about and tried is its truly holistic approach to health. The Maker's Diet incorporates the four pillars of health—which are physical, spiritual, mental, and emotional. The physical health plan incorporates diet, nutrition, exercise, hygiene, and body therapies that emphasize the importance of living in a healthy environment. The message of spiritual health is very clear. Each of us needs to find purpose in our life. We were all created for a reason. We were created to accomplish great things. Our connection with the Creator and His supreme purpose for our lives makes every day worth living. Our mental health is vitally important. The ability to control our thought life and focus on the tasks at hand can shape who we are. Our emotional health and stability are interrelated with each of the other three pillars. We all encounter stress on a daily basis. Our circumstances are not always ideal. Stress and circumstances do not determine who we are. Our ability to handle adversity defines us. The health principles outlined in *The Maker's Diet* can provide you with the framework to achieve health physically, spiritually, mentally, and emotionally.

The Maker's Diet by Jordan Rubin has made a significant difference in my life. I urge you to pay close attention to the principles outlined in this book and share them with the ones you love.

May God bless you and your family with incredible health.

—DR. CHARLES F. STANLEY, SENIOR PASTOR
FIRST BAPTIST CHURCH, ATLANTA, GA
FOUNDER AND PRESIDENT, IN TOUCH MINISTRIES

Introduction

YOU HEAR THE ALARM SCREECHING IN YOUR EAR AS YOU PEER AT the clock, one eye barely open, in disgust. Two "snooze alarms" later, you struggle out of bed, moving slowly and feeling achy, wondering why you feel as if you haven't slept at all.

While you brush your teeth, you look in the mirror and see what must be someone else's face looking back at you. The face is tired with light wrinkling. The beginnings of a double chin are accented by dark circles underneath bloodshot eyes glaring from the mirror image.

You grab your size 16 pants and wonder how, at only age thirty-seven, you are thirty pounds heavier than when you first got married. You go to your kids' rooms, wake them up, and help them get dressed. You head to the kitchen to prepare breakfast for them, sensing a twinge of guilt that it isn't particularly healthy—but then, you are not quite sure what is healthy. There is so much conflicting information regarding health these days.

Despite your promise to yourself that you would start feeding your children healthy foods, it hasn't happened yet. Your daughter is now fifteen pounds overweight, and your younger son has ADD and asthma. You have been secretly hoping they would grow out of their health problems, but your wait continues with no improvements. Even though your doctor tells you their health problems have nothing to do with what they eat, somehow you know better.

You prepare your kids' lunches, making sure they are chock-full of "healthy" carbohydrates such as fortified bread, a fat-free cookie, and a boxed juice drink that says it's healthy (right next to the "10 percent juice" logo).

Your husband runs through the kitchen, already talking on his cell phone. He grabs a Danish and some coffee and kisses you on the cheek as he heads out the door. Looking at him, you don't feel quite as bad about the weight you've put on. He has you beat by five pounds.

You hurry your children out the door. Now it's time for *your* breakfast. You pour yourself a large coffee with nondairy creamer and artificial sweetener and spread margarine on a bagel. You remember to have some orange juice (from concentrate, of course)—the label says it contains as much calcium as a glass of milk.

Then you get a phone call. It's your mother, and she sounds upset. Her arthritis is acting up again, and she wants you to take her back to the doctor. She has been very dependent on you since your father died last year of a massive heart attack. Apparently her new medication isn't working the way the doctor said it would.

If this story sounds a lot like yours, *you are not alone.*

It seems the state of our health as a nation is worse than ever before. Today, nearly 65 percent of American adults are overweight, and almost 30 percent are obese.[1]

People born in the early twentieth century are suffering from diseases of "old age" such as osteoporosis, Alzheimer's, and dementia. They seem to spend many fruitless years of their lives being cared for in assisted living facilities with very little mental or physical function.

The baby boomers of the 1940s and 1950s are clearly the generation of widespread obesity, a health condition leading to diabetes, cancer, and heart disease. It seems that the main reason some baby boomers do not get cancer is because their lives have already been claimed by sudden heart attack.

Then there is my generation, affectionately termed "Generation X"—the first generation of young people to suffer in alarming numbers from chronic degenerative and autoimmune diseases such as multiple sclerosis, lupus, chronic fatigue syndrome, Crohn's disease, Type I diabetes, and even Parkinson's disease. The rates of infertility are staggering, causing more and more Gen-Xers to seek fertility specialists.

Considering all this bad news, it seems our very existence as a species is threatened if we don't change—and change quickly.

I wrote this book because I have some good news for you: *we can change.* We can redirect our own health destiny.

Nearly ten years ago I found myself suffering from an incurable illness. Its effective treatment escaped nearly seventy doctors. Yes, I felt hopeless. Yes, I was afraid. And yes, I felt deserted…but *I wasn't alone.* From the depths of my despair I heard a still, small voice say to me, "Everything is going to be OK."

After visiting what seemed like every doctor on the planet and trying every "miracle" drug, "miracle" diet, and "miracle" supplement, I found myself tearing through the pages of the world's oldest, most sacred, and best-selling book.

What I was looking for in the Bible was not purely spiritual. *I was looking for answers to my many debilitating health problems.* What I found was man's first health plan—and the *only* health program I will need for the rest of my life. This ancient health program literally transformed the life of a seemingly hopeless twenty-year-old, and since I first wrote about it, thousands of people have used these same principles to pull themselves out of the grip of disease and enter the promised land of health.

Read This Book If...
This book may dramatically change and improve your life if:

1. You want to avoid disease and live as healthy as possible with abundant energy and improved physical appearance.
2. You are suffering from disease, feel hopeless, and doubt if you will ever get well, and all of the specialists you have seen offer no answers.

While I make no claims to offer you a "cure-all," I believe this book was inspired by God and that the practical protocol it contains can greatly improve your health. The Maker has given me a program for vibrant health based on His Word and the best available science, in that order. The health principles on which this program is based are essentially the same—yesterday, today, and forever. (See Hebrews 13:8.) You too can enjoy the robust health and freedom from disease by simply following the health plan designed by our Creator.

Remember, the consequences of your health choices will affect many more people than yourself. You owe it to yourself and everyone you care about to return to the Maker's Diet.

Chapter 1

From Tragedy to Triumph: My Personal Journey From Sickness to Health

MOST OF US ENTER THIS WORLD WITH GREAT FANFARE, FEW problems, and no serious health problems. Unfortunately, disease catches many of us later on in life. I was an unlikely candidate for debilitating disease. My father is a naturopathic physician and a chiropractor who made every effort to help his family live the healthy lifestyle he advocated in his practice.

My mother gave birth to me at home with the assistance of four naturopathic students in Portland, Oregon, and I was given no potentially hazardous immunizations. We ate all of the "healthy foods" known at the time. When one of my friends came to our house, he said that he wished he had visited the store on the corner first to get some food he "recognized." He just wasn't too sure about rice milk, soy cheese, or tofu burgers.

I also grew up with a good understanding of the Bible because of the devotion of my parents, who attended a messianic Jewish (Jewish people who believe Jesus is the Messiah) congregation outside of Atlanta, where my family moved after my second birthday.

Throughout childhood and in high school, I was rarely ill—I took antibiotics less than five times. Since I had never been hospitalized, I had no idea what it was like to be in a hospital. I was happy, a good student, and very involved in my local messianic and church ministries.

At the age of seventeen, I went to Florida State University in Tallahassee, Florida, on an academic and athletic scholarship. My extracurricular activities included a spot on the FSU cheerleading squad, campus ministry, singing in a traveling vocal group, and serving as chaplain of my fraternity.

Shattered Dreams

Disease can arrest your fondest dreams and place your life on hold—sometimes permanently. The first signs that my health was failing were periodic feelings of extreme exhaustion, which occurred during my stint as a summer camp counselor. I had always enjoyed an abundant energy level, but I actually fell asleep while riding the bus with some of my camp kids, who kept calling, "Jordan! Wake up!" It was embarrassing to say the least, and it soon became a regular occurrence.

My energy never returned, and without warning I faced an onslaught of other health problems, including nausea, stomach cramps, painful mouth sores, and recurring diarrhea. Believing these were temporary symptoms, I committed to attending a *weeklong* overnight camp four hours from home.

Up Close and Personal With Primitive Bathrooms

Most healthy people consider it difficult to camp out in Florida's simmering summer heat, and my unending nausea made it virtually impossible. The usual "camp chow" wasn't helping. I gulped down quarts of sugary iced tea and became well acquainted with the camp's primitive outdoor bathrooms. I literally ran to the bathroom fifteen or twenty times daily; as a result, I lost *twenty* pounds in *seven* days!

I had an "iron stomach" until that time. When TV commercials played for digestive products, I used to wonder what it felt like to have heartburn or diarrhea. Suddenly I "knew the feeling." These symptoms of extreme sickness and fatigue finally forced me to abruptly leave the camp. A friend had to drive me home because I was too sick to drive myself.

To spare my mom and dad concern, I delivered an Academy Award performance to hide my illness. I didn't want them to block my return to college, scheduled for ten days later. *If I can just hang on until school starts, everything will be fine*, I thought to myself. *I just need to get back into the swing of things.* I visited a local family doctor and told him about my nausea, constant diarrhea, weight loss, "cottonmouth," and fatigue. He immediately tested for viruses (including AIDS). The tests were all negative, which made sense, considering I had never had a blood transfusion or been sexually active. Finally, the doctor prescribed antibiotics and sent me home.

Lean and Mean—but Back in School

Back at Florida State University, the severe gastrointestinal problems continued although I took the antibiotics faithfully. I tried to ignore what was happening to my body, but the symptoms forced me to discontinue my extracurricular activities. I was still active in my local college church ministry, but I quit the cheerleading squad and the fraternity, and I stopped studying for my American College of Sports Medicine exam.

I dropped to 145 pounds from my normal 180 pounds, and I felt as if I was falling apart. Each night I suffered a 104-degree fever and got little sleep between endless trips to the bathroom.

My Father's Dietary Supplements

When I finally explored the nutritional collection my father had packed for me, I found acidophilus, aloe juice, digestive enzymes, fiber supplements, and many other herbal and nutritional products. I made myself believe those products would help me get well.

That was my introduction to what I like to call the "hamster wheel of alternative medicine." Through the years of searching for ways to restore my health, I have come to believe that, while alternative medicine and dietary treatments can sometimes be better alternatives to certain medications, most diets and supplements tend to "over-promise and under-deliver."

In spite of the natural supplements I was taking, my symptoms grew worse, and I was continually hungry. Food just seemed to go right through me. I usually stuck to my "healthy" diet until my friend who worked at a sorority kitchen would bring home leftovers. That sent the diet right out the window.

I lived with seven other guys, and we never missed an opportunity to give each other a hard time. We had a central message board used for jokes, harassing messages, and sometimes "constructive and hilarious criticism" for one another. One of my best friends wrote me a message that accurately reflected my changing physical appearance: "Hey, Jordan, Pee Wee Herman called. He wants his body back!" That may sound cruel, but I laughed, determined to keep a good sense of humor.

Increased Concern

I struggled to attend classes, but I avoided telling my parents how ill I was because I didn't want to leave school. One day as I walked to my music class, my hip cracked as if it had dislocated. I started to realize that something was seriously wrong.

My gastrointestinal problems had become "systemic," which means the pain spread to my joints and other parts of my body. My hip constantly popped out of its socket. I even suffered minor dislocations getting in and out of cars.

I tried different diets along with nutritional supplements after I learned the "cottonmouth" sensation in my mouth indicated oral "thrush," which is caused by a fungus called *Candida albicans*. My father put me on the Specific Carbohydrate Diet to help alleviate the thrush and the diarrhea.[1]

Desperation and a Difficult Diet

Although the diet has reportedly helped some people relieve symptoms, it was difficult for me to follow—especially at college. Unfortunately, I didn't have the self-discipline to stay on such a rigorous diet for very long, and the Specific Carbohydrate Diet didn't relieve my symptoms.

Bathrooms became my obsession. Every life decision hinged on the question, where's the nearest bathroom? My friends stopped inviting me on long drives or to activities in isolated locations. Although I prayed constantly and kept a positive attitude as much as I could, the symptoms refused to cooperate, and relentless misery began to overwhelm me.

Dad Took One Look and...

Finally I admitted to my parents how sick I was, and they arranged a flight home for me the very next day. When I walked in, Doctor Dad took one look at me and strode into action. He took my temperature (it read 105 degrees) and put me into a bathtub packed with ice cubes. As I shivered in the ice water, confused and delirious, I didn't know what was happening, but I remember hearing my dad cry out, "My God, I don't want my son to die."

The next morning I made my *first ever* visit to a hospital, hoping to receive a "cure-all" prescription so I could get back to school. Instead, the "visit" lasted two full weeks! Depression set in as I lay in bed with intravenous fluids and antibiotics going into each arm. It didn't help that the incessant news coverage on TV was the Federal Building bombing in Oklahoma City.

My body was so overridden by infection that inflammation had set in. Doctors prescribed two highly toxic intravenous steroid medications and put me through every test imaginable. I received more x-rays in two weeks than most people receive in a lifetime. The radiologists scanned my upper and lower gastrointestinal tracts; I felt as if they conducted deluxe tours of my gut with a full-sized TV camera!

The results weren't encouraging. The doctor diagnosed Crohn's disease (actually, it was Crohn's colitis), an abnormal inflammation of the small bowel and colon that causes the intestinal wall to thicken. As this disease progresses, eventually the bowel channel narrows and blocks the intestinal tract, robbing it of its ability to absorb nutrients.

One of the "Chosen Few"—Victims

As an added complication, I also had marked duodenitis, an inflammation of the duodenum (the first part of the small intestine) that afflicts less than 1 percent of Crohn's disease patients. As a result, *I was literally starving to death*, so I was put on "total parenteral nutrition" (TPN) to put nutrients directly into my bloodstream.

Infection and pain raged through my body while emotional chaos gripped my mind as I tried to cope with this *incurable* diagnosis of Crohn's disease. Little did I know that my nightmare was just beginning.

My doctor said I could expect to live a "normal life," except for the lifelong need for medication and "a few surgeries." I would be able to father children, but only if I "switched medications" during the process of conception.

Facing the Facts

Though I was not familiar with Crohn's disease, I soon learned that, according to the disease's pattern, my future looked bleak. Crohn's victims experience progressive symptoms of abdominal pain, diarrhea, extreme weight loss, and perhaps premature death. I was told that medications would keep me alive, but I quickly discovered that their side effects were nearly as bad as the disease itself. Science knew of no cause or cure for Crohn's at the time, and my prognosis was very poor.

Dr. Burrill Crohn discovered Crohn's disease in the early 1900s; one of the most famous persons to be diagnosed with the disease was former President Dwight Eisenhower. No one knows for sure, but doctors estimate between 400,000 to 1,000,000 people suffer from Crohn's disease, with 20,000 or more new cases each year. At this writing, diagnoses of inflammatory bowel disease (Crohn's disease and ulcerative colitis) have increased dramatically—less than a decade after my diagnosis. According to some literature, an incredible 85 percent of Americans have suffered from some kind of digestive problem. About two out of every ten Americans have been diagnosed with irritable bowel syndrome, the sales of heartburn medications are booming, and some experts predict Crohn's disease may eventually surpass ulcers as the number one digestive problem in the United States.[2]

Embarrassed by my symptoms, I simply told my friends I was sick and avoided details. I desperately hoped to return to school. Naively, I thought the doctor's "magic bullet" prescriptions would make me well, but health by medication wasn't working. I graduated from intravenous drugs in the hospital to oral medications such as prednisone at home. The first day I took the oral form of prednisone at home, the steroid triggered hallucinations and I began crying uncontrollably. (I also took mesalamine for ulcerative colitis and the antimicrobials Flagyl and Diflucan for the chronic thrush.)

For good measure, the doctors also put me on ciprofloxacin (Cipro), the drug of choice for nonspecific bacterial infections. I topped off this medical cocktail with regular doses of Zantac for the searing heartburn caused by the other medications!

Nighttime Became My Worst Nightmare

Despite all the medications, my condition failed to improve. I still rushed to the bathroom up to thirty times a day. Most of my stools were now bloody, and the severity of the cramps made me want to pull my hair out or bang my head against the wall. But if my days were rough, my nights were worse.

The persistent nocturnal diarrhea produced chronic sleep deprivation. My bathroom visits continued 24/7, occurring every forty-five minutes to an hour. Only rarely did I get more than an hour of unbroken sleep per night. For more than a year, I existed in a state of fatigue and exhaustion—and for good reason. I had an almost unheard of serum iron level of 0 despite my daily iron injections.

Iron is an essential component of hemoglobin, the oxygen-carrying protein in the blood. My low serum levels of albumin indicated I was suffering from a severe wasting disease (cachexia) as well as low immunity and rapid deterioration of all body tissues. My body just wasn't absorbing nutrition, which contributed to my starvation!

Creating More Problems!

My digestive system wasn't absorbing nutrients, a condition called "malabsorption syndrome." And so many toxic drugs were prescribed that their chemical interactions created even more problems than my disease. Taken together, it was quite a shock for a nineteen-year-old who had never been hospitalized before.

Like so many Americans, I did not understand how important the gastrointestinal tract or gut is for optimum health. The gastrointestinal system is an engineering marvel and a creative wonder. It is home to a host of bacteria and other microorganisms, some that are good for the body and some that are pathogenic or "bad."

Scientific and medical research has shown that a proper balance between these intestinal bacteria is key to long-term health. Unfortunately, the modern American diet is literally a candy store for the bad bacteria in the human gut. These bad bacteria love the same sugars, high-carbohydrates, and refined foods that we do.

The final blow to my health was caused by this bacterial imbalance in my digestive system (*dysbiosis*), which led to the breakdown of my body's immune barrier.

A Walking Medical Encyclopedia

Cutting-edge medical researchers now believe that life and death begin in the digestive tract. If your digestive system breaks down, you will likely encounter a host of seemingly unrelated but debilitating illnesses. In the following chart I have listed the disease conditions that were working in my body, with the hope that if you see yourself or a loved one in this profile, you will take courage that your health can be restored as mine has been.

MY PERSONAL DISEASE PROFILE

- *Chronic candidiasis* (or yeast overgrowth): I had the highest level possible.
- *Entamoeba histolytica*, a parasite that causes amebic dysentery
- *Cryptosporidiosis,* a protozoan infection that causes severe intestinal illness
- *Incipient diabetes* (with extremely poor circulation): My lower leg was purple.
- *Jaundice* (besides other liver and gallbladder problems)
- *Insomnia*
- *Hair loss*
- *Endocarditis,* a heart infection
- *Eye inflammation*

- *Prostate and bladder infections*
- *Extreme anemia:* My serum ferritin [iron] level was 0 for over twelve consecutive months.
- *Chronic electrolyte imbalance* due to dehydration
- *Elevated C-reactive protein* indicates chronic inflammation and bacterial infection, pointing to increased risk of heart attack and stroke.
- *Anemia* indicates a shortage of red blood cells in the bloodstream. Only red blood cells carry oxygen to muscle tissues and organs.
- *Chronic fatigue* is a mysterious ailment that includes symptoms of unceasing fatigue, headaches, weakness, aching muscles and joints, and the inability to concentrate.
- *Arthritis* is marked by joint inflammation, stiffness, and pain. My immune system was mistakenly attacking itself. (Crohn's disease is thought by some to be autoimmune in origin. Perhaps my body had begun attacking my own joints.)
- *Leukocytosis* is an abnormal increase in white blood cells—especially immature cells.
- *Malabsorption syndrome*: My body was unable to absorb sufficient nutrients from food, so no matter how much I ate, I was still starving.

Things just got worse despite the treatments I had received in the hospital. I wasn't able to participate in any of life's activities. I was used to being the ringleader who gathered people together. Instead, now I told my friends, "No, I can't come." "No, I really can't do that." I felt bad for my friends who called and wanted to visit. I felt I was disappointing them, along with my parents, my sister, and my grandparents. They were all suffering as a result of my illness, and realizing that filled me with feelings of guilt.

FAMILY MEMBERS SUFFER, TOO

"Where is my brother?"

"Oh, he's in the nurse's office. He's not feeling well. His stomach is bothering him."

The summer camp had *just begun*. How could Jordan get hit with a stomach virus this quickly? He was a counselor at the camp, and I was just entering my teens. I rarely

FAMILY MEMBERS SUFFER, TOO

saw him because he spent so much time at the nurses' office.

He was really sick. I was upset over the whole thing, but no one knew any details about his symptoms. In the end, Jordan had to go home early, leaving me behind at the camp.

Entering camp, Jordan looked very healthy. He was still really muscular, though he had gained some extra weight from eating junk food while away at college. By the end of the six days of camp, he had lost nearly twenty pounds. Things got even worse after my brother returned for his second year at college. He got so sick that he had to come home.

I was already in a rebellious stage, but the combination of worry over Jordan and the big *change* in our lives triggered some hidden anger in me. I loved Jordan, and I was really concerned about his health, but I came to the point where I couldn't believe he would ever get better.

Jordan didn't mean to do it, but his sickness essentially *took my mother from me*. She was always with him trying to find another cure or another doctor somewhere. All of us felt the anger and frustration of our *helplessness*.

As Jordan became sicker and more emaciated, people were more uncomfortable being around him. Yet, even in that difficult time, Jordan was still my brother, and he still had faith that God would one day heal him. In a way, he had become a second father figure for me, too. When I had problems with boyfriends or relationships, Jordan wanted desperately to be my "big brother," but he couldn't do anything. I still remember him telling me over and over again how helpless he felt. He looked like a twig, and all of his hair was coming out. To my young mind it was horrible.

One thing I'll always remember is the time Jordan blacked out in the kitchen and fell face forward toward the floor. I somehow caught him just inches before he cracked his head open. That was only months before he decided to go to California to work with a man who claimed his Bible-based diet would help him. At that point, he was wheelchair bound.

After only three months into his program, when Mom and I flew to California to see him, he actually met us outside the airport and stood up on his own! We were so excited!

FAMILY MEMBERS SUFFER, TOO

He was still thin, and you could tell that he wasn't perfectly healthy—but he was getting better! His hair was still thin and weird looking, but it was starting to grow back.

There are two things I remember the most about that meeting. First, Jordan's attitude was really *positive* (that was missing in the months just before he left for California). And second was something that happened at the beach near Jordan's mobile home: he insisted on picking me up! Then he playfully tried to pick Mom up, too. We have pictures of it all. That was when I knew Jordan's strength was definitely coming back. He was so different from the last time I'd seen him when his arms were frail and he couldn't even speak! Now, we were all filled with hope.

—JENNA RUBIN

Self-centeredness comes easy when you suffer from disease, but it also bothered me to think that I was disappointing others. I tried to keep a positive attitude with my friends, but it is hard to express joy when pain continually pierces your stomach and joints. I can only describe my situation as experiencing the pain of a twenty-four-hour stomach virus or a bad case of food poisoning *day and night* for *two years*.

Though I held to my faith that God would heal me, I was desperate enough to try anything. I grasped at every piece of health literature or booklet "just in case" they contained the answers to my problem. According to all of the information I was reading, my body's healing response had been "turned off" or compromised in some way. My hope was that perhaps some natural method would help reactivate it.

Once I was discharged from the hospital, I joined my father in the search for natural pathways to renewed health. I tried *everything*. Regaining my health became our obsession. Ultimately, our search took me to seventy health practitioners from seven different countries, including medical doctors, naturopaths, chiropractors, immunologists, acupuncturists, homeopaths, herbalists, colon therapists, nutritionists, and dieticians.

Pinpointing the Probable Culprit

Only God knows *why* I got sick, but I have isolated a few key contributors to the situation. As I mentioned, I was fortunate not to receive childhood vaccinations, which create inherent health risks. However, the local school district forced me to receive the MMR (measles, mumps, and rubella) vaccine at the age of fifteen due to a supposed epidemic.

This vaccine has now been implicated in digestive disorders, including Crohn's disease, and in developmental disorders such as autism. Although my symptoms didn't appear for nearly four years after the vaccination, there *seems* to be a causal relationship.

The most probable culprit, however, I believe was my changed diet and lifestyle in college. College life brought a whole new stress level to my existence as well—much of it generated by my own overcommitment of time. And in my quest for athletic supremacy, I adopted a diet that was very high in carbohydrates (mostly from processed grains, dairy, and sugar) and dangerously low in fat and protein. The hard truth is that my college diet was tailor-made for inducing the symptoms of most diseases—especially digestive illnesses.

One More Try

Despite my disappointing experience with the Specific Carbohydrate Diet, I still believed that it would help me if I *stayed on it* without deviations. So I tried it one more time.

I even consulted daily on the phone with Elaine Gottschall, author of *Breaking the Vicious Cycle* (Kirkton Press, 1994). She had worked with a physician, Dr. Haas, to heal her own daughter of ulcerative colitis, a disease very similar to Crohn's disease. However, despite my fanatical adherence to the Specific Carbohydrate Diet for three to six months on three different occasions, it didn't work for me.

That led to personal consultations with some of the foremost practitioners and diet experts in the world. (I must have tried almost every diet ever promoted in print.) I was a patient of the late Dr. Robert Atkins, author of *The Atkins Diet*. I also met with California-based "eicosanoid" guru Barry Sears, Ph.D., author of *The Zone*. Then I consulted with Jeffrey Bland, Ph.D., a highly regarded functional medicine expert and went through several rounds of his detoxification/elimination diet.

Nothing worked. These health professionals were extremely knowledgeable, highly educated, and very sincere about wanting to help me. Each of these diets has many solid underpinnings—yet something was missing that I needed.

During our search of over two years, my father spent approximately $150,000 on natural health treatments for me, including thirty probiotic formulas, countless enzymes, fiber, anticandida and antiparasitic formulas, and numerous immune-boosting and detoxification products.

Willing to Try Anything and Everything

Why did I put myself through such difficult and expensive regimens? I wanted to get better and end the pain. Someone said my liver was the problem, so I decided to detoxify my liver. One "health expert" said he had cured 250 patients with Crohn's disease in the United Kingdom, so I agreed to undergo cell therapy with injectable sheep cells taken from embryos. The needles were huge, but, predictably, the results were nonexistent. I also tried retention enemas, colonics, and even more liver detoxification plans.

I tried "glandulars," or glandular and organ extracts taken from the dried tissues of every conceivable animal organ and gland. I even took adrenal cortical extract, or ACE, an extract of bovine adrenal glands thought to possess the powers of hydrocortisone (once used extensively in medicine).

For nearly a year, I injected myself *seven times a day* with injectable vitamins and minerals using a small needle reserved for insulin injections. I had become so emaciated that when I injected myself in the shoulders and the sides of my hips, I could feel the needle hitting bone.

Got Any Cabbage Juice and Shark Cartilage?

I read that cabbage juice was good for the gut and rich in organic sulfur compounds, so I consumed large amounts of cabbage juice. I did the same with wheat grass juice, Chinese and Peruvian herbs, Japanese kampo, olive leaf extract, and shark cartilage. I tried the macrobiotic diet, the raw food vegan diet, and nitrogenated soy as well.

My desperate hunt for a cure drove me to travel to clinics in Europe, South America, Mexico, and Canada—often in a wheelchair. Without exception, the doctors and health practitioners who treated me characterized my appearance as that of a "concentration camp victim." Despite fragile health, I endured the perils of travel to visit alternative cancer clinics in Mexico and Germany, returning in worse condition than when I left.

Through it all, I drew strength from my faith in God's love for me. I was difficult to live with and at times my hope was dim, but God remained faithful. The psalmist David expressed my pain and revived my hope during daily readings from Psalm 31:

In thee, O LORD, do I put my trust....Bow down thine ear to me; deliver me speedily....I will be glad and rejoice in thy mercy: for thou hast considered my trouble....Have mercy upon me, O LORD, for *I am in trouble*: mine eye is consumed with grief, yea, my soul *and my belly*. For my life is spent with grief, and my years with sighing: *my strength faileth* because of mine iniquity, and *my bones are consumed*....I am forgotten *as a dead man out of mind*....But I trusted in thee, O LORD: I said, Thou art my God. *My times are in thy hand.* ...Make thy face to shine upon thy servant: save me for thy mercies' sake.

—PSALM 31:1–2, 7, 9–10, 12, 14–16, KJV,
EMPHASIS ADDED

False Data Supplied by Scientists for Hire

As I grew more frantic, I tried almost five hundred different "miracle" products (including two or three treatments no rational person would consider). *I know what it is like to be desperate.* I became the *victim*—I choose that word carefully—of many network marketers and mass distributors of health products who made outrageous and unfounded claims with little, if any, scientific substance.

My dad scoured health magazines and called colleagues around the world searching for clinics and therapies that might help. The many machines I hooked up to my body could fill a science fiction novel!

Weird Science From the Outer Reaches of Alternative Health

Some of the practitioners I visited performed various forms of electro-dermal screening (EDS), a method of computerized information gathering based on physics and acupuncture meridians. After one doctor probed me with his EDS machine, he said my illness was due to electromagnetic fields in my house. So I slept in a steel cage placed around my bed. At night I was instructed to shut off the TV and clocks—all electrical devices. (No, it didn't work.) The next EDS practitioner told me that I was having an adverse reaction from a satellite that orbits the earth every seven years. This is what I call weird science from the outer reaches of the alternative health field.

I tried applied kinesiology, a type of chiropractic where different tests for muscle strength and weakness are done on points of your body. I also utilized acupuncture and homeopathy, without relief.

Taking various medications and supplements was my life. When I wasn't visiting a doctor several times a week, I stayed at home in my chair and fantasized while watching cooking shows. (I felt a special bond with Chef Emeril.)

I used all of my spare time puzzling over what products to use and what might help me, and I devoured more than three hundred health and nutrition books. I would locate well-known authors and arrange personal consultations, refusing to meet with anyone but the best.

'Til There Was You

Most of the doctors and practitioners I visited said they could cure me in a short period of time. One after another assured me they had never failed to cure their patients, but they made promises they couldn't keep. Their claims to healing weren't totally unfounded—most of them had *anecdotal* evidence based on patient testimony.

As with so many others who are desperately ill, I was willing to believe and put my faith in them. My frequent bladder and eye infections made it extremely unsettling to travel, but I did it anyway in hope of finding a cure.

One time, while waiting for an airplane to take off, I calmly said to myself, "If this plane went down, it wouldn't be that bad." That was my mental state during the darkest days of my desperate journey. I was not suicidal, but I felt so hopeless. I just couldn't handle the pain anymore. I wasn't actively seeking death, but I reasoned that if I died, at least I could join my Creator and be pain free. Again, it was the psalmist who perfectly expressed my feelings at that point:

> I am troubled; I am bowed down greatly; I go mourning all the day long. For my loins are filled with a loathsome disease: and there is no soundness in my flesh. I am feeble and sore broken: I have roared by reason of the disquietness of my heart....My heart panteth, my strength faileth me: as for the light of mine eyes, it also is gone from me....For in thee, O LORD, do I hope: thou wilt hear, O Lord my God.
> —PSALM 38:6–8, 10, 15, KJV

A last ray of hope drew me to Germany to receive an experimental drug made from the juices of the Venus flytrap plant. (At that time the U.S. Food and Drug Administration did not permit this herbal substance to be imported.)

My Big Fat German Nightmare

My mother accompanied me to Germany. It was a twenty-eight-hour nightmare involving numerous planes and trains. We missed one train because my mom and I couldn't drag our luggage fast enough during a layover; we waited six hours for another. (I used the time locating and frequently visiting the bathroom.) Shortly after arriving in Germany, I was told to discontinue my medications (including prednisone, which I had been taking for over a year). I suffered some devastating withdrawal symptoms, including an inability to catch my breath for three days.

The German medical doctor concluded that my problem rested with my immune system—certain parts were overactive, and others were underactive. I stayed alone in the clinic for six long weeks after financial pressures from my medical bills forced my mother to return to her job as a schoolteacher in the U.S. The therapy produced no positive results; it only left me in the hands of sadly inattentive doctors and nurses.

Mental Problem or Doctor Problem?

Finally the doctor at that clinic egotistically announced that I wasn't getting well because I had "mental problems."

I was a nineteen-year-old who had been forced by illness to drop out of college and abandon my dreams. Thousands of miles and the Atlantic Ocean separated me from family and friends. I was trapped in a German health clinic where no one spoke English; the ceiling of my room was less than five feet high (*ouch!*), and most of the people assigned to care for me seemed to view me more as a nuisance than as a patient. Considering that combination, I suppose it could produce some mental problems in anyone.

Miserable and in constant pain, I felt as if I were imprisoned in my own body. A cloud of despair covered me. Would I ever enjoy a "normal" life again? Would I ever sleep through the night or wake up without pain? Would I ever be healthy again?

It was time to go home, but soon I discovered that making the trip was easier said than done. With great difficulty, I made the trip alone in a cab to the airport with my luggage.

Stranded in Germany

Too weak to walk unassisted on my own, I had to be wheeled into the airport. None of the airline employees at the ticket counter understood

English, and they couldn't find any record of my ticket. I tried to purchase another ticket with my credit card, but it was declined.

That did it. My life seemed to spiral out of control right in front of the ticket counter, complicated by a painful urinary tract infection and pinkeye in both eyes, along with my chronic bowel problems. It appeared I wouldn't get home.

In extreme desperation I quickly prayed: "Lord, I cannot do a single thing. I am putting my life in Your hands. Please help me get out of this situation. I feel completely hopeless." Within minutes my ticket was found, and I boarded the plane. Though I missed my connecting flight, I finally made it home after a thirty-hour ordeal. I cannot describe how relieved I was to be home.

Shortly afterward, I was hospitalized a second time, completely dehydrated with a resting heart rate of 200–260 beats per minute. I couldn't even keep water down, and I weighed only 104 pounds.

"He Won't Make It Through the Night"

My veins were so dry and tapped out that it took a team of nurses and doctors two and one-half hours to insert my IV! I heard one of the nurses say, "That poor boy isn't going to make it through the night."

Hopelessness flooded my being, and all I could do was pray. At that point I was ready to go home and be with my Creator. Though I felt I had lived an incredible life for my young age, I was disappointed that I had never fallen in love and gotten married. In spite of my pain, I thanked my Creator for a wonderful life, committed myself into His hands, and prepared to die.

I finally drifted off into a fitful sleep and awoke to see my grandmother leaning over me with her hand on my forehead. Several nurses entered to announce that they had managed to get a blood return and could hook me up to an IV. I gained ten pounds of water weight in one night and felt a new resolve in my body. (Most normal people would have been in shock.)

I wanted to live, and at last I felt a glimmer of real hope—until the doctors prescribed the same medications I had been given during my first hospital stay. Again I became a human drugstore filled with antibiotics, antifungals, antiparasitics, heartburn medications, and prednisone. When I finally left the hospital and the doctors again switched me from intravenous to oral medications, this once again led to hallucinations. In the words of baseball's Yogi Berra, "It was déjà vu all over again."

Who Would Commemorate Such a Pathetic Sight?

In spite of the hallucinations, I managed to tell my mom, "I want you to take a picture of me." My unusual request completely startled her.

Despite everything I had been through, including hundreds of unfulfilled promises by doctors and health practitioners, I still clung to the hope that God would deliver me.

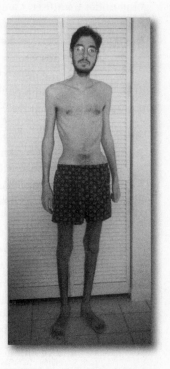

I remember the question my mother asked me: "Why in the world do you want me to take a picture of you?" With all the courage I could muster I softly replied, "Because no one will believe me when I get well. No one will ever believe that I was this sick. I'm getting out of bed, and I need you to take my picture."

I nearly fell in the process, and I needed help to stand up, but we got the picture. All of my options seemed to be exhausted the day my mother snapped that photo. I had a beard at the time only because I was too weak to shave and couldn't afford to cut myself with my unsteady hand.

Two Terrible Choices

The day we shot that picture, I weighed a whopping 111 pounds, but my skin—and my future—still looked dead. One doctor told me that my only hope was to go to Mount Sinai Hospital in New York City for the removal of my large intestines and part of my small intestines. The only other alternative was the "J-Pouch procedure," at the time an experimental procedure to preserve bowel function after a colectomy (the surgical removal of the colon).

Faced with two terrible choices balanced against death or a lifetime of unrelenting pain, I reluctantly decided with my family to go to Mount Sinai and get whatever surgery I needed. My primary physician literally called my condition "the worst case of Crohn's disease" he had ever seen. He doubted I would live long enough to return home.

That revelation forced me to reexamine my "options." The multiple medications I was prescribed only made me feel worse. Yet there was a chance their ill effects might be reversed. The problem with surgery is that it is *permanent*. I had only a little bit of fight left, but I knew I wasn't going under a knife.

FROM PEE WEE HERMAN TO BEST MAN

"Hey, Jordan, Pee-wee Herman called. He wants his body back!"

When I wrote this quip on our "community message board," none of us who lived with Jordan knew how close he would come to death over the next year.

As one of Jordan's closest friends, I literally witnessed from a front-row seat his painful destruction and miraculous reconstruction. I am one of the friends who used to rummage through the Rubin's nutritionally correct kitchen in bewilderment—even to this day I *still* don't know how you get milk from rice.

I watched Jordan struggle with this mysterious sickness, and I saw this extremely active and athletic guy begin to wear down in unexplained exhaustion and lose his zest for life. As Jordan's condition started to progress further, I became unusually alarmed.

Jordan embodied what I thought to be the ultimate health-conscious person with a basically healthy diet, plenty of exercise, a clean lifestyle, and a positive attitude. Throughout his entire high school and brief college life, he didn't consume a single alcoholic beverage or recreational drug, and he practiced sexual abstinence due to his spiritual beliefs. To see him literally waste away before my eyes was very, very difficult.

We had been very involved in activities at church together, and I became the main contact with friends for updates on Jordan's condition. After a long period of trying to dispense hope to them, I found it hard to give any good news—because there just wasn't any.

My best friend was wasting away and dying, and there was nothing anyone could do about it. Some days I would wake up crying, thinking to myself, *This is it. I'm going to lose my best friend.*

One Thanksgiving holiday in the middle of Jordan's darkest time, I decided to read a letter at church that he had written to me in which he declared his healing *by faith*. He quoted me a powerful Bible verse from Hebrews 11:1:

"Faith is the substance of things hoped for, the evidence of things not seen." Jordan believed that true faith could only be proclaimed during the midst of the storm, not in retrospect. Then I performed a song by Steven Curtis Chapman, one of Jordan's favorite artists. I felt that God had really used me to communicate a message to people about faith and friendship.

Things got so bad that one time when I walked into his house and saw him in such an emaciated state, I almost threw up—not out of revulsion but out of *fear.* "How can this person still be alive?" I asked myself. "His leg is thinner than my wrist!"

I felt an intense, gripping, emotional fear over the fact that this person who has so much to give, whose love is so infectious, was sitting in front of me looking as if he had just been liberated from a concentration camp.

Even though it was difficult to be around him because of my grief, I wouldn't leave his side. There were times when Jordan would ask the *why* questions, but 90 percent of the time he was saying, "I'm going to keep my faith. When I get through this, when God heals me, He is going to use me to accomplish great things. I know He has a plan for my life." One of Jordan's favorite Bible verses was Jeremiah 29:11: "'For I know the plans I have for you,' declares the LORD, 'plans to prosper you and not to harm you, plans to give you hope and a future'" (NIV).

I just couldn't understand that. I had to come full circle and witness everything that happened in his life to see that Jordan was right. He had a genuine vision from God, and he knew he would be in front of people one day telling his story.

When Jordan went to California, he asked me to come and help. That "after" picture of Jordan, which has now been seen by millions of people, was taken at Pacific Beach in San Diego, in front of Crystal Pier. Every morning after we drove to Boney's (a health food store) to get raw kefir and raw cheeses, we parked our RV only fifty yards away from Crystal Pier. We would have cheeseburgers for breakfast— you know, *organic* cheeseburgers with whole-grain buns. He was thrilled to have some semblance of his life back, and I was thrilled to have my old friend back.

I was with him the night that he proposed to his wife,

Nicki, and I was the best man in his wedding. Now I have the opportunity to partner with him, sharing the message of hope to those in need. I have witnessed firsthand what God can do in one man's life when that person is yielded to His will.

—JASON DEWBERRY

A Final Ray of Hope

My father extended one last ray of hope to me after I wheeled out of the hospital early in 1996. He contacted an eccentric nutritionist and decided to personally investigate this man's program so that he could avoid getting my hopes up prematurely.

The nutritionist said he believed I was ill because I was not eating *the diet of the Bible.* He based the failure of the doctors who treated me on the fact that they did not base their treatments upon biblical principles.

It made me curious, and I agreed to try his diet. After one day on the program, I smiled for what seemed to be the first time in nearly two years and said, "Mom, I'm going to get well." I had decided to ditch the idea of surgery and give the Bible diet a try—what did I have to lose?

Starting all over again, I stopped taking all nutritional products. Instead, I began to study the Bible to see what people ate thousands of years ago. My studies uncovered an interesting fact: the longest-lived cultures in the world had a few things in common—they consumed "living" foods that *abounded with nutrients, enzymes, and beneficial microorganisms.* And they consumed healthy animal foods that were rich in nutrients. They avoided processed foods filled with "empty" calories that robbed nutrients from the body.

Several weeks later I flew to Southern California (still in my wheelchair) to live closer to the man who would teach me how to eat "God's way." For the first time in my long battle, I saw some improvement in my health after integrating the nutritionist's program with my own findings about nutrition and health from the Bible.

"MOM, I'M GOING TO GET WELL"

No mother should have to see her vibrant, athletic, college-age son fitted for a wheelchair, *but I did.* At 6 feet 1 inch and 180 pounds, Jordan was in incredible shape and on fire for God. He was full of energy and loved life— then he got very sick. After a series of antibiotics, Jordan went back to college weighing 150 pounds. Before long,

"MOM, I'M GOING TO GET WELL"

he showed up at our door weighing only 135 pounds with a 105-degree fever!

My husband and I looked at Jordan and thought, *My goodness, what is wrong with our son?* He wasn't the same person. He could barely walk, and many times he'd faint just walking to the bathroom. No one was able to diagnose Jordan until we found a doctor familiar with his symptoms. He looked at Jordan and immediately said, "Your son has Crohn's disease."

Jordan's health went downhill from there. He progressively got sicker and lost more weight, and his hair began falling out. It was a mother's worst nightmare. We tried many doctors, drugs, and natural therapies; nothing seemed to work. I remember when Jordan had his first upper GI series. As he walked to the X-ray room looking like a very sick old man, he fainted and fell to the floor.

Later, toward the end when we really thought we might lose him, Jordan asked me to take his picture. It was hard to even look at him much less take a picture of him. I wanted to tell him, "Don't wear shorts." It hurt me to see his bony legs and joints—he was just skin and bones. A few of my friends told me, "You have to let him go."

I'm not a negative person, but it was hard to watch my effervescent son have the life sucked out of him. I just cried my eyes out and kept praying for a miracle. I remember weeping all the way back from Germany and praying, "Take care of my son; he's in Your hands. I give him to You, Lord. I have no other choice." It was one of the most difficult and *greatest* things I've ever done.

It was just a few months later that Jordan tried a primitive version of what he now calls *The Maker's Diet* for one week. I will never forget the day he smiled and told me, "Mom, I'm going to get well!" This was the first time I remember Jordan smiling in over a year. On that momentous day Jordan was right—and God was faithful!

—PHYLLIS RUBIN

A Bag of Black Powder

Ten months after I stopped taking all supplements, my father decided to send me *a plastic bag containing a black-colored powder*. (Although he had promised not to send me any other nutritional products, he couldn't help himself.) He said it was a special type of probiotic or friendly bacteria. Unfortunately, I had already tried thirty different varieties of probiotics with no success. How would this be any different?

How could my father expect me to eat this? It looked like dirt! Dad called to encourage me, saying, "It may look like dirt, but it isn't. It contains healthy compounds from the soil."

An article enclosed with the package explained that these nutrients are missing from today's pesticide-sterilized, barren soils. It claimed that the contents of the bag contained far more than trace minerals—it contained vital *organisms* (later called *homeostatic soil organisms*, or HSOs).

These friendly microorganisms have been largely wiped out by the pesticides, herbicides, fungicides, and synthetic fertilizers used on America's farm lands, by pasteurization, and by modern man's disdain for all microorganisms (even those life-supportive "bugs" or microscopic organisms our bodies need for maximum health). After trying well over three hundred different "miracle" nutritional products, I was understandably jaded. But for some reason this black "powder" was different. All of the health research that I had read up to that point validated the fact that our soil is extremely deficient. Deficient soil leads to deficient bodies.

I Added the Black Powder to My Diet

Having nothing to lose, I decided to include the odd-looking dirt organisms in my daily diet. My "biblical" diet consisted of kefir—"naturally fermented milk" from raw goat's and cow's milk; organically raised, free-range, or grass-fed meats; and eggs and meat from healthy chickens. It also included ocean-caught wild fish and natural sprouted or sourdough breads made from yeast-free whole grains, as well as raw nuts and seeds, organic fruits and vegetables, raw sauerkraut, and carrot and other vegetable juices. These "live" foods were filled with beneficial enzymes, vitamins, minerals, and friendly microorganisms.

My health didn't reappear magically in one day; it takes time to overcome years of illness. I actually felt a little *worse* for the first thirty days as my body purged itself of toxins. The nausea increased slightly, my digestion got a little worse, and my energy levels dropped lower than usual.

I was experiencing a *Herxheimer reaction*, or the "die-off" effect that many people experience when they dramatically improve their diet and lifestyles. It is an allergic response to the toxic by-products produced when the body's pH is changed for the better, causing large numbers of pathological organisms, such as harmful bacteria and yeast organisms, to die and exit the body.

The collective effect of this reaction is a temporary worsening of symptoms. In reality, it is indicating that you are responding positively to treatment. Significant improvement should follow this initial detoxification reaction.

Since the time of Hippocrates, it has been understood that the *symptoms* of most diseases represent the efforts of the body to eliminate toxins. Gradually for me, a newfound energy emerged, and I visited the bathroom less frequently. One month after I added the "black powder" to my diet, I noticed a marked improvement in my overall health.

Becoming Something of a Bum

My father purchased a used motor home for me so I could stay close to the beach and breathe the ocean air. I became something of a bum for forty days and nights as I tried to find places to park at night where I wouldn't be arrested or fined. It was an unusual experience for a kid from the suburbs.

Different people came to help me, and I spent each day praying, listening to music, and planning the preparation of my daily "medicine"—food. Amazingly, after my two brutal years of suffering I gained twenty-nine pounds during those forty days, reaching an incredible (for me) weight of 151 pounds!

On my twenty-first birthday, we took an "after" photograph on the beach—four months after I arrived in California. I wasn't completely well at that point, but I was on my way to full recovery. I weighed 170 pounds and felt like the happiest man in the world.

Psalm 30, which I had prayed for so long, was coming to pass. I encourage you to read the entire psalm, but I am including some important verses here:

> I will extol thee, O LORD; for thou hast lifted me up, and hast not made my foes to rejoice over me. O LORD my God, I cried unto thee, and thou hast healed me. O LORD, thou hast brought up my soul from the grave: thou hast kept me alive, that I should not go down to the pit....Thou hast turned for me my mourning into dancing: thou hast put off my sackcloth, and girded me with gladness; to the end that my glory may sing praise to thee, and not be silent. O LORD my God, I will give thanks unto thee for ever.
>
> —PSALM 30:1–3, 11–12, KJV

God worked a miracle in my life. The combination of the biblical diet and the HSOs had restored my health! I gained more than fifty pounds in three months. By December of 1996, after two years of hopeless suffering, I was home in Florida—fully restored and ready to start my life again. Praise God!

By the grace of God, I had done what millions of disease victims desperately hope to do—*I had conquered illness and recovered my health.*

Some Doctors Were Excited, Most Were Skeptical

I immediately told many of the doctors who had treated me about my dramatic recovery through the Maker's Diet and the unique soil organisms I named HSOs. I even mailed them "before" and "after" pictures, fully confident they would all be eager to learn about the regimen that had healed me. Some of them were excited, but *most* were skeptical.

Dr. Morton Walker, a medical journalist who had supplied me information on some of the clinics I visited, asked if he could write an article outlining my amazing story. He published the article in the *Townsend Letter for Doctors and Patients,* a prestigious health publication that focuses on alternative medicine and treatments.[3] The article generated over 2,000 phone calls from doctors and individuals who wanted to try the Maker's Diet along with the HSOs. Overnight I was forced to find a way to distribute the HSOs that had helped me get well, which precipitated the birthing of *Garden of Life,* a health and wellness company that supplies health education and manufactures innovative products based on the dietary principles that helped me. I then went on to earn advanced degrees in nutrition and sports medicine, and continued my studies for doctoral degrees in naturopathy and nutrition.

Discovering Divine Destiny

My mission in life since my recovery is to help people who are sick regain their health and to help the healthy flourish even more. It seems obvious to me that I endured my ordeal for a reason—to discover a major part of the divine destiny for my life.

I can speak with authority on nutrition, disease, and health not because I have "paid my dues" academically (though I have), but because I have personally survived the tortuous walk through the valley of disease and death and emerged triumphant.

At this writing, I have been enjoying good health for nearly eight years and have been free of symptoms and medication for almost nine years. Crohn's disease is supposedly incurable. Because of my experience, I can confirm that no disease is incurable.

Although the disease process in some people may be too advanced for them to recover completely, I am convinced that every person's state of health can be greatly *improved*. By following biblically and historically proven health principles, an individual can return to a diet and lifestyle that will lead to regeneration of the entire body, mind, soul, and spirit.

I remember during my illness telling myself that if I can help just one person who is suffering to overcome his illness, then it will all have been worth it. I have now dedicated my life to teaching others how to attain the level of health and wellness they only dream of.

My studies also taught me a very important truth: *The best way to "cure" disease is to never get it.* I believe that everyone, whether presently healthy or ill, can benefit by incorporating the principles of *The Maker's Diet* into their lives.

This program is for you whether you want to avoid disease, enjoy a long and healthy life, overcome the painful symptoms of illness, lose twenty pounds, or prevent a disease that runs in your family.

My bout with severe illness has made me a stronger person. I can relate to the biblical character Job, who suffered severe loss and extreme illness before God restored his health and increased his fortunes. The Lord has restored to me what was taken away, and He has multiplied it more than I could have ever asked or imagined.

Many would say that my healing and restoration began when I discovered the diet and health secrets of the world's greatest Physician as followed by the world's healthiest people. I believe the spark that ignited the flame of healing in my life was the faith that God allowed my illness for a reason, and if I would trust Him, He would restore my health and direct my path.

Today I am on a mission from God to change people's lives and give them the message of hope and healing. I will spend the rest of my life telling the world the truth that will set them free.

> I waited patiently for the LORD; and He inclined unto me, and heard my cry. He also brought me up out of a horrible pit, out of the miry clay, and set my feet upon a rock, and established my steps. He has put a new song in my mouth—praise to our God; many will see it and fear, and will trust in the LORD.
>
> —PSALM 40:1–3

Chapter 2

The World's Healthiest People

MANY AMERICANS ASSUME THAT THE UNITED STATES IS THE world's healthiest nation. Unfortunately, statistics show that we are not as healthy as we may think.

We *do* enjoy one of the highest standards of living in the world, with extraordinary emergency medical technology and trauma care. The average American has first-class access to emergency health care, but this fact doesn't make us *healthy.* Most people who end up in ambulances and emergency rooms get there because they had an accident or *a health crisis.* And the emergency care they receive is often life saving.

That is quite different from evaluating our national lifestyle as one of healthy living that *prevents* disease. The concept of preventative medicine is only recently getting media attention.

Most Americans eat great quantities of food frequently, based on *convenience.* In fact, the entire fast-food and TV dinner industries have flourished due to our fast-paced lifestyles that demand we eat "convenient" foods.

Unfortunately, the Creator didn't design our bodies to operate at optimum levels on junk food, fast food, or prepackaged foods prepared in microwave ovens. His laws that govern our entire human nature, including our health, bring consequences when violated, whether or not we accept the fact that they are still in place. Elmer A. Josephson, a pioneer who dared to challenge the stream of popular dietary trends, said:

> There is no portion of the commandments of God in general, or of the Mosaic code in particular, that is not based on a scientific understanding of fundamental law. The laws of God are enforced and are as sure as the law of gravity.[1]

All of God's laws are like His law of gravity—*they can't be changed.* Our Creator specifically designed us to function best on the Maker's

Diet. In order to benefit from His plan, we must examine exactly what food is "biblical" and what food is unclean, unhealthy, or unacceptable according to both God and science (in that order).

History reveals that the healthiest people in the world were generally the most *primitive* people as well! Our ancestors rarely died from the diet- and lifestyle-related illnesses that kill most modern people before their time, mainly because they ate more healthfully and had more active lifestyles. They foraged from "first level" food sources such as wild game, fresh-caught fish from the sea or inland waterways, wild berries, nuts, and plant foods.

Under primitive conditions, food is vital for survival; primitive people "ate to live." In our era, we have allowed food to become our idol. Too many people admittedly "live to eat." Most modern men and women have strayed far from the Creator's foods, the same foods that traditionally nourished the world's healthiest people. In our promiscuous society, we say *yes* to virtually every whim and desire of our palate, resulting in a national dilemma of becoming overweight, sedentary, and an increasingly sick population.

The Top Ten (Diseases)

The top ten leading causes of hospitalizations and insurance claims in the United States in 1990 included obesity, diabetes, hemorrhoids (or varicose veins), heart attacks, diverticulosis and diverticulitis, cancer, peptic ulcer, hiatal hernia, appendicitis, and gallstones.[2]

These represent diseases of lifestyle, revealing the hazardous effects of civilization, which are expanding as industrialization and modernization spread to more of the world's nations and cultural groups. These diseases are still uncommon among primitive people groups today, and history indicates they were virtually unknown among the oldest primitive civilizations.

The evidence indicates most ancient "primitive" people consumed a diet very similar to the diet of the Bible and the original intent of our Creator. Of course, other factors figure in our health picture as well—genetics, environmental toxins, lifestyle choices, emotional and mental factors, and cultural trends that affect health—but *diet* remains the *single most influential factor in overall human health*.

Tilt Some Stereotypes

In case, by simply observing its title, you have categorized this book and have classified me as "just another wimpy vegetarian health guru," allow me to tilt some stereotypes for you:

1. I am *in favor* of eating beef, lamb, and other "healthy" red meats.
2. You *should* spend time in direct sunlight.
3. Make sure you take your children out to *play in the dirt.*
4. You will be healthier if you consume *saturated fat* every day.

While I readily admit that we can't go back to the old ways of our primitive ancestors completely, we can learn from their wisdom in order to *overcome* or *avoid* the modern diseases of civilization. We can make our bodies strong and *more disease-resistant* if we take the necessary steps to do so.

The ultimate health wisdom available to us is a diet based on health principles clearly described in the Bible, which I have called "the Maker's Diet." It is remarkably well balanced and extremely healthy. Returning to the Maker's Diet as the ultimate primitive diet, based on instructions from the Creator Himself, is certain to contribute to better health for all who choose to do so.

Ambushed by Our Own Technology

Our own technology and advances in knowledge have ambushed us as our technological and marketing skills advanced far quicker than our digestive tracts.

We process food so it will last for *decades* on a store shelf. (You can purchase an irradiated two-month-old tomato or a twenty-five-year-old prepackaged snack cake.)

Scientists splice together the genes of one species into another to "custom design" a selected end product. Countless forms of these bio-engineered grains and fruits are offered to unsuspecting consumers in America's largest grocery stores—usually with no notice or explanation.

It may sound good, but think about it. This is the twenty-first century with its incredible technological advancements—yet our bodies are still "genetically wired" to function best on the foods favored by our ancestors.

Do You Want to Be Healthier Than Your Neighbor?

One people group stands out among the many primitive cultures studied by anthropologists, health professionals, and nutritional historians.

This group of people carefully restricted scavengers (unclean meats) from their diet, consumed foods rich in nutrients, and lived a lifestyle that kept them free from illnesses and plagues throughout history—as promised in Exodus 15:26. That group was the nation of Israel, the chosen people of God.

The Israelites of antiquity followed a diet established by God and were consistently healthier than all of their neighbors. Regardless of your religious preference, any honest student of the Scriptures must admit that the wisdom of the Bible extends far beyond the spiritual issues to encompass every area of life—including dietary, hygienic, and moral guidelines.

Peter Rothschild, M.D., Ph.D., wrote an unpublished book entitled *The Art of Health*. In a chapter called "Please Don't Eat the Wrapper," he writes:

> It suddenly dawned on us that God, the greatest master nutritionist of all times, has given us an all-purpose diet more than 3000 years ago....
>
> There is abundant historic evidence that reveals that the average Israelite, up to the end of the last century [19th], was much longer lived than the average Gentile. We wish to emphasize that we are referring to the Israelites up to the end of the last century, because up to those years, the overwhelming majority of Jews obeyed God's laws by and large.
>
> However, beginning with World War I, both diet and hygiene began to slacken among the children of Israel all over the planet, until only a small fraction remains true to biblical tradition....worldwide statistics bear witness to their changing eating habits. The trend of longevity is gradually vanishing among the non-observant. It appears that God indeed knew what nourishment to recommend.[3]

In the very first chapter of the Bible, God says, "I give you every seed-bearing plant on the face of the whole earth and every tree that has fruit with seed in it. They will be yours for food" (Gen. 1:29, NIV).

This biblical provision for food, as incorporated into the Maker's Diet, provides a great amount of vitamins, minerals, protein, healthy fats, and "phytochemicals" (the invaluable natural substances in plants that are neither vitamins nor minerals). A wealth of nutrition awaits hurting bodies that are fed liberal doses of fruits, vegetables, herbs, lentils, and properly prepared whole grains (along with the meat, fish, and dairy products introduced later by the Creator).

Apart from the de-branned, bleached, chemically stripped, and "enriched" wheat flour we use to add fat to America's "waist"-land, these biblical "seed-bearing plants" are rare in modern diets. That is unfortunate.

Outdated Legalism

In an odd twist of logic, many religious Americans dismiss the Jewish dietary laws as *outdated legalism,* invalid for the modern era. Yet, they embrace the fundamental truths of the Ten Commandments as universal and timeless. Shouldn't we at least *consider* the Creator's dietary guidelines in the same way?

God gave His *moral law* and His *dietary guidelines* to the Jews at the same time. The moral guidelines preserved spiritual purity, social order, family stability, and community prosperity. These proven "laws" were used by America's founders, who established the Constitution on proven principles from the commandments God gave the Israelites thousands of years ago.

Just as the moral guidelines preserved the culture of Israel, so the dietary guidelines preserved their physical health. God's dietary guidelines are not some narrow-minded religious exercise meant to set apart certain people from their neighbors. They were given by a loving God to *save His people from physical devastation* long before scientific principles of hygiene, viral transmission, bacterial infection, or molecular cell physiology were understood!

Divine Dietary Revision

Many of us have heard the rationale for the "Genesis Diet" championed by many sincere and intelligent health experts. This diet is based on Genesis 1:29, which gave Adam and Eve instructions to eat liberally from the plant foods lavishly provided in the Garden of Eden.

However, *after* humanity's exodus from the Garden of Eden, the proteins unique to animal foods became increasingly important to a race now dependent on heavy labor, speed, and physical strength to survive. God codified approved animal protein sources as recorded in the Old Testament (Leviticus 11; Deuteronomy 14). I have summarized this divine dietary revision in the following chart.

SUMMARY OF THE MAKER'S DIET

1. The foods approved by God as recorded in Leviticus 11 and Deuteronomy 14 superceded "the Genesis Diet" found in the first chapter of the Bible. God declared, "These are the animals which you may eat among all the animals that are on the earth" (Lev. 11:2). Abraham, Moses, Jacob, and Jesus ate biblically clean meats. We aren't in the Garden of Eden, so we all need animal protein. The Bible is specific as to the type:

| a. The meat of animals with a cloven or split hoof that *also* chew the cud (Lev. 11:3) can be eaten. This includes cows, goats, sheep, oxen, deer, buffalo, and so forth. | b. Avoid animals, such as the camel, that chew the cud but do not have cloven or split hooves (Lev. 11:4). This includes, but is not limited to, horses, rats, skunks, dogs, cats, squirrels, and possums. | c. Do not eat swine (pigs). They have divided hooves, but they do no chew the cud. These are *unclean* animals (Lev. 11:7–8). In fact, pigs are so unclean that God warns us not to even touch the body, meat, or carcass of a pig. The Hebrew words used to describe "unclean meats" can be translated as "foul, polluted, and putrid."[4] The same terms were used to describe "human waste" and other disgusting substances. |

2. Eat any fish with fins and scales but avoid fish or water creatures *without* them (Lev. 11:9–10). Those to avoid include smooth-skinned species such as catfish or eel and hard-shelled crustaceans such as crab, lobster, or clams.

3. Birds that live primarily on insects, grubs, or grains are considered clean, but avoid birds or fowl that eat flesh (whether caught live or carrion). They are unclean. (See the extensive list in Leviticus 11:13–19.)

The Bible even describes edible and inedible insects in Leviticus 11:20–23 (foods not normally consumed in North America). Unclean "swarming things" such as lizards, moles, mice, chameleons, and crocodiles are also listed in verses 29–31 to be avoided.

Elmer Josephson, whom I quoted earlier, was a pastor, missionary, and cancer survivor. In his landmark volume *God's Key to Health and Happiness*, he wrote:

> Some ask, why did the Lord make the unclean animals? They
> were created as scavengers. As a rule they are meat-eating
> animals that clean up anything that is left dead in the fields,
> etc. But scavengers were never created for human consump-
> tion. The flesh of the swine is said by many authorities to be
> the prime cause of much of our American ill health, caus-
> ing blood diseases, weakness of the stomach, liver troubles,
> eczema, consumption, tumors, cancer, etc.
>
> The scaleless fish and all shell fish including the oyster,
> clam, lobster, shrimp, etc., modern science discovers to be
> but lumps of devitalized and disease producing filth, because
> of inadequate excretion. These are the scavengers, the gar-
> bage containers of the waters and the seas.[5]

Pork products in particular top the list of favorite foods for many Americans. Some don't even realize their favorite snacks or food items come from swine. The pig did not make the Creator's list of "clean" animals for a very good reason. Clean animals that chew the cud have an alimentary canal and a secondary cud receptacle. Essentially, they have three stomachs available to process and refine their clean, vegetation-based food into "flesh" in a process that takes more than twenty-four hours in general.

Pigs or swine, on the other hand, never limit their diet to vegetation. They will eat anything they can find—including their own young and sick or dead pigs from the same pen.

Josephson claimed the pig's single stomach arrangement was very simple in design and function and that it was combined with a limited excretory organ system: "...*four hours* after the pig has eaten his pol-luted swill and other putrid, offensive matter, man may eat the *same* [swill] second handed off the ribs of the pig."[6]

With impeccable logic, Josephson adds, "Did anything biologically happen to the swine [since Bible times], or did the digestive tract of man have some kind of miracle transformation? No, the Bible, science and experience have all proven the contrary."[7]

Regarding scavengers of the sea, we see media warnings about toxic crabs, clams, and oysters on the East Coast each spring or summer. Why? Scientists literally gauge the contaminate levels of our oceans, bays, rivers, and lakes by measuring the mercury and biological toxin levels in the flesh of crabs, clams, oysters, and lobsters.

Consider Dr. Rothschild's explanation of the toxic effects of what the Bible calls "unclean" foods:

> Do not consume any meat of scavenger animals comprising pork, all shell fish varieties, skin fish which are scale-less fish, scavenger birds, snakes and most reptiles. The reason for this [biblical] prohibition is dual.
>
> The first consists in that the meat of such animals is about ten times more perishable, difficult to preserve, than that of the allowed animals. Frequently people do not realize a piece of meat is already poisonously spoiled until they perceive the toxic symptoms...[and have already] ingested it.
>
> The second reason consists in the scary fact that the...by-products that originate from digesting such scavenger meat are highly poisonous. We're referring specifically to the so-called death enzymes, such as cadaverine, putrescine...these death enzymes are extraordinarily useful in nature. Without their assistance no flesh would revert to dust...they are extremely useful to break down a corpse, but terribly inconvenient in a living human body.[8]

Refined and processed foods

God's dietary guidelines contain no refined or processed carbohydrates and only a very small amount of healthy sweeteners. The typical American diet is just the opposite. We stray far from God's design with an array of techno-foods rich in empty calories, filled with refined carbohydrates, and woefully inadequate in nutrition. In contrast, the totally natural Maker's Diet satisfies us with unprocessed foods harvested directly from the Creator's bounty. Countless healing miracles occur naturally as our bodies process and use these foods with great ease.

Clear-cut hygiene guidelines also accompany the Maker's instructions. Generations of Jewish families followed these instructions and enjoyed remarkable resistance to diseases and plagues, which devastated neighboring people groups with no such guidelines.

Michael D. Jacobson, D.O., a former U.S. Army flight surgeon and family practitioner, noted that in the mid-fourteenth century, bubonic plague wiped out one-fourth of Europe's population in just one year. It returned repeatedly over the next 250 years, killing nearly a fourth of London's population in 1603. England lost nearly half of its total population to this plague. Read history's record of how the Jewish people fared in the face of it:

As the plague continued its scourge, it became apparent that the Jewish people were somehow escaping its death grip. This led many to persecute them. People concluded that it was the Jews who were responsible for the plague, since they were the only ones who were not dying.

The truth is that, hundreds of years prior to the discovery of bacteria, the Jews were protecting themselves from the deadly *Yersinia pestis* microbe by practicing cleanliness and good hygiene.... more than three thousand years before man discovered bacteria, the Creator had given detailed instructions that, if followed, would prevent the spread of such a deadly communicable disease.[9]

Members of my Jewish family have followed kosher dietary guidelines for generations—with a few exceptions. My grandmother always served her family kosher foods in the home but proudly declared, "The only place we eat *traife* (the Yiddish word for biblically unclean meats such as pork and shrimp) is at a Chinese restaurant." Grandma knew that pork and shrimp were biblically unclean foods, but she considered it acceptable to eat them as long as it was not in her home. That "logic" did not change the potential ill effects of those meats, however.

Choosing a Better Way

Some of us diligently verify the claims on prepackaged food reassuring us they are "enriched with 12 vitamins" or that they are "100 percent natural."

The unfortunate truth is that most prepackaged and fast-food products overload our bodies with adulterated fats and refined sugars such as those found in candy, baked goods, and refined grains. (That includes the innocuous hamburger buns and "wholesome bread" wrapped around our "low-fat" grilled chicken breasts.)

Should we give up and just eat twigs, leaves, and berries the rest of our lives? No, we don't have to be that extreme. There is a better way.

The Maker's Diet is a comprehensive lifestyle plan that will help you choose a better way. By way of introducing some general guidelines here, you can choose wild game instead of artificially fattened and estrogen-enhanced slabs of feedlot-raised beef. Reach for naturally fermented raw dairy products instead of antibiotic-laced, hormone-enhanced, and pesticide-tainted pasteurized and homogenized dairy products.

Select wild fish with fins and scales instead of farm-raised varieties dosed with antibiotics. Seek out nutritious fermented or sprouted whole-grain bread (more on this tasty alternative later) instead of commercially produced white bread that can't even sustain insect life. Spice up your life with naturally fermented relishes and condiments instead of sugary sauce substitutes.

The simple biblical principles I have incorporated into *The Maker's Diet* may spare you the misery or help you recover from debilitating modern diseases and health crises such as arthritis, cancer, obesity, diabetes, heart attack, and stroke.

Discard the Myths About Primitive People

Modern society is riddled with myths about primitive people being brutish, savage, and of low intelligence. It permeates our literature and media, but it is still the stuff of myths. We could learn a great deal from our ancestors if we lay down some of our misconceptions about nutrition.

Most of us have an image of our ancestors' primitive lifestyles that paints them as undernourished, animalistic, filthy, and virtually semi-human people plagued by illness and ignorance. In truth, many of our ancestors experienced robust health often until death.

Though a high percentage of people in primitive societies died during infancy or while still young, it was largely because our modern technological benefits, for example, of crisis care, and particularly our knowledge about basic sanitation, were unavailable. (Again, the Jewish people of the Bible were the significant exception because of God's ultramodern sanitation guidelines.)

What Is a Nursing Home?

Your great-great-grandparents probably could not relate to terms like *retirement* or *nursing home*! Most of their generation lived vigorous lifestyles filled with a lot of exercise and consumed a diet that was well suited to their bodies. This combination tended to keep them strong and healthy well into their eighties and beyond.

Though some people in the ancient past failed to live long enough to acquire cardiovascular disease or cancer (two of the major killers in the United States and Europe today), those who *did* live long lives *rarely* acquired these killer diseases.

Cardiovascular Disease Was Nonexistent

Heart disease (as well as cancer) is still rare among isolated primitive groups in the modern era who eat a more primitive, ancestral diet. One clinical study examined cardiovascular disease incidence and related risk factors among 2,300 "subsistence horticulturists" (people who survive on what they grow, gather, or harvest) on Kitava, a tropical island near Papua New Guinea. The title of the study says it all: "Apparent Absence of Stroke and Ischaemic Heart Disease."[10] What was their secret?

As of 1994, these researchers had determined that the modern disease symptoms of sudden cardiac death, stroke, and exertion-related chest pain were still *nonexistent or extremely rare* in Kitavans. It seemed that the most common causes of death included infections, accidents, complications of pregnancy, and senescence (*old age*).[11]

All of the adults had low diastolic blood pressure (all below 90) and were very lean. (Their average weight actually *decreased* after age thirty.) What did they eat most of the time? They lived on Kitava's island bounty of tubers, fruit, fish, and coconut, with very little salt and virtually no access to Western food or alcohol. Oddly enough, 80 percent of the population (both sexes) were daily smokers, supporting the concept that smoking alone is not sufficient to cause cardiovascular disease. The tobacco these native people smoked was, no doubt, grown without the use of toxic pesticides and herbicides and was smoked from a wood pipe or hand-rolled in thin paper free from chemically treated filters and glue. Thus, modern people have even found a way to make smoking even *less* healthy.

One resident was a migrant of sorts. This forty-four-year-old urbanized businessman grew up on Kitava but lived elsewhere. He visited during the survey and agreed to participate anyway. Compared to the resident Kitavan adults, this man had the highest diastolic blood pressure, the highest body mass index, and the highest waist-to-hip ratio.

The contrast strongly indicates that neither the Kitavans nor any native cultures for that matter are *genetically* protected from hypertension or abdominal obesity. Their good health was more certainly *directly linked* to their healthy diet and lifestyle.

The Hidden Cost of Being Thoroughly Modern

Michael Murray, N.D., has written extensively about the absence of modern disease from primitive cultures. He found that a number of aboriginal, primitive societies in Australia, Africa, and South America successfully passed into the twentieth century and enjoyed remarkably low rates of cancer, rheumatoid arthritis, obesity, diabetes, osteoporosis, heart disease, and other "modern" conditions—*until they switched to modern diets.*[12]

Modern civilization has managed to infiltrate the culture of many of these once-isolated societies. Few of them still consume the primitive, simple diets of their ancestors. American travelers are often surprised to find that canned Western-style food, refined sugar, and white flour products are now consumed nearly everywhere on the planet. As you might expect, this transition from primitive diets to modern diets has brought *deadly consequences.*

Explain "This Absence of Cancer"

Appreciation for the virtues of a primitive diet is controversial, but it isn't new. In 1913, the Nobel Prize-winning physician and missionary Albert Schweitzer visited Gabon, Africa:

> I was astonished to encounter no cases of cancer. I saw none among the natives two hundred miles from the coast....I cannot, of course, say positively that there was no cancer at all, but, like other frontier doctors, I can only say that, if any cases existed they must have been quite rare. *This absence of cancer seemed to be due to the difference in nutrition of the natives compared to the Europeans.*[13]

Explorer and anthropologist Vilhjalmur Stefansson searched in vain for cases of cancer among the Inuit peoples while exploring the Arctic. Meticulous diary entries of his experiences and observations appear throughout his book *Cancer: Disease of Civilization.* Stefansson said a whaling ship doctor named George B. Leavitt found only *one cancer case in forty-nine years* among the Inuit of Alaska and Canada.[14]

By the 1970s, breast cancer malignancy appeared frequently among the Inuit women *after they began consuming a modern diet.* Toxic chemicals from our modern foods and industries have contributed to this condition.[15]

Diabetes was rare among Australia's native Aborigines, but now this modern disease appears ten times more often among the Aborigines than among European arrivals. Kerin O'Dea, a professor at Monash University in Clayton, Victoria, Australia, attributes the diabetes increase to dietary changes. The flaws in our modern diet invariably produce modern diseases and a decreased quality of life.[16]

Ironically, the Australian Aborigines *used* to eat great amounts of *fermented* sweet potatoes (a natural source of probiotics and soluble fiber that literally feeds the "good" bacteria of the gastrointestinal tract).

The World's Healthiest People

These potatoes are naturally sweet, but when eaten plain or in fermented form, they seem to reduce significantly the risk of blood sugar imbalances![17] Unfortunately, sweet potatoes in any form rarely make it onto our favorite foods list.

The Surprising Discoveries of Dr. Weston Price

Dr. Weston A. Price was a Harvard-trained dentist with a curious mind and a determination to find root causes. Many refer to him as the "Albert Einstein of nutrition." I consider him to be the greatest nutritionist who ever lived. He was thrust into nutritional research after he became alarmed by the number of cavities, crooked teeth, and deformed dental arches in his young patients.

Price believed dental health is a good indicator of physical health, so he wondered if the epidemic of dental abnormalities was caused by nutritional deficiencies. Solid scientific evidence indicates that all three symptoms Dr. Price noted in his young patients signal physical degeneration and an increased vulnerability to diseases such as heart attacks and cancer.

Dr. Price's search for answers during the 1930s led him to turn from his test tubes and microscopes and launch a six-year expedition on five continents to study primitive societies. He and his wife, Florence, began the study just as many of these societies were adopting modern diets as a result of their exposure to "outsiders." The Prices produced countless photographs and invaluable data on the dental state, dietary habits, and lifestyles of thousands of people in many primitive societies.

This gave Dr. Price the unique opportunity to *compare* people who had grown up with the primitive diet against those in that culture who now consumed modern diets. (Sometimes the individuals lived in the same family or household.)

Price traveled the globe in search of these isolated human groups. He studied the residents of sequestered villages in Switzerland, Gaelic communities in the Outer Hebrides, the Inuit or Eskimo people of Canada and Alaska, native American Indians of North America, Melanesian and Polynesian South Sea Islanders, African tribes, Australian Aborigines, New Zealand Maori, and the Indians of South America.

Primitive Diets Produce Beautiful Teeth, Strong Bodies

Dr. Price found that primitive people consuming their traditional diets exclusively typically enjoyed beautiful straight teeth that were free of decay and strong bodies that demonstrated a remarkable resistance to disease.

He was determined to find the factors responsible for such attributes among so-called "primitives." He concluded that the dental caries (progressive destruction of teeth by decay) and deformed dental arches that produced crowded, crooked teeth and an unattractive appearance were merely a sign of physical degeneration. As he had originally suspected, *nutritional deficiencies* appeared to be the primary cause of this physical degeneration.

Dr. Price reported his findings in the book *Nutrition and Physical Degeneration*.[18] The Prices' astonishing collection of photographs support his finding that primitive people cut off from modern diets generally had perfectly formed teeth and jaws with very little tooth decay. There was a stark contrast between the wide faces, perfect teeth, and perfectly formed dental arches of families who still lived on a primitive diet and the narrow faces, misshapen jaws, and crooked teeth of other family members who consumed modern diets!

Modern Diets Produce Physical Degeneration

Dr. Price concluded that *diet* was the only possible factor accounting for such universal good physical health among primitive people. People who ate the modern diet suffered from physical degeneration, while those on primitive diets did not. He suggested that dietary deficiencies also contributed to poor brain development and associated social disorders such as juvenile delinquency and high crime rates.

Price dared to suggest that modern humans learn from primitives (in an era when it was fashionable to disparage and sneer at primitive people groups), and he strongly urged a return to the primitive diet that made our ancestors so healthy.

> No era in the long journey of mankind reveals in the skeletal remains such a terrible degeneration of teeth and bones as this brief modern period records. Must Nature reject our vaunted culture and call back the more obedient primitives?[19]

When Price analyzed the foods of isolated primitive peoples, he discovered that they provided at least four times the water-soluble vitamins, calcium, and other minerals and at least ten times the fat-soluble vitamins such as A, E, and D found in modern diets! The primitive diets derived these nutrients from *animal foods* such as butter, fatty fish, wild game, and organ meats.

Many "Primitives" Practiced Premarital Nutrition

For many years health practitioners (and most people with a dose of common sense) have understood the importance of good nutrition for mothers during pregnancy. Dr. Price's research revealed that members of primitive cultures have long understood and practiced "preconception nutritional programs" for *both* prospective parents.

However, Price also learned that many tribes required a period of *premarital* nutrition as well for youth planning to be wed. Special foods were often given to maturing boys and girls in preparation for future parenthood, as well as to pregnant and lactating women. Dr. Price found these foods to be very rich in fat-soluble vitamins A and D—nutrients found only in *animal fats*.

Once married, couples seemed to space their children to permit the mother to maintain her full health and strength and to assure the safety and physical excellence of subsequent offspring. The healthy bodies, homogeneous reproduction, emotional stability, and freedom from degenerative ills enjoyed by such primitive societies contrast sharply from modern individuals *existing* on the impoverished foods of civilization—sugar, white flour, pasteurized milk, and convenience foods filled with chemical preservatives and additives.

Dr. Price compared the nutritional intake of primitive groups with their resistance to dental caries and freedom from degenerative processes to the diets of modernized groups who adopted modern foods consisting largely of white flour products, sugar, white rice, jams, canned goods, and vegetable oils.

Virtually without exception, Price discovered that when compared to modernized diets, the primitive diets provided exceptionally high levels of calcium, phosphorus, iron, magnesium, fat-soluble vitamins (A, D, E, K), water-soluble B vitamins (folate, pantothenic acid, thiamin, riboflavin, niacin, B_6, B_{12}), and vitamin C.

Dr. Price's keen observations were first published in 1939 in *Nutrition and Physical Degeneration*. I've summarized just a few samples:[20]

- Switzerland: "The isolated groups dependent on locally produced natural foods have nearly complete natural immunity to dental caries, and *the substitution of modern dietaries* for these primitive natural foods destroys this immunity."

- Outer Hebrides Islands: "I was advised that in the last fifty years the average height of Scotch men in some parts decreased four inches, and that this had been coincident with the general change from high immunity to dental caries to a loss of immunity in a great part of this general district. A study of the market places revealed that *a large part of the nutrition was shipped into the district in the form of refined flours, canned goods and sugar.*"

- Alaska: "We neither saw nor heard of a case (of arthritis) in the isolated groups. However, *at the point of contact with the foods of modern civilization* many cases were found, including ten bedridden cripples in a series of about twenty Indian homes. Some other afflictions made their appearance there, particularly tuberculosis, which is taking a very severe toll on the children who had been born at the center."

- Ethiopia: "In one of the most efficiently organized mission schools that we found in Africa, the principal asked me to help them solve a serious problem of why it is that those families that have grown up in the mission or government schools were physically not so strong as those families who had never been in contact with the mission or government schools."

The pioneering research of Dr. Price provided solid empirical evidence that the primitive peoples he studied did not suffer from obesity, heart disease, digestive problems, or cancer at the rates we do. Thanks in large part to their primitive diets, these people groups enjoyed levels of vibrant health that have virtually been lost to modern civilization.

Health Declined With a Shift to Agriculture

The scientific analysis of skeletal and dental remains of primitive societies from the past suggests that humans before the advent of modern agriculture were stronger, bigger, and healthier than those who lived after that societal change.

In general, the health of our primitive ancestors declined whenever they shifted to agriculture as their primary food supply. This was abundantly clear in a North American research site in the Illinois Valley, one of the few sites in the United States containing an intact mortuary record dating back to when humans first populated the area.[21]

Researchers also uncovered a large amount of archaeological dietary evidence. This allows us to draw some solid conclusions about health and disease in the population of this region.

One site, the Dickson Mounds in Illinois, provides enough information to establish a correlation between increased primary food production and changes in the overall health level. Researchers studied data from three time periods: the Late Woodland period (950–1100 A.D.), the Mississippian Acculturated/Late Woodland period (1100–1200 A.D.), and the Middle Mississippian period (1200–1300 A.D.).

The Late Woodland component is associated with a generalized hunting and gathering economy. Compared to the appearance of these first people at the Dickson Mounds, there is a general increase in the reliance on maize or corn as the primary food crop. The number of skeletons with nonspecific skeletal *infections* greatly *increases as the maize dependence increases.*

By the Middle Mississippian period, the infection rate had more than doubled. It seems the maize-based mono-diet produced severe iron-deficiency anemia in the general population! That, in turn, decreased immunity and allowed for the great increase in infection rates.[22]

In what is now East Georgia, maize cultivation among the "First Peoples" or native Americans occurred only *after* 1150 A.D. Foraging societies before that period moved with their "game" or primary meat sources or scattered far enough apart to live off the land without depleted resources. Once they began to plant and harvest maize, they clustered closer together and lived off of their crops.

Bone Infections Increased With Agriculture-Based Diets

Although these early diets were better than our chemically "enhanced" foods today, they still failed to match the healthy primitive diet patterns based on hunting and foraging for foods. Before the arrival of modern agriculture, the human diet of these primitive peoples consisted mostly of fruits, vegetables, wild heirloom grain and seeds, fish, and meat from wild animals. Our bodies *still crave* these ancestral foods, no matter how we "progress" technologically.

Researchers found clear evidence of increased bone infections among the new "agriculturally based" people groups, along with a general decrease in bone size, stature, and vigor.

Primitive Diets Not All Healthy

However, not all primitive diets are alike. Many of the cultures surrounding the Israelites were "primitive," but they were riddled with diseases instigated by their diets and destructive lifestyles. China allegedly possesses one of the oldest continually sustained cultures on earth. Yet many of the cultures represented in modern China eat foods far removed from biblical guidelines. A headline in the *Palm Beach Post* declared in bold letters, "China's Taste for Critters May Have Aided SARS," referring to the deadly flu-like epidemic that first appeared in China. The article states:

> The possible origin of the SARS epidemic, which has claimed about 600 lives, infected 7,500 people and made places as diverse as China, Taiwan, Hong Kong, Singapore and Toronto no-fly zones in the past two months, has been tentatively traced to civet cats, a delicacy in omnivorous southeast China.
>
> …just as AIDS may have jumped to humans from monkeys, and the Ebola virus from rats, SARS may have found a new host in hungry human beings.[23]

According to the author of the article, civet cats are related to the mongoose. They are clearly unclean animals not meant for human consumption. I couldn't help but make a mental connection between the virtually continuous streams of Hong Kong flu and Asian flu to our shores from the Far East. The article's author added, "The Cantonese have a saying: 'If it flies in the air and it's not an airplane, if it swims in the sea and it's not a submarine, if it has four legs and it's not a table, *eat it.*'"[24]

The Creator's Wisdom

Our Creator established our genetic and nutritional requirements long ago. He caused our ancestors to adapt to the types of foods they could gather, and there is no evidence to suggest that modern humans are any different. Despite our technological advancements, our physical bodies are still designed to consume and thrive on *the same foods* in the *same proportions* that our primitive ancestors ate thousands of years ago!

The wisdom in our physiology and biochemistry cry out for a primitive, biblical diet with plentiful amounts of healthy meat, fish, fruit, vegetables, dairy, grains, nuts, and seeds. We have departed so far from the wisdom of our forefathers that fully 55 percent of the American diet is "new food"—not designed by the Creator or eaten by our ancestors.

If we ever hope to be counted among the world's healthiest people, we must leave behind our disease-producing diets and lifestyle and return to our Creator's dietary guidelines, as incorporated in the Maker's Diet!

Chapter 3

Life and Death in a Long Hollow Tube: The Importance of the GI Tract

AMERICANS SEEM TO ACCEPT POOR HEALTH AS A NORMAL consequence of aging, while many experience poor health while still young. Meanwhile, researchers continue to gather evidence affirming the importance of the *gut* to overall health.

More and more health professionals believe there is life and death in the long hollow tube called the "gastrointestinal tract." Dr. C. Everett Koop, former U.S. Surgeon General, indicated two out of three Americans suffer fatal health problems because of poor dietary choices. That means their problems are centered in their "gut":

> What we eat may affect our risk for several of the leading causes of death for Americans, notably, coronary heart disease, stroke, atherosclerosis, diabetes, and some types of cancer. These disorders together now account for more than two-thirds of all deaths in the United States.[1]

As Americans, we have neglected gastrointestinal health far too long. Most nations and civilizations seem to understand what we have forgotten long ago regarding the critical role of digestive health.

According to scriptures common to the Judeo-Christian tradition, the "bowels," or the "belly," are described as the seat of the emotions. For example, in the Song of Solomon, the Shulamite lover says of her betrothed (Solomon):

> My beloved put in his hand by the hole of the door, and my *bowels* were *moved* for him.
> —SONG OF SOLOMON 5:4, KJV, EMPHASIS ADDED

What modern writer would consider using "bowels" in romantic prose? Surprisingly, the English word *gut* reflects a highly accurate view of the intestinal tract. One dictionary defines *gut* as "the basic visceral or emotional part of a person…the alimentary canal or part of it (as the intestine or stomach)…[and] the inner essential parts."[2]

Several factors linked to modern civilization threaten your internal health, including unsafe vaccinations, environmental toxins, pollutants, the overuse of antibiotics (all the foods they contaminate), and even chlorinated and fluoridated water. Add to the list the burgeoning consumption of alcohol and drugs (prescription and recreation) plus poor diets, and you have only a few of the modern-day enemies endangering your gastrointestinal health!

What Is That "Gut Feeling?"

People are taught from childhood to believe that the brain is essentially the "boss" of the body. While it is true that the brain is the centerpiece of our mental capacity and nervous system, it is also a fact that there are nearly one hundred million nerve cells in the gut alone—about the same number found in the spinal cord!

Fully one-half of your nerve cells are located in the gut, so your capacity for feeling and for emotional expression depends primarily on the gut (and only to a lesser extent on your brain). By the time you add together the number of nerve cells in the esophagus, stomach, and small and large intestines, there are more nerve cells in the overall digestive system than there are in the peripheral nervous system.

Most people would say the brain determines whether you are happy or sad, but they have their facts skewed. It seems the gut is more responsible than we ever imagined for mental well-being and how we *feel*.

You Have Two Brains

Award-winning science writer Sandra Blakeslee specializes in "cognitive neuroscience." She captured the link between our gut and brain perfectly in this quote from one of her numerous *New York Times* articles:

> Have you ever wondered why people get butterflies in the stomach before going on stage? Or why an impending job interview can cause an attack of intestinal cramps? And why do antidepressants targeted for the brain cause nausea or abdominal upset in millions of people who take such drugs? The reason for these common experiences is because each of us literally has *two brains*—the familiar one encased in our skulls and a lesser-known but vitally important one found in

the human gut. Like Siamese twins, the two brains are inter-
connected; when one gets upset, the other does, too.[3]

This "second brain" in the gut is called the "enteric nervous system"
(ENS). This "intestinal nervous system" consists of neurons, neurotransmitters, and messenger proteins embedded in the layers or coverings of
tissue that line the esophagus, stomach, small intestine, and colon. (The
word *enteric* is a Greek term for "intestine.")

The enteric nervous system possesses a complex neural circuitry,
and this "second brain" in your gut can *act independently* from the first
brain in your body. Literally, it learns from experiences, remembers past
actions and events, and produces an entire range of "gut feelings" that
can influence your actions.

Do you remember the gut sensation of what we call "butterflies
in your stomach?" Has anyone ever advised you to "follow your *gut*
instinct?" We regularly hear people say their stomach indigestion
caused nightmares, and patients often tell their doctors that the antidepressants they take for mood swings *also* improved their gastrointestinal symptoms. *Now you know why.*

Two Nervous Systems Form During Fetal Development

Early in our embryogenesis, a collection of tissue called the "neural crest"
appears and divides during fetal development. One part turns into the
central nervous system, and the other migrates to become the *enteric*
nervous system. Both "thinking machines" form simultaneously and
independently of one another until a later stage of development.

Then the two nervous systems link through a neural cable called the
"vagus nerve," the longest of all cranial nerves. (Its name comes from a
Latin root meaning "wandering.") The vagus nerve "wanders" from the
brain stem through organs in the neck and thorax and finally terminates
in the abdomen. This is your vital brain-gut connection.

I've coined the term *gastro-neuro-immunology* to describe the profound influence and importance of this link between our two brains and
its affect on human immune function.

Never Underestimate Your Second Brain

The mass of gray matter between your ears is immensely important to
your well-being, but you should never discount the vital importance of
your "second brain"—the gut.

Dr. Michael Gershon, professor of anatomy and cell biology at Columbia Presbyterian Medical Center in New York City, described the body's second nervous system in his book *The Second Brain*:

> The brain is not the only place in the body that's full of neurotransmitters. A hundred million neurotransmitters line the length of the gut, approximately the same number that is found in the brain.... *The brain in the bowel has got to work right or no one will have the luxury to think at all.*[4]

Around 1899 two English physiologists at University College in London first discovered and described the interaction of hormones at the command of neural cells (ganglion) in the digestive tract. William M. Bayliss and Ernest H. Starling anesthetized dogs and applied pressure to the interior cavity of the intestine. The pressure caused contraction and relaxation followed by a propulsive wave. This propulsive wave or "peristaltic reflex" came to be called the "law of the intestine." It describes the way the intestine propels food through the digestive tract.

Experimental studies demonstrated that "the law of the intestine" operated and digestion continued even when all nerves connecting the bowel to the brain and spinal cord were severed. This convinced the scientists that the enteric nervous system (ENS) was *independent* from the central nervous system.

A German scientist named Paul Trendelenburg confirmed the work of Bayliss and Starling eighteen years later, but the scientific community quickly refocused its interest on the more "exciting" discoveries of the day: chemical neurotransmitters such as epinephrine and acetylcholine.

Scientists Forgot the Second Brain for 100 Years

After a political conflict within the scientific community, disgruntled scientists at the Physiological Society arbitrarily reclassified the enteric nerves as simply part of the "parasympathetic nervous system" and essentially wrote off the discovery of this "second brain" for more than a century.

Interest in the ENS revived between 1965 and 1967 when Dr. Michael Gershon proposed the existence of a third neurotransmitter, *serotonin* (5-hydroxytryptamine, 5-HT), that was both produced in and targeted to the enteric nervous system. Dr. Gershon's proposition was confirmed, and we now know that this neurotransmitter is also found in the central nervous system. Serotonin makes you feel good. It is crucial for emotional health and balance, and it directly affects the well-being and function of your digestive system.

We are still discovering ways the enteric nervous system mirrors the central nervous system. Nearly every substance that helps run and control the *brain* has turned up in the *gut*! Major neurotransmitters associated with the brain—including serotonin, dopamine, glutamate, norepinephrine, and nitric oxide—are found in plentiful amounts in the gut as well.

The Gut Manufactures Opiates and Mood-Controllers

About twenty-four small brain proteins called "neuropeptides" also appear in relatively high amounts in the gut, as well as major cells of the immune system. Researchers have even found plentiful amounts of enkephalins in the gut—a class of natural opiates in the body. The gut is also a rich source of benzodiazepines—psychoactive chemicals that include such popular mood-controlling drugs marketed as Valium and Xanax.

Karl Lashley, whom many consider the founder of neuropsychology, said in 1951, "I am coming more and more to the conviction that the rudiments of every human behavioral mechanism will be found represented even in primitive activities of the nervous system."[5] This link between the brain and the gut is helping researchers understand why people act and feel the way they do.

The Importance of Sleep

Sleep disturbances set up vicious cycles of pain, fatigue, and emotional distress that make sleep even more unlikely. Things don't improve much during waking hours either for people who do not sleep well. Inadequate sleep increases sensitivity to bowel, skin, and muscle stimuli, thus leading to more pain and distress. I know from personal experience that when I don't get sufficient sleep, my digestion suffers as a result.

The brain and gut are much alike. Both have natural ninety-minute cycles. The slow wave sleep of the brain is interrupted by periods of "rapid eye movement," or REM sleep, in which dreams occur. Patients with bowel problems also tend to have abnormal REM sleep, and poor sleep has been reported by many if not most patients with irritable bowel syndrome (IBS) and nonulcer dyspepsia ("sour stomach").

Doctors often treat abnormal REM sleep with mild antidepressants, which may also be effective in treating IBS and nonulcer dyspepsia.

However, some stronger antidepressants make digestive problems worse. Once again this points to a link between sleeping problems and stomach problems. Do the two brains influence each other? Probably.

Sleep may very well be the single most important ingredient for digestive health. And it is important to get enough sleep at the right time. Some researchers believe that every minute you sleep before midnight is the equivalent of *four* minutes of sleep after midnight. Restful sleep will do wonders for your digestion and overall health.

Things Go Wrong When Serotonin Is Robbed From the Gut

Many prescription drugs that affect the brain also affect the gut. Some individuals who take Prozac or similar antidepressants may experience gastrointestinal problems such as nausea, diarrhea, and constipation. These drugs "divert" serotonin from the *body* to the *brain*. Unfortunately, this leaves less serotonin for the cells of the gastrointestinal tract.

Normally, the gut produces more serotonin than any other part of the body. This is important because serotonin is linked with initiation of peristalsis (the rhythmic movement of food through the digestive tract). When that supply of serotonin is reduced or stopped altogether, everything related to food digestion goes wrong.

Small doses of Prozac are often used to treat chronic constipation. However, if a little Prozac *cures* constipation, a lot of Prozac *causes* it!

Opiates also have a powerful effect on the digestive tract because the gut has opiate receptors much like the brain. Dr. Michael Loes, a pain management specialist and author of *The Healing Response*, wrote, "Not surprisingly, drugs like morphine and heroin that are thought to act on the central nervous system also attach to the gut's opiate receptors, producing constipation. Both brains can be addicted to opiates."[6] Many Alzheimer's and Parkinson's disease patients suffer from constipation because these conditions impact the "second" brain in the gut as well as the "first" brain and central nervous system.

Anxious? Follow Your Gut Feeling

Fortunately, the Creator equipped the human gut with its own ways of coping with pain and stress. As I mentioned, the gut produces benzodiazepines, the same pain-alleviating chemicals found in antianxiety drugs such as Valium. It seems the gut is equipped to be your body's anxiety and pain reliever!

If you overeat because you feel anxious, your body may be trying to use the extra food to produce more benzodiazepines. We are not sure whether the gut synthesizes benzodiazepine from chemicals in our foods, from bacterial actions, or from both. We *do* know that extreme pain appears to put the gut into overdrive in order to send benzodiazepine directly to the brain for immediate pain management.

Evidently, if you take care of your gut, it will take care of you. But what happens if you do *not* take care of your gut? Consider again what Dr. C. Everett Koop said in *The Surgeon General's Report on Nutrition and Health* in 1988:

> Food sustains us, it can be a source of considerable pleasure, it is a reflection of our rich social fabric and cultural heritage, it adds valued dimensions to our lives. Yet what we eat may affect our risk for several of the leading causes of death for Americans, notably, coronary heart disease, stroke, atherosclerosis, diabetes, and some types of cancer. These disorders together now account for more than two-thirds of all deaths in the United States.[7]

"Doc, Something's Wrong With My Gut!"

Digestive complaints including everything from hemorrhoids to duodenal ulcers result in more time lost at work, school, and play than any other health-related problem.[8] Interestingly enough, according to epidemiological research done by Drs. Price, Schweitzer, and others, many of these digestive problems were rare or nonexistent less than a century ago!

What did our ancestors know or do that we do not? How can we reclaim the health enjoyed by the ancients? For one thing, they ate a diet similar to the Maker's Diet and maintained physically vigorous lifestyles.

We, on the other hand, tend to take our gut for granted, and it costs us dearly. We continually eat wrong foods that are rarely digested properly. The by-products of incomplete digestion clog the gut with accumulated debris. This coating becomes a perfect breeding ground for dangerous forms of bacteria and other microorganisms.

Good news! There are some very positive things we can do to reverse any damage that has already been done. After Crohn's disease all but decimated my body's digestive system, intestinal cleansing or "detoxification" was one of the keys to overcoming my illness.

Even though I "visited the bathroom" nearly ten thousand times over the two years I was sick, I *still needed to be cleansed.* I went through a natural detoxification process by introducing beneficial microorganisms into my body that helped me regain the natural balance of microflora in my gut.

A couple of years ago, while appearing on a series of television programs devoted to health issues, I took calls from interested viewers. One viewer sent me a medical textbook written in 1896, which examined the problems associated with "autointoxication."

Surprisingly, autointoxication or "self-poisoning" from the bowel was a recognized cause of disease in the early 1900s. Dr. H. H. Boeker stated in 1928, "It is now universally conceded that autointoxication is the underlying cause of an exceptionally large group of symptom complexes."[9] Recent research seems to support these earlier conclusions about intestinal toxemia. Yet, many modern medical practitioners and researchers still dismiss intestinal toxemia as a concept that is "old and outdated."

The "gut" goes from your mouth all the way to the "other end." It is fully self-contained and yet intricately dependent and interlinked with every other major system of your body. It is becoming clearer that anything you consume or that otherwise exerts an influence on the body—i.e., swimming and showering in chlorinated water, swallowing fluoride toothpaste, wearing synthetic clothing, or even cleaning house with powerful chemicals—may indirectly or directly affect your gut and therefore your health.

In fact, virtually every state of health is affected by the GI tract. Even if you break a bone or undergo a surgical procedure, the time required to heal is directly affected by how well your gut is able to process nutrients and detoxify toxins!

And even if you are the most intelligent person in the world, if you fail to fuel your body properly, your brilliant intellect may be dimmed or extinguished through poor nutrition and poor lifestyle decisions.

Digestion: The Law of the Gut

We can accurately say that the digestive process is ruled by the "law of the gut." Simply defined, digestion is:

- A carefully executed decomposition process.
- Carried out by an independent enteric nervous system.

- Supported by an intricate array of *interactive enzymes.*

The food you eat yields only a small proportion of substances usable by your body. The rest is eliminated as two fundamental kinds of waste: metabolic waste and digestive waste. *Metabolic* waste represents the cellular household waste and the breakdown of dead, discarded cells that are constantly being replaced in the body. Most of it is eliminated through the kidneys. (Less than 4 percent exits the body through the bowels.) *Digestive* waste comprises all the breakdown matter from the digestion process that is not absorbed.

If these waste products are not regularly eliminated, they begin to poison the body and blood. Unchecked, this autointoxication may ultimately lead to disease and even death.

Throughout history, people from virtually every nationality have preserved in their folklore an instinctive understanding about the importance of regular elimination in the form of daily, comfortable bowel movements. My Jewish grandmother told me her mother often used an old Yiddish expression to describe her day-to-day digestive health. It perfectly describes this universal understanding about digestion.

If someone asked her, "Mama, are you hungry?" she might reply, "No, *dis bachala teet vay.*" (I've spelled the phrase phonetically.) The translation: "No, my stomach isn't clean." My great-grandmother usually refused to eat until she had a bowel movement that day—she knew how important it was to detoxify the body and cleanse the colon.

Most modern Americans don't follow her criteria; they continue to eat large amounts of harmful foods and, if constipated, simply take a toxic, chemical-based laxative or visit the doctor's office. Unfortunately, disease may visit us quietly as we feast and live foolishly.

It concerns me that we seem to be implanting unhealthy standards of digestion and elimination in our nation at a very young age. Some elementary school children are told in health classes that two bowel movements per week should be considered normal!

Dr. H. H. Boeker believed that over 90 percent of diseases are caused or complicated by toxins created in the intestinal tract by unhealthy foods that are not properly eliminated.[10] Autointoxication occurs when, due to poor elimination, certain toxins escape from the bowel into the blood stream and poison the body, causing a silent form of self-poisoning.

Two Keys to Optimal Health

Guidelines for optimal health and nutrition can be reduced to two vital keys:

1. Optimize the nutrition entering your body.
2. Reduce the toxins in your body.

Virtually every disease can be related to those two guidelines in some way—and it all starts in the small and large intestines.

Caring for your colon

The colon is the number one repository for oxidative stress in the body. We hear a great deal in the media about antioxidants and the danger of free radicals, but very few of us realize most of the free radicals or oxidative damage is generated in the colon during the final stages of the digestion process! This explains why it is good to eliminate waste *daily* rather than have it languish for days in the digestive tract, generating potentially harmful toxins all the while.

Necessary enzymes

Enzymes also play key roles in a healthy gut. Our ancestors enjoyed exceptional health partly because they regularly consumed enzyme and probiotic-rich foods, vital nutrients that remain a mystery to most Americans.

Digestive enzymes help us break down proteins, fats, sugars, starches, and other carbohydrates. Your body requires a steady supply of enzymes to digest food properly and maintain health. Thousands of different enzymes exist in nature, but they may be divided into two basic categories.

The first category, *lytic enzymes*, is designed and programmed to break down only *specified* substances. For example, *proteo*lytic enzymes break down *proteins* only, without affecting fats or sugars. The second category of enzymes, *synthetic enzymes*, focuses exclusively on the process of *synthesis* in the body and is uniquely equipped to help create new substances or structures such as molecules and tissues.

The human body produces most of the enzymes it needs, but certain key enzymes, such as cellulase (an enzyme that breaks down the fiber contained in plant foods), must be obtained from raw vegetables and fruits that enter the digestive system.

These enzymes and the complex processes of the digestive tract are vitally related to your health. If you fail to eat the proper foods or if you abuse your body with dangerous dietary choices, man-made chemicals, or a "burn-out" lifestyle, you could lose more than your "youthful appearance." Enzyme deficiency may also impair your immune function, resulting in illness or disease.

High-speed, high-volume lifestyles and toxic eating habits deprive us of the enzymes we need so desperately. Even worse—they *deteriorate the organs that produce* many of the body's most crucial enzymes. This progressive, overall depletion of enzymes leads to a no-win situation in which we can neither digest the food we eat nor synthesize the materials needed for cell repair and maintenance.

Even a partial enzyme deficiency may lead to the onset of disease. As our enzyme deficiencies grow worse, it gets harder and harder for the body to digest proteins, fats, sugars, starches, and other carbohydrates. The resulting poor digestion can open the door to a great variety of health problems.

Enter the Lymphatic System

The lymphatic system is your body's *front line of defense* against infection and disease. Its primary job is to defend your body from foreign invasion by disease-causing agents such as viruses, bacteria, or fungi.

The lymph system contains a network of vessels that help circulate and filter body fluids. Lymph nodes or glands dot the network of lymphatic vessels and provide meeting grounds for the immune system cells that defend against invaders. They also produce lymph, a pale fluid resembling blood plasma that contains white blood cells. (*Lymph* is a Greek term meaning "a pure, clear stream.")

The lymphatic fluids bathe the tissues of the body and are collected by the lymphatic vessels and discharged into the blood stream. Serious problems arise when lymph glands are blocked and this vital service to the body's cells is eliminated. *Lymphatic congestion* is considered one of the foremost trigger factors for a great variety of serious diseases.

Your GALT

Sixty to 80 percent of the lymphatic system is in your small intestine. Called the *gut-associated lymphoid tissue* (GALT), it is almost synonymous with the term *immune system*. The gigantic task of your GALT is to discriminate between nutritious components and possible antigens passing through your bowel.

Since antigens signal the presence of something that threatens the healthy cells and systems of the body, your GALT alerts the immune system to respond appropriately. When your GALT fails to function properly, your immune health is compromised, and dangerous toxins may escape from the colon into your bloodstream. Numerous illnesses could be released to attack virtually any tissue or organ—even your entire body.

That is why lymphomas (cancer of the lymphatic system) spread so rapidly. The lymphatic system literally goes throughout the length of your body. It has been said that death begins in the colon. And so does life.

Lymphoid organs

While your GALT is the most important of all of the lymphatic systems, the lymphoid organs, or organs of the immune system, are positioned throughout the body. They include the spleen, located at the upper left of the abdomen, which is also a staging ground where immune system cells confront foreign microbes. Pockets of lymphoid tissue appear in many other locations throughout the body as well, such as in the bone marrow, thymus, tonsils, adenoids, Peyer's patches, and the appendix.

This brief description of your body's defense system can help you understand how important it is for you to care for your colon by providing proper nutrition for your body. Avert this deadly scenario of a compromised immune system by avoiding processed and devitalized foods, antibiotics, caffeine, alcohol, chlorine, and other toxins.

Maintain a healthy gut, a free-flowing lymph system, and a healthy immune function by following a daily health program. Include plenty of natural foods from the Maker's Diet, which are rich in enzymes, along with probiotics and a lifestyle that includes movement and exercise.

As you may know, your health is vitally connected to a vast universe of microscopic organisms that thrive in and on every living thing. A wide array of antibiotics has been unleashed to kill and destroy virtually all microorganisms. You are about to learn more regarding the critical need to avoid this "micro-mayhem." Many of these tiny microorganisms—the "good bacteria"—may be both the smallest and best friends you'll ever have.

Chapter 4

Hygiene: The Double-edged Sword

AN OBSCURE RACE OF PEOPLE ATTEMPTING TO CROSS THE SINAI Peninsula about 3,500 years ago received a highly advanced system of disease prevention and medical hygiene. The people followed these instructions and somehow escaped the communicable diseases and social ills that devastated other civilizations over the millennia, as they were promised:

> If you diligently heed the voice of the LORD your God...I
> will put none of these diseases on you which I have brought
> on the Egyptians. I am the LORD who heals you.
> —EXODUS 15:26

What was their secret?

It sure wasn't the prevailing wisdom of the times. Their leader Moses, who received the dietary and hygiene system from God, had been trained as a prince of Egypt in the most "advanced" medical system of his era.

Yet, Moses did not advocate to Israel the sure-fire Egyptian prescription for avoiding epidemics. They did not embrace Egypt's "two vulture feathers" and the promise from a god named "Flame-in-his-face" to save them "from every sickness." History records that the Egyptians treated pinkeye with "the urine of a faithful wife" and favored other treatments such as the "blood of a worm" and a healthy plaster of the latest manure concoction![1]

Forensic examinations of mummified Egyptians indicate the upper-class Egyptians didn't receive much benefit from the best that Egyptian physicians had to offer. They suffered from many of the *same diseases* that afflict us today. (They had a taste for unhealthy foods and a blatant disregard for hygiene.)

The Practice of Advanced Hygiene

In contrast, the Israelites followed advanced hygienic practices according to the divine instructions given to Moses. And they enjoyed an extraordinary resistance to sickness and disease. God's hygiene system is remarkably up to date. In fact, modern hospitals everywhere follow nearly every one of the original guidelines God laid out in the Bible.

For example, the biblical hygiene regimen recorded in Numbers 19:11–22 required strict separation of the corpses of the dead from the living. When a person died, those present and anyone who prepared the body for burial (mandated before sundown) were considered *unclean* for seven days.

Those individuals were to wash their hands, clothing, and utensils with *running water,* extensive scrubbing, and a mild astringent. The water was treated with ashes—a key component of soap for millennia—and administered with hyssop, which contained the antiseptic thymol (the active ingredient in Listerine mouthwash).[2] In addition, this biblical hygiene system required that hands be washed before meals and at other key times to ensure cleanliness.

The Bible also prescribes specific techniques for purifying clothing and key instruments or utensils, along with the safe disposal of human waste, proper burial methods, childbirth procedures, sexual hygiene, feminine hygienic guidelines (for the menses), and more.

Leviticus 13 provides detailed instructions for the diagnosis of the disease called leprosy, with strict guidelines for the purification of fabrics contaminated by the disease. It also called for the quarantine of people with any highly infectious disease.

The Purpose of Advanced Hygiene

Proper hygiene is as essential as diet and exercise to optimum health. You can significantly reduce infections, allergy attacks, and other negative health conditions by cleansing your body of toxins, pollutants, allergens, and disease-causing germs.

The direct relationship between good health and good hygiene has long been established. In fact, *the first cure for cancer* was based in proper hygiene. In the eighteenth century, London's chimney sweeps had an extraordinarily high rate of scrotal cancer until it was learned that those who regularly *washed away* the carcinogenic soot on their skin did not contract the disease![3]

Pioneering modern hygiene

One hundred years later, hundreds of thousands of European women were dying of childbirth fever until a Viennese obstetrician named Dr. Semmelweis rediscovered biblical hygiene. His medical students routinely dissected cadavers barehanded in one room and then walked into the next room to perform pelvic examinations or help deliver babies—*without washing their hands!* Death rates often approached the 50 percent mark.

Dr. Semmelweis went against the grain of established medical practice and asked every doctor and medical student to wash their hands between deliveries (and autopsies). When they did, the death rate dropped by 90 percent! However, Dr. Semmelweis was ridiculed for his hygienic practice, and they insisted on going back to the old way![4] It is estimated that even as late as World War II, poor hygiene caused three times more deaths than battlefield wounds.[5]

Germs don't fly—they hitchhike

We have come a long way since then. We now know that the body's immune system is an autonomic or "automatic" function. The body reacts automatically when it senses an invasion by the disease-causing bacteria, fungi, viruses, and allergens that surround us in our homes, job sites, or backyards. Normally, the human immune system effectively fights off these diseases, but it easily becomes overloaded in today's toxic world. To make matters worse, our transglobal travel rapidly transports new diseases around the world in a day!

We also understand that germs don't fly—they *hitchhike*. Germs generally travel via hand-to-hand contact or hand-to-surface-to-hand transfer. Your hands come into contact with the chief agents of infection on hundreds of surfaces daily, including other hands (and whatever *they* have touched). More than 90 percent of the germs on your hands reside under your fingernails. The same is true for allergens and environmental contaminants.

Unfortunately, it is difficult to reach this area with normal hand-washing techniques. And these germs easily enter the body through the nasal passageways or the tear ducts of the eyes when we touch them—which occurs at least twenty times a day. Typically, your fingertips come in contact with your eyes and nose more than 12,500 times each year. Each time there is the potential of *autoinoculating* yourself with germs, allergens, environmental toxins, and viruses.

Autoinoculation of the eyes and nose from contaminated finger-tips is particularly dangerous because the eyes and nose provide a direct pathway to the upper respiratory tract. (Some diseases enter the body through the mouth, but fluids in the mouth and stomach combat pathogens very effectively.) Upper respiratory problems, including sinus problems, account for eight of every ten visits to doctors' offices. The average adult battles four colds per year (six colds annually for children), and nearly one person in three has allergies.

As with most instinctive human behavior, autoinoculation also serves an important *positive* purpose. When a baby first touches its fingertips to its eyes and nose, it introduces its immune system to the outside world, triggering the production of key antibodies to protect it from infection and to preserve health. This natural process continues throughout life, keeping the immune system "attuned" to changes in the outside world.

Reducing Stress on Your Immune System

The good news is that the potentially deadly autoinoculation process is entirely avoidable. Several years ago, I founded a modern hygiene system called Clenzology, which is scientifically designed to remove the over-load of germs from the immune system.

This program of advanced hygiene represents the first real advance-ment in how we wash since the bar of soap was invented about 150 years ago, allowing the body to defend and protect itself against invasion from diseases more effectively. It addresses the proper cleansing of the areas under the fingernails and the membranes around the eyes and nose. These staging areas for germs are virtually neglected by other popular hygiene methods.

Clenzology preserves the *balance* between the proper function of autoinoculation in building the body's natural defense capabilities and its negative role in promoting infection by mass contamination through the eyes and nose. Careful cleaning under the fingernails and the membranes around the eyes and nose through Clenzology techniques reduces stress on the immune system and helps reduce the occurrence of infectious disease and allergies. Once the overload is removed from the immune system, it can devote energy to eliminating other infections that are present in the body, such as lingering bronchitis or sinusitis.

I have personally been using this simple hygiene program faith-fully morning and evening for several years, and it has kept me virtually free from all respiratory illness and sinus infections. With my frequent North American and international travel, it is comforting to know that I am providing myself a daily measure of protection.

Deterring allergies

Clenzology techniques thoroughly *cleanse* or wash away contaminants, but they do not *sterilize* the fingernail beds and body membranes around the eyes and nasal passages. Sterilization using antimicrobial substances does more harm than good, preventing the immune system from adapting to the outside environment; this is especially important where allergies are concerned.

More than 50 million people suffer from allergies, and the suffering continues even though many have visited allergists, taken tests, tried shots, and ingested recommended drugs. Allergies are caused by *mistaken immune system responses* to harmless substances such as pollen, cat hair, or dust mites. These responses produce defensive immune symptoms such as runny noses and watering eyes.

The allergy industry treats allergies through the exclusive use of drugs that either *desensitize* the immune system toward potential allergens or *suppress* its natural response system altogether. Most of these drugs have multiple side effects and are only marginally effective. While we can't ignore the suffering, we can take a simpler, commonsense approach to the problem.

The concepts of advanced hygiene offer better cleansing techniques that will keep most of the offending substances away from your body (and may even avoid triggering an immune system response altogether).

I am astounded that this simple approach of keeping allergens away from the body is not more prevalent. It is the failure of traditional pharmaceutical allergy treatments (pills, sprays, and injected drugs) to genuinely relieve allergy symptoms that has triggered the resurgent interest in alternative methods of treatment. If you or your family suffers from frequent colds and flu, nagging allergies, upper respiratory problems, weakened immunity, or other chronic health problems, I urge you to try the age-old, proven method of advanced hygiene. For more information on Clenzology, see page 286 or visit www.makersdiet.com.

The Rest of the Microbe Story

The common approach to hygiene has classified all germs (microbes) as "bad." Actually, the Creator designed our bodies to make the maximum use of naturally occurring substances in our environment—including microbes or "germs."

Every day scientists fan out around the globe with spoons and sandwich bags in hand looking for new sources of soil microorganisms in bat caves, jungle clearings, peat bogs, hot springs, undersea volcanoes, and even from mummies. Each exotic locale may yield a completely new discovery of germs—a gold mine of potential pharmaceutical profits. Some leading government officials and scientists in the United States suspect that organisms in our soil may yield powerful new treatments for AIDS, cancer, and other deadly diseases. Even the National Cancer Institute is funding research on soil organisms.

We have just begun to harvest the vast resources of biological "bugs," and the search for new "super antibiotics" is growing more intense. Yet, it seems the pool of known antibiotic formulas is growing less and less effective in the face of ever-mutating "super bugs" and infectious diseases.

Why all the scientific excitement about dirt? Nothing fuels a worldwide hunt like the potential of *finding treasure*. In this case, the treasure is newly discovered microbes, different from any that have been used to date to create antibiotics. Many current antibiotics *come from microbes in the soil*, including streptomycin, the first treatment for tuberculosis, and vancomycin, currently the drug of last resort for the toughest infections.[6] The following are examples of treasure hunters who have discovered valuable microbes:

- An employee of Sandoz Pharmaceutical took a vacation in Norway and gathered a soil sample containing a mold that later led to the development of cyclosporine, the celebrated antirejection drug used in transplants.
- A scientist discovered microbes that can turn starch into sugar in the soil of an Indonesian temple.
- A researcher in Japan picked up a clump of soil from a golf course that produced a drug now used to cure parasitic infections plaguing livestock.

Have You Had Your Packet of 10,000 Species Yet?

Does the subject of dirt seem boring to you? Did you know that one gram of soil—enough to fill a little packet of sugar—can contain as many as 10,000 species of microbes unknown to science, according to Jo Handelsman, a professor of plant pathology at the University of Wisconsin.[7]

Business Week notes, "Now, for the first time, [Handelsman] and her colleagues…are learning to extract the DNA of these mysterious creatures and clone it. They are finding that the microbes differ so profoundly from known bacteria that they could represent entirely new kingdoms of life—as different from other bacteria as animals are from plants. That means that the proteins produced by these creatures could have properties unlike any other known substances." Handelsman said that several new antibiotics have been identified from such soil microbes.[8]

It Takes a Healthy "Community" to Keep Us Healthy

The same article explains the working principles of soil microbes (also called homeostatic soil organisms, or HSOs) that helped turn around my personal health problems, and it gives understanding of why anyone with Crohn's or any other disease may well benefit from them:

> Even human intestines—an environment most people consider pretty familiar—are home to perhaps 10,000 kinds of microbes….Indeed, one of the surprises in the decoding of the human genome was that it contains more than 200 genes that come from bacteria. Microbes not only keep us alive; in some small part, we are made of them.
>
> [Researchers are] now looking at how these largely unknown microbes might play a role in Crohn's disease, an inflammation of the small intestine. [They have] found that the makeup of the mixed "community" of microbes in the intestines changes in people with the disease. A similar thing might happen with tuberculosis…leading [researchers] to wonder whether some diseases might be caused not by a single dangerous microbe, but by a change in the microbial community—an ecological imbalance inside the human body.[9]

Countless numbers of microorganisms live in the soil, in and on plants, and in the human gut. Inside and out we are at one with the earth (or we should be). What depth of incomprehensible wisdom lies in the biblical statement in Genesis 2:7: "And the LORD God formed man of the dust of the [earth], and breathed into his nostrils the breath of life; and man became a living being."

Do Everyone a Favor: Come Home "Dirty"

Through the centuries, our society has migrated from living with too little hygiene (ignorant of the deadly potential of germs) to an environment that is too clean.

In 1989, Dr. David Strachan, a respected epidemiologist at Britain's London School of Hygiene and Tropical Medicine, launched a tidal wave of debate with a complex theorem of human immunology development and disease control, saying, *"We need dirt."*

Dr. Strachan proposed that society's growing separation from dirt and germs may well be the cause of weaker immune systems resulting in the growing incidence of a wide range of maladies.[10] Dr. Strachan advanced the "overcleanliness theory" after noticing that children belonging to large families were much less likely to develop asthma, hay fever, or eczema. He theorized that older children coming home dirty with all sorts of resident soil microorganisms were actually protecting their younger brothers and sisters by exposing their immune systems to microbes and causing them to build antibodies. He may be on to something.

Near-epidemic waves of diseases all but unheard of in previous generations are striking modern societies around the world. (They are still virtually unknown in primitive societies today.) How many people do *you* know who suffer from asthma, allergies of all kinds, irritable bowel syndrome, rheumatoid arthritis, lupus, Crohn's disease, chronic fatigue syndrome, or immune disorders of some kind? The list seems to be endless.

If Dr. Strachan is right (and a growing number of scientists and medical researchers believe he is), then dirt—or to be more specific, the microbes in earth's soil—may be some of our best friends. A recent report in *New Scientist* said researchers have discovered that microorganisms found in dirt influence maturation of the immune system so that it is either functional or dysfunctional.[11]

Long before the factories of the Industrial Age and the existence of modern grocery stores, people tended to get dirty just gathering or harvesting their food. The longest-lived people were exposed to all sorts of microscopic bugs living in the soil. Life in the pre–Industrial Age depended on what grew and lived in and on the earth; "dirt" and "soil" were not negative concepts in the minds of our primitive ancestors.

Reward Offered: My Missing Microorganisms

Technology may be expanding exponentially, but nature is not. We are a part of God's *natural* creation, so most of us will benefit by returning the missing soil microorganisms to our bodies.

So-called "enlightened parents" do everything they can today to keep Junior from getting "dirty." The sad truth is, our environment is too clean! Immune cells that do not have adequate exposure to soil microbes tend to overreact when they do come into contact with them. Too many adults and children have been denied this much-needed exposure to soil microorganisms. The immune systems of children and even adults are overreactive because they are no longer being properly "educated" in the biological playground of life.

To make matters worse, we oversterilize everything with disinfectant dishwashing, hand soaps, and shower gels; disinfectant body lotions and skin bars; and "deodorant soaps" loaded with antibiotic disinfectants such as triclosan. And we sterilize our soil using pesticides and herbicides that destroy beneficial and harmful microbes alike. These agents harm even the natural immune systems of the very plants we try to "help" with our technological advances.

After years of medical and nutritional research, I am personally convinced that our immune systems need regular exposure to naturally occurring soil organisms for long-term health! The immune system of a child deprived of early exposure to soil organisms may seriously overreact when exposed to various benign intruders later in life. It seems to be a consequence of our lost connection with earth that children and adults develop allergies, autoimmune diseases, and certain types of asthma.

Th Cells: Equipped to Defend and Serve

A growing body of evidence implies the immune system will never reach its peak defensive capability against foreign organisms and chemical toxins until we reestablish this lost connection to the earth's soil.

Exposure to these microorganisms "conditions" the human immune system so that it intuitively knows when to produce and activate so-called nondifferentiated T-helper cells (Th cells) that are primarily produced by the thymus gland. These Th cells control the initiation or suppression of the body's immune reactions, and they also regulate many other immune cells. The quality and strength of the immune system are often measured with a classification method called the "Th1/Th2 balance."

Th1 cells promote *specialized* cell-mediated (inside the cell) immunity. These are the quintessential "special forces" that defend the body efficiently. Th1 cells produce only as many germ-zapping antibodies as necessary to stop an invader. Theirs is a *targeted response* with economy of action.

Th2 cells, on the other hand, produce a *mass response* to infection in the form of specialized proteins called *antibodies,* secreted into body fluids by "B" cells (or B-lymphocytes). Th2 cells are the army and navy—the "total response" defenders in your body.

These two infection-fighting forces exist side by side. The body's Th1 cellular immunity force attacks abnormal cells and microorganisms at the site of infection—*inside* the individual cells. Th2 cells trigger the mass production of antibodies to neutralize foreign invaders and substances—*outside* the cells.

A healthy immune system has balanced Th1 and Th2 activity, and it can switch back and forth between the two as needed to eradicate a threat quickly. *Illnesses* result from immune system underresponse and overresponse. For example, the overabundance of Th2 antibodies is implicated in a wide variety of chronic illnesses, including AIDS, chronic fatigue syndrome, candidiasis, chronic allergies, multiple chemical sensitivities (MCS), viral hepatitis, Gulf War syndrome, cancer, lupus, and many other illnesses.

"Organisms 'R' Us"

The soil across the North American continent was exceedingly rich in bacteria and other organisms for thousands of years, and every civilization it supported enjoyed the bounty it produced. After World War II, however, these natural soil organisms were displaced as a result of chemical farming and pesticide usage by commercial agribusiness.

Years ago, the food we harvested from the field was covered with beneficial microorganisms that "became part of us" when we ate the produce. Today, America's soil is essentially sterile. Pesticides and herbicides are believed to be the "total solution" in the natural world. They kill virtually every microorganism they touch, much as our overuse of medical antibiotics has reduced the human gut to a burned-out minefield, destroying the good guys along with the bad guys.

As we have stated, most people aren't exposed to large enough quantities of microorganisms from our soil, dust, air, water, and foods to achieve optimal health on a daily basis. One exception might be veterinarians who specialize in treating large animals. It is estimated they take in large amounts of microorganisms and animal dung involuntarily (primarily through the lungs) when exposed to large herds of livestock.

One veterinarian in the Midwest spends most of his time tending large herds of livestock—on-site in the barns, feeding areas, and fields.

His associates noticed he was virtually impervious to the usual strains of *E coli* and other contaminants in old food and even "chemistry accidents" in the clinic refrigerator. His immune system was like iron, and he very rarely suffered from colds or the usual respiratory complaints, conceivably from his exposure to a wide variety of microorganisms.

For most of us, however, our overly sterile environment, which has virtually severed our healthy relationship to the earth, is seriously weakening our immune systems. And the sterility of our foods isn't helping our immune systems either. We have learned to increase "shelf life" by irradiating or chemically treating our produce and prepared foods to kill microorganisms. These modern, high-tech processing methods used by food manufacturers remove and destroy many of the most important life-giving nutrients in our food.

Drinking an Indiscriminate Killer

Water supplies from wells and rivers once teemed with mycobacteria, including some pathogens that were downright deadly. Chlorine and other disinfectant substances helped make our public water supplies much safer than a century ago, and that is no doubt important to the public health. Unfortunately, most public water purification systems neglect to *remove* the chlorine after it has done its job in the water.

That means that chlorine continues to kill *all* bacteria—even the "good guys" inside our bodies. We're drinking an indiscriminate killer with the government's blessing. Populations in countries with low rates of asthma still drink water with billions of mycobacteria per liter. While I wouldn't advocate drinking impure water to reconstitute the bacteria in your body, I do recommend filtering your tap water with a high-quality purification system (to remove chlorine).

Did You Get Your RDA of Antibiotics?

We have discussed the problem of treating symptoms of disease with antibiotics, since they kill both good and bad bacteria. Even if you don't take antibiotics, you almost certainly consume them in animal products. United States pharmaceutical firms produce more than 35 million pounds of antibiotics each year, and animals receive the vast bulk of them. Growers routinely give big helpings of antibiotics to cattle, pigs, and poultry to prevent infections from spreading in their stressful, crowded quarters. It is so bad that the European Common Market refuses to import livestock from American farms.

Researchers estimate that by consuming just one glass of commercially processed and packaged milk from your local supermarket shelf, you unknowingly ingest the residues of as many as one hundred different antibiotics![12] (Perhaps they should be included in the government's official RDA list of "Recommended Daily Allowances.") This constant exposure to low-dose antibiotics is one reason behind the increase in *antibiotic-resistant bacteria.*

The intestine of a healthy child or adult normally contains billions of bacteria and other microorganisms from up to 10,000 different species. Ideally, the beneficial or benign *bacteria* in your body should outnumber the *cells* of your body by approximately one hundred to one. One side benefit of these friendly bacteria is that they also increase the body's levels of interferon, a powerful immunity-boosting chemical. These beneficial bacteria are your best friends!

Handling the Double-edged Sword

The *beneficial* bacteria in the environment and in your gut serve as your first line of immune defense against the *unfriendly* bacteria and fungi without and within. This is the "doubled-edged sword" of hygiene: to keep your immune system from being overloaded with harmful substances, and still be exposed to the environment enough to "set" and properly program your immune responses for maximum effectiveness.

Adults and children face even more problems in our toxic world when stress, medications, and poor diet combine to reduce *friendly* bacteria to such a great extent that *unfriendly* bacteria begin to thrive. That is exactly what happens when high doses of antibiotics wipe out all the bacteria in your gut.

Once that happens, the race is on to see whether the "good guys" or the "bad guys" recolonize and set up shop in the empty real estate of the sterile digestive system. Unfortunately, if the harmful bacteria gain the upper hand (as they usually do since they thrive on the typical American sugary, high-carbohydrate diet), poor health soon follows.

Get Your Gut Balanced and Get Well

The best way to quickly replenish and stabilize friendly bacteria in the gastrointestinal tract and develop a balanced immune system that reacts only as needed is the regular ingestion of live, fermented, probiotic-rich food and supplementation with homeostatic soil organisms. Homeostatic soil organisms (HSOs), in addition to a diet that includes liberal amounts of cultured or fermented foods including yogurt, kefir, and sauerkraut, will create the proper balance your gut needs to be healthy.

Homeostatic soil organisms produce proteins that the body interprets as *antigens* (a protein from a foreign substance or microorganism that stimulates an immune response). The way the soil organisms stimulate the Th cells of the immune system directly influences other immune cells (especially the B-lymphocytes manufactured in the bone marrow), and they trigger production of *nonspecific* or *unprogrammed* antibodies.

Unprogrammed antibodies have not been preprogrammed to *overreact* to foreign substances. They remain free and available for specific assignment to points where they are needed. Constant exposure to soil organisms helps to reeducate the body's Th cells so they become more "tolerant" of foreign cells, helping them to mount only necessary immune responses without excess. It is as if the HSOs send the immune cells "back to school" to learn their jobs all over again and perform them even better.

Regular ingestion of HSOs produces a significant reservoir of extra antibodies ready for targeted response, greatly increasing the effectiveness of an individual's immune system. (Unfortunately this reservoir appears to diminish when HSO ingestion ends.) It seems that homeostatic soil organisms help to restore the lost link between the human body and the earth.

While speaking at a nutritional seminar in 1999, I met a board-certified gastroenterologist named Joseph Brasco, M.D., who was seeking new options for his patients with gastrointestinal disorders. Dr. Brasco had read about my recovery from Crohn's diseases in an article published in the *Townsend Letter for Doctors and Patients* and had already seen significant improvement in many of his patients by combining diet modification with HSO supplementation. He is but one of many respected medical professionals who are turning to the Maker's Diet and HSOs to restore health to their patients. Dr. Brasco and I have since become close friends, and he and I have coauthored the book *Restoring Your Digestive Health* to help those suffering from digestive problems.

Reverse the Vicious Cycle

Unfortunately, people who are sick or who are recovering from a sickness tend to seek out "comfort food" such as milk shakes, breads, pastas, cookies, and fries. These are the very foods that promote the rapid growth of disease-causing bacteria! This dysbiosis, or bacterial imbalance in the gut, results in abnormal fermentation in the small intestine.[13]

Fermentation is somewhat desirable in the large intestine because it produces butyrate and other short-chain fatty acids that nourish the cells of the intestinal wall.[14] In the small intestine, however, the growth of yeast, fungi, and/or fermenting pathogenic bacteria may damage the gut lining, cause toxic by-products to be absorbed, and impair the absorption of vital nutrients.[15] Instead of eating junk food and feeding the vicious cycle, you can improve the microbial balance in your gut by consuming the nutrient-rich live foods in the Maker's Diet as well as supplemental HSOs.

Antibiotic Bandages Cover More Serious Issues

Individuals who make repeated use of broad-spectrum antibiotics, oral contraceptives, and steroid medications may set up conditions for over-growth of opportunistic organisms in their bodies that are not controlled by drugs or that are able to recolonize rapidly once antibiotic treatment has ended, causing more disease symptoms. In this way, excessive antibiotic treatments become "temporary bandages" placed over more serious health issues with far-reaching consequences.

In short, it is easier to treat *symptoms* than to do the extensive medical sleuthing it takes to get to the root cause of patients' complaints. Medical science routinely resorts to antibiotics to deal with recognized symptoms, without assuring treatment or elimination of the cause of those symptoms.

Yeast and fungal organisms are especially aggressive in weakened intestinal systems. When antibiotics kill the harmful bacteria they are targeting, they also indiscriminately decimate the friendly bacteria in the body. This allows other harmful bacteria, yeast, and fungi in the body, which are normally held in check by the friendly bacteria, to begin to multiply profusely, causing other disease conditions.

For example, the overgrowth of *Candida albicans*, an especially potent yeast-like fungus, leads to a potentially serious condition called *candidiasis*. It may inflame the tongue, mouth, or rectum, cause vaginitis, or trigger a range of mental and emotional symptoms, including irritability, anxiety, and even depression. Many allergies have been causally linked to candida yeast overgrowth. It sometimes goes undetected because symptoms initially may appear to be innocuous digestive disorders such as bloating, heartburn, constipation, and diarrhea.

Secret Abuse at the Pharmacy

Doctors, pharmacists, and consumers alike face a critical need to use antibiotics in a safe and effective manner. The abuse of antibiotic medication often starts with our children. According to the American Academy of Pediatrics, 95 percent of the children in the United States will receive treatment with antibiotics for a middle ear infection by age five. Some children will tolerate it; others will not fare as well once the antibiotics destroy their population of beneficial bacteria.

Research has shown that the prevention and treatment of dysbiosis and dysbacteriosis are among the most challenging problems doctors face today![16] When dysbiosis sets in, creating imbalance between the protective or "friendly" bacteria and the "unfriendly" bacteria, even normally harmless organisms encountered may produce illness.

Studies implicate intestinal bacterial imbalances as a basis for conditions ranging from recurrent infections and immune breakdown to chronic fatigue.[17] Dysbiosis may leave us predisposed to ailments such as diarrhea, constipation, irritable bowel syndrome, colon cancer, allergies, vaginitis, increased susceptibility to infection, food cravings, lack of mental clarity, hypoglycemia, and many more conditions. Most doctors would rarely connect the cause of these illnesses to the microbial populations of the gastrointestinal tract.

Gut Problems Are Only the Beginning

Dysbiosis may also affect body tissues far from the intestinal site, including the brain, joints, muscles, and the immune system. Dysbiosis, the imbalance of microorganisms in the gut, really "export their misery" very effectively. Symptoms are diverse and may include headaches, learning disorders, insomnia, immune dysfunction, behavioral disorders, chronic fatigue, joint pain, and nutritional deficiencies.

Other more familiar conditions may also be traced to an imbalanced gastrointestinal tract microbial population. These include irritable bowel syndrome, Crohn's disease, fibromyalgia, leaky gut syndrome, wasting disease, diverticulitis, hemorrhoids, and breast and colon cancer.

Where the Gut Hits the Wallet

Contrary to the popular notion that "ignorance is bliss," where your health is concerned, ignorance can be costly at best and deadly at worst. Digestive diseases and other conditions related to unhealthy intestinal flora imbalances have an enormous impact on our health and the nation's financial bottom line as well.

New technologies and new drugs have revolutionized the understanding and treatment of peptic ulcer disease and gastrointestinal esophageal reflux disease (GERD). Everyone hopes that *future* research will reduce the economic and healthcare costs related to diagnosing and treating digestive diseases. But I believe we could benefit right now by tapping proven wisdom from the *past*.

Your body desperately requires healthy intestinal flora because your health depends on it. A healthy gastrointestinal system has a balance of approximately 85 percent "good" bacteria to 15 percent "bad" micro-organisms. Unfortunately, most of us show the *reverse ratio*. My own nearly fatal struggle with Crohn's disease is a severe example of what happens when microbial imbalance abounds. If our ignorance about hygiene contributes to the problem, then we should determine to educate ourselves. The benefits we reap will be immense.

The following chart summarizes the simple steps you can take to restore and maintain a healthy gut.

STEPS TO A HEALTHY GUT
1.   **Restore your connection to the soil.**
•   You may not be comfortable making mud pies, so I recommend that you do a little gardening, hike in the mountains, or supplement your diet with homeostatic soil organisms. A growing number of scientists, nutritionists, and medical doctors are convinced this is the most effective way to enhance the healing response of the body.
2.   **Reap the benefits of HSO supplementation.**
•   Most people who begin HSO supplementation in concert with healthy dietary choices see a rapid and overall improvement in bodily functions and natural immunity to disease and infection.
•   Cholesterol levels tend to drop while energy levels increase; many notice an enhanced resistance to disease-causing organisms such as colds and flu. We have even seen increases in serum enzymes and normalization of serum albumin, indicating improved lymphatic flow and removal of lymphatic blockages.

STEPS TO A HEALTHY GUT
• Soil organisms also produce substances called bacteriocins, which act as natural antibiotics to kill almost any kind of pathogenic microorganisms and to set up a protective shield in the gut.
• Hardy HSOs survive the harsh environment of the gut. Unlike traditional probiotics, HSOs seem to be much hardier and are better able to survive the harsh environment of the intestine until they reach the location where they are most needed in the gut.
• Soil organisms seem to be especially well equipped to establish colonies in the entire digestive system, starting in the esophagus and ending in the colon. They attach themselves to the walls of the digestive tract and burrow behind any putrefaction lining the intestinal walls where they consume or destroy unfriendly microorganisms. The waste products are then dislodged and flushed out of the body in the normal evacuation process.
• HSOs also seem to act aggressively against protozoa, worms, and other parasites within the intestines and related organs and tissues. Even *Candida albicans*, along with other yeast and molds, is obliterated.

Do You Need an Immune Boost?

The natural detoxification of the intestinal tract promoted by HSOs increases the body's ability to absorb nutrients. It also strengthens the immune system by removing mucoid plaque that covers the gut-associated lymphoid tissues (GALT), and it boosts the body's ability to fight off infectious viruses and bacteria.

If these statements sound a little far-fetched, remember that scientists from the world's leading research institutions, governmental health agencies, and pharmaceutical firms are scouring the soils of the earth for more soil organisms from which to create their medicines. The following list briefly describes the health benefits scientists attribute to the consumption of homeostatic soil organisms (HSOs):[18]

- *Pool new RNA/DNA in the cells.* HSOs provide a rich source of coded instructions for the cells to reactivate their own repair called DNA and RNA. HSOs appear to work in a symbiotic (mutually beneficial) relationship with body tissues by creating a pool of extra DNA/RNA raw materials. This reserve is immediately available upon demand, accelerating the healing process when cells are damaged by wounds, burns, surgical incisions, and infections.

- *Quench free radicals by creating superoxide dismutase (SOD).* HSOs produce superoxide dismutase (SOD), a powerful antioxidant. Unless extinguished at once, free radicals attack any physiological molecule, causing cancers and other tissue damage. SOD works enzymatically as a first-line defense against free radicals, stopping them cold before they can cause organ damage.

- *Stimulate alpha interferon production.* HSOs seem to stimulate the production of the polypeptide *alpha interferon* (a molecular protein and a key immune system regulator). The scientific community long ago recognized the virus-fighting ability of alpha interferon. They synthesized the alpha interferon to treat a variety of illnesses, including hepatitis. (Unfortunately, it is extremely costly, inefficient, and has many adverse side effects.)

- *Stimulate the production of human lactoferrin.* A substance present in homeostatic soil organisms stimulates the formation of human lactoferrin, one of the body's iron-carrying proteins. The iron carried by the lactoferrin protein is released to healthy cells and not available to feed pathogenic microorganisms or contribute to iron overload.

The newly recognized ability of soil organisms to aid our quest for healing and maintaining good health is one of the most exciting breakthroughs in modern health. (Isn't it ironic that we are talking about soil organisms as old as the earth?)

I would urge anyone with intractable autoimmune conditions, allergies, low energy, inability to gain weight, fibromyalgia, and chronic fatigue syndrome to take advantage of HSOs. Parents of children with chronic middle ear infections would do well by their children to give them HSO supplementation as well. For more information on HSOs, see pages 74–79.

Will You Choose a Road Less Traveled?

Even though they were virtually unknown just two hundred years ago, we now know these invisible organisms, good and bad, play vital roles in our health—and, potentially, in our destruction. We have discussed three simple steps to guard our health from the bad guys and strengthen it with the good guys:

1. First, we balance the double-edged sword of hygiene by *cleansing* rather than sterilizing our bodies (particularly under the fingernails and around the eyes and nasal passages) using Clenzology. This permits *exposure* to the environment without *overload*.
2. Second, we feed our bodies healthy living foods from the Maker's Diet.
3. Third, we repopulate and strengthen the living environment in the gut with HSOs.

These are three relatively simple steps to improved health. However, most of us are careening down a different path, following what I call the "modern prescription for illness." It is an easily accessible path of least resistance—simply follow the standard American diet (SAD), consume whatever you find at America's fast-food restaurants, and fill your homes and bodies with toxic chemicals hidden in common items that advertisements make you believe you can't live without. The destination is the same for all travelers—illness that could be avoided by taking a road less traveled.

HOW TO KNOW IF YOU HAVE DYSBIOSIS

Dysbiosis is a health condition of living with intestinal flora that has harmful effects, due to putrefaction, fermentation (carbohydrate intolerance), deficiency, or sensitization. The following lists include many of the symptoms and major causes of dysbiosis.

Common symptoms
- Abdominal pain or cramps
- Colon cancer
- Constipation or diarrhea
- Distention/bloating

HOW TO KNOW IF YOU HAVE DYSBIOSIS

- Fatigue/fatigue after eating
- Flatulence (excessive gas)
- Bad breath
- Body odor
- Food allergy
- Hypoglycemia
- Inability to lose weight
- Irregular bowel movements
- Irritable bowel syndrome
- Itchy anus
- Leaky gut syndrome
- Poor complexion
- Poor digestion
- Rheumatoid arthritis
- Spastic colon

Major causes

- Decreased immune function
- Decreased intestinal motility (constipation)
- Drugs—especially antibiotics, oral contraceptives, and cortisone-like medications
- Intestinal infection
- Maldigestion and malabsorption
- Poor diet—excessive carbohydrates, sugar, and trans fats
- Stress—including long-term emotional stress

Chapter 5

How to Get Sick:
A Modern Prescription for Illness

UNDER IDEAL CONDITIONS, EVERYONE WOULD BE BORN PERFECT and without flaws. In reality, we *all* carry genetic and metabolic weaknesses and are constantly bombarded and attacked by potentially harmful bacteria, viruses, fungi, and industrial toxins.

I'm convinced that we all have predetermined weaknesses in our bodies. Mine was the gut, but yours may be the lungs, the cardiovascular system, the blood, or the kidneys.

If we eat unhealthy foods and adopt unwise lifestyles, we may well see these predetermined weaknesses present themselves as devastating symptoms. Unfortunately, many of us exist in a state of subclinical illness (often unawares). That means we can't afford to go through life without taking certain precautions.

In my case, I will take extra care with my diet and lifestyle for the rest of my life because I don't want a replay of my illness. I will resist medications of any kind—especially antibiotics. And unless I'm forced at gunpoint, I will never knowingly take another vaccination.

How to Get Sick

I focus extensively on wise food and dietary decisions elsewhere in this book, but in this chapter I examine a short list of nonfood danger areas that may threaten our long-term health. In fact, if you want to "get sick," follow these twenty-seven recommendations of the "world," and you will achieve just that. But if you, like majority of us, want to remain healthy as long as possible, go against these twenty-seven suggestions if at all possible. The list may surprise you. Be sure to examine the evidence and reasoning for each item to see why it made the dubious list I've called "How to Get Sick."

1. Stay out of the sun.

Civilizations throughout history have understood that the sun is vital to human health. The human skin uses the energy from the sun to manufacture vitamin D for the body. This hormone/vitamin is important for many reasons, including its role in strengthening immune system function and proper mineral absorption.

Critics claim that exposure to the UV rays of the sun cause higher rates of melanoma and other forms of skin cancer. This might be true for a small population segment—those with compromised immune systems who don't consume adequate nutrients (especially healthy fats). However, the people who actually get the most exposure to sunlight in different parts of the world exhibit the lowest incidence of skin cancer. The only logical explanation is that exposure to sunlight is not unhealthy.

What is unhealthy is exposure to sunlight with the diets we consume. Rex Russell, M.D., notes that when sunlight activates the phytochemicals in healthy foods, consumption of these foods not only blocks the harmful effects of UV rays, but they also produce "antiviral, antibacterial, and anticancer components, as well as pest repellents."[1]

2. Go to bed after midnight.

This is a great way to get sick. From biblical times to just before the Industrial Revolution, people used to go to sleep and rise with the setting and rising of the sun. This is the natural way to link your peak activity to the body's natural hormonal rhythms.

Dr. Joseph Mercola believes the timing of your sleep affects its quality. He says, "The more hours that you can sleep before midnight, the better off you will be."[2] He cites a study published in the *Lancet* (a respected medical journal in Great Britain) indicating chronic sleep loss produces serious symptoms mimicking the effects of aging and the early stages of diabetes (including age-related insulin resistance and memory loss).[3] And finally, according to the late Elmer Josephson, "Authorities tell us that one hour of sleep before midnight is equivalent to four hours afterward."[4]

3. Never let them see you sweat.

Any attempt to artificially prevent perspiration is very unhealthy because perspiration is the Maker's method of safely cooling the body while excreting numerous toxins. Suppressing this natural sweat response in your underarms or other areas blocks the body's cleansing process and the natural flow of the lymphatic system. Interference in normal lymphatic function may increase the risk of breast cancer. The products most often used to stop perspiration contain forms of aluminum, which has been linked to Alzheimer's disease or other neurological problems; triclosan, an antimicrobial absorbed through the skin that poses some risk to the liver; and zirconium-based compounds that can cause underarm granulomas.[5] For more information about these products and possible alternative choices, see David Steinman & Samuel S. Epstein, M.D., *The Safe Shopper's Bible* (New York: Hungry Minds, Inc., 1995).

4. Take megavitamins.

The use of massive amounts of vitamins and minerals is very unnatural—especially the popular and cheap synthetic and isolated "vitamins" created in chemical plants and widely sold in discount retail stores. The human body was not designed to consume such artificial products, especially in such excessive amounts. Nature prevents us from consuming 20,000 mg of vitamin C in one day because it is impossible to consume three hundred oranges (a natural source of vitamin C) in one day. Even if you could, it would produce one major colon cleanse! Vitamins and minerals that have not been incorporated into an organic matrix—a natural food form containing all necessary cofactors—may actually be very harmful to the body. It is better to supplement healthy food and beverage choices with living food supplements known as homeostatic nutrients rich in vitamins and minerals. This is a balanced form the body can absorb and utilize.

5. Use fluoride toothpaste and mouthwash, and drink fluoridated water.

Fluoride is extremely poisonous—especially the salt-based form used in toothpaste and mouthwash. (Besides, its effectiveness is questionable at best.) A top EPA scientific advisor voiced the opinion that "since recent federal government tests have shown that fluoride appears to cause cancers at levels less than ten times the present maximum contamination level, this would ordinarily require that all additions of fluoride to water supplies be suspended and treatment be instituted to remove naturally occurring fluoride."[6] That would be enough warning for me! (By the way, I have no evidence that the EPA ever suspended fluoridation operations.) Choose nonfluoridated alternatives for oral hygiene and be safe.

6. Use artificial sweeteners and avoid sugars.

As bad as sugar can be in its various forms, artificial sweeteners are worse! Some are downright deadly because of their carcinogenic properties and their use in such high-volume products as diet soft drinks and sugar-free foods. Chief among sinners is aspartame, which is marketed as NutraSweet or Equal. Renowned diabetes expert Dr. H. J. Roberts believes there is a clear scientific link between aspartame and increased incidence of brain tumors, seizure disorders, chronic headaches, and hyperactivity in children.[7] As for saccharin, the cancer-causing labels that accompany its use still apply. The newcomer on the block is sucralose (used in Splenda), but the jury of scientific research still seems to be awaiting further testimony on this one. (If the Maker didn't produce it "as is," then it probably isn't much better than the other synthetic sugar substitutes.)

7. Shower every day, but don't bathe (take a bath).

Excessive showering—even in the purest water—can actually rob your hair and body of the natural oils.[8] It can also alter your body's pH (especially if you're using certain alkaline shampoos and soaps). Then you have the added problem of heavily chlorinated public water supplies (see below). If the Maker has a preference, it might be the use of ritual bathing that combined bathing (washing in a shallow bath) with sprinkling (showering for brief periods). This combination is especially beneficial for the thorough but gentle cleansing recommended for the female genital area.

8. Swim in chlorinated pools (and drink and shower with chlorinated water).

Chlorine is an effective bacteria killer, although some strains of bacteria are developing a resistance to chlorine. Unfortunately, chlorine is an indiscriminate killer that kills both friendly and unfriendly bacteria. It also eats through lead pipes, corrodes most metals, and harms cells and DNA strands in virtually every living thing it touches. Chlorine also introduces to our water supplies some highly carcinogenic chemicals called trihalomethanes (THMs). Studies show a strong link between chlorinated water supplies with elevated THM levels and cancers of the bladder, kidney, liver, pancreas, gastrointestinal tract, urinary tract, colon, and brain.[9] It is risky enough to drink chlorinated tap water, but the mass exposure created by swimming in chlorinated pools or taking extended hot showers in heavily chlorinated water is much more dangerous. (The heat opens skin pores and increases the already high absorption rate of chlorine through the skin.) Dogs exposed to chlorine (this is the ingredient used to bleach white bread) get the running fits, a disorder similar to many psychiatric disorders in humans.

9. Don't breast feed your baby.

Mothers, consider breastfeeding your children if you don't want them to risk the trauma of numerous childhood diseases and if you don't want to pay the hospital bills. It will also reduce your risk of developing breast cancer by 25 percent, and it may lower the risk of postpartum depression! Mother's milk contains cells that attack harmful bacteria in the baby's system, and it is able to form antibodies that destroy invading viruses as well. Mother's milk is the Maker's perfect food for babies, delivered in the close bonds of maternal intimacy.[10]

10. Get tattoos.

Scripture warns against piercing the skin. (See Leviticus 19:28.) Body piercing and tattoos can easily introduce potentially deadly infections and toxic foreign substances into the body and bloodstream. Some health providers warn that even tiny puncture wounds might block important electrical nerve impulses just under the skin.

11. Get all of your immunization shots.

Despite massive media and government public relations campaigns to the contrary, certain childhood immunization injections may pose considerable risks to children. Most adults today received one to five immunizations in childhood, but schoolchildren today receive an average of twenty-two or more immunizations—most of them administered while the brain and nervous system are still developing!

An epidemic of juvenile autism and other neurological and developmental disorders sweeping through America's school-age children generally coincides with the introduction of certain mandatory immunizations. A growing body of scientific and medical research appears to link this dangerous health trend to these childhood immunizations.

Vijendra K. Singh, Ph.D., an eminent neuroimmunologist from the Department of Biology and Biotechnology Center at Utah State University, hypothesized in research published internationally "that a measles virus-induced autoimmune response is a causal factor in autism, whereas HHV-6 via co-infection may contribute to pathophysiology of the disorder. Although as yet unproven, I think it is an excellent working hypothesis to explain autism, and it may also help us understand why some children show autistic regression after the measles-mumps-rubella (MMR) immunization."[11]

Dr. Singh's findings seem to confirm the results of a similar study published in the *Lancet* in 1998 by Dr. Andrew Wakefield and co-workers of the Royal Free Hospital in London, indicating a possible link between MMR vaccination, Crohn's disease of the bowel, and autism.[12] Most states allow philosophical and religious exemptions from mandatory immunization programs should you decide this is the way to go.

12. Travel in airplanes often.

Some people who spend a lot of time at high altitudes experience problems with infertility and oxygen production in the body. The body adapts well to high altitudes for short periods of time, but not for long periods. Animals dwelling at heights of thirteen to fourteen thousand feet have much more difficulty conceiving and instinctively return to lower pastures for breeding. Some researchers believe the atmospheric pressures and radiation to which airplane travelers are exposed are the equivalent of hundreds of CAT scans and pose the greatest oxidative stress on the human body.[13] (Who wants to be trapped in a small room with hundreds of sneezing, coughing people?)

13. Expose yourself often to electromagnetic energy.

Everywhere you go, you run into electromagnetic fields (EMFs) from television sets, microwave ovens, cell phones, and local media transmission towers. Studies conducted over the last two decades imply possible association of EMFs with miscarriages, birth defects, leukemia, brain cancers, breast cancers, and lymphomas.[14]

Hospital body scans (x-rays and their computerized cousin, computerized axial tomography [CAT scans]) and magnetic resonance imaging (MRI) expose us to especially high levels of EMFs. One MRI delivers radiation equal to one hundred conventional x-rays. These diagnostic tools are potentially deadly if used indiscriminately. Cellular phones may pose dangers to brain tissues due to the close proximity of delicate brain tissue to powerful EMF transmitters.

The good news is that most EMF exposure can be avoided or limited because it occurs in the home through the use of electric blankets, microwave ovens, hair dryers, television sets, and computers. Avoid getting too close to these devices while in use. Use regular blankets instead of electric ones, and make sure all appliances and electrical installations in your home are in working order with all protective devices and protocols in place.

14. Use a lot of skin care products, cosmetics, hair care products, nail care products, shampoos, soaps, perfumes, shaving cream, suntan lotion, and antibacterial soaps.

Beware of skin care products that cause harm by destroying the skin's natural pH and by introducing dangerous toxins to the body. Hair-coloring products used by approximately 40 percent of U.S. women, particularly brown and black hair products, are associated with increased incidence of Hodgkin's lymphoma, multiple myeloma, Hodgkin's disease, and 20 percent of all non-Hodgkin's lymphoma! (There are several brands of natural hair-coloring products that are relatively safe.) Also avoid products containing DEA or TEA—these ingredients often contain carcinogenic nitrosamine impurities. Toluene, a neurotoxic substance that triggers asthma attacks and causes asthma in previously unaffected people, was found in every fragrance sample tested by the EPA in 1991. The fragrance industry routinely uses 884 toxic substances. As for shampoos, many of the most common ingredients break down into formaldehyde.[15] For detailed information on things to avoid and where to find good alternatives, see *The Safe Shopper's Bible* and *Diet for a Poisoned Planet*. As for antibacterial soaps, most of them contain triclosan, which may be absorbed through the skin and pose a risk to the liver. Plenty of regular soap, sufficiently heated running water, and thorough scrubbing will do the job just as well with no side effects. Clenzology is the best cleansing plan I've found to date.

15. Take lots of medications.

Every medicine has a side effect. There may a time and place for the use of medication, but much of the prescription activity in the U.S. perpetuates health problems by treating symptoms rather than their root causes. Medications such as antibiotics, oral contraceptives, and corticosteroids may cause major problems with the gastrointestinal terrain, damage the immune system, cause liver problems, and alter enzyme function. The practice of taking a baby aspirin a day to prevent heart attacks is dangerous, for instance. Aspirin can cause bleeding in the intestinal track and can be toxic to the liver. You get similar health benefits with no side effects by consuming foods in the Maker's Diet such as cold-water fish, fruits and vegetables high in antioxidants, and certain botanicals that naturally reduce the Cox-2 enzyme and provide other anti-inflammatory benefits.[16]

16. *Get your cavities filled with mercury.*

For more than 150 years, the dental profession has carefully avoided using the term *mercury* when describing the material used to fill tooth cavities for millions of Americans. They called it "silver amalgam," "silver fillings," or "amalgam fillings." The true composition of dental amalgam is 45 to 55 percent mercury, with about 30 percent silver and other metals such as copper, tin, and zinc. Mercury is a heavy metal toxin. According to BioProbe, an independent non-profit watchdog agency, vapor released continuously from mercury amalgam fillings in your mouth can produce "neurological and psychiatric symptoms...such as depression, irritability, exaggerated response to stimulation, excessive shyness, insomnia, emotional instability, forgetfulness, confusion, and vasomotor disturbances such as excessive perspiration and uncontrolled blushing. Tremors are also common in individuals exposed to mercury vapor." The organization cites one estimate that approximately "26 million amalgam bearers whose allergies may be causally related to their mercury/amalgam dental fillings" would benefit by replacing mercury amalgam fillings with safer alternative materials.[17] It may be difficult to find a dentist in your area who will fill your cavities with more natural materials, but it isn't impossible. The movement is growing despite significant opposition from the American Dental Association and state dental boards. Recent court challenges have begun to change the picture, however. Vivian Bradshaw Black offers another expert opinion on the subject in her article "Diet and Nutrition Principles": "The human body is able to take rock, dolomite, mercury and other toxic metals from sucking it all day in tooth fillings; dirt, toxic chemicals, plastics etc., and such things should not even be introduced to the mouth if health is desired."[18]

17. *Do aerobic exercise.*

While I believe strongly in the need for regular exercise, my research indicates that high-intensity aerobic exercise producing a very high elevated heart rate for long periods of time through vigorous exercise such as jogging or running on hard surfaces is essentially unnatural to the body. Exercise as the body was designed to by incorporating the principles of Functional Fitness. (See Appendix B.)

Typically, human beings in virtually every culture engaged in the anaerobic type of functional exercise common to regular labor or work functions on the farm, at sea, or while hunting wild game. Long-distance walking or slower-paced labor functions may have been punctuated by intense but relatively brief bursts of physical labor or high-speed movement.

Intense aerobic exercise may lower immune response and create more oxidation through stress than anaerobic exercise (strength training). Marathon runners often struggle with decreased resistance to viruses and bacterial infections in peak training seasons. They also battle chronic ligament and joint problems that grow progressively worse in intensity and long-term degeneration of organs and tissues.

18. Wear contact lenses and receive implants of other foreign objects such as silicone breast implants.

Media reports constantly feature horror stories of movie stars (and ordinary people) whose lives were ruined after receiving silicon implants that burst, hardened within their bodies, or inflamed nearby tissues. Even contact lenses, especially the soft lens variety offered for long-term wear, pose significant infection risks to the wearers under certain conditions. These products offer certain conveniences and cosmetic benefits, but remember that they are still foreign substances that the Maker never intended for us to insert into the human body. I am convinced they pose risks to our immune systems.[19]

19. Live in a toxic home with toxic paint, carpet, mold, paraffin candles, etc.

You could fill a small library with the books and official research reports written on this subject. Do some research if you or your family suffer from allergies or unexplained physical symptoms. Many popular building materials, including plywood, particle board, treated lumber, adhesives, paint, paint thinners, insulation, paint strippers, carpets, and carpet pads—even decorative paraffin candles—contain highly toxic materials such as formaldehyde, chloroform, lead vapor, arsenic, and countless other toxins. They can enter your living area as gaseous vapors and increase the toxic load of the body. Add to that the problem of toxic black molds, and you have a very toxic home. For detailed information on this subject, see *The Safe Shopper's Bible* by David Steinman and Samuel S. Epstein, M.D., *Diet for a Poisoned Planet* by David Steinman, and *Toxic Relief* by Don Colbert, M.D.

20. Wear synthetic fabrics.

The Maker's natural fibers produce the ideal clothing for the human body. Such natural fibers as wool and cotton are far better for the human body because they "breathe" and are better suited to handling human perspiration while preserving balanced body temperatures in hot or cold climates. Synthetic fibers often come from petroleum-based resins and other unnatural sources. Unfortunately, even conventionally grown cotton is often contaminated with numerous pesticides and chemical dyes. For details and safe sources of cotton clothing, see *The Safe Shopper's Bible*.[20]

21. Breathe with shallow breaths.

The Maker gave you two lungs with an amazing air capacity. Unfortunately, most of us use only a fraction of our lung capacity, and we suffer for it. Infants are instinctive "belly breathers," but most of us have learned to breathe from our chest in short, shallow breaths that resemble a pant more than a deep breath. The body (the brain and nervous system in particular) thrives on abundant oxygen. Proper breathing relieves stress and lowers blood pressure. Breathe from the abdomen or "belly" instead of from the chest. If your stomach moves outward when you take a deep breath (and any breath for that matter), then you have learned the secret of breathing fully from the diaphragm.

22. Swallow your food without chewing well (or at all).

Chewing is extremely important to proper digestion. The chewing reflex signals the body to release saliva containing the salivary enzyme ptyalin, a form of amylase, which begins to break down carbohydrates. Parotid glands behind the ears signal the thymus gland to produce T-cells just in case the food contains toxins or pathogens. The ultimate goal of the process is to deliver food to the stomach in a liquid state. I'm convinced that my habit of "wolfing down food" in chunks contributed to the development of Crohn's disease in my body. Horace Fletcher, who lived in the early 1900s, had a wasting disease known as Addison's disease, which produced major digestive problems and weight loss. Mr.

Fletcher allegedly cured himself by chewing each mouthful of food thirty-five to fifty times. His story inspired others who began chewing their food thoroughly; they called themselves "Fletcherizers." Don't go calling yourself a "Rubinizer," but I do recommend chewing each bite twenty-five to fifty times as needed—especially when eating foods high in carbohydrates such as grains, sugars, and starches. Always eat sitting down, and avoid watching TV, arguing, or doing something that requires concentration.

23. Use plastic food storage products, the popular food wraps, and re-use plastic drinking bottles.

Plastic products release or leach carcinogenic toxins into foods. The toxicity is increased when foods contain high amounts of water or when they are highly acidic. Water is one of nature's most effective solvents, and it is effective at drawing out toxins from plastic. According to *The Safe Shopper's Bible*, cling film contains carcinogenic by-products such as di-2-ethylhexyl phthalate (DEHP) and di-2-ethylhexyl (adipate) (DEHA), while plastic wrap contains residual traces of vinylidene chloride.[21] As for aluminum wrap, you already know it's bad. Some aluminum inevitably leaches into foods it touches. (If you wash and reuse plastic water bottles, be aware that researchers say repeated washing and reuse of disposable water bottles may accelerate the breakdown of the plastic, increasing your exposure to potentially harmful chemicals. Do not use plastic water bottles more than twice at the most.)

24. Eat grocery store produce and processed foods treated with pesticides, herbicides, animal growth hormones, and antibiotics; don't forget hybridized, irradiated, and genetically altered foods.

What a mouthful—literally! Pesticides and herbicides comprise one of the world's most deadly classes of chemical compounds. If a pesticide or herbicide kills one thing, it will probably kill, mutate, or seriously damage a whole host of other things. The problem with these compounds is that they tend to stay on the fruit, vegetable, or plant they were applied to. Then there is the cumulative affect of adding the toxins from our water, air, food, and buildings year after year.

Animal growth hormones don't go away after an animal is butchered, prepared for market, or cooked. They go right into our stomachs and continue their work. Nor do they disappear from the milk of a cow treated with antibiotics. It is estimated that one glass of commercial, nonorganic milk purchased from a grocery story may contain the residue of up to one hundred antibiotics!

Many of the meats we eat come from animals fed antibiotic-laden feeds. Growth hormones in our food supply are blamed for causing the abnormally early menses of young girls and for the overabundance of female hormones in young men. (Female hormones are given to milk cows to increase milk production.)

Most pesticides are known carcinogens, and some of them pose as counterfeit versions of the female hormone estrogen. These xenoestrogens may promote cancer by stimulating estrogen receptors in the body.[22] Hybridized foods are also very unhealthy with potentially deadly side effects. God says to eat every seed-bearing plant after its own kind. Hybridized, seedless watermelons or grapes cannot reproduce, and they may not be the healthy food sources we think they are. Genetically modified foods can be really dangerous, and irradiated foods offer many of the same problems and dangers as other forms of radiation. The government may reassure us they are safe, but the same government put U.S. soldiers at risk by encouraging them to stand in the open and watch the early tests of the atomic bomb—with disastrous results. Of course, they too were assured they were totally safe.

25. Wear tight underclothing.

The body's lymph system is absolutely crucial to the immune system. It is the first line of defense against cancer cells, toxins, and viral and bacterial attacks. Lymph nodes that are compressed or blocked by tight underclothing such as bras or other tight clothing may not allow the lymph system to be properly cleansed. It is conceivable that this may help contribute to the development or proliferation of cancer in the body. Women should not wear bras to bed.

26. Undergo surgery to remove "unnecessary body parts."

No one knows how many children fell victim to the medical myth common years ago that it was best to remove the tonsils to ensure the child wouldn't get tonsillitis—after all, the tonsils served no useful purpose anyway. This myth has since been disproved and discarded, but other equally arrogant myths persist about the supposedly useless appendix, an appendage that "lost its purpose in the process of evolution somewhere." The truth is that the appendix and the tonsils are lymphoid tissues serving a very necessary purpose! They are not unnecessary as some doctors may say.

If it was there when you were born, chances are your Maker intended for it to stay there until you die. Besides, you take your life in your hands every time you agree to enter a hospital for surgery. The risk of infection, surgical error, surgical complications, or dangerous drug interaction may be far greater than most of the problems you face outside of the hospital.

27. Visit your medical doctor often.

While I am thankful for all of the wonderful medical breakthroughs and excellent emergency medical care available in this country, you might want to know that according to the *Journal of the American Medical Association*, doctors are the third leading cause of death in the U.S., causing 250,000 deaths every year.[23] I know it sounds as if I have an ax to grind, but I don't. Most doctors are sincere, hard-working professionals who try to do their jobs well. However, the American healthcare system is not healthy. It is downright unhealthy at times because it has skewed its entire care system toward dispensing health out of a drug container.

The author of the article, Dr. Barbara Starfield of the Johns Hopkins School of Hygiene and Public Health, noted that a quarter of a million deaths occurred due to a physician's activity, manner, or therapy—including 12,000 unnecessary surgeries, 7,000 medication errors in hospitals, 20,000 "other errors" in hospitals, 80,000 infections acquired in hospitals, and 106,000 "non-error, negative effects of drugs." (And these are the low estimates.) The report also notes that of the thirteen nations included in an international ranking of healthcare quality, the United States ranked twelfth, or second from the bottom![24]

Many Americans have filled every one of these twenty-seven prescriptions for illness. Their bodies struggle to overcome an unbearable toxic load while fueled with poisonous processed junk food or non-nutritious prepackaged foods.

If the day comes when you are stricken with chronic sickness and pain, a desperate search for health will begin. Perhaps I have some hard-won advice that might help you avoid such a day, but the choice is up to you.

Chapter 6

The Desperate Search for Health

MILLIONS OF MIDDLE-AGED AMERICAN MOMS AND DADS, COLLEGE students, and even younger teens sense that something is terribly wrong with their health. They just don't know what to do about it. Best-selling health books offer ever-changing "flavors of the month" fad diets, while the media blow like a leaf in the wind telling us to eat a certain food one day and to avoid it the next.

So how does an exhausted forty-two-year-old mother lose weight safely while finding the energy to keep up with a vanload of active teenagers and younger children? How does she keep her husband off the heart-attack treadmill and help her mother overcome the painful bouts with arthritis and an embarrassing overactive bladder?

Most moms know better than to take these questions to their local HMO or even their busy family physician. Though moms may not have a wall full of degrees, most moms run long on common sense—they *have* to. Something inside tells them that none of the small health "miracles" they hope for will come from a pill bottle—or from a man or woman in a white coat.

Philosophy of Conventional Medicine

Conventional medicine sends its troops into battle against disease armed solely with surgery, pharmaceuticals, and invasive therapies (including chemotherapy and radiation). Anything outside the ironclad realm of a knife, a pill, or an x-ray machine is considered voodoo or worse. The genuine "maintenance" of health is simply beyond the scope of this "take-two-tablets-and-call-me-in-the-morning" philosophy.

Though "maintenance" of health is mentioned often in the world of allopathic or nonconventional medicine, the practical function of defining and preserving genuine good health is beyond the reach of most conventional medical doctors because of their consuming focus on the "cut, poison, and burn" approach to treating disease. Most medical doctors totally exclude basic nutrition from their treatment plans. Indeed, they have little educational background to do otherwise.

The prevention of disease and maintenance of health do not begin in the emergency room or intensive care ward of a hospital; they begin with the lifestyle choices you and I make every day.

I am thankful for the surgical expertise in the United States, but I am convinced that if the masses follow genuine biblical nutritional and lifestyle principles, we would largely remove the need for most of the work done in surgical suites and pharmacies! America's surgeons would be reduced to their excellent and vital roles in trauma and emergency medicine due to accidents and other special cases.

In general, physicians have little or no training in nutrition. Yet, many physicians confidently tell patients that diet has nothing to do with their sickness—even patients like myself with severe bowel disorders! As a result, many people leave their physician's office with a prescription and a nagging feeling that their symptoms are "all in their head."

Priorities for healthcare are changing.

The last decade witnessed a grassroots rebellion among millions of people whose lifestyle-related conditions and growing chronic health problems were not addressed by modern medicine. Even when presented for treatment, their conditions would not respond to conventional medical protocols. Feeling as if they have been "kicked to the curb" by a sometimes arrogant and rigid medical system, these people have turned en masse to complementary and alternative healthcare.

Though conventional medicine "declared war" on cancer, heart disease, and other killer diseases, it is definitely losing these battles despite vast expenditures on research. Some might convincingly argue that conventional medicine—as it is currently practiced in the United States—is actually shooting itself (and us) in the foot.

People are changing their priorities regarding healthcare. In fact, the authors of a study published in the prestigious *New England Journal of Medicine* in 1993 suggested that *more people seek out complementary and alternative health practitioners than conventional medical doctors*—this despite the fact that the insurance industry generally refuses to pay for these services! (The same study noted that up to 70 percent of patients may not reveal their use of "unconventional treatment" to their physician.)[1]

Stephen E. Straus, M.D., director of the National Center for Complementary and Alternative Medicine (NCCAM) for the National Institutes of Health, told a House subcommittee, "Approximately 42 percent of U.S. healthcare consumers spent $27 billion on CAM therapies in 1997."[2] I suspect these are very conservative figures.

Essentially, the *shortcomings* of conventional medicine have spawned countless forms of alternative treatment. Before you include me in that group of unconventional medical practitioners, let me candidly tell you that many of these "alternatives" are as suspect as their conventional counterpart! Care must be taken to ascertain that an alternative approach to healthcare is scientifically based and fundamentally sound, as we will discuss.

As I have stated, most of you will never need emergency and trauma medical services for disease-related conditions if you adopt the Maker's Diet and make wise lifestyle choices. Should you develop cancer or some other disease that is not immediately life threatening, your first order of treatment should be to adopt the principles that would have kept you from disease in the first place. Remember that great saying: "An ounce of prevention is worth a pound of cure."

Dr. Strauss made a prediction in his testimony before the House subcommittee: "In future years, these interventions will be integrated into conventional medical education and practice, and the term 'complementary and alternative medicine' will be superseded by the concept of '*integrative medicine.*'"[3] I must agree with him; we can do more together than we can ever accomplish apart.

However, I discovered during my battle with a supposedly incurable disease that once you step outside of the relatively *predictable* world of conventional medicine, you find yourself on a very *unpredictable* hamster wheel of alternative medicine. It is virtually impossible to wade through the hundreds of "miracle diets," pills, potions, and health programs out there—and I do mean "out there."

Empty promises and flashy marketing campaigns aside, many of these "alternative treatments" are incredibly expensive, and some may actually endanger your health. I know from painful personal experience that people who are desperate to get well or to regain some measure of health may grasp at every straw that offers hope. (Some may have even been told by a well-meaning nutritionist to eat straw at one time or another.)

Step-by-step programs offering inflated guarantees of success are the most dangerous attractions. Something inside us desperately longs to return to the health and active lifestyles we once enjoyed. There is a tremendous temptation to plug in to any promising program that tells us to simply "follow along."

Perhaps most people can't name all of the minerals the body needs or explain why we need protein or vitamin B_{12}, and that is all right. On the other hand, I refuse to insult your intelligence with simplistic health maxims and ridiculous promises without explaining the functional basis for the health therapy and lifestyle changes you may choose to embrace.

Before we examine the functional basis for the Maker's Diet, let's analyze briefly some of the more popular health diets available, which you have perhaps tried already. What you learn will help you make informed choices for your personal lifestyle. For this synopsis, we will include the following:

- Standard American diet (or "SAD")
- Vegetarian diet (the Genesis and Hallelujah diets)
- Raw-food diet
- Anticandida diet
- Balanced macronutrient ratios diet (the "Zone" diet)
- Ketogenic or "low-carb" diet (Atkins' and South Beach diets)
- Food-combining diets
- Blood-type diet

The Standard American Diet (SAD)

The "standard" American diet typically might include a doughnut or muffin with coffee and orange juice for breakfast followed by a mid-morning bagel with cream cheese. Lunch would likely be a turkey sandwich with some chips and a soft drink—or a hefty fast-food burger with extra cheese, a large order of french fries, and a "super-sized" soft drink. The afternoon hours would feature an "energy-boosting" candy bar from a vending machine with another soft drink. Dinner promises a meat-and-potatoes entrée with a roll and margarine, some green beans for the health-conscious, and some ice cream for dessert.

Since you are reading this book, you may already know this diet amounts to a prescription for poor health at best and disaster at worst.

Virtually *any* departure from this diet will make you feel better. There is very good reason that I refer to the standard American diet by its acronym—SAD!

The Vegetarian Diet
(Also Called the Genesis or Hallelujah Diet)

Vegetarian diets rank as perhaps the oldest of all specialty diets. Some people turn to vegetarian diets because of religious or philosophical beliefs, while others shun meats for fear of heart disease or to avoid the supposedly "bad" saturated fats found in animal foods.

Vegetarianism has the *appearance* of a great lifestyle. To clarify terminology, while all *vegetarians* avoid meat, fish, and fowl, *lacto-ovo-vegetarians* add dairy and eggs, and *lactovegetarians* say *yes* to dairy but *no* to eggs.

Vegans (no, they are *not* from another planet) usually consider themselves purists because they won't eat *any* animal products. Their motto is "never to eat anything that has or comes from something that has a face." (Many won't even eat honey because honey is produced by bees.)

Variations of the diet include the *fruitarian* diet (no definition needed) and the popular *Hallelujah* and *Genesis* diets based on God's early instructions to Adam and Eve in the Garden of Eden to eat only grains, nuts, seeds, legumes, fruits, and vegetables (Gen. 1:29).

Pure vegetarianism plays into all the food phobias prevalent in our very phobic society. It attributes virtually every problem of humanity to the consumption of meat, animal fat, and animal products (and to those who provide them).

Benefits

The chief benefit of the vegetarian diet is that with its focus on fruits and veggies and its avoidance of junk food, it decreases the toxic burden on the body. It is of tremendous value as a *short-term cleansing diet*.

Downside

The purist vegan diet is totally unsuitable for a long-term diet, however, because it deprives the body of essential nutrients available only from meat and animal products. These nutritional deficiencies pose potentially deadly consequences to long-term health.

Stephen Byrnes, Ph.D., N.D., the author of *Diet & Heart Disease* and *Digestion Made Simple*, published an in-depth article entitled

"The Myths of Vegetarianism" in the *Townsend Letter for Doctors and Patients*.[4] This article is the primary source for the following information about vegetarianism.

The goal of Dr. Byrnes was not to "bash" vegetarians but to correct the myth that vegetarianism is somehow healthier for people than any diet associated with the consumption of meat or animal products, which vegans believe is a prescription for sickness and death. Proponents of vegetarianism justify this claim with a number of secondary myths that are widely cited but totally unsupported by scientific evidence. They include the following:

Myth: Meat consumption contributes to famine and depletes the earth's natural resources. The myth behind the myth is the simplistic idea that the solution to world hunger is for people to become vegetarians. It is based in the claim that livestock dominate agricultural land that could be used to raise grains to feed the world's starving masses. The fact is, two-thirds of the earth's landmass is unsuitable for farming, but easily provides food for grazing animals.

To the charge that animals are fed grain that could more efficiently be used to feed the world's starving masses, Byrnes points out that two-thirds of the plants and plant products fed to animals are unsuited for human consumption. Both the animals and the plants are renewable resources, in no danger of depletion.

People do need to eat an abundance of plant products for good health, but the problem has never been a shortage of these foods, rather their equitable distribution as well as widespread poverty. Even the Population Reference Bureau attributed the world hunger problem to poverty, not eating meat, and did not consider mass vegetarianism to be a solution to world hunger.

Myth: Vitamin B_{12} can be obtained from plant sources. This may be the most dangerous myth of all. Vegans who do not supplement their diets with vitamin B_{12} will eventually succumb to anemia—a potentially fatal condition. According to Byrnes, several studies indicate most, if not all vegans, have impaired B_{12} metabolism and low vitamin B_{12} concentrations. Vegans simply do not get this vitamin from their diet, since it can only be found in animal products, especially eggs, fish, red meat, and organ meats. Besides anemia, a deficiency in vitamin B_{12} can also cause fatigue and neurological disorders. It is essential for cell division, energy, and the formation of red blood cells. The only reliable sources for vitamin B_{12} are animal products (especially organ meats and eggs) and to a lesser degree, dairy products.

Many vegetarians believe they get vitamin B_{12} from eating tempeh (fermented soybean cake), spirulina (a type of algae), and brewer's yeast. Though these foods actually contain compounds called B_{12} analogs, these compounds cannot be metabolized by the body. Some researchers believe that spirulina, although a generally healthy food, actually depletes vitamin B_{12} because the B_{12} analogs compete with vitamin B_{12} and inhibit the metabolism of the vitamin.

Vitamin B_{12} is produced by fermenting bacteria in the large intestine, as vegans claim, but it must have "intrinsic factor" from the stomach to be absorbed. Thus, this fermentation by-product is unusable by the body.

Myth: Our needs for vitamin D can be met by sunlight. It is true that the body, in particular the skin, catalyzes the conversion of cholesterol into vitamin D. However, this conversion only occurs in the presence of relatively rare UV-B rays, which are present only at certain times of the day, at certain latitudes, and at certain times of the year. Even then, depending on one's skin color, it would take as long as two full hours of continual sunning to get 200–400 IUs of vitamin D. Recent research indicates adults need even higher amounts of this vitamin.

A limited number of plant foods contain the "plant form" of vitamin D called D_2, but clinicians have reported disappointing results using D_2 to treat conditions such as rickets, which are related to a vitamin D deficiency. Concerns about vitamin D deficiencies and rickets in vegetarians and vegans always exist because the full-complex form of this vital nutrient is only found in animal fats.

Myth: The body's needs for vitamin A can be entirely obtained from plant foods. This vitamin is all-important to the human diet because it allows the body to use proteins and minerals, enhances the immune system, fights infection, and ensures proper vision and reproduction.

The true form of vitamin A, or retinol, is found only in animal fats and organs such as liver. The body is able to convert beta carotene from plants into vitamin A if bile salts are available, but bile secretion in the body is stimulated by the consumption of fat. Even then, the conversion isn't very efficient. Butter and full-fat dairy foods from pastured cows are rich sources of vitamin A, as is cod liver oil.

Myth: Meat-eating causes osteoporosis, kidney disease, heart disease, and cancer. This claim does not reconcile with the facts of history and anthropological research. All of the diseases mentioned have occurred primarily in the twentieth century, whereas people—and long-lived people at that—have been eating meat and animal fat for thousands of years! The truth is that recent studies demonstrate that vegan and vegetarian diets predispose women to osteoporosis.

As for kidney disease, meat contains complete proteins and vitamin D, both of which help maintain pH balance in the bloodstream. Meats God has provided, such as beef, fish, and lamb, are good sources of magnesium and B_6, which help limit the risk of kidney stones.

Nothing in nutritional science supports the claim that eating meat causes cardiovascular problems. The French eat large amounts of meat and enjoy low rates of heart disease, and the same is true in Greece. The claim that eating meat causes cancer is based on a flawed study by Dr. Ernst Wynder in the 1970s, who said there was a link between animal fat intake and colon cancer. The "animal fats" turned out to be vegetable fats. Historically, studies of meat-eating peoples—including the people of the Bible—show they had very little incidence of cancer.

Myth: Saturated fats and dietary cholesterol cause heart disease, atherosclerosis, and/or cancer—and low-fat, low-cholesterol diets are healthier for people. This claim rooted in the flawed "liquid lipids" hypothesis has been used to promote vegetarianism as the best insurance against heart disease. The theory that saturated fats and cholesterol clog arteries has been effectively disproved by a number of highly respected scientists from many nations. Studies have shown that "arterial plaque is primarily composed of unsaturated fats, particularly polyunsaturated ones, and not the saturated fat of animals, palm or coconut." The real culprit is "trans-fatty acids" in such supposedly "healthy" foods as margarine, vegetable shortening, and foods made with them. A Swedish study confirmed previous findings linking vegetable oil intake with higher breast cancer rates.

The Framington Heart Study, often cited as "proof" of this myth, actually found that the residents of Framington, Massachusetts, who ate more saturated fats, cholesterol, and calories had the lowest serum cholesterol levels! Vegetarian diets do not protect against heart disease or atherosclerosis. Recent studies have shown vegetarians to have higher homocysteine levels in their blood. (Homocysteine is a known cause of heart disease.)

Myth: Vegetarians live longer and have more energy and endurance than meat-eaters. One English vegetarian guidebook claimed that vegetarians "can expect to live nine years longer than meat-eaters." A witty commentator called this fictitious life expansion, "indulging in a bit of wishful thinking." A massive study of heart disease by Russell

Smith, Ph.D., showed that death rates actually decreased as animal product consumption increased among some study groups![5] The longest-lived peoples on earth have all been meat-eaters, and the anthropological data from primitive societies do not support the contention that vegetarians live longer than meat-eaters.

Myth: Consumption of meat and saturated fat has increased in the twentieth century, with a corresponding increase in heart disease and cancer. The hard statistics say the opposite. Butter consumption dropped by more than two-thirds over the last century, but the incidence of heart disease and cancer has skyrocketed.

Beef consumption has risen, but meat-eating societies have lived virtually free of cancer and heart disease for centuries, so this cannot be a sole factor. What has kept pace with the rise of heart disease and cancer is our consumption of trans-fatty acids, packaged foods, processed vegetable oils, carbohydrates, and refined sugar—items virtually unavailable to primitive societies of long-lived meat-eaters. I think you know where the blame should land.

Myth: Soy products are adequate substitutes for meat and dairy products. In Asia soy products are never used as a primary food! They are used as condiments or in traditionally fermented forms. Unfermented soybeans and soy products are high in phytic acid, an antinutrient that carries minerals out of the body. Vegetarians are known for their frequent mineral deficiencies. The high phytate content of grain and legume-based diets is to blame. Processed soy products are rich in trypsin inhibitors, which inhibit protein digestion! Some recent research indicates that soy's phytoestrogens (or isoflavones) could be causative factors in breast cancer, penile birth defects, infantile leukemia, and depressed thyroid function. They have caused infertility in every animal species studied so far!

Myth: The human body is not designed for meat consumption. Human physiology clearly refutes this false claim. The stomach's production of hydrochloric acid is unique to meat-eaters—it activates protein-splitting enzymes (and it is something not found in herbivores). Then there is the human pancreas, which produces a full range of digestive enzymes for handling both animal and vegetable foods. Our very physiology (and dental structure) demonstrates we are "mixed feeders" or omnivores.

Myth: Animal products contain numerous, harmful toxins. Dr. Byrnes comments, "If meat, fish, and eggs do indeed generate cancerous 'ptyloamines,' it is very strange that people have not been dying in droves from cancer for the past thousand years."[6] It also seems strange to me that our Creator would recommend such foods, and that Jesus and the disciples would eat them, thereby validating them. Commercially raised or farmed meat and animal sources may have some harmful contaminants in them (as do commercially farmed plant foods), but this can be avoided by consuming range-fed, organic meats, eggs, and dairy products largely free of man-made chemical toxins.

Myth: Eating meat or animal products is less "spiritual" than eating only plant foods. I am satisfied to know that Abraham prepared a calf for three angelic visitors. Isaac, Jacob, David, and Moses all ate meat, and Jesus partook of meat at the Last Supper, sharing fish with the disciples. (I also understand that Muslims celebrate Ramadan with lamb before fasting.)

Most vegetarians are really "grain-etarians," "sugar-tarians," or "starch-etarians." The excessive consumption of carbohydrates can drive up insulin levels and jeopardize overall health. Health problems typically associated with vegetarianism include anemia, pallor, listlessness, and poor resistance to infection.

The Raw-Food Vegan Diet

Raw-food advocates never cook food before eating it, believing this weakens the potency of vitamins and minerals, destroys enzymes, and possibly introduces toxins. (One version of the raw-food diet suggests eating raw meat as well as raw fruits and vegetables.)

Their premise is that cooking destroys food enzymes that help with digestion. By preserving these enzymes, we are able to digest food properly and assimilate nutrients.

Benefits

The raw-food diet shares all the advantages of the vegetarian diet, which are earned by eating plenty of organic fruits, vegetables, and nuts—foods rich in the antioxidants (including vitamins C, E, and beta carotene) that prevent free radicals from damaging body tissue.

Downside

The raw-food diet *also* shares all the drawbacks of the vegetarian diet. The raw-food diet is notoriously lacking in quality protein, unless raw animal foods are included. This diet is very difficult to stay on and can be dangerous with today's tainted food supply and lack of minerals, vitamins (most notably vitamins A, D, and B_{12}), and essential fatty acids obtainable only from animal foods and/or animal fat.

Some raw-food advocates supplement their raw-vegetarian diet with raw animal products such as unpasteurized dairy products, raw eggs, uncooked meats, poultry, and fish. This combination offers many benefits, but they may be outweighed by the risk of raw-food contamination due to parasites.

In addition, some foods are easier to digest when cooked; people with gastrointestinal illnesses simply cannot tolerate a predominantly raw-food diet. Humans lack the enzyme cellulase, which is necessary for digesting plant fibers. And undesirable intestinal microbes can ferment undigested sugar and fiber, which may produce gas, inflammation, and severe pain in certain individuals. I believe a healthy diet contains a combination of raw and cooked foods with plenty of raw foods. Those in seasonal climates will usually be better off consuming more cooked foods in the winter and more raw foods in the summer.

The Anticandida (Antiyeast) Diet

Many women are drawn to the antiyeast diet because of chronic battles with candida in the form of vaginal yeast infections and a myriad of other health problems often attributed to systemic candida infections. Candidiasis, or chronic yeast overgrowth, is a disease caused by a yeast fungus, *Candida albicans*. This yeast often breeds in the throat, mouth, digestive tract, vaginal tract, and on the skin.

However, this same yeast has valuable functions in the digestive tract *as long as* it is kept in check by other more beneficial microorganisms in the intestine. Once it grows out of control, this seemingly harmless yeast turns into an aggressive fungus that can cause serious intestinal problems and infections of the vagina, mouth, and throat. (The latter two are known as "thrush.")

In its most serious form, the candida fungus *grows into and through the walls of the intestine*, allowing food particles, toxic waste, and yeast waste products to seep into the bloodstream. This serious condition is called *leaky gut syndrome*. Many cases of candida occur after taking antibiotics that kill *all* bacteria in the gut. Candida microbes, resistant to antibiotics, remain active and *take over,* when the friendly bacteria that would normally keep them in check soon die out.

Benefits

The anticandida diet is an attempt to starve the candida fungus by eliminating sugar in every form, including foods and beverages that contain sugar, plus fresh fruit and fruit juices because candida yeast feeds on sugars. Foods fermented with vinegar such as soy sauce, beer, vinegar, sauerkraut, and pickles are also avoided as they may cause an exacerbation of the condition. Naturally fermented foods using probiotic cultures are highly recommended in the fight against candida. Avoiding these foods also lowers carbohydrate consumption, which can help people balance blood sugar and hormones. It may also aid in weight management.

Downside

The standard medical community does not recognize candidiasis as a condition. Also, it may be diagnosed much too often among alternative medicine practitioners, who too readily blame yeast overgrowth for symptoms when the root cause is the lack of balance in the gut flora and immune system that keeps *Candida albicans* in check. Anticandida diets can be very difficult to follow, and they exclude many healthy foods, including fruit and honey. Following the Maker's Diet and adding probiotic supplements, especially HSOs, are extremely effective against candida and other fungi, working to create a healthy balance of flora.

Balanced Macronutrient Ratios Diet ("the Zone")

The balanced macronutrient ratios diet advocates eating macronutrients (carbohydrates, protein, and fat) *in the ratio* of 40 percent carbohydrate, 30 percent protein, and 30 percent fat. Promoters claim this diet will help you lose weight, live longer, and lower the risk of heart disease.

Dr. Barry Sears created the "40-30-30 diet" or "the Zone" diet and promoted it in his popular "Zone" books (sounding one of the first alarms about the danger of carbohydrate overconsumption). His goal is to produce a more balanced biochemical state in the body by reducing carbohydrate intake to 40 percent while increasing protein intake to 30 percent.

This diet focuses on two blood-sugar hormones—*insulin*, the fat-storing hormone, and *glucagon*, the fat-releasing hormone—and on a group of short-acting bioactive chemicals known as *eicosanoids*, which promote inflammation.

Benefits

Balancing macronutrient ratios is a great improvement over the high-carb, low-fat diet. This philosophy leads to more balanced blood sugar levels and a reduction in inflammation. It often leads to weight loss also.

Downside

The Zone diet fails in some respect to address the *quality* of the food you eat. There is also a noticeable shortage of the fat-soluble vitamins A and D in this diet. Dr. Sears strongly endorses soy protein isolates, which new research suggests can be highly allergenic and estrogenic; this can be problematic for men and certain women. Soy is an inferior protein source containing high levels of phytic acid. (Exceptions are naturally fermented forms of soy.)

My recommendation? Follow the Maker's Diet, which is packed with super nutrition, healthy carbohydrate intake, and the highest quality protein and fat from sources such as naturally raised meat, poultry, fish, eggs, and fermented dairy products. As we will discuss, this diet lowers insulin and inflammation levels naturally, thus reducing the levels of "bad" eicosanoids in the body, while also promoting healthy weight levels and reducing inflammation.

The Ketogenic "Low-Carb" Diet

Name the most popular diets in America for the second half of the last decade; they will probably be ketogenic or "low-carb" diets. These diets include *Dr. Atkins' New Diet Revolution, Protein Power,* and the *South Beach diet.* The Atkins' Diet has enjoyed increased publicity and popularity due to recent studies acknowledging the diet's effectiveness as a weight-loss program. All of these diets call for eating large amounts of protein and very small amounts of carbohydrates.

These low-carb diets essentially mimic fasting or starvation by reducing carbohydrate intake enough to induce a physical state called *ketosis,* in which body metabolism speeds up and hunger urges are suppressed. Starved of glucose from carbohydrates, the body resorts to burning ketones, chemicals the body produces from fat.

Benefits

With the combination of hunger suppression, consuming fewer calories, and burning fat reserves—people on ketogenic diets lose weight. Some promoters even claim that you can eat *all the fat you want* and still lose weight, which obviously sounds attractive. The body can tolerate the ketogenic diet without substantial harm for certain periods of time.

Under the supervision of a knowledgeable physician, a ketogenic diet can be used to manage a host of illnesses, including obesity, GI disorders, childhood epilepsy, and certain types of brain tumors.

Downside

The popular do-it-yourself versions of the ketogenic diet cater to current tastes and whims without discrimination about food choices. This makes low-carb diets really *high-fat diets*, not high-protein programs. The dietary suggestions for these regimens often make it very difficult to maintain a healthy ratio of omega-6 to omega-3 essential fatty acids. Some of the recommended foods are *very dangerous* according to the biblical dietary guidelines, as incorporated in the Maker's Diet. For instance, the late Dr. Robert C. Atkins suggested that dieters treat themselves to a heaping helping of *pork rinds*, calling them "the zero carbohydrate consolation prize for corn or potato chip addicts."[7] Many low-carb diets advocate the consumption of artificial sweeteners such as aspartame and sucralose, which may pose significant health risks.

The Food-Combining and Acid/Alkaline Diets

If Adam and Eve sat down in the garden for a hearty "food-combining" meal, you would see them carefully separate certain foods from others. Many advocates believe that alkaline-forming foods are essential because humankind *evolved* from the alkaline environment of the ocean.

Even aside from its nonbiblical origins, the problem with the food-combining diet is that most of its suppositions are *not based on scientific fact* or *historical evidence.* No empirical evidence suggests that the body has trouble digesting certain foods when eaten in combination.

The *acid-alkaline* diet, which divides food into alkaline-forming and acid-forming foods, is the first cousin variation of the food-combining diet. It sets a goal of eating 80 percent alkaline-forming foods and 20 percent acid-forming foods.

Benefits

Since most people tend to be overly acidic, both of these diets can be beneficial for those switching from a primarily junk-food diet. After learning about the food-combining diet years ago, I never eat melon with any other food, in accordance with food-combining adage, "Melon: eat it alone or leave it alone." Many people experience improved digestion by avoiding certain combinations of foods. If you notice certain food combinations are tough on your gut, it's best to avoid them. For the average person, however, most healthy foods eaten in combination are just fine and have been for thousands of years.

Downside

People on acid-alkaline and food-combining diets experience all the same challenges as those on vegetarian diets. Due to the lack of animal foods, they run the risk of long-term nutrient deficiencies.

The Blood-Type Diet

I call the "blood-type diet" an *evolution-based diet* because its promoters believe our food requirements "evolved" with mankind over 40 million years since prehistoric times in essentially four "flavors" corresponding conveniently with the blood types—O, A, B, or AB. This is a diet philosophy popularized by Peter D'Adamo, N.D., in his best-selling book *Eat Right for Your Type* (Putnam, 1997).

He maintains that modern people with type O blood are descended from the earliest humans, who were physically active and ate a diet composed mostly of the meat of large herbivorous mammals, with little or no grain. As "modern cavemen" with type O blood, you also require large amounts of meat and lots of exercise.

Type As descended from agrarian humans, are more docile, thrive on vegetables and fruit, and should avoid meat and dairy products. Type Bs descended from nomadic herders, thrive on dairy products, and require only moderate exercise. Type ABs do not handle meat well; they should eat fish, grains, and soy-based foods.

Proponents of the blood-type diet claim that lectins, specialized proteins in foods such as cereals and beans, are incompatible with certain blood types, causing many ailments such as kidney failure, arthrosclerosis, and food allergies.

Benefits

The diet's virtues appear to be that it is essentially a low-calorie, healthy diet. For people who typically eat junk food, adopting the blood-type diet will be an improvement, allowing them to take in fewer calories, exercise more, naturally lose weight, and feel better.

Downside

Aside from being unbiblical, this diet is viewed as a fad by the scientific community and many nutritionists in alternative circles. Its thesis is unproven and without solid anthropological evidence.

New Age Programs

Once you depart from the solid foundation of biblical, historical, commonsense nutrition, you enter no-man's-land of "New Age" programs, unusual therapies, and odd diagnostic contraptions. Let the buyer beware!

You will find very motivated and sincere people who claim each of these programs worked for them. I tried many of them during my desperate search for health, but nothing restored my health except the biblically grounded and scientifically proven foods of the Maker's Diet. I know that desperate times require desperate measures, but before you commit to some alternative, extra-biblical diet from the bestseller list, take a chance on the historically correct and life-giving principles of the Maker's Diet.

In the years since I recovered my health by following this protocol, I've been able to help thousands of others overcome serious health problems, turning their tragedy into triumph. In the next chapter, you will meet several of these people who tell their dramatic "success stories." Consider their seemingly hopeless health crises, and then share their surprise and joy in discovering the commonsense biblical diet that turned their lives around.

Chapter 7

Seven Victims Find Victory

DISAPPOINTMENT IN MODERN CONVENTIONAL MEDICINE IS THE hard reality experienced by millions of Americans. Some maintain they were lied to and even discarded by healthcare systems and providers. Others simply exhausted all of their options in a search for health that was forever lost to disease, accidents, or nutrition-related health problems.

While personal testimonies cannot take the place of scientifically controlled studies or independent research, neither should they be ignored or set aside. They are a vital part of the process of scientific inquiry and discovery.

I have selected seven people who experienced significant results on the Maker's Diet. They represent a cross-section of people who first sought help through standard medical healthcare without success and were desperate to recover their health, as God intended them to enjoy. Some had been disappointed with the conventional and alternative medical community. Others received life-saving procedures but discovered that to regain their total health required more than was available from the conventional medical system.

Suffering the "System"

Let me affirm again that I understand that most doctors, nurses, and other healthcare providers are sincere, highly gifted, and dedicated in their work. However, they are part of a larger healthcare system in this country that is motivated by goals that may not have the public's best interest at heart. Some for-profit health maintenance organizations (HMOs), for instance, have won nationwide disdain for their tendency to maximize profits while minimizing healthcare services and expenditures to protect those profits.[1]

Some hospitals and medical clinics, largely underwritten by private insurance and Medicare, are quickly earning the same questionable reputation. Far too often, government bureaucrats and insurance under-writers, along with pharmaceutical companies, are influencing key medical treatment decisions, rather than the patients and their health-care providers.

Since Medicare and most insurance companies refuse to pay for many advanced diagnostic tests or any treatment not listed as a *standard medical procedure*, many doctors simply follow the status quo. They avoid many proven alternatives, including virtually everything in the realm of proper nutrition and genuine health maintenance.

A typical scenario

The story is all too familiar, beginning with the long delays in crowded waiting rooms packed with sick people who are sneezing, coughing, and hacking uncontrollably. After being whisked into an anti-septic white room, you wait another thirty minutes before seeing the doctor, who finally appears for a rushed ninety-second interview and to prescribe medications. The result is predictable: you take your prescription with you on the way out past the small receptionist window, and then you make the weary run to your friendly hometown pharmacist for the promised "cure in a bottle."

Add to that the ever-increasing problems of incorrect prescrib-ing, overprescribing of antibiotics, missed diagnoses, late diagnoses, and understaffed and underpaid hospital workers existing in a fog of fatigue, often working in overcrowded conditions in buildings housing a host of deadly microbes, communicable diseases, and infectious staph infestations. Taken together, you have a prescription for disaster! As my mother says, "The worst place for a sick person to be is in the hospital."

Each of the individuals introduced below came to me in despera-tion after every other medical promise had failed. Feeling helpless and almost hopeless, they agreed to try the Maker's Diet. The first testimo-nial is from my grandmother, which I'm telling from my viewpoint with her permission.

• •
Rose Menlowe
• •

"Jordan, are you OK? Can I get you anything? Do you need your IV changed?"

The voice was very familiar to me. I heard that voice night after night as I came in and out of delirium in the hospital—it was the loving voice of Rose, my tough, full-of-life, Jewish grandmother.

This matriarchal champion stood by me in my battle to survive Crohn's disease. Just three years after my full recovery, as I was enjoying life again and launching into my life's mission in addition to planning my wedding, which was only three months away, Grandma Rose found herself in a life-and-death battle with cancer. According to her doctor, things weren't looking good.

In late spring of 1999, she began experiencing excruciating stomach pain and threw up constantly. Laboratory tests conducted in Florida kept coming back normal, and doctors wrote it off as a tough virus.

Grandma Rose went to Atlanta for a visit with my aunt and uncle but almost immediately began feeling even worse. She had to be lifted out of bed and helped in and out of the shower. Days turned into weeks of pain and nausea, difficulty in keeping food down, dry heaves, and excruciating abdominal pain.

The pain became so unbearable that Grandma fell into despair. She even asked my uncle to give her pills so she could "end it all." When he refused, she asked to be taken to the emergency room. Desperate to end the pain, she agreed to follow the gut instinct of a surgeon she had never met. He was certain *something* dangerous was going on that could only be found through exploratory surgery.

Facing the facts

My mother heard about it and was furious. (She shares the natural distrust of "knife-happy" surgeons common to many in the natural health community.) But this time the doctor was right. When Grandma emerged from the anesthesia, the surgeon confirmed what she secretly suspected—she was dying.

He had found multiple malignancies hidden beneath the larger internal organs (which helps explain why they escaped detection earlier). The malignancies included a goblet cell carcinoid in her appendix and stage IV ovarian cancer that had spread to her lymph nodes and portions of her small and large intestines. Ovarian cancer cells were also found in the pleural fluid (located in the cavity surrounding the lungs).

The surgeon removed all of the cancer he found, removing both ovaries, the appendix, some of the lymph nodes, and portions of the small and large intestines. But the ovarian malignancy was extremely advanced, and the cancer had spread to other sites.

Since Grandma Rose was in her late seventies and in a weakened state, chemotherapy and radiation were out of the question. The doctor told Rose she had two years to live at most. He told her family it was closer to *six months*—if that long.

Grandma Rose called me and said, "Jordan, you were my first grand-child. I want to do something so I might live to see you married. Maybe you can help me. Maybe you can find something for me." I had never heard her voice sound so weak before.

As we talked, I realized just how similar her trial was to my own. Her condition was extremely painful, and no one seemed to believe her description of the symptoms at first. She didn't know what was wrong, and the unrelenting suffering had stolen her hope—and her smile. (My aunt and uncle used to sneak my baby cousin Ethan past the hospital staff to visit Grandma Rose in her room—he was the only one who could get a smile out of her.)

Immediately after her surgery, my grandmother became very depressed, sensing that she was going to die. "I was praying that I would live long enough to go to your wedding," she confided to me later.

She had lost thirty pounds, felt terrible, and had lost her will to live—except for one remaining hope she really wanted to somehow attend my wedding in Florida just a few months away.

A painful challenge

Though the stakes were almost unbearable, I had no choice but to meet the challenge of my grandmother's terminal illness. All of her con-ventional medical options were exhausted.

I understood that I had to find a way to strengthen Grandma's immune system to suppress her cancer cells and promote healthy cells. She needed more than an increase in white blood cells and cytokines in her body—these components needed to be highly activated as well.

Tumor cells secrete *"transforming growth factor-beta"* (TGF-b), which renders immune cells inactive or ineffectual—even in large num-bers. This factor also inhibits proliferation of T-cells, reduces the cancer cell-killing power of tumor necrosis factor-alpha, and inhibits the ability of macrophages, our immune system's first line of defense, to destroy invaders. The result: the body believes its defense system is effectively attacking cancer cells when it isn't.

In addition to putting Grandma on the Maker's Diet, my research led me to particular *polysaccharide peptides* or *glycoproteins* that enhance macrophage and natural killer cell production and efficacy. They are found in greatest abundance in edible fungi and germinated grains and seeds. These compounds enhance production of cytokines, which facilitate cell-to-cell communication and optimize immune function. I had a hunch that these glyconutrients might overcome some of the deceptive methods of TGF-b.

Glyconutrient compounds were abundant in most primitive diets, but they are virtually absent from modern Western diets heavy in refined foods. Edible mushrooms are the richest source of these compounds (the healing powers of mushrooms have been known for more than five thousand years). However, positive research findings on the medicinal powers of mushrooms have become prominent in research literature only in the last twenty years.[2]

Several varieties (*not* including the popular button mushroom from the grocery store) offer immunomodulatory, lipid-lowering, antitumor, and other beneficial or therapeutic health effects without any significant toxicity.[3] These benefits are so promising that some of the most potent anticancer drugs under development by pharmaceutical scientists are based on the glyconutrient compounds found in these mushrooms.

Mushrooms are too fibrous and difficult for the body to easily break down, so I had to overcome this problem if I hoped to tap into the healing powers of these natural fungi. Grandma Rose needed an effective delivery system to help her benefit from the prototype formula I had prepared for her.

In the process of my own healing from Crohn's disease, I had pioneered the use of a fermentation process using more than fourteen species of homeostatic soil organisms and other lactic-acid producing microorganisms. I used this probiotic "starter" to ferment or "predigest" the ten mushrooms, aloe vera, and the herb cat's claw in the formula and unlock the active ingredients.

By applying what I now call the "Poten-Zyme" process, Grandma Rose's body was able to utilize all of the "body ready" phytochemicals and phytonutrients available in my herb and mushroom compound without placing stress on the digestive tract. My grandmother began taking my prototype formula, combined with the Maker's Diet, immediately following her surgery.

Rose: blooming again!

"Not only did I gain my weight back," Grandma Rose says, "but my energy level and physical appearance improved to the point that I feel and look better than I can recall in the last thirty years! My digestion improved dramatically. But most importantly, according to my regular follow-up CAT scans, I am cancer free! Even the fatty liver that I developed (probably due to metabolic imbalance) is gone now."

Only three months after radical abdominal surgery, Grandma Rose attended my wedding. She was still moving slowly at that time, but she was able to dance with me to a song I had recorded and that I sang especially for her. What a special victory it was for us.

On Labor Day 2001, Grandma Rose described her victorious battle with cancer before the Cancer Control Society's twenty-sixth annual convention in Universal City, California. "Four years after the discovery of my cancer, my CAT scans show no evidence of cancer. My energy levels are that of a twenty-year-old. With help from my grandson, I hope to see my great-grandchildren grow up." She received a standing ovation.

Bob N.

On September 26, 2002, I was given the life-changing news that I had stage III lymphoma cancer. Immediately, I started researching the available treatments and diet changes that would give me the best chance for a quality life and help me live the longest possible amount of time.

After consulting with my doctor and praying about what God wanted me to do, I chose to go with chemotherapy. After receiving five treatments, my hair fell out, and I was fighting nausea and fatigue.

When my son called to tell me about Jordan Rubin's incredible story and his health program called the Maker's Diet, I immediately jumped on a plane and flew down to West Palm Beach to get the facts "straight from the horse's mouth." After meeting with Jordan personally and being introduced to the Maker's Diet, I decided to continue chemotherapy while following the diet, food supplement, and lifestyle program very diligently.

My oncologist warned that after my next series of treatments for stage III lymphoma cancer I would feel extremely weak and nauseated—much more than the initial five treatments.

On November 8, my doctor insisted that I go on disability because my energy level and blood count would drastically drop in the next few weeks.

On November 28, I began the Maker's Diet, including the food supplements recommended to me. I also followed Dr. Rubin's suggestion to observe a seven-day juice fast to detoxify and cleanse my system. I was sixty-five pounds overweight and had little energy to do anything at the time.

On December 3, I took my next chemotherapy treatment and waited for my energy level to hit the bottom as predicted. To my delight and surprise, the nausea and fatigue were almost nonexistent! According to the doctor, my blood counts never dropped. What a difference the diet change and food supplements made!

The nurses at the doctor's office asked how I was feeling—they couldn't believe I was feeling so good! I told them about the Maker's Diet, and they noted it on my chart.

On December 23, I received the toughest chemotherapy treatment yet (five separate drugs), and *the results were the same*—very little side effects. My son and his family flew up to Tennessee on Christmas Day to visit with us. Would you believe that we had nine people in the house for one week and that I did the grocery shopping for everyone, cooked most of the meals, and entertained four grandchildren (all under five years of age)? Where did I get the energy I wasn't supposed to have? I am convinced I owe it to the Maker's Diet.

On January 8, I stopped the program for about three days, just to see how I would do. Without the nutrients from the Maker's Diet, I found myself extremely weak and hardly able to get up off the couch. I started back on the program again on January 12 and regained my strength the next day! That convinced me more than ever that the Maker's Diet was what made the difference!

"The lymph nodes have shrunk back to normal, and there is no sign of cancer anywhere!" (Bob's doctor)

On January 15, 2003, my cancer was restaged by CAT and PET scans. The doctor, who is normally very low key, came bouncing energetically into the examination room and shouted, *"This is incredible. In my fifteen years of practice, this is the best lymphoma scan report I have ever seen. The lymph nodes have shrunk back to normal, and there is no sign of cancer anywhere!"*

My wife and I were overcome with joy and excitement at the awesome report and answer to so many prayers. Not only was I progressing better than anyone expected, but also I had lost twenty-five pounds and was feeling better than I had in years! Now that my cancer is in remission, I will continue following the Maker's Diet, expecting it to keep the cancer away for good!

Doug M.

My journey began when I decided to make one last-ditch desperation attempt to correct a deteriorating physical condition that had plagued me for five long years.

During the winter of 1998, I experienced recurring symptoms of heartburn that rapidly progressed into a chronic acid reflux condition. I was unable to digest my food (regardless of what I ate) without bringing it back up repeatedly. This took place over and over for forty-five minutes to an hour after each meal.

This painful condition began to wreak havoc on me physically, emotionally, and socially, as my eating habits became increasingly erratic. I often ate in seclusion to avoid any embarrassment associated with this condition, which I later learned was called GERD (gastroesophageal reflux disease).

I did some research and learned that GERD is a generic term applied to any common acid reflux or heartburn condition. I soon learned that my particular case of GERD was anything but common when I went to my doctor seeking a diagnosis and a conventional medical remedy. That doctor's visit began an eighteen-month barrage of seemingly endless paperwork and referrals as I bounced from one "specialist" to the next within my HMO health insurance plan.

After running a number of diagnostic procedures (upper GI series, upper endoscopy, stomach-emptying study, manometry tests, etc.), my gastroenterologist finally determined that I had a severe case of GERD. It was complicated by a gaping hiatal hernia, a duodenal ulcer, and an abnormally slow-emptying stomach, which emptied at a rate 75 percent slower than normal for a male my age. The prognosis wasn't good.

These complications, combined with the substantial reflux I was experiencing, made it very difficult to treat my GERD symptoms. It seemed that each health practitioner I sought for medical advice told me that GERD symptoms as complex and severe as mine were the leading cause of esophageal cancer. I was ready to exhaust every effort to combat this disorder.

So began a three-year search during which I tried three conventional prescription remedies, two mail-order prescriptions from Canada (not approved yet in the U.S.), and one prescription from Europe. Each "remedy" provided a host of side effects such as constant nausea, sleeplessness, and headaches—but none of them alleviated the reflux.

My desperation and hopelessness grew with each futile attempt at a cure. Finally, a specialist at the University of Miami Hospital told me my last remaining option was an uncommon surgical procedure called a Laparoscopic Nissen. It would require the removal of the upper third of my stomach so it could be tied around the bottom of my esophagus. I avoided this grisly procedure by ignoring my problem for the next two years. When I could no longer stand the constant burning sensation in my throat and the haunting fear of life-threatening throat cancer, I contacted the specialist.

One day in early December of 2002, I finally caved in and agreed to my doctor's constant plea that immediate Laparoscopic Nissen surgery was the only solution. Reluctantly, I scheduled a preoperative appointment with the hospital.

On the very same day that I scheduled my preoperative appointment, fate took a lucky turn. I just "happened" to share the details of my circumstances with a co-worker whom I really didn't know. That conversation became a life-altering moment. The guy's next sentence was, *"Have you ever heard of a doctor named Jordan Rubin?"*

I said *no* without showing a shred of interest, and my attention faded even further when he described Dr. Rubin as some kind of holistic health practitioner. I thought, *If conventional modern medicine can't provide an answer, what chance would a holistic approach provide?* The co-worker was so persistent that he persuaded me to look at Jordan's Web site.

That is when I was introduced to Jordan's amazing personal chronicle of his own life-and-death battle with Crohn's disease. I felt a newfound inspiration budding inside me. I knew this could be my last opportunity to avoid being butchered like a guinea pig. What happened next was nothing short of miraculous.

I excitedly called the contact number on the Web site, and the customer service representative on the other end sounded strangely familiar. He was an old friend and co-worker of mine who was also a childhood friend of Jordan Rubin. He arranged a consultation for me with Dr. Rubin. Every day since this meeting has been nothing short of amazing.

The day I began the Maker's Diet was my last day with GERD!

Jordan's confidence impressed me immediately during my initial consultation. I distinctly remember the kind and determined look in his eyes as I described my symptoms and mentioned that I had already booked a preoperative appointment for esophageal surgery. His confidence radiated from what he had overcome personally, and he had an absolute belief in his program. Yet, all he said was, "If you're willing, I think I can help." The reassuring way he made this simple statement gave me a sense of optimism and hope I hadn't felt since my troubles began.

Jordan familiarized me with the Maker's Diet, recommending a dietary program and whole-food nutritional supplements, going to great lengths to describe the synergistic effect his program would have on my prevailing symptoms and on my overall health as well.

This was extremely exciting to me because for months I had been experiencing a number of other symptoms that alarmed me. I was almost embarrassed to discuss these "other" symptoms with Jordan, fearing he would consider me to be some kind of hypochondriac. Yet, I felt I needed to make the most of this once-in-a-lifetime opportunity.

I went on to describe the strange malaise spells I'd get every three to four weeks that lasted two or three days. The achy, bone-tired lethargic feeling rendered me almost nonfunctional for days at a time. (I realize now that it may have been chronic fatigue syndrome.)

Surprisingly, Jordan was able to relate and empathize with everything I described to him because he had been down that road himself—and he had emerged triumphant. Our conversation that day marked a turning point for me. I *knew* I was on the right path, and I fervently began the Maker's Diet. I was unwaveringly determined to finally restore the most vital asset I possessed—my health.

I began the protocol on December 16, 2002, and—God is my witness—that was the *last day* I ever experienced GERD! I can still hardly believe it's true. I haven't had one iota of regurgitation from the very first dose of Omega-Zyme (a digestive enzyme product formulated by Dr. Rubin).

December 16 also marked the first day I began keeping a health/food journal to religiously document my progress by briefly describing how I feel every day and recording what I eat. The protocol Jordan put me on included Omega-Zyme, Primal Defense, RM-10, FYI, Springs of Life, Acid Defense, Perfect Food, Extra-Virgin Coconut Oil, Olde World Icelandic Cod Liver Oil, and lastly (yet most importantly) my strict adherence to the Maker's Diet.

Today I still have absolutely no sign of the GERD or any of the related heartburn symptoms, and my energy levels continue to even out and become more and more consistent with each passing day.

There's really no way to appropriately thank someone who has given you so much of your life back...and I don't exaggerate when I say that. However, there's one thing that I can do—I can simply pass along the miraculous results I've enjoyed with Jordan's program. And I pray that many of you who are suffering will read my story and hold on to the hope that your prayers can be answered, beginning with the belief in Jordan's simple statement, "If you're willing, I think I can help."

Christian S.

January 5, 2001 was a day that drastically altered the course of my life forever. It was a cool Florida winter day, with a temperature of 65 degrees, slightly overcast skies, and strong prevailing winds. And there I was, lying on the ground in agonizing pain. *This can't be happening*! I thought to myself.

Only split seconds earlier, while on patrol as a security guard for a luxury community, I was struck by a rather large SUV. The incident happened at lightning speed, but the moment seemed to last for an eternity.

Life throws a curve ball once in a while, and this was a doozy. I was on top of the world at the time. I had just ended my service with the United States Air Force and was looking forward to serving the community as a deputy sheriff in West Palm Beach, Florida. Even more exciting at the time, my amateur boxing career was on the verge of exploding.

After the accident, my self-esteem hit a downward spiral, and I found comfort in a lot of things—but my favorite was food. I could no longer train, and my future plans just went up in flames. I couldn't get out of bed for weeks, plenty of time for me to get well acquainted with two very good friends of mine—Ben & Jerry (ice cream). As time went on, so did the pounds. In two years I ballooned from a muscular six foot, 200-pound physique to a marshmallow body shape type weighing in at 270 pounds. I didn't even recognize the person I saw in the mirror.

The more depressed I felt, the more I ate. It was a vicious cycle I didn't know how to break. I kept my natural defense mechanism on the alert for any possible fat joke that came my way so I could beat people to the punch line and make the joke on myself before others had the chance. That was the way I handled the feeling of rejection from all of my fit and thin friends.

I tried other ways to lose weight, but as a former athlete, the only effective method I had ever known was working out. The two herniated disks in my lower back and my bum left knee, along with the additional weight gain, removed that exercise option. (Despite repeated attempts, problems with my insurance prevented me from getting the surgery I desperately needed.)

The "decision"

Life is all about decisions. This was one decision I had to make: Would I keep living in this overweight, achy, tired, and depressed body? Or would I take back the control of my health I had forfeited and decide to do something about it?

I was introduced to a health program called the Maker's Diet shortly thereafter. At first I dismissed it as just another diet, but I couldn't get it out of my mind. Fed up with my predicament and facing my upcoming wedding, the choice was simple. I don't believe in coincidences; I believe God gave me the unique opportunity to follow the Maker's Diet. Just from the name I knew that God was in complete control and had heard my cries for help. If you are reading this today, it is not by coincidence; this diet may very well be *your* answer as well.

Feeling good and back in the gym!

I saw results immediately. Losing five pounds my first week only excited me and furthered the faith I had in the diet. The funny thing was that I thought that being on a diet meant limiting the amount of food I was eating. With the Maker's Diet, I felt as if I was eating more than I ever had before.

When I started the program, my back and knee were still bothering me, so I wasn't even able to exercise. After the second week, people started noticing and commenting on how good I was looking. Trust me, with my low self-esteem, I was sopping it up like a sponge in water.

The weight kept pouring off as I adhered to the diet and nutritional supplements, but my health wasn't the only thing that was improving. My self-worth was increasing as well. I woke up excited about life again, and I wasn't afraid to walk in front of the mirror without my shirt on. My knee and back pain decreased more and more over a period of time, and my energy level skyrocketed from where it was before.

Within twelve weeks I had dropped forty pounds and was down to 230 pounds. Another fantastic result is that my back pain and knee pain have improved so much I am back in the gym and playing basketball.

Simple Conclusion

One by one, desperate people just like Rose, Bob, Christian, and Doug contact me for help. While I do *not* consider myself a miracle worker, I *do* have great confidence in my Teacher, affectionately called "the Great Physician," who heals all our diseases (Ps. 103:3). Nothing matches His wisdom concerning His creation, including the ideal human diet and natural treatments for our most common ailments.

Before you examine the "nuts and bolts" of the Maker's Diet, I wanted you to consider its effect on these people who were desperate for any glimmer of hope in their health situation—including my own grandmother, who prayed for just a few more months of life! They represent a great number of people who enjoy restored health today as a result of making the decision to try the Maker's Diet. In fact, just a few months before publication of this book, many of the staff members at our local church finished the Maker's Diet 40-Day Health Experience. They are looking and feeling better, and many are experiencing a level of health they never thought possible. Isn't God awesome!

I want to end this chapter with three of their "before" and "after" stories.

JoAnn D.

"Before"

I am sick and tired of being sick and tired. I think that pretty well sums it up. I guess I have had minor health problems all my life, and I got used to them. As you get older, though, they seem to become more noticeable. All through my married life, my husband has had his share "in sickness" and very little "in health." I can't say they have been major issues, but they are enough for him to start his day with, "How are you feeling today?" I appreciate his love and concern, and I know he really wants to know. After thirty years he even measures the pause between the time he asks the question and the time it takes me to answer. My number one goal for this forty-day experience is to look like I feel so wonderful that my husband's first question every day is not, "How are you feeling today?"

An important goal is to spend more time with the Lord and really relax. Other goals are to not go to bed and wake up with a headache; my blood pressure to stabilize throughout the month; migraines to go away; nails to grow; and hair to quit falling out.

"After"

I am still in shock. I never thought I would win! I never win...and I won the biggest prize! WOW! Go figure...me...a winner!

Now let me tell you what I won—my health. I did reach my goal. I feel wonderful inside and out. I feel younger and more alive. I don't feel sick and tired all the time, and I find myself smiling more. I have been a PR person for quite sometime, and I found myself having to force myself to sound happy. Now it just comes bursting out. I guess now I will have to train myself to control it.

As for my other goals:

1. Not to go to bed and wake up with a headache: the headaches have stopped.
2. For my blood pressure to stabilize throughout the forty days: I had one elevation, and it was not even "that" time of the month. (Speaking of "that" time of the month, we never knew it was coming. I had no BP elevations or mood swings, and it was a lighter, more normal flow.)
3. Migraines to go away: I did not have one the whole forty days!
4. Nails to grow: they did not grow healthy
5. Hair to quit falling out: still falling out, but then it started from blood pressure medication many years ago. I knew it would not stop falling out overnight.

I have never guessed myself to be a selfish person, but I have to admit I did not think about what these forty days would do for my husband...or our marriage. My husband has needed to lose weight for quite sometime, and I knew he would feel better once he did. I never gave thought to how "we" would feel.

My heart melted when he came home from work one night and announced, "I feel great!" He has lost a significant amount of weight (he started dieting in the middle of July) and knows he has more yet to lose. He is not depressed over that fact. He sees it as a challenge now and eagerly exercises and is careful to eat correctly (since beginning the Maker's Diet). He has not been tempted by candies or goodies at work. I am so proud and pleased for him. But I also think the Lord softened his heart to be open to this opportunity.

And the grand prize—that happened November 1, 2003. We were invited by a special couple to attend the fiftieth anniversary ball at our local Elk's club. I was wearing the evening gown I wore to our daughter's wedding rehearsal dinner. My husband was wearing the same white dinner jacket and tuxedo pants. I cannot remember my husband ever looking so handsome—nothing too tight, nothing uncomfortable. He looked at me and said, "You are looking real sexy!" And I felt it. I was so happy inside and out. I may have taken a little longer than most to feel well, but I sure do!

"You are looking real sexy!" sure outclasses "How are you feeling today?" As I stated earlier, all through my married life, my husband has had more than his share "in sickness" and very little "in health." I think that is about to change!

· ·
Carolyn G.
· ·

"Before"

In 1994 I became very ill with mononucleosis, which I never seemed to recover from. I spent months at a time during the following two years taking antibiotics and penicillin. I eventually had a tonsillectomy done and saw some improvement, but never complete healing. I still suffer from fatigue on a daily basis. I never wake up refreshed and find it difficult to get through the day without enough energy. I also get sick very easily; if I am around someone who is ill, I am sure to get what they have.

I have also been diagnosed as having a spastic colon, now called IBS (irritable bowel syndrome), suffering from severe bloating, constipation, irregular bowel movements, distension, and cramping. This has been a chronic, difficult thing to deal with over the years.

A year ago I was engaged in a regimented exercise and eating routine with a personal trainer, which produced excellent results for a time. I toned up and ate only low-sodium and low-sugar foods. I was feeling well physically and had more energy during the day, but I knew it wasn't actually a program that would heal my body or that I could do long term. The food choices were extremely limited, and I lost the drive to put in the amount of time it took to be in that program.

Unfortunately, over the last year, I have become so busy with my job and master's degree course load that I have neglected my health greatly. I have doubled my dress size, going from a size 6 or 8 to a size 12 or 14.

Currently, I am quite unhappy with my physical health. I feel unfit and unsatisfied, yet I haven't made sufficient time in my daily schedule to prioritize my health.

I look forward to the forty days as a time set aside to concentrate on healing and learning how to eat well. I am specifically targeting my physical health, hoping to both lose weight and cleanse my bowels of any disease.

I believe by faith that God is truly going to use the Maker's Diet to bring healing to my body. I hope to gain self-discipline in eating and exercising well, and I hope to make the Maker's Diet a priority in my life practices.

"After"

I cannot say enough about my journey through the Maker's Diet 40-Day Health Experience. I have been challenged and blessed beyond measure by my involvement. I have seen critical changes in my overall health, which I have been praying for desperately over the years.

I believe that I finally got some answers about what foods I need to avoid for optimal health. It is amazing how getting educated about proper nutrition—removing toxins, hormone-enhanced, chemically altered food, and introducing food in its natural form as our Maker created it—can change one's complete perspective about food and enhance well-being.

For the first time in my life I have begun to recognize how my body actually responds to foods not on the Maker's Diet. I had three difficult days where I ate foods off the diet, and each day I was able to see and feel the negative results of those choices within hours. My stomach cramped up and became distended. I got headaches and felt foggy and fatigued. It is almost like these foods are toxic to my body; my body wanted to repel them immediately. I am now certain that I am literally "allergic" to particular foods I had been eating on a frequent basis before starting this diet. My body just can't process them.

I have more energy than before. Typically, I used to require a nap on both Saturday and Sunday afternoons to get myself ready physically for another week of labor. I can honestly tell you that I only took one nap on the whole diet! There were some days where I thought, *I should lie down and rest*, only to find that I was not tired! This is truly amazing for me. It has made me far more productive at work as well. I have an intense job researching and writing all day, and I have found that I concentrate better, process more quickly, and am more efficient.

Much of the reason I am sure I have had more energy is that my sleep has been more restful. My gut and my brain are working together! The three or so times I ate food off the diet, I didn't sleep nearly as well...there is definitely a connection. I'm sure my bowels are being cleansed as well. This has been a huge prayer concern for me. I believe with all my heart that the Super Seed and Living Multi combined with the whole foods have helped my body learn how to absorb good bacteria and expel bad bacteria.

I've also found that my skin has become very clear and clean. This is the biggest area that I have gotten comments from others. They have noticed a glow in my skin and a reduction in tiny lines around my eyes. I attribute this to removing chemicals, hormones, and pesticides from my foods and from using the hygiene kit. I have not missed one single opportunity to use the hygiene system. It has changed my life. In the past I have always gotten sick from flying on a plane. I have had two round-trip flights since being on this diet, and I have not had a sniffle— let alone the ear infections and bronchial infections I typically get. I refuse to give up the hygiene system...it is a total jewel that I treasure.

It has been wonderful to do this diet with my boyfriend. We have prayed about targeting particular areas such as diet *before* we commit in marriage. It has been wonderful to support one another, get educated together, and cook together. We've spent a lot more time at home because this diet has simplified our life perspective; it's been invaluable for us. He said to me, "We are starting a legacy of health for our family." And we have. I am excited to work with him as one to build a family on God's wisdom and provisions. Proverbs 24:3–4 says, "Through wisdom a house is built, and by understanding it is established; by knowledge the rooms are filled with all precious and pleasant treasures." God has provided us with this wisdom through the Maker's Diet.

There is so much to say about how the Maker's Diet has impacted me. I could write my own book! I am so thankful for the opportunity I've had to take part in this diet. It has changed my life forever.

Kim V.

"Before"

My incentive about getting serious about my weight problem has begun with the start of this diet. For the last several years, I have been at my heaviest weight ever. I was always active in high school and college, and since hitting my mid-thirties, I have not changed my diet. I wouldn't say I'm a bad eater. I don't snack a lot, and I drink lots of water. I just tend to eat two big meals a day, sometimes not even breakfast. Only within the last three weeks have I begun an exercise program.

I have been a children's pastor for thirteen years, and it is a very rewarding and fulfilling ministry for me. But it does come with a lot of stress. I moved here two and a half years ago having no family and knowing only two people, and they have moved within this last year. It's been an adjustment for me—adjusting to the weather (I'm a Tennessee girl), people, and large church dynamics. That has had and still has an effect on my mental and emotional health, which I believe has affected my physical health. I do see how stress affects your weight. The only thing I feel I have going for me is my spiritual health, and as with everyone, during difficult times the enemy tries to use it against me.

From past experiences, I know how good I feel about myself when I am in shape. I do not feel good about my appearance now. I hide my weight very well. Plus, I am constantly tired when leaving work and sometimes have to work hard at making myself work out. But I am committed to that as I will be committed to the forty days of the Maker's Diet.

My goal is that this will jump-start my metabolism, give me more energy, and change my lifestyle of eating habits. I don't just want this to be a forty-day fad and then go back to putting in the "old tapes." I'm ready for new tapes. I'm ready to start feeling good about myself again and having a body—a temple—to reflect a healthy image. I desire balance in the areas of physical, mental, spiritual, and emotional health.

"After"

Wow! It's been an unbelievable forty days! Words can only briefly touch on how I feel. As stated in my "before" essay, I was not liking the way my body looked, and that affected many areas in my life. But I can definitely say today that I feel like a new person.

I have been totally committed to this plan and faithfully working out three times a week. I have seen and felt a significant difference. My overall attitude is becoming healthier. I was determined to stick with the Maker's Diet even through the detox and occasional cravings for "bad" foods.

I gave up all caffeine, and I am only drinking water. I ate the foods that were recommended and came up with some new recipes. I have not spent this much time thinking about the foods to eat and preparing them as I have these last forty days. Now it has become part of my daily ritual—a habit.

As I stated in my "before" essay, this is not going to be a forty-day only plan; my goal is to make it a lifestyle. My whole being—spiritual, mental, physical, and emotional—is healthier and happier. I'm beginning to see the *in-shape* Kim that I used to know years ago. I started out with a goal of losing a certain amount of weight, and I'm halfway there.

Chapter 8

Return to the Maker's Diet

THE SIMPLE REASON THE MAKER'S DIET CAN POSITIVELY AFFECT SO many different health problems is that it improves the health of the entire body, especially *the digestive tract*, which affects virtually all other bodily systems. The healing of the digestive system in turn positively affects the immune system, endocrine system, heart, lungs, blood supply, brain, and total nervous system. This proven health protocol involves a conscious return to the proteins, fats, carbohydrates, and additional micronutrients originally provided by our Creator for His highest creation, mankind.

As we discuss the basis of the Maker's Diet, we will refute some popular myths about the basic food groups. To the uninitiated, let me warn you—you may be *shocked*! Much of the information you are about to read has been confirmed by numerous double-blind, placebo-controlled, scientific studies conducted over many years as well as by thousands of years of history. Rest *un*-assured, you have *not* read this information in the popular magazines, books, and television programs with agendas supposedly leading us to better health.

Understanding Our Roots

Just one hundred years ago or less, the diet of the average American was dramatically different from our SAD (standard American diet) table fare today. Widespread corporate "mono-agriculture" with concentration on single-crop specialties and chemical fertilizers and pesticides was unheard of then, so the typical diet consisted mostly of fruits, vegetables, wild grain and seeds, fish, raw, unpasteurized dairy products, and meat from wild animals. (Of course, the menu varied significantly with locale and availability of food types.)

Since the Creator made us with a perpetual pattern in mind, it should not surprise us to discover that we crave the foods, in their natural state, that our ancestors consumed. Our physical bodies were engineered as marvelous, highly tuned machines, genetically set for nutritional requirements established from the beginning of time.

Human physiology and biochemistry are geared for the foods the Creator intended for us to eat, not for the high-speed output of modern food "processing" plants or fast-food windows. (By my estimate, more than half of the "foods" commonly consumed today were not eaten by our ancestors.)

Our ancestors consumed 30 to 65 percent of their daily calories (and up to 100 grams of fiber a day) from a wide variety of fresh fruits and vegetables. That is why, long before the discovery of vitamins, people who had access to healthy foods lived extremely long lives without vitamin deficiencies or major illnesses. Their protein needs were met by consuming pasture-fed animals, wild game, and fish that were rich in highly beneficial omega-3 fatty acids and CLA (conjugated linoleic acid). These fats protected our ancestors against diseases such as cancer, diabetes, and heart disease.

The Maker's Proteins

The word *protein* is derived from the Greek word *proteus*, which literally means of primary importance. It is translated into Latin as "primaries," that is, the primary constituent of the body.[1] The human body requires twenty-two amino acids to build body organs, muscles, and nerves (and much more). It also has the capacity to convert amino acids into proteins that combat invading protozoa, bacteria, and viruses, and that have the ability to communicate internally. Altogether, your body builds or uses around fifty thousand different proteins, including five thousand specialized proteins called enzymes!

Under normal conditions, the healthy human body is able to manufacture all but eight of the twenty-two amino acids from healthy food sources entering the body. These eight *essential* amino acids must come from other sources outside the body. If even *one* of these eight essential amino acids is missing, the body is unable to synthesize the other proteins it needs—no matter how much protein you eat![2] Animal protein is our only complete protein source, providing all eight essential amino acids. When we fail to get the essential amino acids and protein we need, we begin to lose myocardial (heart) muscle, which may contribute to coronary heart disease.[3]

Properly prepared (germinated or fermented) seeds, legumes, and cereal grains represent the best sources of protein in the vegetable kingdom, but they—along with all other plant foods—are low in tryptophan, cystine, and threonine. Other sources are low in additional protein components, which is why many vegetarians emphasize eating from a variety of vegetable sources.

Popular protein powders (protein isolates) derived from soy, egg whites, whey, and casein are usually manufactured using high temperatures or harsh chemical processes that leave the protein virtually useless. Studies show that soy protein isolates in such powders tend to be "high in mineral-blocking phytates, thyroid-depressing phytoestrogens and potent enzyme inhibitors that depress growth and may even cause cancer."[4]

Three key essential amino acids crucial to the health of the brain and nervous system are methionine, cysteine, and cystine; these amino acids are abundant in eggs and meat. While the consumption of organic fruits and vegetables is an obvious and important foundation of the Maker's Diet, the human body cannot function optimally without certain proteins and fats available *only* from animal sources (and the Maker's proteins are rarely if ever supplied by man's mass production techniques).

Animal products purchased from grocery stores are prone to contamination from pesticides, herbicides, and chemical fertilizers as well as the common overuse of antibiotics and growth hormones in large-scale commercial feedlots, making these food sources downright dangerous.

For these and other reasons, we only recommend animal proteins from beef, lamb, goat, buffalo, venison, elk, and other clean red meats; fish with fins and scales from oceans and rivers; chicken, turkey, and other poultry raised in a free-range setting or organically and grass-fed. We also recommend "clean" meats harvested from wild sources. These are all becoming more widely available in your grocery store or local health food store. (We have listed a number of excellent sources for these proteins Appendix B.)

Under no circumstances do we recommend pork or pork products, shellfish, or any of the other biblically unclean meats, such as the popular ostrich and emu, as sources of protein.

The Maker's Fats

As I have mentioned throughout this book, the Bible gives incredible information on health, especially diet. The foods eaten by the Israelites made them the healthiest people on the planet during that time period. In reading the dietary instructions of the Bible, many health-conscious people seem to ask the same question: How could the Creator claim "fats" are healthy food sources for human beings? Doesn't He know that saturated fats and cholesterol are the main causes of heart disease and cancer?

Good saturated fats?

Contrary to the myth, perpetuated since the late 1950s, supposedly linking saturated fat and dietary cholesterol with coronary heart disease, many saturated fats are actually good for you! This truth may not be easy to believe, but it is still true, nevertheless.

Michael DeBakey, the famous heart surgeon, studied 1,700 patients with hardening of the arteries and found *no relationship between the level of cholesterol in the blood and the incidence of atherosclerosis.* The Medical Research Council found that men eating butter (a key biblical fat) ran half the risk of developing heart disease as those eating margarine (a man-made fat that is often indigestible and toxic). A study comparing Yemenite Jews in Israel who ate butter with those consuming margarine and vegetable oils yielded similar results.[5]

Saturated fats are not the "dietary demons" behind modern diseases. The truth—according to the Bible, anthropological evidence from past civilizations, and recent scientific research—makes it clear that saturated fats play a crucial role in body chemistry.

Sally Fallon, a renowned nutritional researcher, and Mary Enig, Ph.D., an international expert in the field of lipid (fat) biochemistry, coauthored *Nourishing Traditions*, and listed some key roles of saturated fats:[6]

- Saturated fatty acids constitute at least 50 percent of all cell membranes.
- At least 50 percent of dietary fat we consume should be saturated, otherwise calcium cannot be effectively incorporated into the skeletal structure.
- Saturated fats actually *lower Lp (a)*, a key substance in the blood that indicates proneness to heart disease.
- Saturated fats protect the liver from alcohol and other toxins, such as those contained in nonsteroidal anti-inflammatory drugs (NSAIDs).
- Saturated fats enhance the immune system.
- Without saturated fats, we cannot properly utilize essential fatty acids such as the all-important omega-3 fatty acids.

- Saturated 18-carbon stearic acid and 16-carbon palmitic acid provide *the preferred fuel for the heart,* which is why the fat around the heart muscle is highly saturated.

- Short- and medium-chain saturated fatty acids found in butter, coconut, and palm oil have important antimicrobial properties. They protect us against harmful microorganisms in the digestive tract.

The authors summarize their study with this astounding statement: "The scientific evidence, honestly evaluated, does not support the assertion that 'artery-clogging' saturated fats cause heart disease. Actually, evaluation of the fat found in clogged arteries reveals that only about 26 percent is saturated. The rest is unsaturated, of which more than half is polyunsaturated."[7]

The author of the study cited by Fallon and Enig, Uffe Ravnskov, M.D., Ph.D., writes:

> Studies of African tribes have shown that intakes of enormous amounts of animal fat [do] not necessarily raise blood cholesterol; on the contrary it may be very low. Samburu people, for instance, eat about a pound of meat and drink almost two gallons of raw milk each day during most of the year. Milk from the African Zebu cattle is much fattier than cow's milk, which means that the Samburus consume more than twice the amount of animal fat than the average American, and yet their cholesterol is much lower, about 170 mg/dl.[8]

Heart disease should be blamed not on animal fats or cholesterol, but upon excess consumption of vegetable oils, hydrogenated fats, and refined carbohydrates; vitamin and mineral deficiencies; and the reduction or disappearance of antimicrobial fats from the food supply (from animal fats and tropical oils).[9]

Most crucial fats for health

The Maker's fats are essential for good health and maximum protection from disease. You find them in natural vegetable and animal sources. Many people do not realize that animal proteins and fats appear together for a reason—we need fat to properly assimilate protein and minerals. Perhaps our most important fats (and those we lack the most) are the omega-3 fatty acids, found in cod liver oil, high omega-3 eggs, and ocean-caught fish such as salmon, mackerel, and sardines. Small amounts are available in meat, poultry, and dairy products from grass-fed animals.

A word of caution: With the rising popularity of salmon, more and more distributors, grocery chains, and restaurants have turned to *farm-raised salmon* to meet demand, which is contrary to the Maker's design for salmon. Research has shown that the omega-3 fatty acids so abundant in ocean-caught salmon are changed into omega-6 fatty acids when they are farm-raised, which creates an imbalance of these nutrients for your body. Always ask for ocean-caught salmon—especially the varieties from cold Alaskan waters, which offer a healthful *balance* of omega-3 and omega-6 fatty acids.[10]

The liberal consumption of omega-3 fatty acids is crucial for negating the effects of the overabundance of omega-6 linoleic acids and hydrogenated fats in most American diets—a combination linked to excess inflammation and tumor formation when in the presence of carcinogens and certain enzymes in cells lining the colon.[11]

Beware of hydrogenated fats

Many *hydrogenated* fats (liquid fats injected with hydrogen gas at high temperatures under high pressure to make them solid at room temperature) are heavily promoted as "health foods," but scientific findings say otherwise. The production process converts them into indigestible *trans-fatty* acids. Hydrogenated fats have been associated with cancer, atherosclerosis, diabetes, obesity, immune system dysfunction, low-birth-weight babies, birth defects, decreased visual acuity, sterility, difficulty in lactation, and problems with bones and tendons.[12]

The Maker's Diet focuses on the balanced intake of *natural* fats occurring in ocean-caught fish, cod liver oil, omega-3 eggs, and grass-fed, organic, and free-range meats. It also includes animal products such as butter, cheeses, and full-fat lacto-fermented dairy products such as yogurt and kefir, as well as raw milk and cream from goats, sheep, cows, and other biblically "clean" mammals.

The Maker's Carbohydrates

Carbohydrates are the *starches* and *sugars* produced by all plants, synthesized by the body from proteins and fats, and "refined" by humans until they become "negative" calories that leach nutrients from the body rather than replace them.

Table sugar (sucrose) and its first cousin, refined and bleached wheat flour, are the stripped-down and nutrition-less versions of naturally occurring foods from nature. These refined products were virtually unknown before A.D. 1600, but they have certainly made their mark on the human race over the last four hundred years.

A sugar revolution

Sugar in all of its commercial forms has taken America by storm. Nearly two hundred years ago, the average American consumed about 10 pounds of sugar per year. Today, we gladly push aside healthier fare to gather fully *one-fourth* of our annual calorie intake from sugar—which is about 170 pounds of sugar each year for each of us![13]

How would you like to see a grocery stock worker drop a heavy pallet of 170 one-pound bags of sugar beside your bed? Would you be willing to sit down and eat a bowl full of sugar every fourth meal (and nothing else)? As bizarre as that may sound, according to the statistics, *most of us are doing just that!*

When two United Nations agencies, the World Health Organization (WHO) and the Food and Agriculture Organization, released the results of a study on how to halt the epidemic of obesity-linked diseases worldwide, they also issued a bold warning to reduce the percentage of sugar-based calories to no more than 10 percent in 2003.[14]

Immediate protests and indignant news releases arose from the Sugar Institute (their news release carried the headline "Sugar Association Continues Disapproval of Release of Misguided WHO Diet and Nutrition Report"[15]), the Grocery Manufacturers of America (GMA), and the U.S. National Soft Drink Association, among others. *I wonder why?*

The saddest part of the picture for me is the official stance of the U.S. government—the leadership of a nation that leads the world in obesity. The U.S. government's "Dietary Guidelines for Americans" and official USDA guidelines include only a weak warning to consume sugar "in moderation" (while recommending *fluoridated water* as the *preferred* method of protecting teeth from cavities). And it directs the nation to consume even *more carbohydrates* from its newly revised "food pyramid."[16]

This is the same dietary picture and lifestyle that may put one out of every three Americans at risk of developing diabetes (one in two for Hispanic children), according to K. M. Venkat Narayan, M.D., chief of the diabetes epidemiology section at the Centers for Disease Control in Atlanta.[17] Meanwhile, the U.S. National Academy of Sciences' Institute of Medicine actually recommends that *sugar could make up 25 percent of calories!*[18]

GRANDMA ROSE'S DIET	My Grandma Rose was born on a farm in Poland where they consumed fruits and vegetables straight from the garden; eggs from free-range chickens; dairy straight from the cow and goat; cold-water fish such as sardines; cod liver oil; and meats from grazing animals. They pressed flaxseed and poppy seed into oil, using their own mill. "I used to eat lignan cakes as snacks with black sourdough bread," she recalls. "We used to break off pieces from the flax cakes and dip them in fresh oil right from the press."
	Grandma is a cancer survivor today thanks in part to the Maker's Diet. I am convinced her problems began after her family emigrated to America, where she fell in love with white bread and ate a lot of junk food loaded with sugar, including cakes and doughnuts from the bakery. I can imagine that there are many similar stories of immigrants losing their health after coming to "the land of plenty."

A more natural way

The Maker's carbohydrates—including natural sugars—come directly from nature without so-called refinement or enrichment. There are two types of natural sugars found in carbohydrate foods. The first type consists of *disaccharides*, which are chains of two simple sugars. Disaccharides include sucrose (table sugar), lactose (milk sugar), maltose, and many others. Foods containing disaccharides include sugar, grains, potatoes, corn, and noncultured dairy products. These foods can be difficult to digest unless they are consumed in their "predigested form" (i.e., after they have been soaked, sprouted, and/or fermented).

The second type of sugar in carbohydrate foods consists of *monosaccharides*, which are "single" sugars found in fruits, vegetables, nuts, seeds, fermented or sprouted grains, and dairy products. These are more easily digested. To eat carbohydrates the Maker's way, only include whole-grain products in your diet that have been properly treated through soaking, sprouting, or fermenting that converts disaccharides to monosaccharides, and that reduces or eliminates phytates, which are not easily digested and can actually cause nutrient deficiencies.

These natural carbohydrates include wholesome whole-grain sour-dough and sprouted-grain breads and cereal grains, soaked and fermented lentils, beans, and other legumes. They also include soaked seeds and nuts, fresh fruits and vegetables, and fermented vegetables.

Before the advent of mass-manufacturing processes, it was common for long-lived peoples to soak their grains overnight and then allow them to dry in the open air until they were partially germinated or *sprouted*, or to go through an ancient leavening process. From these grains they made breads and other foods.

We now know these processes effectively remove the *phytates* from the outer covering of the natural grains. Phytates are substances that contain phosphorus in acidic form as well as powerful *enzyme inhibitors* that combine with (or "grab") minerals in the intestinal tract and block their absorption. Without this scientific understanding, our ancestors were preparing their food in a way that enhanced digestion and health.

Some of the most toxic phytates appear in the extruded form of sugary breakfast cereals lining the shelves of America's grocery stores! According to Fallon and Enig, "Studies show that these extruded whole grain preparations can have even more adverse effects on the blood sugar than refined sugar and white flour!"[19] Dr. Edward Howell, one of the great enzyme scientists of the twentieth century and author of *Food Enzymes for Health and Longevity* (Lotus Press, 1994), observed that the products of our "modern" mechanized harvesting techniques lack something our forefathers possessed in abundance—*digestible* or *bioavailable* nutrition.

Modern techniques decrease nutrition value.

While modern techniques for harvesting crops definitely multiplied *efficiency* exponentially, they have also decreased the nutrition value to the same degree. Dr. Howell noticed that the old harvesting techniques helped preserve and enhance the nutrition value of the grain. After cutting the mature grains in the field, farmers would gather the stalks and loosely bind them upright in sheaves and let them stand overnight in the field before threshing them (or removing the grain from the grass stalks) the following day. This allowed the grains to germinate or sprout.

Germination initiates a chemical transformation in the seed grains that naturally neutralizes the phytates or enzyme inhibitors the Creator put on the exterior of the seeds. The seeds are activated or come alive, making all of the nutrition within the seed available for digestion. These *germinated* seeds of wheat and barley and the bread made from them were of great importance in biblical times. This living "staff of life" supplied easily digestible, life-giving carbohydrates.

However, the people of the Bible didn't wolf down great quantities of carbohydrates as we do. They actually ate significantly less food than we do today. They didn't consume a "high-carbohydrate" diet—they consumed a lower-carbohydrate diet by today's standards. It was common for people in biblical times to eat only one meal a day at times. And the grains they did eat were healthy, sprouted, or germinated grains with lower amounts of disaccharides and phytates.[20]

The Maker's Dairy

Despite the modern hype and controversy over dairy products, the Bible makes it clear that milk produced by clean animals such as cattle, sheep, and goats is a viable food acceptable for human consumption.

The biggest problems with modern dairy products come from our habit of "tinkering" with dairy animals and their milk products to "make them better." Dairy farmers today selectively breed dairy cows and inject them with growth hormones to boost their annual milk production from 500 pounds to 3,000 pounds. That gives us lots of hormone-laced, antibiotic-rich milk—for our enjoyment.

Rather than allow the cows to feed on grass in the field, they pump them full of high-protein soybean meal. The cows, in turn, produce incredible amounts of milk for two years—and then suffer chronic mastitis (infections of the nipples) and shorter life spans. The milk we receive in such high quantities is very low in nutrients—especially compared to the highly nutritious milk produced by grass-fed cows and other animals.

Unhealthy milk processing

Early and primitive societies understood the incredible value of milk products. Butter and cream in particular provide a treasure trove of vitamins, enzymes, and fats that promote healthy bodies and long life. In the days before refrigeration, virtually every society practiced time-honored methods of fermentation to preserve and prepare dairy products for consumption over time.

Modern milk producers routinely pasteurize milk by heating it at high temperatures to destroy undesirable bacteria. This process destroys all of the beneficial organisms in milk, along with all of the enzymes (considered the "final test" for successful pasteurization). It also alters vital amino acids, reducing our ability to access the protein, fats, vitamins, and minerals in milk. (In reality, modern sanitation standards, sterile, stainless steel holding tanks, and milking technology have made pasteurization largely *unnecessary* today.)

Milk producers also "add" powdered milk and synthetic vitamin D_2 or toxic D_3 to "low-fat" milk to make it thicker. Then they "homogenize" the mixture so fat particles remain in suspension—making them indigestible in the intestine but highly likely to pass through the intestinal wall, directly into the bloodstream.

Making better choices

Always choose butter over margarine or other "low-fat spreads." Seek out raw goat's milk or raw cow's milk. It may be difficult, but the search will be worth it. (Appendix B lists nationwide sources of raw dairy.)

Goat's milk in particular is *very* good for human consumption because it is easily digestible. (It digests in only twenty minutes versus three hours for pasteurized cow's milk.) It contains less lactose (the type of sugar in milk that many find hard to digest) and is filled with vitamins, enzymes, and protein. Sixty-five percent of the world's population drinks goat's milk.

Look for raw milk cheeses in health food stores, and learn how to make your own kefir, whole-milk yogurt, and other fermented dairy products. (The fermentation process makes most dairy products very digestible for sensitive people.)

The Maker's Fiber

For thousands of years before the birth of America's corporate processed food giants, Americans ate foods barely one step from their natural state as the Creator intended. Vegetables were harvested from the garden just outside the back door and prepared for the table; fermented vegetables were enjoyed during the winter. Fruits were plucked from the family fruit trees and vines.

The nutritious parts of these foods that could be digested were effectively passed through the intestinal wall into the bloodstream. The remainder—the *fiber*—consisting of the cell walls (cellulose), hemicellulose, pectin, lignans, gums, and mucilage that were indigestible continued the journey through the colon to final elimination.

Fiber: friend or foe

Fiber comes in two forms. *Insoluble fiber* cannot be broken down at all, while *soluble fiber* dissolves in water. Fiber is vital to the body because it promotes regular bowel movements, prevents constipation, increases the elimination of waste matter in the large intestine, and pressures the rectum muscles to loosen and expel waste without undue pressure on delicate rectal tissues.

Bran fiber became popular after a British missionary surgeon named Dr. Dennis Burkitt announced the results of pioneering studies in the 1970s noting that rural Africans on high-fiber diets had far less colon cancer than people in the West. Burkitt had already distinguished himself by being the first to discover and describe what is now called "Burkitt's lymphoma" in 1958. His later discovery of a primitive people who had almost no diabetes, constipation, or irritable bowel syndrome seemed to support the conclusion that the Africans' high fiber intake accounted for their good intestinal health.[21]

Dr. Burkitt's basic premise was right, in my opinion, but the American media and health culture took "the fiber hypothesis" in a totally different direction. While the African tribesmen Dr. Burkitt studied rarely ate *grains*, the idea was promoted in America that eating large amounts of *bran* fiber from whole-grain wheat would help prevent colon cancer, diverticulosis, hemorrhoids, and colonic polyps.

For thirty years, the grain-fiber hypothesis (especially from bran) was considered the gospel truth. However, the truth is that bran fiber actually *aggravates* many of these conditions. I couldn't eat bran fiber during my battle with Crohn's disease, and I won't touch it today due to the high amount of mineral-blocking phytates it contains.

Fiber found in grain is a *carbohydrate*. The overconsumption of high-carbohydrate grain-based foods such as bran, fibrous breakfast cereals, whole-wheat bread (nonsprouted or fermented), and soy, which all contain high amounts of phytates, is a primary cause of intestinal disease and other diseases!

Friendly fiber

The Maker's recommended fiber sources, the kind of fiber that promotes colon health, are found in *low-carbohydrate*, high-fiber foods. These foods include broccoli, cauliflower, celery, and lettuce, as well as soaked or sprouted seeds, nuts, grains, and legumes. Berries and other small fruits along with fruits and vegetables with edible skins are also good sources of low-carbohydrate fiber. Besides providing the right kind of fiber, these foods are rich in vitamins, minerals, and antioxidants.

Another form of helpful fiber, called *mucilaginous* fiber, also helps relieve constipation and soothes inflamed tissue in the lining of the gut while decreasing transit time for proper elimination. Lowered transit times mean that toxins are quickly flushed out before they putrefy in the colon. Mucilaginous fiber is found in chia and flaxseeds.

The Maker's Fermentation

I once heard a man say that the creation of the refrigerator is one of the worst inventions for our health. Before artificial refrigeration, fermentation was the "poor man's" (or should we say "rich man's"?) "refrigeration" to preserve his food in a healthy way. Few Americans from urban and suburban areas know anything about preserving food in this way. Most of the people in the world—including people of Europe, Asia, Africa, South America, and various Third World and emerging nations—still depend on fermentation to preserve foods and to protect them from dangerous organisms in other foods and drinks.

Thousands of years ago, Abraham served his best meat, dairy, and fermented cream curds to entertain his angelic visitors:

> So Abraham hurried into the tent to Sarah. "Quick," he said, "get three seahs of fine flour and knead it and bake some bread." Then he ran to the herd and selected a choice, tender calf and gave it to a servant, who hurried to prepare it. He then brought some curds and milk and the calf that had been prepared, and set these before them.
>
> —GENESIS 18:6–8, NIV

It is said the Chinese fermented cabbage as far back as six thousand years ago. And according to Annelies Schoneck, the Roman emperor Tiberius always took a barrel of sauerkraut (fermented cabbage) with him when he made the long voyages to the Middle East.[22] Fermentation is especially effective in releasing important nutritional compounds through "pre-digestion" that would otherwise pass through the human digestive system, undigested and unused.

Modern vinegar-based fermentation techniques used for large-scale commercial production do *not* produce the same benefits as *lactic acid fermentation*, which is driven by beneficial microorganisms. This natural biological activity produces enzymes that break down foods into usable compounds and inhibits putrefying bacterial growth.

Every long-lived culture in the world has consumed fermented vegetables, dairy, and meat. Aboriginal peoples of Australia buried sweet potatoes in the soil for months before removing and consuming them. The proliferation of lactobacilli and other friendly microorganisms in fermented vegetables enhances their digestibility, increases vitamin levels, and produces helpful enzymes as well as natural antibiotic and anticarcinogenic substances.

The same thing happens in lacto-fermented sauerkraut described in ancient Roman manuscripts, and in pickled green tomatoes, peppers, and lettuce in Russia and Poland. Asian peoples make legendary pickled preparations of cabbage, turnip, eggplant, cucumber, onion, squash, and carrot (including Korean *kimchi*, a lacto-fermented condiment of cabbage with other vegetables and seasonings, and Japanese pickled vegetables).

American lacto-fermented foods include the full range of pickled vegetables, relishes, eggs, and many native fruits—plus nearly all of the fermented products carried over from Europe, Asia, and nations south of the border.

Easy do-it-yourself lacto-fermented dairy products such as yogurt, kefir, cheeses, cottage cheese, and cultured cream (also called *crème fraish*) are exceptionally healthy and nutritious. (If you are lactose-intolerant, you should know that the healthful "probiotic" bacteria involved in the lacto-fermentation process feed on the lactose in milk, leaving behind galactose, an easily digested monosaccharide sugar.)

The Maker's Enzymes, Living Vitamins, and Minerals

When the Creator provided protein, He placed it in close proximity to healthy fats needed for proper assimilation of the protein. He also provided *enzymes* as a type of divine "match" to light the fires of digestion.

Enzymes are specialized proteins that trigger, facilitate, and accelerate chemical reactions, while remaining unchanged in the process. These natural catalysts are found in all *living* organisms, especially raw or uncooked food.

There are three types of enzymes: *digestive*, *metabolic*, and *food* enzymes. The three *digestive* enzymes are *proteases* (to digest protein), *amylases* (to digest carbohydrates), and *lipases* (to digest fat). These enzymes help the body break down food so it can be absorbed in the small intestine. The body itself manufactures *metabolic* enzymes that direct body functions and digestive enzymes. Food enzymes are found only in uncooked raw foods. One such enzyme, cellulase, breaks down plant fiber known as cellulose and makes it digestible.

Cultural enzyme deficiency

Prolonged heat kills all enzymes, as does cooking, processing, and pasteurization. That is why we should eat raw foods along with our cooked foods. Lacto-fermented foods are especially rich in beneficial digestive enzymes of all types.

Dr. Howell, whom we mentioned earlier, maintained that every human being is born with a finite or fixed number of enzymes. This is, perhaps, the central theme of his classic work *Enzyme Nutrition*.[23] Because these vital enzymes are limited, it is important to provide as many outside enzymes as possible from raw food sources.

Unfortunately, the vitamin and mineral content of American vegetables and fruits has declined over the last half century due to the overuse of chemical fertilizers and other chemical additives, as well as "mono-farming" techniques that do not promote the natural replenishment of the soil. In addition, Americans are consuming fewer servings of even these "less-potent" fruits and vegetables, while loading up on junk food virtually devoid of all nutrients. This national eating pattern has produced widespread nutrient and enzyme deficiencies, thus leading to a number of health problems.

For many concerned individuals, the solution to nutritional deficiencies was to turn to vitamin and mineral supplements. Unfortunately, what passes for vitamin and mineral supplements in grocery stores, pharmacies, and even "health food" stores often amounts to little more than isolated or synthetic, lifeless chemicals. Worse yet, these are laboratory-produced synthetic substitutes for food nutrients that were never meant to be assimilated apart from their natural form in food.

Over 50 percent of the population take vitamin or mineral supplements to improve energy and performance and to reduce the risk of deadly diseases such as cancer, heart disease, and diabetes.[24] Despite widespread use of vitamin and mineral supplements since their introduction only some fifty years ago, the incidence of those major diseases has skyrocketed! Even more surprising is the lack of scientific research showing the efficacy of multivitamin/mineral supplements.

A new form of living vitamins and minerals is about to change all of this. These *homeostatic nutrients* provide vitamins and minerals in the natural form our Creator intended—as living food. They provide all of the necessary cofactors required for assimilation by the body, and they are literally "alive" with probiotics and enzymes.

The early results of university research being conducted on homeostatic nutrients show that consumption of these nutrients not only improves energy and performance but also reduces risk factors for cancer, heart disease, and diabetes! [25]

Research conducted by Dr. Price led him to believe that without fat-soluble vitamin A (retinol) from animal sources such as butterfat, egg yolks, liver, and other organ meats, the body cannot utilize protein, minerals, or water-soluble vitamins. He also discovered what he called *Activator X*—or the X Factor—a fat-soluble nutrient that acts as a catalyst to mineral absorption. Activator X is found in cream from grass-fed animals, organic liver, and fish eggs.[26]

In addition, there are seven "macrominerals" (calcium, chloride, magnesium, phosphorus, potassium, sodium, and sulfur) and at least thirty trace minerals that are essential to life. If present in only minute amounts, these minerals prevent certain diseases and promote proper body function. The natural sources for minerals include nutrient-rich foods, beverages, broths, and living multivitamins with homeostatic nutrients.

The Maker's Top "Healing" Foods

More and more, history and science are confirming that the Creator's provisions for mankind's need for food are still the best choices for ensuring health and quality of life today. The following section reviews some of these top biblical foods that you can choose to include in your diet for health and longevity.

Fish and fish oil

If you follow the precise biblical recommendations for the Creator's seafood, you can ensure health and avoid disease. (See Leviticus 11:9–12.) Fish is a wonderfully rich source of protein, potassium, vitamins, and minerals. For those who simply don't get enough cold-water fish, it is imperative that you take a form of high-quality cod liver oil every day. Today we understand scientifically that fish and cod liver oil:

- Thin the blood
- Protect the arteries from damage

- Inhibit blood clots (antithrombotic)
- Reduce blood triglycerides
- Lower LDL blood cholesterol
- Lower blood pressure
- Reduce risk of heart attack and stroke
- Ease symptoms of rheumatoid arthritis
- Reduce risk of lupus
- Relieve migraine headaches
- Fight inflammation
- Help regulate the immune system
- Inhibit cancer in animals (and possibly humans)
- Soothe bronchial asthma
- Combat early kidney disease

Much of the healing powers of fish reside in the omega-3 fatty acids that are particularly highly concentrated in cold-water fish such as salmon, sardines, bluefish, herring, lake trout, mackerel, sablefish, whitefish, bluefin tuna and anchovies, as well as in cod liver oil.

Doctors have prescribed cod liver oil for more than two hundred years for a number of ailments, including rheumatism and arthritis. (It was believed it could "lubricate the joints.") It took until 1985 for doctors to officially recommend (in the *New England Journal of Medicine*) that arthritis sufferers could benefit from eating fish once or twice a week! (In the case of arthritis, the omega-3 oils *do* "lubricate" the joints!)

Three villains inside our bodies cause heart attacks and stroke: *plaque,* which can clog arteries and dangerously restrict blood flow; the *accumulation of platelets* (sticky pieces of blood cells), which clump together and form clots; and the sudden, unexplained *spasms of blood vessels*, which can throw the heart out of kilter or halt the flow of blood to the brain, causing strokes. Studies show that cod liver oil high in omega-3 fats EPA and DHA reduces or eliminates all three risks. The higher the levels of omega-3 fatty acids in the blood, the lower your blood pressure and your risk of heart disease and cancer![27]

In study after study, cod liver oil has been acknowledged to play a role in the development of the brain, the rods and cones of the retina of the eye, the male reproductive tissue, skin integrity, lubrication of the joints, and the body's inflammatory response. This has made it a recommended first-response treatment for early symptoms of autism and other neurological child-development problems.[28]

Grains of the Bible: barley and wheat

God described the Israelite's Promised Land as "a land of *wheat* and *barley*" (Deut. 8:8, emphasis added). Was it coincidence that the young boy in John 6:9–13 brought Jesus five *barley loaves* with which He fed thousands? Barley has been consumed for thousands of years and is known to improve potency, vigor, and strength. Roman gladiators at times were called "barley eaters" because they ate barley before their contests for bursts of strength.

While barley and wheat can be valuable, their *young sprouts* known as cereal grasses are considered by some to be true "miracle" foods. These grasses contain four essential compounds largely absent from our diets:

1. Antioxidant enzymes
2. Trace minerals
3. Chlorophyll
4. High-quality vegetable proteins

You can obtain the juice from young wheat and barley grasses by juicing them yourself or by consuming a green superfood powder containing the dried cereal grass juices. (See Appendix B.)

Cultured dairy from goats, cows and sheep

"You shall have enough goats' milk for your food, for the food of your household, and the nourishment of your maidservants" (Prov. 27:27). The milk consumed in biblical times differed much from the milk we consume today. The milk of the Bible came from cows and goats and was consumed straight from the animal (it was not pasteurized or homogenized), or it was immediately fermented. These "live" foods provide excellent health benefits in contrast to today's pasteurized, homogenized, often skimmed and "refortified" milk, which is not only less nutritious but also can be potentially harmful and a major cause of allergies and even heart disease.

It was virtually impossible to keep milk fresh in those days, so the people "borrowed" the fermentation process used to make wine or sourdough bread and used it to preserve their dairy products. The result was what we know today as yogurt, cheese (soft and hard), and what is sometimes called *curds* in the Bible (called butter or butter curds in some translations). Here are some of the recently discovered health benefits of high-quality *fermented* dairy:

- It provides calcium that builds bone in children, and it also helps prevent or slow the development of osteoporosis that plagues so many elderly.
- It lowers high blood pressure and cholesterol.
- It attacks bacterial infections, especially those that cause diarrhea. It soothes stomach linings irritated from drugs or harsh foods.
- It prevents dental cavities and chronic bronchitis.
- It stops the growth of some cancers, including colon cancer.
- It boosts mental alertness and energy.

High-quality fermented dairy can come from cow's or goat's milk. Many people find that they attain better results by consuming goat's milk rather than cow's milk. Below are some of the health benefits attributed to goat's milk consumption.

- Goat's milk is less allergenic. (It does not contain the complex proteins that stimulate allergic reactions to cow's milk.)
- Goat's milk does not suppress the immune system.
- Goat's milk is easier to digest than cow's milk. (An old statistic showed that goat's milk will digest in a baby's stomach in twenty minutes, whereas pasteurized cow's milk takes eight hours. The difference is in the structure of the milk.)[29]
- Goat's milk has more buffering capacity than over-the-counter antacids. (The USDA and Prairie View A&M University in Texas have confirmed that goat's milk has more acid-buffering capacity than cow's milk, soy infant formula, and nonprescription antacid drugs.)[30]
- Goat's milk alkalinizes the digestive system. It actually contains an alkaline ash, and it does not produce acid in the intestinal system. Goat's milk helps to increase the pH of the blood stream because it is the dairy product highest in the amino acid L-glutamine. L-glutamine is an alkalinizing amino acid, often recommended by nutritionists.[31]

- Goat's milk contains twice the healthful medium-chain fatty acids, such as capric and caprylic acids, which are highly antimicrobial. (They actually killed the bacteria used to test for the presence of antibiotics in cow's milk!)[32]
- Goat's milk does not produce mucus; it does not stimulate a defense response from the human immune system.
- Goat's milk is a rich source of the trace mineral selenium, a necessary nutrient, however, for its immune modulation and antioxidant properties.[33]
- When consuming milk or yogurt, I usually recommend goat's milk sources. However, high-quality dairy products from grass-fed cows can be excellent as well. (See Appendix B to find two fantastic dairies producing outstanding products that truly fit the Maker's design.)

Olive oil

The olive branch has symbolized peace throughout history, and olives and olive oil have been used as powerful remedies for a wide variety of ills. Olive oil is one of the most digestible of all fats. A diet rich in olive oil contributes to longevity and reduces the wear and tear of aging on the body tissues, organs, and the brain. It reduces the risk of heart disease and cancer, and it can protect against stomach ulcers.

I believe high-quality extra-virgin olive oil should not be used in cooking, as some of the nutrients in olive oil become less effective when heated. I recommend that it be mixed into food once it has cooled.

Small fruit (figs, grapes, and berries)

Figs are mentioned more than fifty times in the Bible and are the first fruit specifically named in Scripture (Gen. 3:7). Whether fresh or dried, figs have been prized since ancient times for their sweetness and nutritional value.

Grapes were the first crop Noah planted after the flood (Gen. 9:20). They were made into wine and vinegar or eaten fresh or dried. We now know that grapes fight tooth decay, stop viruses in their tracks, and are rich in other ingredients that many researchers believe may lower risk of cancer.

Berries such as blueberries, strawberries, blackberries, and raspberries, while not mentioned explicitly in the Bible, are super foods containing some of the highest levels of antioxidants known to man. Blueberries contain antioxidant compounds that show promise in reversing some of the effects of aging, especially cognitive function. Raspberries contain notable anticarcinogenic compounds, are low in calories, and are high in fiber. They make a great addition to the diet.

Soups/stocks

Stocks and soups appear in biblical diets, as we see in Judges 6:19, and meat and fish stocks are virtually universal fixtures in traditional cuisine in France, Italy, China, Japan, Africa, South America, Russia, and the Middle East. Chicken soup, widely considered a "cure all," is sometimes called *Jewish penicillin*. Fish soup enjoys the same reputation in the Orient and South America.

Properly prepared meat stocks are extremely nutritious and contain minerals, cartilage, collagen, and electrolytes all in an easily absorbable form. Also, meat, fish, and chicken stocks contain generous amounts of natural gelatin, which aids digestion and helps heal many intestinal disorders, including heartburn, IBS, Crohn's disease, and anemia. Science has confirmed that broth helps prevent and mitigate infectious diseases.

Healthy saturated fats (high-vitamin butter, coconut oil)

Butter from grass-fed cows, extra-virgin coconut oil, and animal fats have nourished human beings for several thousands of years. However, for the last five decades Americans avoided these fats based on erroneous advice and, instead, increased their consumption of polyunsaturated and hydrogenated fats. As we have mentioned, in direct correlation, the rate of heart disease has increased, as has obesity and many immune system disorders. It is time to return to healthy fats from whole, grass-fed, cow butter; extra-virgin coconut oil; and properly raised animals.

Whole-milk butter produced from cows eating *rapidly growing green grasses* is loaded with vitamins A, D, and E. It is also high in Activator X, which significantly increases the effectiveness of vitamin A's ability to stimulate a person's immune system, as described by Dr. Weston Price.[34] It also contains a healthy balance of omega-6 to omega-3 fatty acids, as well as CLA. (These characteristics are seriously compromised once a cow has any grain introduced to its diet.)

CLA is strictly a product of bacterial function and is virtually non-existent in cow-milk fat during any period when grain is in the diet. For many types of cancer, CLA 9-11 is proven to prevent and retard tumor cell growth.

The quality of Activator X and other vitamins is directly related to the quality of the grass/forage the cow is eating. The faster the grass is growing when the cow is grazing it, the higher the vitamin content. Make sure to buy butter from grass-fed cows. The first telltale sign that the butter you are consuming is from grass-fed cows is its yellow color.

Extra-virgin coconut oil is one of the healthiest saturated fats available (despite the misguided advice of so-called health experts warning against the saturated tropical oils such as coconut and palm oils). Coconut oil can tolerate extremely high heat, unlike polyunsaturated vegetable oils. Use extra-virgin coconut oil in cooking, baking, and in smoothies. It is a stable, healthy saturated fat that does *not* elevate undesirable (LDL) cholesterol; it reduces the symptoms of digestive disorders, supports overall immune functions, and helps prevent bacterial, viral, and fungal infections.

Extra-virgin coconut oil is great for people suffering from candida yeast infections, due to the presence of caprylic acid and antifungal fatty acids contained in the oil. Extra-virgin coconut oil has also been shown to help balance the thyroid and improve metabolic function, which may result in weight loss.

Honey

The Creator chose to use *honey* to describe the abundance of the Promised Land, calling it the land of "milk and honey" (Exod. 13:5). Honey is one of the most powerful healing foods we have at our disposal. Generations of grandmothers prepared hot honey drinks to soothe sore throats, calm frayed nerves, and ensure a good night's sleep. Asthmatics often swear by honey's ability to help them breathe easier. Honey wipes out bacteria that cause diarrhea. And honey may eliminate such disease-causing bacteria as *salmonella, Shigella, E. coli,* and *cholera*.

The Bible implies a strong influence of butter and honey on brain function. "Curds [butter] and honey He shall eat, that He may know to refuse the evil and choose the good" (Isa. 7:15). The brain is made of mostly fat (which butter provides), and it runs on glucose (of which honey is an excellent source). Always look for high-quality honey produced locally and sold in its raw and unheated form—this preserves its rich storehouse of naturally occurring enzymes and bee pollen.

Pomegranate

Pomegranate is called the fruit of royalty in the Bible and is one of the richest sources of antioxidants. Pomegranates contain high amounts of ellagic acid, an antioxidant with proven anticancer properties and excellent benefits for female health.

Wild animal foods

Grass-fed red meat, poultry, and wild game have nourished humans for thousands of years. Grass-fed beef, buffalo, lamb, goat, and venison are valuable sources of nutrients that protect and enhance the immune and circulatory systems. They contain cysteine, glutathione, coenzyme Q_{10}, carnitine, MSM, CLA, several B vitamins, zinc, magnesium, and vitamins A and D as well as omega-3 fatty acids.

Properly raised red meats provide an excellent source of complete proteins. Lamb and goat represent two of nature's best sources of carnitine, a fat-soluble nutritional factor that helps drive fatty acids into the cells for energy use. (Carnitine supplements are standard therapy for congestive heart failure and high triglycerides, and they are helpful during recovery after a heart attack.) Free-range pastured chicken, turkey, and duck are good sources of protein, fatty acids, and fat-soluble vitamins. Chicken and turkey contain generous amounts of tryptophan, a natural sedative.

Seeds (soaked and sprouted)

These rich sources of nutrients become real nutritional power-houses when they are soaked and sprouted. The germination process (sprouting) produces vitamin C and increases carotenoids and vitamin B content, especially B_2, B_5, and B_6. Even more importantly, *sprouting neutralizes phytic acid*, a substance present in the bran of all seeds that inhibits the absorption of calcium, magnesium, iron, and zinc. Sprouting also neutralizes enzyme inhibitors present in all seeds. This is important, because these inhibitors can neutralize our own precious enzymes in the digestive tract, which is one reason many people seem to get a stomachache or excess gas after consuming large amounts of seeds. Sprouting can also inactivate certain toxins found in seeds. (For instructions on soaking or sprouting seeds, please see Appendix A.)

Omega-3 eggs

High omega-3 eggs are nature's nearly perfect food. Eggs contain *all known nutrients except for vitamin C!* They are good sources of fat-soluble vitamins A and D as well as certain carotenoids that guard against free-radical damage to the body. They also contain lutein, which has been shown to prevent age-related macular degeneration.

When possible, buy eggs directly from farms where the chickens are allowed to roam free and eat their natural diet, or purchase eggs marked DHA or high omega-3 eggs (they contain a healthy balance of omega-3 to omega-6). Despite the unfounded cholesterol scare of the last fifteen years, eggs can be a healthy addition to anyone's diet; they can actually help reduce the risk of both heart disease and cancer.

Cultured/fermented vegetables

Fermented vegetables such as sauerkraut, pickled carrots, beets, or cucumbers are some of the most health-giving foods on the planet. Raw cultured or fermented vegetables provide the body with beneficial microorganisms known as probiotics and an abundance of enzymes. They are also a rich source of many vitamins, including vitamin C, and are very easy to digest. Sauerkraut (fermented cabbage) contains nearly four times the cancer-fighting nutrients as unfermented cabbage and is the primary source of vegetable nutrition in many countries where the winters are cold. Cultured/fermented vegetables are very easy to make and are readily available at health food stores everywhere. (See Appendices A and B.)

Organ meats

Although native peoples have always prized the inner organs of game and domestic animals, irrational and unscientific fears about cholesterol have driven organ meats, like liver and heart, out of Western diets. Organ meats are the most nutrient-dense part of animals, but even natural health authorities routinely tell people not to eat organ meats for fear of consuming toxins found in these organs (especially liver).

It is true that the liver filters toxins from the body, but the benefits derived from consuming liver from organically raised, grass-fed animals far outweigh any negatives. Liver is one of nature's richest sources of vitamins A, D, B_6, B_{12}, folic acid, iron, glutathione, and various fatty acids. Raw liver figures prominently in many world-renowned alternative cancer protocols, including the Kelley and Gerson programs.

Fermented beverages

It is difficult to think of popular modern beverages that qualify as healthy beverages. It is time to return to the lacto-fermented beverages that have supplied beneficial probiotics, enzymes and minerals, rapid hydration, and enhanced digestion to people throughout the world. Some typical fermented beverages include kefir, grape cooler, natural ginger ale as well as kombucha and kvass. (For instructions on how to make homemade fermented beverages, please see the beverage section in Appendix A.)

These lactic-acid-containing drinks help relieve intestinal problems, including constipation, and promote lactation, strengthen the sick, and promote overall well-being and stamina. They are considered superior to plain water in their ability to relieve thirst during physical labor. Many scholars believe that the "new wine" consumed in the Bible was a nonalcoholic lacto-fermented beverage.

Green vegetables

Green leafy vegetables are some of the most nutrient-dense foods on the planet, including many nutrients not found in any other foods. Greens contain large amounts of beta carotene and virtually every mineral and trace element. Many experts believe that ideally we should be consuming between three and five servings of green leafy vegetables per day. If you can't get enough greens from food, try juicing fresh greens or supplementing with a powdered green superfood drink containing dried juices of wheat and barley grass and other vegetables.

Your Creator knows better than anyone does what makes your body function at its peak capacity while remaining free of disease. He designed the bounty of the earth and a wide variety of foods to be the cornerstone of a long and healthy life. The first and most dramatic step anyone can make toward renewed or greater health is to return to the Maker's Diet, which is based on the sound nutrition principles given to us in the Scriptures.

Your Creator is also vitally concerned with the spirit and soul living inside your body. He knows that you are not just what you *eat*—you are also what you *think*.

Chapter 9

You Are What You Think

FROM THE MOMENT THE CREATOR PLANTED THE FIRST HUMAN IN the middle of an incredibly complex creation, we have scrambled to accumulate, organize, analyze, categorize, label, and understand knowledge about the created universe.

Since we are *finite* or limited creatures, we must break things down into bite-sized portions to learn and understand them. It is critical to consider how we perceive our universe and our personal world, for that perception (world-view) will largely determine our existence.

During and after the Reformation—and especially during the twentieth century—it became popular among certain intellectuals to dismiss the spiritual side of the human race in favor of two broad philosophical viewpoints:

1. We are purely animal life forms operating solely as highly evolved organisms driven by chemical reactions.
2. We are evolved life forms with highly advanced mental capacities that have "evolved" into more or less "spiritual" beings, creating our own gods as we need them.

Neither of these views of mankind is expressed in the Scriptures. And they have produced tremendous problems as they have infiltrated the scientific and philosophical communities, gradually influencing the way we view life and approach physical, mental, and even spiritual issues.

For example, some psychiatrists view humans as purely chemical or organic beings whose every mental state is created by or dramatically influenced by chemical reactions. Therefore, in their view, every mental malady we face can be isolated to chemical imbalances and "fixed with a pill." That godless way of thinking is demeaning and narrow-minded at best. The Scriptures warn:

> The fool says in his heart, "There is no God."...The LORD
> looks down from heaven on the sons of men to see if there
> are any who understand, any who seek God.
>
> —PSALM 14:1–2, NIV

God created us in His image (Gen. 1:27), and God is a Spirit (John 4:24). Therefore, we are *spirit* beings who have *souls* (mind, will, emotions) and who live in physical *bodies*. Our "parts" cannot be divided without skewing or misunderstanding the whole.

God made you a complex, interrelated being, fully integrated and interdependent. Even alternative and holistic health practitioners fall into the same error often made in conventional medicine—they try to fix one *system* or *function* instead of addressing the whole person: spirit, soul, and body.

I'm convinced that the Creator knew what He was doing when He created us, and I believe His Word is the foundation for total health: spiritual, mental, and emotional, as well as physical. I am thankful for science and human advances in medicine and nutrition, but where science presumes to dismiss the Creator's foundational principles, I am convinced *His pattern* provides us with a better approach to life.

We must emphasize the *whole being*—body, soul, and spirit—and provide the individual with all of the tools needed to maintain or recapture complete health and wholeness.

It is clear from Scripture that in each person, spirit, soul, and body are very closely linked. The early computer term "G-I-G-O" (garbage in, garbage out) may best describe the most crucial "equation" available for the human condition. You and I are not computers, but the formula really does apply to virtually *every* area of human existence. If I allow "garbage" into my body, mind, or spirit, I can expect to "express" garbage. I have it on the highest authority:

> For as he thinketh in his heart, so is he: Eat and drink, saith
> he to thee; but his heart is not with thee.
>
> —PROVERBS 23:7, KJV

> For whatever is in your heart determines what you say. A
> good person produces good words from a good heart, and an
> evil person produces evil words from an evil heart.
>
> —MATTHEW 12:34–35, NLT

As examples of modern ways to entertain "garbage," consider the following scenarios:

- If you eat junk food, excessive amounts of sugar and preservatives, and favor the unclean foods the Creator warned us about, then you will almost certainly reap an unpleasant harvest of failed health later in life.
- If your friends and close associates are people who use "recreational" drugs, get drunk, and are promiscuous, then you are likely to fall into a very dangerous lifestyle yourself sooner or later.
- If you fill your mind with unhealthy and unwholesome images of pornography, violence, fractured relationships, and scornful attitudes about God, eternal values, and godly living, you will begin to *act out* what you *put in*.

What You Do Begins With What You Think

In most cases, the things you do and say begin with the things you *think* and *believe*. You are barraged by stressing circumstances and challenges every day. How do you deal with them? (Or do you even try?)

Imagine your life as a glass filled to the halfway mark with water. How would you describe your "life"? Is your glass "half full" or "half empty"? Your answer may reveal a lot about your thought life and life view. A positive view would say "half full," considering what you have; a negative view would say "half empty," focusing on what you don't have.

Stress is a natural part of life; some experts say that stress *is* life. Psychologist and author Dr. Kevin Lehman said the best definition for stress he has ever found was, "The wear and tear on our bodies produced by the very process of living."[1] He explained that stress comes from good things as well as bad circumstances, but trouble comes when it goes on for days and weeks. As he put it:

> It reminds me of buying the best Die-hard battery you can find, but if you have a habit of leaving the lights on, even a Die-hard finally runs down.[2]

Develop Your Stress Management Skills

Stress comes at you from at least four sources:

1. Outward circumstances over which you have *no* control

2. Circumstances or influences over which you *do* have control
3. *Inward* attitudes, beliefs, and thought patterns
4. Internal *physical* conditions

For maximum health, it is important to become skilled in handling stress according to the Creator's principles.

According to Dr. Michael D. Jacobson, cortisol and DHEA are two of the most critical stress hormones produced by your body. Cortisol is a steroid hormone that affects your body in ways very similar to prednisone. (It blocks inflammation and suppresses the immune system.) DHEA is the balancing hormone that reverses the effects of cortisol. (DHEA has antiaging effects, boosts the immune system, and exerts key influence on sex hormones—thus, fertility.)[3] Both are produced by the adrenal cortex, which is directly affected by your brain. One of the important keys to achieve a healthy life is to eat a diet and live a lifestyle that promote a healthy balance of DHEA and cortisol. When the two hormones are in balance, we experience excellent health physically, mentally, and emotionally.

The adrenals also produce the neurotransmitters *adrenaline* and *noradrenaline*. They also help regulate blood pressure as well as salt and water balance through the production of *aldosterone*, an *antidiuretic hormone*. Excess adrenaline can wreak havoc on the human digestive system, skin, heart and circulatory system, and mental state. And excess cortisol, with its powerful immunosuppressive powers, may even open the door to runaway infection, cancer, hyperthyroidism, poor wound healing, diabetes, infertility, and mental instability.

Anger, resentment, unforgiveness, and a desire for revenge all trigger the classic "alarm triad" response to stress, which involves *adrenal gland hypertrophy* (swelling), *thymus and lymph gland atrophy* (shrinkage), which indicates the suppression of the immune system, and *gastric inflammation*.

Is It Really Worth It?

These age-old "life-shorteners" were well documented in Scripture long before scientists and researchers set out to quantify the effects of negative emotions on our bodies. At last we are beginning to catch up to the Creator's wisdom. Is it really worth the dangerous cost to hold on to anger or unforgiveness? Are we really willing to destroy ourselves in a quest for revenge?

When it comes to stress, it seems that the body can handle the day-to-day emergencies and surprises without any problem—but when stress hangs on, it drains the adrenal system, making a "crash" inevitable.

In contrast, studies have shown that people "who experienced an episode of deep appreciation or love for five minutes saw their IgA levels [an antibody secreted in saliva and other body fluids as a first line of defense against infection] rise to 40 percent above normal and stay elevated for six hours."[4]

Even simple lifestyle adjustments can make a significant difference in your stress levels.

- If you feel too busy to get away from the telephone or cell phone, then your stress-buster may be an answering service or simply the "off" switch on your phone.
- If you usually eat "on the run," choose to sit down when you eat, and turn off the television or radio. Don't allow your thoughts to be occupied with worry, irritation, or uncertainty. Focus on your meal and on pleasant thoughts. I recommend conversation with good friends during meals or reading something uplifting, such as God's Word.
- Get proper rest. There is simply no substitute for quality sleep. Sleep is so vital to health that I often refer to it as the most important non-nutrient you can get.

The Deadly Stress of Fear

Unmanaged stress can kill you. It may be the single most important "trigger" of heart attacks. A report in the *Journal of Clinical Basic Cardiology* said that "sudden cardiac deaths" increased significantly during the Northridge earthquake in California in January 1994 and in the Israeli civilian population during the first days of the Gulf War in 1991. The 58 percent increase in mortality was due to an increase in mortality from cardiovascular diseases *on the day* of the first strike on Israel by Scud missiles. Female death rates increased 77 percent, while male mortality increased 41 percent.[5]

Though the Scud missiles launched against Israel in the first Gulf War in 1991 did very little real damage, obviously they were deadly in another way, because people are people, not mere *chemical organisms*. These effects of fear on the body confirm the very real link between the spirit, soul (mind and emotions), and body. This connection is strong enough to touch our pocketbooks! Some experts have estimated that stress accounts for as much as 75 percent of all visits to a physician![6]

Beware the Dangerous Unity of Dysfunction

I am convinced that we help create many of our problems through wrong thinking, poor decision making, and poor dietary choices. When these factors unite and start working together against us, sickness or death may not be far behind. The problem of arteriosclerosis perfectly illustrates this kind of dangerous "unity" in dysfunction.

Arteriosclerosis is a generic term for several vascular diseases in which the arterial wall becomes thickened and loses elasticity. Atherosclerosis, which involves fat deposits on blood vessel walls, is the most common and serious vascular disease.

Vascular disease, which affects the brain, heart, kidneys, other vital organs, and extremities, is the leading cause of morbidity and mortality in the U.S. and in most Western countries. There were almost 1 million deaths due to vascular disease in the U.S. in 1994 (twice as many as from cancer and ten times as many as from accidents).[7]

Sudden stress is the most common "trigger" for fatal heart attacks because it is able to "crack" the smooth covering of plaque common in people with atherosclerosis. This sets off a fatal chain reaction in the blood vessel that becomes clogged with plaque, which then dams up or shuts off blood flow to the heart—triggering a heart attack.

According to Dr. Michael Miller, mental stress "is associated with impairment of the endothelium, the protective barrier lining our blood vessels. This can cause a series of inflammatory reactions that lead to fat and cholesterol build-up in the coronary arteries and ultimately to heart attack."[8]

Anyone—whether he or she is a a health-conscious layperson or a health professional—who doubts the effect of the thought life on physical well-being should consider the "partial list" of diseases *caused or worsened* by emotional stress compiled by S. I. McMillen, M.D., and David E. Stern, M.D., in the revised and updated edition of the landmark book *None of These Diseases*.[9] The list was compiled from results of twenty-eight separate medical research studies and texts specifically offered as references for doctors, students, and researchers seeking further proof.

Doctors McMillen and Stern said emotional stress *causes* or *worsens* the following health problems:

- Digestive system disorders
- Circulatory system disorders
- Genito-urinary systems disorders
- Nervous system disorders
- Glandular disorders
- Allergies and immune system problems
- Inflammation of muscles and joints
- Infections
- Inflammatory and skin diseases
- Cancer

If you or someone you love suffers from any of the conditions on that list, let me reassure you there is hope. As depressing as the facts about stress may appear, you do not have to become a *victim* of stress! Countless numbers of people have overcome the negative effects of stress in the worst possible situations involving stressors beyond their control. Dr. McMillen nearly died of a bleeding ulcer before he learned how to successfully manage stress. His life and death crisis inspired the writing of the classic book *None of These Diseases*, in which he wrote:

> Our reaction to stress is an important key to longer, better living. When we feel stressed out, will we give up or keep going? Will we see it as an irritation or a challenge? Will we blow a fuse or let it charge us up? We hold the key. We can decide whether stress will work for us or against us—whether stress will make us better or bitter.[10]

Negative Thoughts, Negative Words

In his book *What You Don't Know May Be Killing You*, Don Colbert, M.D., described the story of a Jewish Holocaust survivor during World War II from Warsaw, Poland.[11] When the Nazis discovered that he spoke German, they forcibly separated him from his wife, two daughters, and three sons—and then they mowed his family down with machine guns right in front of his eyes.

Author and psychiatrist George Ritchey was with the American troops who liberated the death camp survivors—including this man. Ritchey described this man's life in *Return From Tomorrow*: "For six years he had lived on the same starvation diet, slept in the same airless and disease-ridden barracks as everyone else, but without the least physical or mental deterioration." This miraculous survivor had no control over his outward circumstances. In fact, he shared the same misery inflicted on millions of Jewish victims.

What was his secret? He told Dr. Ritchey, "I had to decide...whether to let myself hate the soldiers who had done this...I had seen, too often, what hate could do to people's minds and bodies. Hate had just killed the six people who mattered most to me in the world. I decided then that I would spend the rest of my life, whether it was a few days or many years, loving every person I came into contact with."[12] This man immediately went to work with the liberators, working fifteen to sixteen hours per day serving his fellow death camp survivors. Dr. Colbert observed, "He had learned the secret that *negative thoughts* lead to *negative words*, which lead to *negative attitudes* and *emotions*."[13]

A vital key: Remove negativity

One of the keys to my own recovery was to remove negative thinking and negative statements from my life. When I went to California to live with the man who taught me the first principles of how to eat foods from the Bible, he forced me to examine my negative thinking. Basically, he gave me no choice.

I stayed in his home, and we studied the Bible in family meetings every day. He would not tolerate any negativity. I used to sit in the meetings wearing a frown, which had become a regular part of my wardrobe for two years. He eventually made me sit in another room because he didn't want his kids to learn that negative demeanor from me! His tough standards of conduct amounted to a rough boot camp for my soul.

I had no one to complain to because the family was not allowed to entertain negative words. And somehow the positive principles he taught were wearing off on me. I remember thinking as I left the bathroom one time, *I may have a stomachache in ten minutes, but right now I am fine, so I am healed.* And I started believing my positive statement and thanking God for my healing. I learned to count my blessings for the few moments that I had when I was free from pain and nausea. It was a valuable lesson in learning how to live a moment-to-moment life of thanksgiving.

One night, after several weeks on the biblical diet, I finally believed that I was healed. I would no longer focus on the negative or on what would happen tomorrow or in the next hour. I had to take *conscious steps* to make the change from negativity to thinking positive thoughts, but it was worth it! If I could only say *positive* things (which were all that were allowed in that home), I had to find the positive in my seemingly negative situation. When I had a short time in which I didn't feel agonizing pain, I started to say, "I am well for this moment." I discovered that faith is not just something you say—it is something you live, moment by moment.

The impact of this change in my thinking was a huge factor in my healing. I believe that faith and positive thinking, based on God's Word, are vital keys to recovering and maintaining health. That is why faith the size of a tiny mustard seed can move mountains. (See Matthew 17:20.) When I was sick, I was unhappy; I didn't have tangible joy, *but* I had faith. That was the seed—or foundation—from which my miracle could "grow."

Psychologist Dan Baker discovered virtually the same thing after dealing with the devastating death of his infant son, Ryan. The author of *What Happy People Know*,[14] he said that after his son's death, he "wanted to wrestle with God and rewrite history." He said, "Happy people are hugely resilient on the whole. One thing happy people know is that they don't get to be happy all the time. They can appreciate the moments, the little victories, the small miracles and the relationship with one another."[15]

The "Placebo Effect" Phenomenon

It is a commonly known fact that approximately three out of every ten people will see their symptoms or behavior change significantly simply by being told and then believing they have received a valuable treatment for a physical condition. In fact, researchers *count on this* happening every time they conduct a scientific "double-blind" study.

As Dr. Michael Jacobson explained in his book *The Word on Health: A Biblical and Medical Review of How to Care For Your Body and Mind*:

> In a typical study, it is expected that around one-third of the placebo group [the group of subjects who receive a "sugar pill" or fake treatment exactly like the real dose] *will actually show as much benefit* as if they were on the actual medication. This improvement may be due simply to the positive physical changes that can take place when a person believes that he is getting better.[16]

The placebo effect is especially strong with people who have no "anchor" of absolute truth and faithfulness in their lives. Personally, I am convinced that if one hundred *healthy* people were told by a physician they had incurable cancer and that they only had six months to live, approximately thirty of them would die—that's how powerful faith, even in the negative, can be.

The "placebo effect" is yet another indication pointing to the power of our thought life over physical conditions. I am not advocating some "mind-over-matter" therapy here, but this phenomenon gives us a hint about the marvelous tool for health and power God has given us in the human mind. It is no wonder the apostle Paul said that we should take every thought captive. (See 2 Corinthians 10:5.)

Recently, two Danish researchers questioned the validity of the placebo phenomenon. In a report entitled, "Are 'Dummy Pills' a Dumb Idea, or Do They Really Help?", their findings questioning the effect of placebos outside of their use as a baseline for comparison in clinical trials were presented.[17] However, John Bailar III, M.D., Ph.D., found faults with the study and called the negative conclusions "too sweeping."[18]

The fact is, most doctors *know* a treatment is sometimes useless, but because many patients demand medication, they oblige. For example, they may prescribe antibiotics that a patient demands, perhaps even considering the antibiotics to be a placebo that will help the patient get well by *thinking* he has been given a cure. The downside to this practice is that, while I *know* the placebo effect may possibly help the patient, I am very concerned about the havoc wreaked in the digestive and immune systems by such indiscriminate use of antibiotics and other medications.

Placebo versus faith

Dr. Jacobson makes a big distinction between the placebo effect and the power of faith—and so do I. The placebo effect is based on a person's belief or presumption in a *falsehood*, while faith is based on nothing less than the nature, faithfulness, and absolute *truth* of God and His eternal Word.

In my search for health, I had plenty of opportunities to experience improvement from the placebo effect—I believed in almost every one of the so-called "cures" I tried at the hands of seventy doctors and health practitioners. But the truth is that none of them helped me. It took *faith* in God's Word—and obedience to it—to really trigger a turnaround in my life.

Faith is powerful, and it produces hope. Hope begins with knowing that your Creator cares about you and that He has a plan for your life.

> "For I know the plans I have for you," declares the LORD,
> "plans to prosper you and not to harm you, plans to give you
>   hope and a future."
> —JEREMIAH 29:11, NIV

Doctors McMillen and Stern noted a 1995 Harvard Medical School Conference in which a study was reviewed documenting that *weekly churchgoers in Maryland* were less likely than people who didn't attend church regularly to die from heart attacks (50 percent), emphysema (56 percent), cirrhosis (74 percent), and suicide (53 percent). Similar results were found in studies of different population groups at three different medical teaching universities.[19]

The Power of Prayer

All of the great heroes of the Bible, from Abraham to Hannah (the mother of the prophet Samuel) to John the Beloved, were people of fervent faith and devotion. One after another, they demonstrate the power and peace available through prayer and communion with the Creator of all.

People of faith have known the truth regarding power in prayer since time began. Now, even the secular worlds of psychology and medicine are finally catching on. Studies are popping up all the time promoting the power of prayer (or meditation). Hospitals across the land have bolstered their "prayer therapy" for the sick and recovering.

Biblical prayer incorporates more than words—it often includes the healing touch of caring people of faith, and the results are often nothing less than miraculous. In the very least, they are comforting in times of need.

The Healing Power of Laughter

The Bible tells us, "A merry heart does good, like medicine, but a broken spirit dries the bones" (Prov. 17:22). Dr. Don Colbert noted that research conducted by the Department of Behavioral Medicine at the UCLA Medical School into the physical benefits of happiness proved conclusively that "laughter, happiness and joy are perfect antidotes for stress." Colbert added, "A noted doctor once said that the diaphragm, thorax, abdomen, heart, lungs—and even the liver—are given a massage during a hearty laugh."[20]

Dr. Michael Miller from the University of Maryland told attendees at an American Heart Association Conference, "We don't know why laughter protects the heart....We know that exercising, not smoking and eating foods low in saturated fat will reduce the risk of heart disease. Perhaps regular hearty laughter should be added to the list." In a BBC interview, Dr. Miller said, "The [doctor's] recommendations for a healthy heart may one day be exercise, eat right and *laugh a few times a day*!"[21] Adding my professional opinion: "You gotta laugh a little!"

Moral of the Story

Here is the moral of this chapter: when I started to *believe* I was well and to give thanks to God for the *moments* of well-being I experienced, I began to get well. That memorable moment when I asked my mother to take my picture at 111 pounds, when I was barely able to stand, demonstrated the seed of faith that sparked my healing. It was that mustard seed of faith that eventually moved the mountain of illness in my life.

A seemingly far-fetched, ridiculous-sounding, positive thought, word, or action that you can choose to express in your moment of desperation can act as a seed of faith that will spark the healing process for you. As you meditate on God's Word and pray, daring to quote His promises for your healing, your faith will grow, and you will receive your miracle as I received mine.

> Faith is the substance of things hoped for, the evidence of things not seen.
>
> —HEBREWS 11:1

Chapter 10

Stop, Drop, and Roll!

ELEMENTARY SCHOOLCHILDREN HEAR IT OVER AND OVER AGAIN: "If your clothing catches fire, just *stop, drop, and roll!*" This fire safety formula has some genuine application to the problem of physical, mental, and spiritual burnout as well.

When it comes to your health, if you sense the heat of life on your backside and smell the smoke of imminent burnout billowing around you, just stop, drop, and roll—more literally, *rest, fast,* and *exercise.*

Just as the original manufacturer of an automobile provides detailed information and maintenance schedules for maintaining maximum performance and utility of that car, so your Creator has provided detailed instructions and maintenance schedules for preserving peak performance for *you.*

Even if your friends confuse you with the "Energizer bunny," you still need regular periods of rest.

Stop: We All Need a Sabbath Rest

Every working creature needs a Sabbath rest—that goes for people, animals, and even the soil! People and animals need a break every seven days, and even the soil prospers with a break at least every seven years. Every wise farmer understands the need to put fields and crops in rotation so the soil can replenish at least one growing season every seven years.

Dr. Mark Virkler cited a study comparing two identical farming soils. One was farmed continuously for eight years while the other was allowed to stand fallow or not farmed. The soil from the field that had no Sabbath rest contained 1,097 parts per million (ppm) nutritional solids, while the fallow or rested field soil yielded an astounding 2,871 ppm of nutritional solids! That is almost two-thirds more nutritional solids than the over-farmed soil![1]

Elmer Josephson noted that the anti-God government that seized the reins of France after the bloody French Revolution decided to increase the entire nation from a seven-day workweek to a ten-day cycle. Before long, the nation's horses and mules became diseased and died at alarming rates. After scientists investigated, "they found that a return to the seventh day principle was necessary to physical welfare, health, and long life...as someone has said, 'The donkeys taught the atheists a lesson in practical theology.'"[2]

Rest is crucial to the health of your body and soul. Sleep is an absolute and undeniable necessity of life. Lengthy and regular periods of rest are equally important over the long haul. Europeans are far ahead of Americans in this area. By my observation, it is normal for many European families to take extended vacations each year for periods averaging between four and ten weeks! Most Americans struggle just to take a two-week vacation every few years (and many take no vacations).

Besides giving us the night for regular sleep, the Creator programmed people and animals to rest completely every seventh day. When we tinker with His design, things start to unravel. Even the Creator rested on the seventh day. (By the way, you rest by *stopping* all labor—even the *mental* labor that has been proven to be more exerting to the adrenal system and the entire body than physical labor.)

Do you need a good reboot?

One of the first things I learned about personal computers was that many of the seemingly serious problems with a computer can be "fixed" by turning it off! This allows the circuits to reset themselves in the absence of an electrical current. When you "reboot" or turn on the computer again, everything turns up clear and fine in many cases. So it is with the body. Sometimes it is enough just to reboot, to "stop and rest."

Drop (Your Fork): Fasting

Other times the situation calls for much more; it requires that you *drop the fork* and rest. This is what the Bible calls *fasting*.

Biblical leaders such as David, Daniel, the prophets, Jesus, and Paul often launched great ministries after extended periods of fasting. Entire nations and cities declared fasts in times of crisis or during times of repentance and soul-searching.

Fasting is the Creator's high-powered spiritual tool for receiving a "breakthrough" in body, soul, and spirit. People in virtually every civilization and culture have an instinctive understanding of the power of fasting—from listening to the "voice" of their natural bodies, if from no other source. Anyone who has been sick understands that in times of sickness, hunger pangs tend to end. Any attempt to bypass those signals and eat often results in violent regurgitation or other discomfort.

Don't worry! Fast and be happy!

The Bible describes numerous fasts that varied according to type, length, and purpose.

- The three-day "Esther fast" is considered a "crisis fast." (See Esther 4:16.) It is a *total* fast from all food and liquids for three days. Many people observe this fast when they face difficult decisions, worries, or spiritual concerns. However, due to our poor level of health and the abundance of toxins, total fasts—abstaining from all food *and water* or liquids—should not be attempted today.

- The ten-day "Daniel fast" is a modified fast with virtually unlimited applications. It is named after the biblical Daniel and his Hebrew companions who fasted from rich (and possibly unclean) meats and wine, choosing to consume "pulse" or vegetables instead. The results were phenomenal. (See Daniel 1:12–15.) It is interesting to note that after Daniel and his friends "outperformed" all of the others who ate the usual foods, they *continued on this diet for three years*. (See Daniel 1:5, 14–16.)

- You may choose a fast that eliminates sugar, caffeine, carbonated soft drinks, junk foods, pasteurized dairy products, commercial breakfast cereals, or pork products. It is an excellent way to break free from food addictions or habits and to launch a healthier lifestyle.

- Daniel also completed a very serious *21-day water-only fast* as well. Make sure you confer with your health professional before beginning such a fast. Extended water fasts should only be performed under strict supervision of a licensed physician. Some health conditions make this a very risky choice—it is better to be safe than sorry.

- Moses and Jesus both completed miraculous *forty-day total fasts* (without liquids), but I wouldn't recommend it—*without a miracle*. Serious damage is done to internal organs and body chemistry beyond the three-day point of dehydration.

- Many people have completed *forty-day water and diluted juice fasts* (using diluted low-acid fruit or vegetable juices). However, these fasts should only be undertaken with great care and under the supervision of a health professional. Doing this *repeatedly* has been known to trigger permanent undesirable metabolism changes in the body. (I know of one man who completed more than fifteen such fasts; he was formerly slim and trim, but he developed ongoing problems with obesity and blood sugar regulation.)

"Take some chicken broth, and call me in the morning!"

The average person feels much better and lives healthier by observing a one-day cleansing fast each week. Many health practitioners are returning to the proven wisdom of selected fasting in the treatment of major toxicities (a prominent feature of certain cancer therapies). Some involve "monofasts" where people eat only one food or fast from a particular food group. Sometimes they recommend that people go on a chicken broth fast, which is a modified fast.

History has proven that the body can heal itself from many serious conditions by fasting, and today the healthcare community is beginning to catch on. Even a partial-day fast can be beneficial. This is why I recommend a weekly one-day partial fast from dinner to dinner in my forty-day health program, which is outlined in chapter twelve.

The body heals while it fasts—it undergoes an important regeneration process during our nightly break from activity and eating. That is why our first meal is called *breakfast*—we are *breaking* the *fast* that heals.

Dr. William L. Esser followed the progress of 156 patients at his West Palm Beach retreat center in Florida who agreed to go on therapeutic fasts of various lengths. He reported on the fasting of 156 people who complained of symptoms from thirty-one medically diagnosed diseases, including ulcers, tumors, tuberculosis, sinusitis, pyorrhea, Parkinson's disease, heart disease, cancer, insomnia, gallstones, epilepsy, colitis, hay fever, bronchitis, asthma, and arthritis. The shortest fast among these 156 patients lasted five days; the longest lasted fifty-five days. Only 20 percent of his patients fasted as long as Dr. Esser recommended; however, the results are as follows:[3]

- 113 completely recovered.
- 31 partially recovered.
- 12 were not helped.
- 92 percent improved or totally recovered.

Selected forms of fasting may bring improvement to a number of physical conditions including arthritis, intestinal problems, obesity, and even diabetes.

Note: If you have a physical condition and are considering a fast, make sure you consult with your health professional first. In general, *anyone with diabetes or hypoglycemia* should only observe a fast with the approval and ongoing supervision of a healthcare provider knowledgeable in the management of blood sugar and insulin as related to diabetes. Pregnant or breast-feeding women should not fast at all!

Join the coated tongue and bad breath crowd.

Observing water-only or liquids-only fasts in today's toxic world may place a considerable toxic burden on the body, but at times the benefits far outweigh the difficulties. What difficulties? Arthur Wallis, author of *God's Chosen Fast: A Spiritual and Practical Guide to Fasting*, outlines a few difficulties for us:

> The pores of the skin, the mouth, the lungs, the kidneys, the liver and of course the bowels are all involved, so the medical experts tell us, in this physical spring-cleaning. The unpleasant taste in the mouth, coated tongue and bad breath are all part of the process.
>
> There is the familiar "fasting headache," mostly caused by the reaction of the body to the sudden cessation of tea and coffee, sugar and other stimulants—a mild "withdrawal" symptom as the body accustoms itself to being without the caffeine drug.... There is also the tendency to sleeplessness, bouts of abdominal discomfort, nausea, dizziness and of course weakness.
>
> ...It is a physical and spiritual medicine, and our usual

verdict on such, however well the pharmacist may sugar-coat
the pill, is: "Unpleasant, but good for you."[4]

Wallis also presents a list of benefits from fasting that include bright eyes, pure breath and skin, and a renewed sense of well-being, adding, "A Christian worker after only a five-day fast declared, 'I feel as though I've got a brand-new stomach.' A digestive weakness he had for years disappeared."[5]

Finally, understand that the most crucial time of any fast is *at the end* when you begin to reacclimatize your cleansed digestive system to foods once again. Do not gorge yourself on breads, meats, or even large amounts of vegetables. Your stomach literally shrinks during the fasting process. It will stretch out again, but this should happen gradually.

Be sure to break longer fasts with broths and nonacidic liquids such as raw vegetable juices, vegetables, fruits, and raw cultured dairy the first day. Then gradually work your way back to a regular diet over a period of two to four days, depending on the length and extent of your fast. Consult some of the excellent books on fasting available at bookstores for more detailed information in this area.

Roll: Move, Exercise, Get Up, and Do Something!

The advice to "roll" for anyone whose life seems to be going up in flames is simple and easily followed.

God created us to *live, move, work, play, overcome obstacles,* and *win victories* throughout life. He never intended for us to sit around and wait for death.

Some confirmed couch potatoes have confidently justified their lackadaisical approach to life by quoting the passage from the King James Bible, "For bodily exercise profiteth little" (1 Tim. 4:8). They conveniently forget that Timothy probably walked everywhere he went and got more exercise in one day than most people do today in a week. Modern translations more accurately paint the picture and remove the "lazy boy loophole," saying, "For physical training is *of some value*" (1 Tim. 4:8, NIV, emphasis added).

What was it you were waiting for again?

We have a world to explore and master, and we can't do it if our bodies are accumulating fat and our muscles, joints, and internal organs are breaking down. We all need exercise.

For about three decades, the extended-exertion theory of aerobic exercise has ruled supreme in medical and physical fitness circles. This theory maintains that maximum health comes from exercising the cardiovascular system to elevated or maximum stress levels for *sustained or unbroken time periods* (usually thirty minutes or more). The belief is that this trains or strengthens the cardiovascular system much as a bodybuilder exercises muscles through applied stress to achieve maximum size or strength.

This may be true; however, the weakness of this theory comes from its foundation in the flawed "clogged artery/high cholesterol" theories of cardiovascular disease. Lower cholesterol rates have no connection with lower incidences of heart attack or heart disease; it is better to use the genuinely accurate homocysteine levels and oxidative stress as risk factors.[6]

Unfortunately, the stressful and artificial nature of sustained aerobic exercises has worn out joints and cartilage and inflicted serious chronic sports injuries at rates higher than anyone predicted. Even worse, aerobically fit people with low cholesterol levels are dropping dead from heart attacks just as often as those who *never* exercise and have terrible cholesterol levels. This may be due to the fact that people who regularly perform aerobic exercise for long periods of time experience a weakened immune system. This drop in immunity makes them prime targets for infections.

We *do* need exercise for maximum health, but high-stress aerobic exercise just doesn't seem to be delivering as promised.

Exercise should mirror real life

From my research, I am convinced the Creator's prescription for exercise more closely resembles real-life activities involved in the daily patterns of work and play.

The longest-lived peoples in human history usually walked everywhere they went, trailed their animals and herds, hunted wild game on foot, built rugged shelters, or cultivated fields at an active pace each day with intermittent periods of rest. They knew *nothing* about aerobic exercise, treadmills, or running tracks, but they were masters at *anaerobic exercise*—activities that incur an "oxygen debt" through temporary or briefly sustained exertion.

Current fashion fads aside, we don't need to look as muscular as the people we see on television or on magazine covers, but *anyone* can certainly be a lot healthier with a nutritious diet and moderate exercise.

I am not completely against aerobic exercise, but if your goal is to live a healthier life free of disease and needless health complications, there are certain exercises that are much better for your overall health.

Walking

My description of the oldest physical activity of the human race can be expressed in one word: *walking*. Even before Eve, Adam was assigned the task to care for God's garden—a job that could not be done without *walking*. Subsequent development of our species demanded even more walking.

A brisk two-mile walk (with long strides and vigorous arm movement) every day increases enzyme and metabolic activity and may increase calorie burning for up to twelve hours afterward![7]

Don't waste time looking for choice parking spots *close* to your destination—choose a spot *far away* and *walk* there. This takes care of two important priorities at once—you get what you came for, *and* you're getting healthful exercise, too! (And forget the elevators and escalators—take the stairs.) Take a walk on the beach or to the corner store; just don't buy junk food for the return trip. Ride a bicycle, stroll through your neighborhood, and "walk the mall" when the weather doesn't cooperate.

Functional fitness

Functional fitness is a system of exercise that is truly holistic. Functional fitness utilizes movements that are natural to the body; it enhances the health and strength of every muscle. Unlike traditional bodybuilding, functional training focuses on improving the strength of the body's core (the abdominals and lower back), which also houses many of our most important organs.

Functional fitness can be used to achieve great results by people of all walks of life, from the professional athlete who wants to improve performance to the grandmother who wants to climb the stairs to her bedroom more easily. Functional training (fitness) expert Juan Carlos Santana says it best: "Function is a duty or purpose of a thing—or what something is intended for. One of the main things that the body is intended for is to provide structure and movement. Therefore, functional training (fitness) would be any training that enhances the body's structure and/or movement."[8]

There is no doubt in my mind that *functional fitness* is the most effective exercise and fitness system available. I feel it truly deserves to be used officially as the Functional Fitness Exercise Program. (For more information on Functional Fitness, see Appendix B.)

Deep-breathing exercise

Even deep-breathing exercises will increase the fat-burning metabolism of your body and "boost your brain" with a rich dose of oxygen. Deep breathing offers benefits that might make a major difference in your health. Your lungs are larger at the bottom than at the top, but most people in America are "top breathers." We live on the shallow breaths common to the sick and the sleeping.

Learn to breathe "from the gut." You know you are breathing from the diaphragm if you see your stomach move in and out. If the only thing that moves or expands is your chest, then you are still living on a shallow percentage of the divine potential for deep breathing.

Deep breathing literally "massages" and moves the soft internal organs inside your rib cage, allowing your lymph system to rid itself of collected toxins and to collect even more. Only deep breathing allows you to tap the "bonus power" of your lower lungs.

Newborn babies *instinctively* deep breathe—watch and learn at the next opportunity. We actually "learn" how to "shallow breathe" and rob ourselves of the breath of life. Singers, stage performers, broadcast announcers, and professional athletes pay great sums to voice coaches and breathing coaches to learn how to breathe, project the voice, and achieve maximum strength through diaphragm breathing (which is what they did *naturally* as babies). Here is a quick course just to get you started:

1. Sit or lie down and relax.
2. Place a hand your abdomen to see if it expands as you breathe. If only your chest moves with your breaths, you are "shallow breathing."
3. Breathe deeply through your mouth, and breathe "all the way down to your belly button." Your abdomen (stomach) should rise as you inhale (not your chest).
4. Hold your breath for a few seconds, and then exhale slowly and fully. Learn to recognize the sounds and sensations of long, slow, deep breaths as your Maker intended.[9]

With more practice, you will revert back to the instinctive deep-breathing way you began life.

Rebounding

One way to get the exercise you need is *rebounding,* in which you use a portable mini-trampoline to jog, jump, hop, twist, or step walk in place. One respected advocate of rebounding uses the devices and rebounding techniques in his rehabilitation program. According to James White, Ph.D., director of research and rehabilitation in the physical education department of the University of California at San Diego (UCSD), "When you jump, jog and twist on this [rebounder] device, you can exercise for hours without getting tired. It's great practice for skiing, it improves your tennis stroke, and it's a good way to burn off calories and lose weight."[10] Dr. White believes it is more effective for fitness and weight loss than cycling, running, or jogging—while producing fewer injuries.

If you are stuck indoors, try some "rebounding" exercise in which you jump on a mini-trampoline. Rebounding is very good for the lymphatic system, the circulatory system, and the spine (while sparing your joints and ligaments).

Even a little helps

We are much less active than we used to be, but even a little exercise goes a long way. An article in *Consumer Reports on Health* described a study of 13,000 men and women at the Cooper Institute for Aerobics Research in Dallas, Texas. The researchers conducted the eight-year study hoping to prove the value of consistent aerobic exercise, based on how long the volunteers could stand to exercise on a treadmill.

> As fitness increased, the death rate fell. But by far, the *biggest drop in mortality*—60 percent for men, nearly 50 percent for the women—occurred between *the most unfit volunteers* and *those who were just slightly more fit.*[11]

Regardless of where you land on the exercise scale, this should make you feel better. Even if you don't exercise at all, you can begin to improve your health immediately by starting to exercise *now.*

I hope this chapter has served as a "tune-up," a service warning light in your health dashboard. Even if you faithfully follow the guidelines and food recommendations of *The Maker's Diet,* you will need to practice the philosophy of "stop, drop, and roll" on a regular basis.

Don't wait until you smell smoke—learn to read your body's symptoms and discern the familiar warning signs. At the first sign of fire or flames burning where they shouldn't be, stop everything to *rest, fast, and exercise* a little. It doesn't take much to recharge your battery.

Even when you are trying to do everything right, there may be those times when you need some of the Maker's medicine. Fortunately for us, He has supplied them in abundance. In the rigors of daily life, you may need to take a hot/cold shower, anoint yourself with essential oils, listen to music that soothes the soul, and allow the warmth of a hot bath soak deep into your aching bones. This may seem like a description for a day at the spa—but it's just biblical medicine.

Chapter 11

Biblical Medicine: Herbs, Essential Oils, Hydrotherapy, and Music Therapy

THE PROPHET EZEKIEL PROVIDED US WITH A FASCINATING, biblical portrait of divine health when he spoke of healing leaves and refreshing fruit:

> Along the bank of the river, on this side and that, will grow all kinds of trees used for food; their leaves will not wither, and their fruit will not fail. They will bear fruit every month, because their water flows from the sanctuary. Their fruit will be for food, and their leaves for medicine.
> —EZEKIEL 47:12

Send someone from our Western civilization for medicine, and they will head for the nearest pharmacy. Send someone from East Asia or Central and South America (who has not been "Westernized") for medicine, and they would more likely head for the nearest herb garden or herbal outgrowth in the wild. They may return with herbs or essentials oils extracted from the herbs of the field.

An herb is defined as a "seed-bearing annual, biennial or perennial that does not develop persistent woody tissue but dies down at the end of a growing season" [unlike a tree for instance] or "a plant or plant part valued for its medicinal, savory or aromatic qualities."[1] The Maker's herbs were humanity's first medical resource. They remain an important source of healing and nutritional support, although many in our Western culture don't realize it.

A botanist named Dr. David Darom has identified and photographed eighty kinds of plants mentioned in the Bible that are still growing in Israel today![2] And according to Rex Russell, M.D., thousands of herbal ingredients have been identified by chemists, and the pharmaceutical industry is constantly searching for more plant ingredients to isolate and mass distribute in purer forms. Dr. Russell went on to say, "25 percent of all drugs still come from herbs."[3]

Herbs and spices are incredible sources of antioxidants with antimicrobial and anti-inflammatory properties. According to James Balch, M.D., herbs have an important advantage over isolated drugs. The powerful chemicals they contain treat specific health problems while other ingredients in the herbs "balance" those chemicals, making them less toxic while improving their medicinal effectiveness.[4]

Medicinal herbalist James A. Duke, Ph.D., former chief of the USDA Medicinal Plant Laboratory and author of *Herbs of the Bible: 2000 Years of Plant Medicine*, states, "The Bible mentions 128 plants that were part of the everyday life of ancient Israel and of its Mediterranean neighbors."[5] Dr. Duke goes on to provide a detailed list of fifty of the most important healing and fragrant herbs noted in Scripture.

The Bible often mentions herbs, although it rarely goes into great detail about the use of healing herbs. However, herbs were so highly valued in biblical times that herb or "vegetable" gardens spawned murder plots and national atrocities. King Ahab's wife, the infamous Jezebel, took matters into her own lethal hands when Naboth refused to sell his vineyard. (The New International and New American versions translates it "vegetable garden.") Naboth was wrongfully stoned, and King Ahab suddenly had the garden he always wanted. (See 1 Kings 21:2–13.)

Natural herbs still offer us medicines for inducing healing, preserving health, and improving our quality of life. I've listed but twenty-one of the top biblical herbs to whet your appetite so you can learn how they can improve your life. Many of these herbs are used as seasonings, some are edible in salads or soups, and some can be used to make teas. It is very beneficial to incorporate these wonderful substances into your everyday diet.

Twenty-one of the Maker's Most Healing Herbs

Of the fantastic variety of herbs the Creator gave to us, which are ever being studied and their healthful uses documented, I consider the following twenty-one herbs to be among the top healing herbs known to man.

1. Aloes

The aloes of the Bible were used in several forms. Nicodemus evidently blunted or neutralized the bitter smell of the bitter aloes he brought with one hundred pounds of myrrh before wrapping the body of Jesus. (See John 19:39–40.) Though it may not be the true aloe of the Bible, aloe vera "sailed the ocean blue" with Columbus. It continues to appear in countless American kitchens and bathrooms as front-line treatment for burns and skin irritations.

Aloe vera also purges the stomach and lower intestines when taken internally (exercise caution here), and it aids healing of open sores. It has anesthetic and antibacterial properties and literally increases blood or lymph flow in small vessels where it is applied topically. Use it for teenage acne. In addition, try heating an actual aloe vera leaf and applying it directly to abscesses, bruises, skin inflammations, gumboils, or even sprains, as the Yucatecs do.[6]

2. Black cumin (*Nigella sativa*)

This biblical herb, popular in breads and cakes, is used medicinally to purge the body of worms and parasites. An Arab proverb calls it "the medicine for every disease except death." These seeds taste hot to the tongue and are sometimes mixed with peppercorns in Europe. Black cumin oil contains nigellone, which protects guinea pigs from histamine-induced bronchial spasms (perhaps explaining its use to relieve the symptoms of asthma, bronchitis, and coughs). The presence of the anti-tumor sterol, beta sitosterol, lends some credence to its use in folklore to treat abscesses and tumors of the abdomen, eyes, and liver.[7]

3. Black mustard (*Brassica nigra*)

The Greeks were the first to name this herb. It grew wild along the Sea of Galilee. Its seeds contain both a fixed and an essential oil. It has been used in plasters and has been applied externally to treat numerous conditions such as arthritis and rheumatism. According to Dr. Duke, recent research revealed five compounds in mustard that inhibit cancer caused by exposure to tobacco smoke! Mustard applied to skin surfaces causes blood vessels to enlarge and shed body heat, which explains its use for treating congestion in head afflictions, neuralgia, or muscle spasms. Steam produced by hot water poured over bruised mustard seeds is good for colds and headaches.[8]

4. Cinnamon (*Cinnamomum verum*)

This delightful herb was part of the holy anointing oil used to anoint the priests and vessels in the tabernacle of Moses (Exod. 30:22–25). It was also mentioned in setting the stage for romance (Prov. 7:17–18).

And ancient Chinese used cinnamon to treat health conditions in China as early as 2700 B.C.

Originally imported from India and Sri Lanka in Bible times, this herb has become one of America's favorite spices. It calms the stomach and may even prevent ulcers. Recent research indicates cinnamon contains benzaldehyde, an antitumor agent, along with antiseptic properties that kill bacteria-causing tooth decay and disease-causing fungi and viruses. It may even prevent urinary tract infections (UTI) and infestations of candida. Dr. Duke reports that USDA researchers discovered that cinnamon reduces the amount of insulin necessary for glucose metabolism in Type II diabetes. *One-eighth teaspoon of this herb triples insulin efficiency!* (Warning: Although the substance is a powerful germicide, do not consume straight cinnamon oil. It may cause vomiting or kidney damage.)[9]

5. Coriander (Coriandrum sativum)

In its green form, this herb, also known as *cilantro* and *Chinese parsley*, has been used traditionally as a remedy for acid indigestion, neuralgia, rheumatism, and toothaches. History records its use as early as 1550 B.C. for culinary and medicinal purposes. It was one of the medicines employed by Hippocrates around 400 B.C. There is some research that shows cilantro can aid in the elimination of harmful metals from the body, including mercury, lead, and cadmium. Coriander contains twenty natural chemicals possessing antibacterial properties that help control body odor; as mentioned, its essential oil treats indigestion and excess gas.[10]

6. Cumin (Cuminum cyminum)

Cumin, which has incredible antioxidant properties, was used in biblical times as a medicine and appetite stimulant. It has also been traditionally used as a remedy for arrhythmia (abnormal heartbeat), asthma, dermatitis, and impotence. The oil of this aromatic seed was used as a disinfectant, perhaps because it is bactericidal and larvicidal, and it possesses anesthetic properties.

Dr. Duke notes, "My research shows that the spice contains three pain-relieving compounds and seven anti-inflammatory properties. If I had carpal tunnel syndrome, I would add lots of cumin to my curried rice and other spicy dishes."[11]

7. Dandelion (Taraxacum officinale)

One of the candidates for the bitter herbs eaten at Passover, dandelion has been used traditionally as a remedy for cancer, diabetes, hepatitis, osteoporosis, and rheumatism. Contemporary herbalists recommend dandelion almost exclusively as a diuretic for weight loss. (It *provides* potassium rather than depleting it as diuretic drugs do.) Its leaves are rich in vitamin C and contain more beta carotene than carrots, and its roots act as a diuretic and purgative useful for treating kidney and liver disorders.[12]

8. Dill (*Anethum graveolens*)

This common ingredient for modern do-it-yourself "picklers" was so historically valued that the ancient Israelites were required to *tithe* from their supplies. The ancient Greeks and Romans also cultivated dill as a kitchen herb. Dill has been used traditionally as a remedy for cancer and estrogen deficiency, and research supports dill's three-thousand-year use as a digestive aid and remedy for excessive intestinal gas.

Dill seed oil inhibits the growth of several bacteria that attach to the digestive tract. As a tea, it soothes stomach and intestines, relieving upper respiratory ailments. Its oil is so strongly antibacterial that it inhibits organisms such as *Bacillus anthracis*. Dill contains various phytochemicals that act as insecticides; enhance estrogen levels; fight infection, bacteria, and insects; and act as a uterine relaxant.[13]

9. Henna (*Lawsonia inermis*)

This fragrant herb yields a dark red dye popular among Egyptian women and still used for chemical-free brownish chestnut hair dye formulas today. It was also used in cosmetics and for dying anything and everything that could be dyed. Dr. Duke reports that mummies exhumed after three thousand years in a tomb still had traces of henna dye on their nails! Henna contains lawsone, an active antibacterial and fungicide often used to treat fungal infections of the nails.[14]

10. Fenugreek (*Trigonella foenum-graecum*)

This herb may be what the Bible calls "leeks." It has long been considered the "cure-all" treatment for ailments in the Middle East. Dr. Duke reports that fenugreek's bittersweet seeds contain five compounds that appear to help diabetics lower blood sugar.[15]

11. Frankincense (*Boswellia sacra*)

Frankincense, one of the three gifts presented to Jesus by the Magi in

Matthew 2:10–11, was not native to Israel. This "milk" of the frankincense shrub came from sap seeping through cuts made in the bark of the plant. It was also one of the four exclusive components used to make holy incense for the tabernacle of Moses and is still used by the Roman Catholic church. It is used in a number of very expensive perfumes and colognes today.[16]

12. Garlic (Allium sativum)

This ancient herb has more going for it than its unmatched flavor. It is an effective infection fighter, and it even discourages irritating and potentially dangerous mosquitoes and ticks. It is a painkiller, it stimulates the immune system, and it is helpful for treating asthma, diabetes, and high blood pressure. According to Dr. Rex Russell, "Population studies indicate an inverse relationship between *the amount of garlic consumed* and *the number of cancer deaths* in a given population!"[17]

13. Hyssop (Hyssopus officinalis or Origanum syriacum)

This herb, also called marjoram, is harvested in dry places among rocks. A spice, a tonic, and a digestive aid, hyssop was the Bible's "brush of salvation" for spreading the blood of lambs on doorposts to spare the Israelites from the death angel in Egypt. It was also used in purification ceremonies to cleanse those who came into contact with lepers or corpses. Hyssop stops bleeding (as an astringent) and effectively masks odors; it has been used traditionally as a remedy for colds, inflammation, and rheumatism; it has also been used as a digestive aid.[18]

14. Juniper (Juniperus oxycedrus)

This conifer "undergrowth" still grows in Israel and is likely to be the "algum" timber King Solomon requested of Hiram, king of Tyre, in 2 Chronicles 2:8–9. It yields two forms of "cade oil" prized for use in men's fragrances, antiseptic soaps, and as a smoked flavor in meats. Cade oil has long been used to treat skin parasites in animals, and it is finding new uses as a treatment for human psoriasis, eczema, and other skin and scalp conditions.

Dr. Duke reports that researchers recently identified certain lignans in some junipers that could be used in the production of etoposide, a drug used to treat testicular and lung cancers. They also found a potent antiviral compound in junipers that inhibit viruses linked with the flu and herpes.[19]

15. Milk thistle (Silybum marianum)

This ancient herb native to Samaria and parts of Israel has been used as a liver remedy for two millennia, perhaps because it contains silymarin, a natural compound that prevents and repairs liver damage and even regenerates damaged liver cells. The German government has approved milk thistle seeds and extracts for use in treating cirrhosis and chronic liver conditions. It has also been shown to lower blood sugar and insulin levels in diabetics and to help prevent gallstones. Milk thistle may be grown in home gardens. Its seeds contain eight anti-inflammatory compounds that aid in healing skin conditions and infections.[20]

16. Mint or horsemint (Mentha longifolia)

Mint or "sweet-scented plants" are mentioned in two Gospels where Jesus scolded the Pharisees for gladly giving a tenth of their garden herb harvest to God while failing to honor Him in far more important matters. (See Matthew 23:23; Luke 11:42.) The Jewish people enjoyed mint with their spring Passover feasts and placed mint on the floors of their synagogues. Some species of mint are used to treat Alzheimer's disease and to flavor candies, gum, toothpaste, and liqueurs. They are also used as digestive aids. Peppermint oil is antiallergenic and is used in aromatherapy to stimulate brain activity.[21]

17. Myrrh (Cistus inanus or Commiphora erythraea)

According to Dr. Duke, there are 135 varieties of myrrh found throughout Africa and Arabia. Myrrh oil was used in the purification of Esther and the other virgin candidates to prepare them to appear before King Xerxes. (See Esther 2:12.) It was administered both as oils for the exterior and as edible substances for internal cleansing. Persian kings even wore myrrh in their crowns. This expensive, fragrant herb was used to make the holy anointing oil used in the tabernacle of Moses and was one of the gifts given to Jesus Christ by the Magi.

Myrrh was a cure-all treatment in Mesopotamia, Greece, and the Roman Empire. Myrrh used in a mouthwash can stop infections, and the herb is an effective treatment for bronchial and vaginal infections.[22] Myrrh contains a compound called "furanosesquiterpenoid," which deactivates a protein in cancer cells that resists chemotherapy, according to researchers at Rutgers University. This compound has proven effective against leukemia, breast cancer, and cancers of the prostate, ovaries, and lungs.[23]

18. Nettle (Urtica dioica)

"Stinging nettles" get their name from the Latin term *urtica* ("to burn") because the tiny hairs on the leaves cause a burning sensation when touched. (The poison is similar to that in bee stings and snakebites.) Mentioned in the Book of Job, nettles may contain substances that alleviate arthritis symptoms; they are also rich sources of vitamins A, C, and E as well as many antioxidants.[24]

19. Saffron (Crocus sativus)

This flowering herb served as a condiment, sweet perfume, and coloring agent in biblical times; it was the world's most expensive spice. One ounce of saffron requires 4,300 flowers.[25] Each autumn, saffron flowers are picked in the morning when they first open because the three orange-scarlet stigmas inside the flowers must be taken before the flowers wilt.[26]

Saffron dyed the clothes and hands of Jewish spice merchants yellow in the Middle Ages, so they were often called "saffron merchants." Saffron yellow was used to mock Jews for centuries, but never so cruelly as in Nazi Germany's requirement that all Jews wear armbands bearing a yellow Star of David. Saffron was used medically in tinctures for treating gastric and intestinal problems and is considered antispasmodic, expectorant, sedative, and a stimulant in small doses. It is also helpful for bladder, kidney, and liver ailments.[27]

20. Spikenard (Nardostachys grandiflora or jatamansi)

A woman of the streets won eternal fame when she humbly anointed Jesus with an alabaster box filled with *spikenard*, worth a year's wages. The plant was imported from India, and the oils were used in cosmetics and perfumes and medically dispensed as a stimulant. The spikenard's rhizome, or large root, contains *jatamansi*, a compound used to treat epilepsy. Infusions are used to treat epilepsy, hysteria, heart palpitations, and chorea. Spikenard oil may help treat auricular flutter, and it acts to depress the central nervous system and relax skeletal and soft tissue muscles.[28]

21. Turmeric (Curcuma longa)

This herb and spice possesses tremendous anti-inflammatory and antioxidant properties. Much of the research conducted on turmeric has been done in India, and it shows this herb may be beneficial as a wound treatment, digestive aid, liver protector, and heart tonic. It is a potent spice for cooking and flavor enhancement, and in powdered form it is antioxidant. It is a reliable chemical indicator that changes color when in contact with alkaline and acid substances. Turmeric's essential oil has been proven to exhibit anti-inflammatory and antiarthritic qualities. It is a pain reliever older than aspirin that rivals the newest exotic painkillers in its ability to relieve aches and pains, without upsetting the stomach.[29]

I highly recommend the use of biblical herbs as an integral part of any healing regimen. Try to add these herbs and spices to your daily diet, or take a nutritional supplement containing oil-based extracts of these life-giving substances. To locate health products containing many of the aforementioned herbs, please see Appendix B.

The Maker's Healing Oils

The Bible mentions at least thirty-three species of *essential oils* and makes more than one thousand references to their use in maintaining wellness, acquiring healing, enhancing spiritual worship, emotional cleansing, purification from sin, and setting apart individuals for holy purposes. Why are they missing from our lives today?

These essential oils were inhaled, applied topically, and taken internally. According to David Stewart, Ph.D., "Seventy percent of the books in the Bible mention essential oils, their uses, and/or the plants from which they are derived."[30] We are constantly learning more about essential oils, but we should consider their immense value when we understand the importance, mentioned so many times in Scripture, given to them by the Creator.

We *do* know that essential oils have the *highest ORAC* scores of any substance in the world. The oxygen radical absorbance capacity (ORAC) scale measures the antioxidant powers of foods and other substances. Four important biblical essential oils greatly outperform the highest-ranking fruits and vegetables in existence. For example, one ounce of clove oil *has the antioxidant capacity of 450 pounds of carrots, 120 quarts of blueberries, or 48 gallons of beet juice.*[31]

Essential oils are composed of very small molecules that are able to pass through the blood-brain barrier freely or pass through the skin and reach every part of the body in minutes. If you place a drop of cinnamon or peppermint oil on the sole of your foot, you may taste it on your tongue in less than sixty seconds.

The fourteen *principle* biblical essential oils I have listed below contain three unique classes of compounds. The first are *phenylpropanoids*, which are antiviral and antibacterial; they are able to clean and reprogram "receptor" sites in individual body cells. The second are *sesquiterpenes*, possessing a variety of healing properties and the ability to reprogram scrambled or damaged DNA coding. And the third are *monoterpenes*, which deliver oxygen directly to cells and possess anti-carcinogenic properties.

Personal benefits

Perhaps we should consider that the divine instructions for biblical anointing affected the physical realm far more than we formerly believed. You may enjoy significant health benefits by utilizing essential oils for yourself, your family, and your home.

I encourage you to anoint yourself with an essential oil and investigate these claims for yourself. Place a few drops of one of the biblical essential oil blends on your palm, making several clockwise circles with your fingers. Then rub your palms together and cup them over your nose and mouth (but make sure you avoid touching your eyes). Deeply inhale the aromatic vapors, then run your fingers and palms through your hair. It won't make your hair "oily," but it will transform the way you feel.

A great way to use essential oils is to put five to ten drops into a warm bath. That is a true healing treat. You can also rub a few drops of these oils into the soles of your feet. You can even gain benefit from inhaling directly from the bottle. If you have small children, try applying essential oils to their stuffed animals or to the inside of their pillowcase each night.

The following list is fourteen of the most useful essential oils with a brief description of their positive effects on the body.

1. Myrrh (Commiphora myrrha)

In days of old, pregnant mothers anointed themselves with myrrh for protection against infectious diseases and to elevate feelings of well-being. It was also used in ancient times for skin conditions, oral hygiene, embalming, and as an insect repellent. In modern times, myrrh is used to balance the thyroid and endocrine system, support the immune system, heal fungal and viral infections, and to enhance emotional well-being.

2. Frankincense (*Boswellia carteri*)

In biblical times, frankincense was used as holy anointing oil, to enhance meditation, for embalming, and in perfume. Frankincense was used to anoint the newborn sons of kings and priests, which may have been why it was brought to baby Jesus. Today it is used to help maintain normal cellular regeneration, to stimulate the body's immune system, and as an aid for people suffering from cancer, depression, allergies, headache, herpes, bronchitis, and brain damage resulting from head injuries.

3. Cedarwood (*Cedrus libani*)

Cedarwood was used traditionally in ritual cleansing after touching a dead body, unclean animals, or anything else considered biblically "unclean," such as the bedding of someone who had died. Cedarwood was also used in the cleansing of leprosy and the cleansing of evil spirits. It has been used by cultures around the world for embalming, medicine, disinfecting, personal hygiene, and skin problems. Today cedarwood is used as an insect repellant, hair loss treatment, and for tuberculosis, bronchitis, gonorrhea, and skin disorders (such as acne or psoriasis). Cedarwood has the highest concentration of sesquiterpenes, which can enhance cellular oxygen.

4. Cinnamon (*Cinnamomum verum*)

Cinnamon and cassia are actually two species of the genus *Cinnamomum* and have similar fragrances. Both are very effective antibacterial and antiviral agents that God provided to protect the Israelites from disease. They support the human immune system in the battle against influenza and cold viruses—simply inhale them or put them on the soles of your feet. (Do not apply these powerful oils to sensitive areas of the body since they may be slightly caustic and irritating in these areas. If irritation occurs, apply vegetable oil immediately to "cool off" the skin.)

5. Cassia (*Cinnamomum cassia*)

Cassia was an ingredient in Moses' holy anointing oil. Cassia, a cousin of cinnamon, is a potent immune system enhancer.

6. Calamus (*Acorus calamus*)

This ancient essential oil is rich in phenylpropanoids and is usually used in combination with other essential oils. It was used in holy anointing oil and incense and for perfumes. It was an aromatic stimulant and a tonic for the digestive system. Today it is used to relax muscles, relieve inflammation, support the respiratory system, and clear kidney congestion after intoxication. It is taken orally, inhaled as incense, and applied topically over the abdomen.[32]

7. Galbanum (Ferula gummosa)

Historically, galbanum was used as holy anointing oil, perfume, and in various medicines. Today, galbanum is used to treat acne, asthma, coughs, indigestion, muscle aches and pains, wrinkles, and wounds as well as to balance emotions.

8. Onycha (Styrax benzoin)

This essential oil comes from tree resin and is the most viscous of all essential oils. It has a characteristic vanilla-like fragrance and was used as a perfume, was blended into anointing oils, and was used to heal skin wounds and comfort, soothe, and uplift. Today it is used to stimulate renal output and treat colic, gas, and constipation. It may help control blood sugar levels. It is also inhaled for sinusitis, bronchitis, colds, coughs, and sore throats. It soothes skin irritations and wounds. It is inhaled, applied topically in wound dressings, and massaged into the skin.[33]

9. Spikenard (Nardostachys jatamansi)

In biblical times, spikenard was used as a perfume, medicine, mood enhancer, and preparation for burial. Modern science has shown it to relieve allergies, migraines, and nausea. Spikenard supports the cardiovascular system and calms the emotions.

10. Hyssop (Hyssopus officinalis)

As a principal cleanser in biblical times, hyssop was used in many purification rituals and to drive away spirits. Modern science has shown that hyssop can be used to relieve anxiety, arthritis, asthma, respiratory infections, parasites, fungal infections, colds, flu, and wound healing. Hyssop metabolizes fat, increases perspiration, and can aid the body's detoxification of harmful chemicals. Hyssop can provide help to balance emotions.

11. Sandalwood (Santalum album)

Used by the ancients for assistance in meditation, sandalwood is also an aphrodisiac and was used in embalming. Sandalwood contains sesquiterpenes that deprogram misinformation and carry oxygen at the cellular level. It can be used in skin care, to enhance sleep quality, to support the female reproductive and endocrine systems, and to provide relief in urinary tract infections.

12. Myrtle (Myrtus communis)

Myrtle was used in various ceremonies in biblical times that involved purification from ritual uncleanness. Today, myrtle can be used to balance hormones, soothe the respiratory system, battle colds and flu, and treat asthma, bronchitis, coughs, and skin conditions (including acne, psoriasis, and blemishes).

13. Cypress (Cupressus sempervirens)

Ancient healers used this essential oil to treat arthritis, laryngitis, swollen scar tissue, and cramps. Today cypress is used to support the cardiovascular system and promote emotional well-being in times of loss or stress. It also promotes the production of white blood cells and boosts natural defenses. It is generally massaged along the spine, on armpits and feet, and over the heart and chest.[34]

14. Rose of Sharon (Cistus ladanifer)

Used historically as a perfume and to elevate mood, Rose of Sharon is used today as an antiseptic, immune enhancer, and for calming the nerves.

I highly recommend the use of biblical essential oils on a daily basis. Inhaled directly or used in therapeutic baths, these oils can make a subtle but powerful difference in our lives. (To locate biblical essential oils, please refer to Appendix B.)

The Maker's Hydrotherapy

Is it any wonder that water helps heal us when a large percentage of our bodies are composed of water? Men and women have found refreshment and healing in water since the beginning of human history. The Greeks and Romans built elaborate baths that are still standing, and more recently an American president plagued by polio made a pilgrimage to natural mineral baths in Hot Springs, Arkansas, seeking healing for his aching joints.

"Water healing," or hydrotherapy, is simple and inexpensive in its various forms:

- **Bathe by immersion** when you want to soak your sore body in a bath. Simply immerse yourself for twenty minutes or so in 95-degree water to soothe nerves, relax muscles, and ease bladder and urinary problems. Add healing herbs, salts, or essential oils to increase the effectiveness of the bath.
- **Showers** often best meet the needs of sore shoulders, upper back, and necks.
- **Sitz baths** are simply shallow baths deep enough to immerse the bottom and hips (and ease the various physical ailments and pains found in those areas).
- **Bathe your extremities**—the feet and hands—in one or two buckets or containers large enough to hold them.

There are many ways to use hydrotherapy for the health of your body. Here are just a few:

- Warm up cold feet with a fifteen-minute bath in hot water. For tired feet, go with a cold foot bath.
- For aching or arthritic feet or hands, use *two* buckets or containers of water, one with hot water and the other with cold. Alternate your feet or hands between the hot bath (sixty seconds) and the cold bath (twenty seconds) for a total of twenty minutes.
- The most effective way to get your blood flowing and to stimulate circulation is to take a shower and *alternate between hot and cold water* for a minimum period of fifteen minutes (one minute hot followed by one minute cold). You should make the water as hot as you can handle without burning your skin and as cold as you can handle it without pain. Alternate between hot and cold at least seven times during this period. If one area in particular is sore, then make sure the water is hitting that area directly if possible.

The Maker's Music Therapy

Two biblical examples that illustrate the virtually untapped power of music stand out to me: When King Saul fell victim to an evil spirit, all it took was David playing his harp to bring deliverance and sweet relief. (See 1 Samuel 16:23.) When the Israelites encircled impregnable Jericho and blew their trumpets and shouted as commanded by God, the walls came tumbling down "without a shot." (See Joshua 6.)

Music therapy as a healing art is beginning to make great inroads in the treatment or rehabilitation of patients battling with autism, Alzheimer's, and Parkinson's disease. It seems to exhibit a unique property of organizing or reorganizing cerebral function that has been damaged.

Music is a gift from God that possesses healing and delivering powers, so we should use this gift wisely. The best proof of the power of music is your own heart. *How many times have you been emotionally and spiritually moved by music?*

King Saul knew enough to call for the minstrel David when the "blues" set in. You should prepare lists of your favorite music, and then play the music often. See if it doesn't lift your spirits. Certain types of music, particularly what we call "classical" music and cultural music, can bring about great health benefits. A good time to listen to music is during exercise, which can be very inspiring.

If you feel overwhelmed by the stresses of the day, I recommend that you listen to your favorite *worship music*, and join in. In my experience, worship and music are virtually indivisible. Of course, worship cannot be limited to music, but it can certainly play a major role in its expression. Consider these words of wisdom by a noted spiritual leader, musician, and author:

> Worship is like breathing: You were created to do it all the time. It's a lifestyle. When everything imaginable comes against you, worship God. When things finally go your way, worship Him. (Of course, it's easier to worship in the good times.) Nothing else will be as creative as worship, because you are doing more than expressing faith in the sovereign God. You are creating an atmosphere in your own heart and circumstances that releases faith and enables you to say, "My God is in control of this."[35]

I encourage you to tap into the power of the Maker's music and allow it to drain away the stress, build up your soul, and enhance your health. The right music at the right time can calm you, excite you, awaken you, or put you to sleep. It is a divine tool from the loving hand of God to make everyday life a little healthier.

Moving Forward

We would think it foolish for someone to squander a free membership to an exclusive health spa or exclusive golf country club. Yet, how often do we take the time to partake of God's bounty of healing herbs, essential oils, the relaxation of a soothing hot bath, and soothing and inspirational music?

If you sense it is time for a significant change in your life, it is most likely to happen with a clear-cut decision and a period of commitment. God has typically used the time period of forty days to accomplish significant life events. If you are serious about making a break from the past and starting over again in your quest for maximum health, strength, and vitality, then you are ready to begin the Maker's Diet as a forty-day, life-changing experience.

Chapter 12

The Maker's Diet:
Your 40-Day Health Experience

AS WE HAVE SEEN, DIETS AND HEALTH FADS LITTER THE LANDSCAPE of American culture, but the Maker's original plan for your optimal health and wellness is no fad. The Maker's Diet is at once ancient and new, timely yet timeless. Best of all, *it works!* Unlike other diets or health programs, the Maker's Diet is designed to improve the four pillars of health—physical, spiritual, mental, and emotional.

This is the final stretch, the place where the Maker's Diet can become a reality and produce a richer life for you. My goal was to present the principles of this healing protocol to you as clearly as possible. I felt compelled to develop a scientifically sound, real-life plan *that you could live with!*

Here it is, laid out in a simple and *doable* forty-day program. Many times in the Bible when God wanted to trigger a significant "turnaround" on earth, He instituted a *forty-day plan*. We see this demonstrated in the lives of Noah, Moses, Elijah, Ezekiel, and Jesus (Gen. 7:4; Exod. 24:18; 1 Kings 19:8; Ezek. 4:6; Matt. 4:2; Acts 1:3). Are you ready for your significant "turnaround" to restore optimal health to your body—physically, spiritually, mentally, and emotionally? This forty-day investment will pay a lifetime of dividends for you and for those you love.

The Maker's Diet 40-Day Health Experience incorporates the same biblical dietary and lifestyle principles that saved my life. In addition, as a result of my years of research and experience with patients, I estimate *it is at least ten times as effective* as the early version of the program that I used to regain my health and break free from the bondage of disease!

As of this writing, I have been off all medications for nine years and am extremely healthy. After suffering the ravages of continuous exposure to powerful medications, including catabolic steroids, for years, I have regained my normal weight (195 pounds at 6 feet 1 inch). I work out, play recreational sports, and am happily married with a child on the way. I am still awed by this miracle, considering that I used to wonder if I would *live long enough* to see my twenty-first birthday.

If an injection, pill, or experimental therapy could have freed me from my painful disease, I would have paid any amount of money to get it. (And we *did* spend hundreds of thousands of dollars in our futile search for a cure.)

God definitely healed me, but He did it in the natural, practical way I have shared with you—through the Maker's Diet. My mother says it best; I was healed "as I feasted on the Word of God" and applied His principles—including dietary—to my life. Believe me, these principles of divine health are completely reproducible in your life, too.

Experience Forty Days That Will Change Your Life Forever!

Now it is your opportunity to experience the first forty days of the rest of your life—forty days that will change your life forever! The Maker's Diet 40-Day Health Experience is divided into three two-week phases. These three phases are easy to follow, and each features foods that are extremely healthy and delicious.

This plan is designed for results; your success depends significantly on your diligence in following the plan. Every effort has been made to keep the recipes simple and the ingredients widely available. You may experience moments of discouragement when dealing with a new recipe or when facing a week without your favorite junk food or dessert, but it is well worth it to persevere through those times—your future health depends on it.

The Maker's Diet 40-Day Health Experience is designed to attack the three *i's*—insulin, infection, and inflammation. By balancing *insulin*, you can improve physical, mental, and emotional health, and in turn you balance blood sugar, sharpening concentration and enhancing mood. By reducing *infection*, you can lessen the toxic burden placed on your body by your daily contact with germs. By lessening *inflammation*, you can reduce aches and pains and decrease risk factors for such diseases as heart disease and cancer. By attacking these three *i's*, you can improve appearance and enhance energy, and you can begin to reverse the process of accelerated aging and live life the way you were meant to live it.

Here are some helpful tips to make your forty-day health experience a successful one.

1.   When you begin phase one and avoid consuming certain foods and chemicals that you were addicted to (such as sugar, artificial sweeteners, caffeine, preservatives), you may experience temporary withdrawal symptoms such as headache, flu-like symptoms, increased carbohydrate cravings, less energy, mood swings, or even temporary changes in bowel habits. This may also happen due to the increased cleansing of toxins from the body. This "detox reaction," as it is sometimes called, is an indication that the program is working and is usually short lived. Make sure to increase your water intake, and if your body is telling you to rest, it is best to do so.

2.   If you mess up and go off the program, do not beat yourself up! You are only one meal away from success. No one is perfect. If you are put in a situation where you must eat foods not recommended on a particular phase of the program (and you better have a really good excuse), it is better to consume all of these "forbidden" foods in a one-hour time period rather than several hours or the entire day. Consuming high-carbohydrate or high-calorie foods within a one-hour time period will minimize the amount of insulin your body can produce or overproduce; this will minimize the amount of fat you will store and limit the damage that will be done.

3.   Make time for fun. I recommend at least one day per week to be a fun day. Don't do anything that resembles work. If you can plan your fun day outside, that is even better. Being outside in the sun and breathing fresh air is very healthy.

4.   Get out in the sun. It is important to spend time in the sun. Exposure to sunlight can be very beneficial for your health and can aid in the balance of hormones, enhance mood, and help to build strong bones.

5.   Take time to chew your food. Digestion of carbohydrate

foods begins in the mouth. When you eat starchy, high-carbohydrate foods, it is of the utmost importance to chew each mouthful of food thirty-five to seventy times. That may seem like quite a chore, but it will benefit you immensely. Chewing your food not only aids in digestion, but also the action of chewing can stimulate the body to produce certain chemical hormones that enhance mood as well.

6.   Don't eat when you're angry, sad, scared, or anxious. These emotions all shut down digestion. When you are emotionally out of balance, it is better not to eat at all. I mentioned earlier that when we eat sugar, our immune system can be depressed for up to six hours. We also learned that when we are angry, our immune system can be depressed for up to six hours. So if you go and eat a doughnut while you're angry, half of your day is ruined!

The basic, intermediate, and advanced levels

As you will see in the instructions for each phase of the program, there are tools or products recommended to help you achieve your goals quickly and easily. These tools will help ensure your success and enable you to improve your health on all levels—physically, spiritually, mentally, and emotionally. Each product is designated as basic, intermediate, or advanced in the instructions for each phase.

If you go on the basic program, you will be using three core products. The intermediate program uses the three core products plus two additional products. The advanced program incorporates all products from the basic and intermediate levels and adds four additional products. Based on a number of factors (finances, discipline, desire, or a hectic travel schedule), you may choose to use all of the tools and begin at the advanced level or use only the core products and begin at the basic level.

Based on my experience and research, the more tools you take advantage of, the better your results will be. However, if you are already healthy, on a budget, or simply don't have the time or discipline to "do the program" in its entirety, you will still have excellent results no matter what level you choose. For those people hoping to overcome challenging health symptoms, we recommend embarking at the advanced level.

Three phases

You will also see that there are three phases. Here are some guidelines to determine what phase you should start on. If you are significantly overweight or obese, or if you have health problems, I recommend you start on phase one. If you are extremely healthy and want to stay that way, or even improve your health, you may start on phase three. Even if you start on phase three, I believe it will be the healthiest program you have ever been on. However, I believe it is a good idea for everyone to start on phase one at least for a few days in order to reset your metabolism and attack the three *i*'s (insulin, infection, and inflammation).

Tackle your 40-day health experience with a friend or a whole group of friends. This program is ideally undertaken in a small-group setting. (See Appendix B for a small-group curriculum to help you on your journey.) If you want to experience real results in your life, it will take some determination on your part—but achieving your dream of superb health is a worthwhile goal.

I designed each phase of the Maker's Diet to produce noticeable results, but not through dangerous, quick-weight-loss gimmicks that cause you to gain more weight after the program than you lose while going through it. The all-important third phase shows you how to continue on the path that leads to health *for life!* I have done my part. Now it is your turn as you begin the Maker's Diet 40-Day Health Experience.

Phase One: Days 1–14

AS WITH VIRTUALLY ANY IMPORTANT TASK OR ENDEAVOR, *THE WAY you start* significantly affects the results you enjoy at the finish. Phase one of the Maker's Diet is designed to stabilize insulin and blood sugar, reduce inflammation, reduce infection, enhance digestion, and help balance the hormones in your body. This should help you better manage your weight in a healthy manner and significantly improve your overall health.

Best of all, the components of phase one should greatly reduce your risk of incurring disease. It effectively helps your body reduce insulin sensitivity and balance the omega-3/omega-6 ratio that is so vital to balance levels of inflammation and enhance the health of your immune system, which will reduce chances of infection.

Temporary Food Limitations

After reading through this forty-day program, you will notice that phase one restricts disaccharide-rich carbohydrate foods such as grains, pastas, breads, sugar, potatoes, corn, beans, and legumes. While it is true that the people of the Bible consumed a diet that contained liberal amounts of grain and other carbohydrate foods, they were higher-quality, lesser-processed carbohydrates, therefore much easier to digest. And since they ate smaller quantities of food (some believe as much as six times less food than we do), their typical diet was close to a modern lower-carbohydrate diet.

Also, these people would have eaten extremely healthy diets since birth, so they weren't hampered by increased insulin sensitivity, endocrine imbalances (including thyroid problems), infection, inflammation, and digestive problems common to people who have been reared with the standard American diet (SAD). Since phase one is designed to *correct* these harmful imbalances, it must *temporarily* limit even healthy foods such as fruits, whole grains, and honey while allowing for the liberal consumption of protein foods, vegetables, and healthy oils.

The Prayer Factor

The Maker's Diet 40-day health experience begins and ends each day with prayers of thanksgiving, prayers for healing, and prayers of petition. As we discussed, it has now been scientifically proven that prayer works. Try repeating these prayers daily to experience how the God of the ages will work a miracle in your life. I've developed these prayers from many different biblical passages. Even if you have never prayed before, God promises that His Word will never return void (empty), but it will prosper in the thing for which He sends it (Isa. 55:11). We can trust God's promises. The following prayers can serve as guidelines for you.

A morning prayer for healing

> *Father God, I thank You for creating me in Your image. I praise You that I am fearfully and wonderfully made. I confess that You are the God that heals, my Great Physician. I ask You to heal my body from the top of my head to the soles of my feet. I pray that You would regenerate every bone, joint, tendon, ligament, tissue, organ, and cell of my body. This is the day that the Lord has made; I will rejoice and be glad in it.*

An evening prayer for restoration

> *Father God, I thank You for sustaining me today. I thank You that You are made perfect in my weakness. Your grace is sufficient for me. I thank You that Your steadfast love never ceases and Your mercies are new every morning. You say in Your Word that mourning may come for a night, but the new day will bring gladness. Bless me with a healing night's sleep. Restore unto me the joy of my salvation. Help me to stay on the path that leads to life.*

The Purpose Factor

The alignment of Life Purpose to start each day will spell the difference between success and failure. This simple but profound exercise of two to five minutes before the day gets too crazy will produce sustained passion, motivation, and purpose that will illuminate even the most mundane situations and events.

This exercise is a time of alignment and reflection on what is most important to an individual's life including health, happiness, and productivity. Realignment oscillation cycles should take place every ninety minutes to realign for a quick two- to five-minute splash of energy and focus. Starting each day with purpose coupled with a regular routine to check-in every ninety minutes throughout the day will be the key to sustaining the Maker's Diet and that will produce the lasting results desired![1]

Phase One: Foods to Enjoy

Meat (grass-fed/organic is best)

- Beef
- Lamb
- Venison
- Goat
- Veal
- Buffalo
- Elk
- Meat bone soup/stock
- Liver and heart (must be organic)
- Beef or buffalo sausage or hot dogs (no pork casing—organic and nitrite/nitrate free is best) (Use sparingly in phase one.)

Fish (wild freshwater/ocean-caught fish is best; make sure it has fins and scales!)

- Salmon
- Tuna
- Scrod
- Haddock
- Pompano
- Trout
- Orange roughy
- Snapper
- Herring
- Whitefish
- Halibut
- Cod
- Grouper
- Mahi mahi
- Wahoo
- Tilapia
- Sea bass
- Mackerel
- Sole
- Fish bone soup/stock
- Salmon (canned in spring water)
- Tuna (canned in spring water)

- Sardines (canned in water or olive oil only)

Poultry (pastured/organic is best)
- Chicken
- Cornish game hen
- Guinea fowl
- Turkey
- Duck
- Poultry bone soup/stock
- Chicken or turkey bacon (no pork casing—organic and nitrite/nitrate free is best)
- Chicken or turkey sausage or hot dogs (no pork casing—organic and nitrite/nitrate free is best) (Use sparingly in phase one.)
- Liver and heart (must be organic)

Eggs (high omega-3/DHA is best)
- Chicken eggs (whole with yolk)
- Duck eggs (whole with yolk)

Dairy
- Goat's milk yogurt (plain)
- Homemade kefir from goat's milk (See Appendix B.)
- Soft goat's milk cheese (See Appendix B.)
- Goat's milk hard cheese
- Sheep's milk hard cheeses

Fats and oils (organic is best)
- Oil, butter (ghee)
- Goat's milk butter
- Avocado
- Cow's milk butter, organic
- Extra-virgin coconut oil (best for cooking)
- Extra-virgin olive oil (not best for cooking)
- Flaxseed oil (not for cooking)
- Hempseed oil (not for cooking)
- Goat's milk butter (not for cooking)
- Raw cow's milk butter, grass-fed (not for cooking)
- Expeller-pressed sesame oil
- Coconut milk/cream (canned)

Vegetables (organic fresh or frozen is best)
- Broccoli
- Squash (winter or summer)
- Asparagus
- Beets
- Cauliflower
- Brussels sprouts
- Cabbage
- Carrots

- Celery
- Eggplant
- Garlic
- Okra
- Spinach
- Peas
- String beans
- Cucumber
- Pumpkin
- Onion
- Lettuce (leaf of all kinds)
- Mushrooms
- Peppers
- Tomatoes
- Artichoke (French, not Jerusalem)
- Leafy greens (kale, collard, broccoli rabe, mustard greens, etc.)
- Raw leafy greens (endive, escarole, radicchio, arugula, frisse, etc.)
- Sprouts (broccoli, sunflower, pea shoots, radish, etc.)
- Sea vegetables (kelp, dulse, nori, kombu, hijiki)
- Raw, fermented vegetables (lacto-fermented only, no vinegar)

Beans and legumes (soaked or fermented is best)

- Small amounts of fermented soybean paste (miso) as a broth
- Lentils

Nuts and seeds (organic, raw, or soaked is best)

- Almonds (raw)
- Hempseed (raw)
- Sunflower seeds (raw)
- Hempseed butter (raw)
- Pumpkinseed butter (raw)
- Pumpkinseeds (raw)
- Flaxseed (raw and ground)
- Almond butter (raw)
- Sunflower butter (raw)
- Tahini, sesame butter (raw)

Condiments, spices, seasonings (organic is best)

- Salsa (fresh or canned)
- Guacamole (fresh)
- Celtic sea salt
- Herbamare seasoning
- Umeboshi paste
- Tomato sauce (no added sugar)
- Apple cider vinegar
- Mustard
- Omega-3 mayonnaise
- Soy sauce (wheat free), tamari
- Raw salad dressings and marinades (see recipes)
- Herbs and spices (no added stabilizers)
- Pickled ginger (preservative and color free)
- Wasabe (preservative and color free)
- Organic flavoring extracts (alcohol based, no sugar added), i.e., vanilla, almond, etc.

Fruits (organic fresh or frozen is best)

- Blueberries
- Blackberries
- Cherries
- Lemon
- Strawberries
- Raspberries
- Grapefruit
- Lime

Beverages

- Purified, nonchlorinated water
- Natural sparkling water, no carbonation added (i.e., Perrier)
- Herbal teas (preferably organic)—unsweetened or with a small amount of honey or Stevia
- Raw vegetable juice (beet or carrot juice—maximum 25 percent of total)
- Lacto-fermented beverages (see recipes)
- Certified organic coffee—buy whole beans, freeze them, and grind yourself when desired; flavor only with organic cream and a small amount of honey.

Sweeteners

- Unheated, raw honey in very small amounts (1 Tbsp. per day maximum)

Miscellaneous

- Goat's milk protein powder (See Appendix B.)

Phase One: Foods to Avoid

Meat

- Pork
- Bacon
- Veggie burgers
- Ostrich
- Ham
- Sausage (pork)
- Imitation meat product (soy)
- Emu

Fish and seafood

- Fried, breaded fish
- Eel
- Shark
- Catfish
- Squid
- Avoid *all* shellfish, including crab, clams, oyster, mussels, lobster, shrimp, scallops, and crawfish.

Poultry
- Fried, breaded chicken

Luncheon meat
- Turkey
- Ham
- Roast beef
- Corned beef

Eggs
- Imitation eggs (such as Egg Beaters)

Dairy
- Soy milk
- Almond milk
- Rice milk
- Avoid all dairy products other than those listed in "Foods to Enjoy."

Fats and oils
- Lard
- Shortening
- Safflower oil
- Sunflower oil
- Cottonseed oil
- Margarine
- Soy oil
- Canola oil
- Corn oil
- Any partially hydrogenated oil

Vegetables
- Corn
- White potato
- Sweet potato

Beans and legumes
- Soy beans
- Black beans
- Navy beans
- Garbanzo beans
- Tofu
- Kidney beans
- White beans
- Lima beans

Nuts and seeds
- Honey-roasted nuts
- Macadamia nuts
- Hazelnuts
- Peanuts
- Cashews
- Nuts or seeds dry or roasted in oil
- Walnuts
- Pecans
- Brazil nuts
- Peanut butter

Condiments, spices, seasonings
- All spices that contain added sugar

- Commercial ketchup with sugar
- Commercial barbecue sauce with sugar

Fruits
- Avoid all fruits except berries, grapefruit, limes, and lemons. This includes apples, bananas, apricots, grapes, melon, peaches, oranges, pears, dried fruit, and canned fruit.

Beverages
- Alcoholic beverages of any kind
- Fruit juices
- Sodas
- Chlorinated tap water
- Pre-ground commercial coffee

Grains and Starchy Carbohydrates
- Avoid *all* grains and starchy foods, including bread, pasta, cereal, rice, oatmeal, pastries, and baked goods.

Sweeteners
- Sugar
- Maple syrup
- Heated honey
- Fructose or corn syrup
- All artificial sweeteners, including aspartame, sucralose, Acesulfame K
- Sugar alcohol, including sorbitol and xylitol

Miscellaneous
- Milk or whey protein powder from cow's milk
- Soy protein powder
- Rice protein powder

Your Daily Regimen

I have detailed for you a daily regimen for each phase of the protocol. And I have given you sample menus for several days of each two-week phase. Always refer to the "foods to enjoy" for the phase in which you are participating in order to create your own healthy, delicious meals with a wide variety of natural, healing foods and beverages. And enjoy the wonderful recipes included in Appendix A.

You will notice the designations basic, intermediate, or advanced by each component of the daily regimen. Whether you follow the basic, intermediate, or advanced recommendations will depend on your state of health, available time, and budgetary allowances. Your results from this program will depend on your commitment level and discipline.

"Partial-fast" days

I have recommended a partial fast one day per week in each phase. (I recommend Thursday as it is much more difficult to fast during the weekend.) On the partial-fast days you will not be eating breakfast or lunch. You should still consume your cleansing drink and other supplements. This partial-fast day allows the body to cleanse and rebuild. Make sure to consume lots of fluids during your partial-fast day, especially raw vegetable juices and pure water. To gain maximum spiritual benefit from your partial-fast days, I recommend praying each time you experience hunger.

Remember to follow the daily regimen diligently in order to reap the greatest results. You may want to copy some of these pages and keep record of your progress by checking the boxes when you have completed each part of the daily regimen.

You can find these products listed in Appendix B, Garden of Life Companion Guide to Healthy Living.

Daily Regimen for Phase One: Days 1–14

Morning hygiene

CHECK HERE	Clenzology (Basic). Clenzology is a simple program that is designed to greatly reduce infectious germs that enter the body. This is accomplished without the use of antibacterial soaps or detergents. Clenzology thoroughly cleanses the hands, underneath the fingernails, and the mucous membranes of the eyes and nasal cavities as well as the sinuses. Clenzology takes approximately three minutes twice per day. It can greatly reduce the amount of stress placed on your immune system, leading to better health and fewer colds and flus. Use as directed. (See page 286.)
CHECK HERE	Aromatherapy A.M. (Advanced). Use three drops of a biblical aromatherapeutic blend in the palm of your hand. Rub your hands together, cup them in front of your face, and gently inhale through your nose three or four times. You may then rub the remaining oil into your scalp or into the soles of your feet. (See page 286.)
CHECK HERE	Purification A.M. (Advanced). Take 1–2 two capsules with 8 ounces of pure water. (See page 284.)

Morning cleansing drink (intermediate)

CHECK HERE	Mix 2 tablespoons of a whole-food fiber blend and 1–2 tablespoons or 5 caplets of a green superfood blend with HSOs in 8 to 12 ounces of purified water or diluted vegetable juice. Shake vigorously and drink immediately. (See page 284.)

Morning tune-up

CHECK HERE	Morning prayer (See page 200.)
CHECK HERE	Morning purpose (See page 201.)
CHECK HERE	Exercise ten to fifteen minutes. Choose one: Functional Fitness, rebounding (page 176), or breathing exercises (page 175).
CHECK HERE	Listen to music that uplifts and energizes while you exercise.

Breakfast

CHECK HERE	See the sample breakfast menus on pages 210–211.

Breakfast supplements (Basic)

CHECK HERE	Living multivitamin/mineral with homeostatic nutrients, 2–3 caplets. (See page 283.)

Lunch

CHECK HERE	See the sample lunch menus on pages 210–211.

Lunch supplements (Basic)

CHECK HERE	Living multivitamin/mineral with homeostatic nutrients, 2–3 caplets.

Afternoon cleansing drink (Intermediate)

CHECK HERE	Mix 2 tablespoons of a whole-food fiber blend and 1–2 tablespoons or 5 caplets of a green superfood blend with HSOs in 8 to 12 ounces purified water or diluted vegetable juice. Shake vigorously and drink immediately.

Dinner

CHECK HERE	See the sample dinner menus on pages 210–211.

Dinner supplements (Basic)

CHECK HERE	Living multivitamin/mineral with homeostatic nutrients, 2–3 caplets.
CHECK HERE	Icelandic Cod Liver Oil (basic): 1 teaspoon to 1 tablespoon based on sun exposure. If you receive more than two hours of direct sunlight per week, you may take 1–2 teaspoons. If you receive less than two hours of direct sunlight per week, you may take 1 tablespoon. (See page 284.)

Evening snack

CHECK HERE	See sample snack menus on pages 210–211.

Evening wind down

CHECK HERE	Evening prayer
CHECK HERE	Exercise ten to fifteen minutes. Choose one: Functional Fitness, rebounding (page 176), or breathing exercises (page 175).
CHECK HERE	Listen to music that uplifts and energizes while you exercise.

Evening hygiene

CHECK HERE	Clenzology (Basic). Clenzology is a simple program that is designed to greatly reduce infectious germs that enter the body. This is accomplished without the use of antibacterial soaps or detergents. Clenzology thoroughly cleanses the hands, underneath the fingernails, and the mucous membranes of the eyes and nasal cavities as well as the sinuses. Clenzology takes approximately three minutes twice per day. It can greatly reduce the amount of stress placed on your immune system, leading to better health and fewer colds and flus. Use as directed. (See page 286.)
CHECK HERE	Aromatherapy P.M. (Advanced) Use three drops of a biblical aromatherapeutic blend in the palm of your hand. Rub your hands together, cup them in front of your face, and gently inhale through your nose three or four times. You may then rub the remaining oil into your scalp or into the soles of your feet. (See page 286.)

PHASE ONE

	Purification P.M. (Advanced) Take 1–2 two capsules with 8 ounces of
CHECK HERE	pure water. (See page 284.)

In bed before 10:30

Sample Menus for Phase One

Day 1

Breakfast

Fried eggs (prepared any way you desire: over-easy, medium, or well. Fry in extra-virgin coconut oil or butter.)
Stir-fried veggies

Lunch

Tuna Salad (page 243)
Raw carrots and celery

Dinner

French-style London Broil (page 248)
Green salad

Evening snack

½ cup strawberries with 1 ounce of raw goat's milk cheese

Day 2

Breakfast

Vegetable Frittata (page 240)

Lunch

Coconut Milk Soup (page 233)

Dinner

Wild Alaskan Salmon With Pecan Pesto (page 242)
Green salad
Cultured vegetables

Evening snack

Carrot, celery, and raw almond butter

Day 3

Breakfast
> Onion, Pepper, and Goat Cheese Omelet (page 240)
> Avocado slices with seasoning

Lunch
> Oriental Red Meat Salad (page 235)

Dinner
> Coconut Milk Soup (page 233)
> Easy Broiled Halibut (page 241)
> Green salad

Evening snack
> Goat's milk yogurt, raw honey, vanilla, and blueberries

Day 4

Breakfast
> None (partial-fast day)

Lunch
> None (partial-fast day)

Dinner
> Cultured veggies
> Green salad
> Tuna Steaks, Oriental Style (page 243)

Evening snack
> None (partial-fast day)

Phase Two: Days 15–28

CONGRATULATIONS! YOU FINISHED PHASE ONE, THE MOST DIFFICULT part of the Maker's Diet 40-Day Health Experience. It was a tough two weeks, but I trust you are convinced it was well worth it.

You should feel much better already. If your goal is to lose unwanted pounds and inches, you are probably feeling pretty good right about now. If it's more energy you desire, you are probably surprised by the surge of new energy you are now feeling. Your digestion has improved, your energy levels have increased, your skin looks better, and your cravings are under control. Let me assure you that you are well on your road to optimal health!

What to Expect

As a result of the healing process that has begun, phase two introduces (or reintroduces) a *greater variety of foods* into your daily diet, including fruit, nuts, and seeds. In phase two, you may continue to enjoy all of the foods from the "foods to enjoy" list in phase one while adding the new foods listed for phase two.

You will *continue* to lose excess weight, though many people lose weight at a slower pace during this phase. The health goal at this point may not be to achieve dramatic weight loss, but to continue to move toward your *ideal* weight as you enjoy greater benefits of enhanced health.

Be encouraged. The Maker's Diet 40-Day Health Experience helps you *return* to your optimal health levels by restoring your immune system, balancing blood sugar, and creating healthy eating habits that will, hopefully, last a lifetime.

Remember, you are *not* trying to squeeze yourself into someone's fanciful idea about how everyone should look. By returning to "the Manufacturer's specifications," your body will naturally return to its ideal weight, shape, and strength levels—all without *dangerous side effects!*

By the end of phase two, you should really be feeling *good* about yourself because you will have accomplished what very few people even dare to try: you *changed* your life for the better!

Phase Two: New Foods to Enjoy

Feel free to add the following new foods for phase two and enjoy them along with the "foods to enjoy" from phase one. As in phase one, you can find sources for the products listed in Appendix B, Garden of Life Companion Guide to Healthy Living.

Meat (grass-fed/organic is best)
• All meats listed in phase one

Fish (wild freshwater/ocean-caught fish is best—check for fins and scales!)
• All fish listed in phase one

Poultry (pastured/organic is best)
• All poultry listed in phase one

Eggs
• Fish roe or caviar (fresh, not preserved)

Luncheon meat (organic and nitrite/nitrate free is best)
• Turkey, sliced (free range, preservative free)
• Roast beef, sliced (free range, preservative free)

Dairy (organic, grass-fed is best)
• Homemade kefir from raw or nonhomogenized cow's milk
• Kefir from pasteurized, nonhomogenized cow's milk
• Raw cow's milk hard cheeses
• Cow's milk cottage cheeses
• Cow's milk ricotta cheese
• Cow's milk plain whole-milk yogurt
• Cow's milk plain kefir
• Cow's milk plain sour cream
• Raw goat's milk

Fats and oils (organic is best)
• Expeller-pressed peanut oil

PHASE TWO

Vegetables (organic fresh or frozen is best)
- Sweet potatoes
- Corn
- Yams

Beans and legumes (soaked or fermented is best)
- White beans
- Kidney beans
- Tempeh (fermented soybean)
- Black beans
- Navy beans

Nuts and seeds (organic, raw, soaked is best)
- Walnuts (raw)
- Hazelnuts (raw)
- Pecans (raw or soaked and low-temperature dehydrated)
- Macadamia nuts (raw)
- Brazil nuts (raw)

Condiments, spices, seasonings (organic is best)
- Ketchup (no sugar)
- All-natural salad dressings (no preservatives)
- All-natural marinades (no preservatives)

Fruits (organic fresh or frozen is best)
- Apples
- Grapes
- Peaches
- Pears
- Kiwi
- Pomegranates
- Guava
- Apricots
- Melon
- Oranges
- Plums
- Pineapple
- Passion fruit

Beverages
- Raw vegetable juice (beet or carrot—maximum 50 percent of total)
- Coconut water

Sweeteners
- Unheated raw honey (up to 3 tablespoons per day)
- Stevia

Miscellaneous
- Same as phase one

Phase Two: Foods to Avoid

Meat
- Pork
- Bacon
- Ostrich
- Imitation meat product (soy)
- Veggie burgers
- Ham
- Sausage (pork)
- Emu

Fish and seafood
- Fried, breaded fish
- Eel
- Shark
- Catfish
- Squid
- Avoid *all shellfish*, including crab, oyster, mussels, lobster, shrimp, scallops, and crawfish.

Poultry
- Fried, breaded chicken

Eggs
- Imitation eggs (such as Egg Beaters)

Luncheon meat
- Ham
- Corned beef

Dairy
- Soy milk
- Almond milk
- Rice milk
- Avoid all commercial dairy products including milk, ice cream, cheese, and yogurt.

Fats and oils
- Lard
- Shortening
- Safflower oil
- Sunflower oil
- Cottonseed oil
- Margarine
- Soy oil
- Canola oil
- Corn oil
- Any partially hydrogenated oil

Vegetables
- White potato

PHASE TWO

Beans and legumes
- Soy beans
- Tofu
- Garbanzo beans
- Lima beans

Nuts and seeds
- Peanuts
- Honey-roasted nuts
- Nuts or seeds roasted in oil
- Peanut butter
- Cashews

Condiments, spices, seasonings
- All spices that contain added sugar

Fruits
- Bananas
- Papaya
- Mango
- Canned fruit
- Avoid *dried fruits*, including raisins, dates, figs, prunes, bananas, mango, and papaya.

Beverages
- Alcoholic beverages of any kind
- Fruit juices
- Chlorinated tap water
- Sodas
- Pre-ground commercial coffee

Grains and starchy carbohydrates
- Avoid *all* grains and starchy foods in phase two, including bread, pasta, cereal, rice, oatmeal, pastries, and baked goods.

Sweeteners
- Sugar
- Heated honey
- Maple syrup
- Fructose and corn syrup
- All artificial sweeteners, including aspartame, sucralose, and Acesulfame K
- Sugar alcohol (including sorbitol, maltitol, and xylitol)

Miscellaneous
- Milk or whey protein powder from cow's milk
- Soy protein powder
- Rice protein powder

Daily Regimen for Phase Two: Days 15–28

Morning hygiene

CHECK HERE	Clenzology (Basic). Clenzology is a simple program that is designed to greatly reduce infectious germs that enter the body. This is accomplished without the use of antibacterial soaps or detergents. Clenzology thoroughly cleanses the hands, underneath the fingernails, and the mucous membranes of the eyes and nasal cavities as well as the sinuses. Clenzology takes approximately three minutes twice per day. It can greatly reduce the amount of stress placed on your immune system, leading to better health and fewer colds and flus. Use as directed. (See page 286.)
CHECK HERE	Aromatherapy A.M. (Advanced). Use three drops of a biblical aromatherapeutic blend in the palm of your hand. Rub your hands together, cup them in front of your face, and gently inhale through your nose three or four times. You may then rub the remaining oil into your scalp or into the soles of your feet. (See page 286.)
CHECK HERE	Purification A.M. (Advanced). Take 1–2 capsules with 8 ounces of pure water. (See page 284.)

Morning cleansing drink (intermediate)

CHECK HERE	Mix 2 tablespoons of a whole-food fiber blend and 1–2 tablespoons or 5 caplets of a green superfood blend with HSOs in 8 to 12 ounces of purified water or diluted vegetable juice. Shake vigorously and drink immediately. (See page 284.)

Morning tune-up

CHECK HERE	Morning prayer (See page 200.)
CHECK HERE	Morning purpose (See page 201.)
CHECK HERE	Exercise ten to fifteen minutes. Choose one: Functional Fitness, rebounding (page 176), or breathing exercises (page 175).
CHECK HERE	Listen to music that uplifts and energizes while you exercise.

Breakfast

CHECK HERE	See the sample breakfast menus on pages 219–220.

PHASE TWO

Breakfast supplements (Basic)

CHECK HERE	Living multivitamin/mineral with homeostatic nutrients, 2–3 caplets.

Lunch

CHECK HERE	See the sample lunch menus on pages 219–221.

Lunch supplements (Basic)

CHECK HERE	Living multivitamin/mineral with homeostatic nutrients, 2–3 caplets.

Afternoon cleansing drink (Intermediate)

CHECK HERE	Mix 2 tablespoons of a whole-food fiber blend and 1–2 tablespoons or 5 caplets of a green superfood blend with HSOs in 8 to 12 ounces purified water or diluted vegetable juice. Shake vigorously and drink immediately.

Dinner

CHECK HERE	See the sample dinner menus on pages 219–221.

Dinner supplements (Basic)

CHECK HERE	Living multivitamin/mineral with homeostatic nutrients, 2–3 caplets.
CHECK HERE	Icelandic Cod Liver Oil (basic): 1 teaspoon to 1 tablespoon based on sun exposure. If you receive more than two hours of direct sunlight per week, you may take 1–2 teaspoons. If you receive less than two hours of direct sunlight per week, you may take 1 tablespoon. (See page 284.)

Evening snack

CHECK HERE	See sample snack menus on pages 219–221.

Evening wind down

CHECK HERE	Evening prayer
CHECK HERE	Exercise ten to fifteen minutes. Choose one: Functional Fitness, rebounding (page 176), or breathing exercises (page 175).
CHECK HERE	Listen to music that uplifts and energizes while you exercise.

Evening hygiene

CHECK HERE	Clenzology (Basic). Clenzology is a simple program that is designed to greatly reduce infectious germs that enter the body. This is accomplished without the use of antibacterial soaps or detergents. Clenzology thoroughly cleanses the hands, underneath the fingernails, and the mucous membranes of the eyes and nasal cavities as well as the sinuses. Clenzology takes approximately three minutes twice per day. It can greatly reduce the amount of stress placed on your immune system, leading to better health and fewer colds and flus. Use as directed. (See page 286.)
CHECK HERE	Aromatherapy P.M. (Advanced) Use three drops of a biblical aromatherapeutic blend in the palm of your hand. Rub your hands together, cup them in front of your face, and gently inhale through your nose three or four times. You may then rub the remaining oil into your scalp or into the soles of your feet. (See page 286.)
CHECK HERE	Purification P.M. (Advanced) Take 1–2 two capsules with 8 ounces of pure water. (See page 284.)
CHECK HERE	Healing bath (optional) (See Appendix B for recommended bath salts and essential oils.)

In bed before 10:30

Sample Menus for Phase Two

Day 15

Breakfast
Cottage cheese or ricotta cheese
Pineapple
Sliced almonds

Lunch
Uptown Salad (page 234)

Dinner
Venison Steaks With Marinade (page 249)
Sweet potatoes with butter
Steamed vegetable medley

Evening snack
Balanced Vegetable Juice (page 254)

PHASE TWO

Day 16

Breakfast
> Garden Herb Omelet (page 240)
> 1 orange

Lunch
> Salade Nicoise (page 235)

Dinner
> Chicken With Oregano and Mushrooms (page 243)
> Corn on the cob
> Steamed broccoli and carrots with butter

Evening snack
> Apple slices
> Almond butter and honey

Day 17

Breakfast
> Easy Soft-boiled/Hard-boiled Eggs (page 239)
> Avocado with salsa

Lunch
> Chicken Soup/Stock (page 232)

Dinner
> Red Snapper Mexican Style (page 242)
> Black beans
> Easy Vegetable Salad (page 234)

Evening snack
> Mixed raw nuts (almonds, walnuts, pecans, Macadamia nuts)
> Apple slices
> 1 ounce cheese

Day 18

Breakfast
> None (partial-fast day)

Lunch
None (partial-fast day)

Dinner
Ginger Carrots (page 236)
Mushroom Soup (page 233)
Green salad
Grilled chicken breast
Pan-fried sweet potato in coconut oil or butter

Evening snack
None (partial-fast day)

PHASE TWO

The Maker's Diet: Phase Three

Days 29–40 (and Beyond)

THIS PHASE MARKS THE "MOUNTAINTOP EXPERIENCE," THE WINNER'S circle, the Olympic Gold of a challenge conquered and a battle won. You will now enter phase three in the fifth week of the program.

Phase three is the *maintenance phase* of the diet. It is specifically designed to allow and encourage healthful eating of foods from each food group. In this phase, you will reacquaint yourself with healthy grain foods and foods higher in sugars and starches, such as potatoes.

You may notice that phase three of the Maker's Diet does not mandate a daily snack. (I know you looked forward to them). The good news is, if you want to have a snack, choose one at any time—*but only from the acceptable foods.*

Your weight should stabilize in this phase, and you can expect other key areas of your health picture to continue to improve. Having reached this phase, you have managed to establish considerable self-control, so it should be much easier not to "cheat."

If you do venture off the Maker's Diet, perhaps during the holidays, on a vacation, or another special event such as an extravagant birthday or anniversary celebration, you can always go back to phase one or two for a week or two to get back into the groove. This option is always available, and you will find it to be a great tool in your journey on the path that leads to health—for life!

Remember, as in phase one and phase two, you can find the recommended foods and products listed in Appendix B, Garden of Life Companion Guide to Healthy Living.

Phase Three: More New Foods to Enjoy

Meat (grass-fed/organic is best)
- All meats listed in phase one and phase two

Fish (wild freshwater/ocean-caught fish is best—check for fins and scales!)
- All fish listed in phase one and phase two

Poultry (pastured/organic is best)
- All poultry listed in phase one and phase two

Eggs (high omega-3/DHA or organic is best)
- All eggs listed in phase one and phase two

Luncheon meat (organic is best)
- All luncheon meat listed in phase two

Dairy
- All dairy listed in phase one and phase two

Fats and oils (organic is best)
- All fats and oils listed in phase one and phase two

Vegetables (organic fresh or frozen is best)
- All vegetables listed in phase one and phase two

Beans and legumes (soaked or fermented is best)
Along with beans and legumes listed in phase one and phase two, add:

- Pinto beans
- Split peas
- Lima beans
- Black-eyed peas
- Red beans
- Garbanzo beans
- Broad beans
- Edamame (boiled soybeans) (in small amounts)

Nuts and seeds (organic, raw, soaked is best)
Along with nuts and seeds listed in phase one and phase two, add:

- Almonds (dry roasted)
- Almond butter (roasted)
- Pecans (dry roasted)
- Sunflower seeds (dry roasted)
- Pumpkinseeds (dry roasted)
- Walnuts (dry roasted)
- Tahini (roasted)
- Macadamia nuts (dry roasted)

PHASE THREE

- Pumpkinseed butter (roasted)
- Sunflower butter (roasted)
- Peanuts, dry roasted (must be organic) (in small quantities)
- Peanut butter, roasted (must be organic) (in small quantities)
- Cashews, raw or dry roasted (in small quantities)
- Cashew butter, raw or roasted (in small quantities)

Condiments, spices, seasonings (organic is best)
- All condiments, spices, and seasonings listed in phase one and phase two

Fruits (organic fresh or frozen is best)
Along with fruits listed in phase one and phase two, add:
- Banana
- Papaya
- Mango
- Canned fruit (in its own juices)
- Dried fruit (no sugar or sulfites): raisins, figs, dates, prunes, pineapple, papaya, peaches, and apples

Beverages
Along with beverages listed in phase one and phase two, add:
- Raw, unpasteurized vegetable juice
- Raw, unpasteurized fruit juice
- Organic wine and beer (in very small amounts)

Grains and starchy carbohydrates (whole-grain, organic, soaked is best)
- Sprouted, Ezekiel-type bread
- Sprouted Essene bread
- Fermented whole-grain sourdough bread
- Whole-grain kamut or spelt pasta (in small quantities)
- Quinoa
- Buckwheat
- Kamut (in small quantities)
- Oats (in small quantities)
- Barley (in small quantities)
- Brown rice (in small quantities)
- Amaranth
- Millet
- Sprouted cereal
- Spelt (in small quantities)

Sweeteners
Along with sweeteners listed in phase one and phase two, add:
- Maple syrup

Miscellaneous
- Selected healthy snacks (a few times per week) (See Appendix B.)
- Trail Mix (page 258)
- Organic chocolate spreads
- Carob powder
- Zesty Popcorn (page 258)

Phase Three: Foods to Avoid

Meat
- Pork
- Bacon
- Veggie burgers
- Emu
- Ham
- Sausage (pork)
- Ostrich
- Imitation meat product (soy)

Fish and seafood
- Fried, breaded fish
- Eel
- Shark
- Catfish
- Squid
- Avoid *all shellfish*, including crab, oyster, mussels, lobster, shrimp, scallops, and crawfish.

Poultry
- Fried, breaded chicken

Eggs
- Imitation eggs (such as Egg Beaters)

Luncheon meat
- Ham
- Corned beef

Dairy
- Soy milk
- Almond milk
- Processed cheese food or singles
- Rice milk
- Avoid all commercial dairy products, including milk and ice cream.

Fats and oils
- Lard
- Shortening
- Margarine
- Soy oil

- Safflower oil
- Sunflower oil
- Cottonseed oil
- Canola oil
- Corn oil
- Any partially hydrogenated oil

Nuts and seeds

- Nuts roasted in oil
- Honey-roasted nuts

Condiments, spices, seasonings

- All spices that contain added sugar

Fruits

- Canned fruits in syrup

Beverages

- Fruit juices
- Chlorinated tap water
- Alcoholic beverages of any kind
- Sodas
- Pre-ground commercial coffee

Grains and starchy carbohydrates

- White rice
- Instant oatmeal
- Baked goods
- Bread (except sprouted or sourdough)
- Pastas (except whole-grain kamut or spelt)
- Dried cereal (except sprouted)
- Pastries

Sweeteners

- Sugar
- Fructose or corn syrup
- Sugar alcohol, including sorbitol and xylitol
- All artificial sweeteners, including aspartame, sucralose, and Acesulfame K
- Heated honey

Miscellaneous

- Soy protein powder
- Milk or whey protein powder from cow's milk
- Rice protein powder

Daily Regimen for Phase Three: Days 29–40 (and Beyond)

Morning hygiene

CHECK HERE	Clenzology (Basic). Clenzology is a simple program that is designed to greatly reduce infectious germs that enter the body. This is accomplished without the use of antibacterial soaps or detergents. Clenzology thoroughly cleanses the hands, underneath the fingernails, and the mucous membranes of the eyes and nasal cavities as well as the sinuses. Clenzology takes approximately three minutes twice per day. It can greatly reduce the amount of stress placed on your immune system, leading to better health and fewer colds and flus. Use as directed. (See page 286.)
CHECK HERE	Aromatherapy A.M. (Advanced). Use three drops of a biblical aromatherapeutic blend in the palm of your hand. Rub your hands together, cup them in front of your face, and gently inhale through your nose three or four times. You may then rub the remaining oil into your scalp or into the soles of your feet. (See page 286.)
CHECK HERE	Purification A.M. (Advanced). Take 1–2 capsules with 8 ounces of pure water. (See page 284.)

Morning cleansing drink (intermediate)

CHECK HERE	Mix 2 tablespoons of a whole-food fiber blend and 1–2 tablespoons or 5 caplets of a green superfood blend with HSOs in 8 to 12 ounces of purified water or diluted vegetable juice. Shake vigorously and drink immediately. (See page 284.)

Morning tune-up

CHECK HERE	Morning prayer (See page 200.)
CHECK HERE	Morning purpose (See page 201.)
CHECK HERE	Exercise fifteen to twenty minutes. Choose one: Functional Fitness, rebounding (page 176), or breathing exercises (page 175).
CHECK HERE	Listen to music that uplifts and energizes while you exercise.

Breakfast

CHECK HERE	See the sample breakfast menus on pages 229–230.

PHASE THREE

227

Breakfast supplements (Basic)

CHECK HERE	Living multivitamin/mineral with homeostatic nutrients, 2–3 caplets. (See page 283.)

Lunch

CHECK HERE	See the sample lunch menus on pages 229–230.

Lunch supplements (Basic)

CHECK HERE	Living multivitamin/mineral with homeostatic nutrients, 2–3 caplets.

Afternoon cleansing drink (Intermediate)

CHECK HERE	Mix 2 tablespoons of a whole-food fiber blend and 1–2 tablespoons or 5 caplets of a green superfood blend with HSOs in 8 to 12 ounces purified water or diluted vegetable juice. Shake vigorously and drink immediately.

Dinner

CHECK HERE	See the sample dinner menus on pages 229–230.

Dinner supplements (Basic)

CHECK HERE	Living multivitamin/mineral with homeostatic nutrients, 2–3 caplets.
CHECK HERE	Icelandic Cod Liver Oil (basic): 1 teaspoon to 1 tablespoon based on sun exposure. If you receive more than two hours of direct sunlight per week, you may take 1–2 teaspoons. If you receive less than two hours of direct sunlight per week, you may take 1 tablespoon. (See page 284.)

Evening snack

CHECK HERE	See sample snack menus on pages 229–230.

Evening wind down

CHECK HERE	Evening prayer
CHECK HERE	Exercise fifteen to twenty minutes. Choose one: Functional Fitness, rebounding (page 176), or breathing exercises (page 175).
CHECK HERE	Listen to music that uplifts and energizes while you exercise.

Evening hygiene

CHECK HERE	Clenzology (Basic). Clenzology is a simple program that is designed to greatly reduce infectious germs that enter the body. This is accomplished without the use of antibacterial soaps or detergents. Clenzology thoroughly cleanses the hands, underneath the fingernails, and the mucous membranes of the eyes and nasal cavities as well as the sinuses. Clenzology takes approximately three minutes twice per day. It can greatly reduce the amount of stress placed on your immune system, leading to better health and fewer colds and flus. Use as directed. (See page 286.)
CHECK HERE	Aromatherapy P.M. (Advanced). Use three drops of a biblical aromatherapeutic blend in the palm of your hand. Rub your hands together, cup them in front of your face, and gently inhale through your nose three or four times. You may then rub the remaining oil into your scalp or into the soles of your feet. (See page 286.)
CHECK HERE	Purification P.M. (Advanced). Take 1–2 two capsules with 8 ounces of pure water. (See page 284.)
CHECK HERE	Healing bath (optional) (See Appendix B for recommended bath salts and essential oils.)

In bed before 10:30

Sample Menus for Phase Three: Days 29-40 (and Beyond)

Day 29

Breakfast
Berry Smoothie (page 256)

Lunch
Sliced turkey and avocado sandwich on toasted sprouted or whole-grain sourdough bread
Carrot and celery sticks

Dinner
Barbecue style chicken breast
Pan-roasted red bliss potatoes
Steamed asparagus

PHASE THREE

Day 30

Breakfast
Tomato Basil Omelet (page 240)
1 orange or grapefruit

Lunch
Uptown Salad (page 234)

Dinner
Lamb Chops (page 247)
Baked potato with butter
Steamed vegetables (carrots, peas, broccoli)

Day 31

Breakfast
Fried eggs
Blueberry Pecan Pancakes (page 253)

Lunch
Green salad
Chicken Soup/Stock (page 232)

Dinner
Green salad
Easy Broiled Halibut (page 241)
Steamed broccoli

Day 32

Breakfast
None (partial-fast day)

Lunch
None (partial-fast day)

Dinner
Raw Sauerkraut (page 236)
Green salad
Beef Soup (page 231)
Chicken Fajitas (page 244)
Sprouted tortillas
Salsa, guacamole, sour cream

Evening snack
None (partial-fast day)

Appendix A

The Maker's Diet Recipes

Soups and Stocks
BEEF SOUP/STOCK

About 6 lb. beef marrow and knuckle bones	3 celery stalks, coarsely chopped
1 calf's foot, cut into pieces (optional)	Several sprigs of fresh thyme, tied together
5 lb. meaty rib or neck bones	1 tsp. dried green peppercorns, crushed
4 or more quarts cold, filtered water	1 bunch parsley
3 onions, coarsely chopped	¼ cup vinegar
3 carrots, coarsely chopped	

Good beef stock must be made with several sorts of beef bones. Knuckle bones and feet impart large quantities of gelatin to the broth; marrow bones impart flavor and the particular nutrients of the bone marrow; and meaty rib or neck bones add color and flavor.

Place the knuckle and marrow bones and calf's foot (optional) in a very large pot; cover with water. Let stand for one hour. Meanwhile, place meaty bones in a roasting pan and brown at 350 degrees in the oven. When well browned, add to the pot along with vinegar and vegetables.

Pour fat from roasting pan, add cold water, set over a high flame, and bring to a boil, stirring with a wooden spoon to de-glaze. Add this liquid to the pot. Add additional water, if necessary, to cover the bones, but the liquid should come no higher than within 1 inch of the rim of the pot, as the volume expands slightly during cooking. Bring to a boil. A large amount of scum will come to the top. It is important to remove this with a spoon. After you have skimmed, reduce heat and add the thyme and crushed peppercorns.

Simmer stock for at least 12 hours and for as long as 72 hours. Just before finishing, add the parsley. Let it wilt and remove stock from heat.

You will now have a pot of rather repulsive-looking brown liquid containing globs of gelatinous and fatty material. It doesn't even smell particularly good. But don't despair. After straining, you will have a delicious and nourishing clear broth that forms the basis for many other recipes in this book.

Remove bones with tongs or a slotted spoon. Strain the stock into a large bowl. Let cool in the refrigerator, and remove the congealed fat that rises to the top. Reheat and transfer to storage containers.

Note: Your dog will love the leftover meat and bones.

VARIATION: LAMB STOCK
Use lamb bones, especially lamb neck bones. This makes a delicious stock.

From *Nourishing Traditions* by Sally Fallon. Used by permission.

CHICKEN SOUP/STOCK

1 whole chicken (free range, pastured or organic)	6 celery stalks, coarsely chopped
2–4 chicken feet (optional)	2–4 zucchinis
3–4 quarts cold-filtered water	4–6 Tbsp. extra-virgin coconut oil
1 Tbsp. raw apple cider vinegar	1 bunch parsley
4 medium-sized onions, coarsely chopped	5 garlic cloves
8 carrots, peeled and coarsely chopped	4 inches grated ginger
	2–4 Tbsp. Celtic sea salt

If you are using a whole chicken, remove fat glands and gizzards from the cavity. By all means, use chicken feet if you can find them—they are full of gelatin. (Jewish folklore considers the addition of chicken feet the secret to successful broth.) Place chicken or chicken pieces in a large stainless steel pot with the water, vinegar, and all vegetables except parsley. Bring to a boil, and remove scum that rises to the top. Cover and cook on low heat for 12 to 24 hours.

The longer you cook the stock, the richer and more flavorful it will be. About five minutes before finishing the stock, add parsley. This will impart additional mineral ions to the broth.

Remove from heat, and take chicken out of pot. Let it cool, then remove meat from the carcass. Reserve for other uses such as chicken salads, enchiladas, sandwiches, or curries. (The skin and smaller bones, which will be very soft, may be given to your dog or cat.) Strain the stock into a large bowl and reserve in your refrigerator for use as a base for other soups.

VARIATIONS: TURKEY STOCK AND DUCK STOCK

Prepare as chicken stock using turkey wings and drumsticks or duck carcasses from which the breasts, legs, and thighs have been removed. These stocks will have a stronger flavor than chicken stock and will profit from the addition of several sprigs of fresh thyme tied together during cooking.

From *Nourishing Traditions* by Sally Fallon. Used by permission.

FISH STOCK

3 or 4 whole carcasses, including heads, of non-oily fish such as sole, turbot, rockfish, or snapper	Several sprigs fresh thyme
	Several sprigs parsley
2 Tbsp. extra-virgin coconut oil or butter	1 bay leaf
2 onions, coarsely chopped	½ cup dry white wine or vermouth
1 carrot, coarsely chopped	1 Tbsp. apple cider vinegar

Melt coconut oil or butter in a large stainless steel pot. Add the vegetables and cook very gently, about 30 minutes, until they are soft. Add wine and bring to a boil. Add fish carcasses and cover with cold, filtered water. Add vinegar. Bring to a boil. Take the time to carefully skim off the scum and impurities as they rise to the top. Tie herbs together and add to the pot. Reduce heat; cover and simmer for at least 4 hours or overnight. Remove carcasses with tongs or a slotted spoon, and strain the liquid into pint-sized storage containers for refrigerator or freezer.

The carrot will add a delicate sweetness to the stock when it has been reduced. Do not be tempted to add more carrots to the stock, or your final sauce will be too sweet!

From *Nourishing Traditions* by Sally Fallon. Used by permission.

COCONUT MILK SOUP

1½ quarts homemade fish or chicken stock	• 1 Tbsp. grated fresh ginger
1½ cups coconut milk and cream	• 2 Tbsp. fish sauce (optional)
1 lb. chicken or fish, cut into small cubes	• 2–4 Tbsp. lime juice
3 jalapeño chilies, diced, or ½ tsp. cayenne pepper, dried	• Chopped cilantro for garnish

Simmer all ingredients until meat is cooked through. Garnish with cilantro. **SERVES 6–8.**

From *Nourishing Traditions* by Sally Fallon. Used by permission.

MUSHROOM SOUP

2 medium onions, peeled and chopped	• 1 piece toasted whole-grain sprouted or sourdough bread, broken into pieces
3 Tbsp. extra-virgin coconut oil or butter	• Freshly ground nutmeg
2 lb. fresh mushrooms	• Sea salt or fish sauce and pepper to taste
Butter and extra-virgin olive oil	• Sour cream or creme fraiche
1 quart chicken stock	
½ cup dry white wine	

The mushrooms must be very fresh! Sauté the onions gently in extra-virgin coconut oil or butter until soft. Meanwhile, wash mushrooms (no need to remove stems) and dry well. Cut into quarters. In a heavy cast-iron skillet, sauté the mushrooms in small batches in a mixture of butter and olive oil. Remove with slotted spoon and drain on paper towels. Add sautéed mushrooms, wine, bread, and chicken stock to onions; bring to a boil, and then skim. Reduce heat and simmer about 15 minutes.

Blend soup with a handheld blender. Add nutmeg and season to taste. Ladle into heated soup bowls and serve with cultured cream. **SERVES 6.**

From *Nourishing Traditions* by Sally Fallon. Used by permission.

RED MEAT CHILI

3 lb. coarsely ground beef, buffalo, or game	• 1 Tbsp. ground cumin
Extra-virgin olive oil	• 2 Tbsp. dried oregano
¼ cup red wine	• 2 Tbsp. dried basil
2 cups homemade beef stock	• ¼ to ½ tsp. red chili flakes
2 onions, finely chopped	• 4 cups cooked, soaked kidney beans
2–4 small green chilies, hot or mild, seeded and chopped	• No-oil chips for garnish
2 cans tomatoes, briefly chopped in food processor	• Chopped green onions for garnish
	• Creme fraiche or sour cream for garnish
3 cloves garlic, peeled and mashed	• Avocado slices for garnish
	• Chopped cilantro for garnish

Brown meat until crumbly in a little olive oil in a heavy pot. (Olive oil may not be necessary if the beef contains a lot of fat.) Add remaining ingredients. Simmer about 1 hour. Serve with garnishes. **SERVES 8–12.**

From *Nourishing Traditions* by Sally Fallon. Used by permission.

Salads

EASY VEGETABLE SALAD

1 head romaine, Boston, or red lettuce (or mixed greens)	2 plum tomatoes, seeded and chopped
½ zucchini, quartered	½ red onion, sliced
½ cucumber, quartered	2–3 oz. raw cheddar cheese, grated
	Dressing of your choice

Place enough lettuce to cover the bottom of your salad bowl, then add a layer each of the other items, then another layer of lettuce, repeating until all ingredients are used up. Serve the dressing on the side, or mix into the entire salad and serve. **SERVES 4.**

From *The Lazy Person's Whole Food Cookbook* by Stephen Byrnes. Used by permission.

UPTOWN SALAD

Romaine, Boston, red lettuce, or mixed greens	½ red onion, sliced
4 oz. turkey breast or roast beef	½ avocado, sliced
½ red pepper	2–3 oz. Gorgonzola cheese, grated
½ cucumber, quartered	Dressing of your choice
1 tomato, sliced	

SERVES 1.

By Brian Upton. Used by permission.

ITALIAN SALAD

1 head romaine	1 small red onion, finely sliced
1 bunch watercress	½ cup small seed sprouts
1 red pepper, seeded and cut into a julienne	2 carrots, peeled and grated
1 cucumber, peeled, seeded, quartered lengthwise, and finely sliced	1 cup red cabbage, finely shredded
1 heart of celery with leaves, finely chopped	1 cup cooked chickpeas
	¾ cup Basic Salad Dressing (page 237) or garlic dressing

This is a good, basic salad. Children love it. The secret is to cut everything up small. Remove the outer leaves of the romaine, slice off the end, and open up to rinse out any dirt or impurities, while keeping the head intact. Pat dry. Slice across at ½-inch intervals. Place romaine in your salad bowl, then watercress, then add chopped vegetables in different piles. Finally strew sprouts and garbanzo beans over the top for an attractive presentation. Bring to the table to show off your creation before tossing with dressing. May be served with grated Parmesan cheese. **SERVES 6.**

VARIATION: MEXICAN SALAD

Use Mexican dressing rather than Basic Salad Dressing or garlic dressing. Omit chickpeas. Top with a sprinkle of pepitas, or thin strips of sprouted wheat tortillas, sautéed in olive oil until crisp.

From *Nourishing Traditions* by Sally Fallon. Used by permission.

ORIENTAL RED MEAT SALAD

1½ lb. beef flank steak, or similar cut from lamb or game	1 tsp. grated fresh ginger
½ cup lemon juice	Pinch of red pepper flakes
6 Tbsp. soy sauce	2 Tbsp. toasted sesame seeds
2 Tbsp. extra-virgin olive oil or expeller-expressed peanut oil	½ lb. snow peas, steamed lightly and cut into quarters at an angle
1 Tbsp. toasted sesame oil	1 pound bean sprouts, steamed lightly
	1 red pepper, seeded and cut into a julienne

Using a sharp knife, score the flank steak or red meat pieces across the grain on both sides. Broil 3 or 4 minutes to a side, or until meat is medium rare. Transfer to a cutting board and let stand for 10 minutes. Meanwhile, mix lemon juice, soy sauce, oils, ginger, and red pepper flakes together. Cut the meat across the grain on an angle into very thin slices, then cut these slices into a julienne. Marinate with soy sauce mixture for several hours in refrigerator. Mix with sesame seeds and vegetables just before serving. **SERVES 6.**

From *Nourishing Traditions* by Sally Fallon. Used by permission.

SALADE NICOISE

6 portions fresh tuna steak, about 4 ounces each	1 lb. French beans, blanched for 8 minutes and rinsed under cold water
Extra-virgin olive oil	2 dozen small black olives
6 cups baby salad greens or frise lettuce	2 cups herb dressing, made with finely chopped parsley
6 small ripe tomatoes, cut into wedges	
6 small red potatoes, cooked in a clay pot	

Brush tuna steaks with olive oil, and season with sea salt and pepper. Using a heavy skillet, cook rapidly, two at a time, for about 4 minutes per side. Set aside.

Divide salad greens between 6 large plates. Garnish with tomatoes, potatoes, beans, and olives. Place steaks on top of greens. Add dressing. This is delicious with sourdough bread or pizza toasts. **SERVES 6.**

From *Nourishing Traditions* by Sally Fallon. Used by permission.

TUNA TAHINI SALAD

2 large cans water-packed tuna, drained and flaked	Melted butter and extra-virgin olive oil
¼ tsp. cayenne pepper	⅓ cup toasted pine nuts
2 cups tahini sauce (see below)	Cilantro sprigs for garnish
4 medium onions, thinly sliced	Toasted, sprouted, or sourdough bread or sprouted crackers

Mix tuna with cayenne pepper and 1 cup sauce. Meanwhile, strew the onions on an oiled cookie sheet; brush with mixture of melted butter and olive oil, and bake at 375 degrees until crisp. Mound tuna on a platter. Scatter onions and pine nuts on top. Garnish with cilantro, and serve with dehydrated, sprouted, whole-grain crackers and remaining sauce. **SERVES 6–8.**

From *Nourishing Traditions* by Sally Fallon. Used by permission.

TAHINI SAUCE

2 cloves garlic, peeled and coarsely chopped	1 Tbsp. unrefined flaxseed oil
1 tsp. sea salt	1 cup water
½ cup tahini	½ cup fresh lemon juice

Place garlic in food processor with salt. Blend until minced. Add tahini and flaxseed oil and blend. Using attachment that allows addition of liquids drop by drop and with motor running, add water. When completely blended, add lemon juice all at once and blend until smooth. Sauce should be the consistency of heavy cream. If too thick, add more water and lemon juice. **MAKES 2 CUPS.**

From *Nourishing Traditions* by Sally Fallon. Used by permission.

Vegetables

General preparation guidelines: Do not boil vegetables unless this is required to eat them. Steam your veggies for a few minutes, then add butter or ghee, seasonings, and serve. You can also sauté your vegetables in extra-virgin coconut oil. Raw veggies with a healthy dressing or dip are also good.

EASY SAUTÉED GREENS

1 quart spinach or other greens	Sea salt/pepper to taste
Extra-virgin coconut oil	

Wash the spinach or greens in several waters. Remove all stems and brown leaves. Heat extra-virgin coconut oil in skillet. Place leaves in the skillet and cover. Cook till wilted, stirring occasionally. Season as you like. **SERVES 6–8.**

From *The Lazy Person's Whole Food Cookbook* by Stephen Byrnes. Used by permission.

Cultured Vegetables

GINGER CARROTS

4 cups grated carrots, loosely packed	2 Tbsp. whey (if not available, add an additional
1 Tbsp. fresh ginger, grated	1 tsp. salt)
2 tsp. sea salt	

This is the best introduction to lacto-fermented vegetables we know. The taste is delicious, and the sweetness of the carrots neutralizes the acidity that some people find disagreeable when first introduced to lacto-fermented vegetables. Ginger carrots go well with fish and with highly spiced meats.

In a bowl, mix all ingredients and pound with wooden pounder to release juices. Place in a quart-sized, wide-mouth Mason jar and press down with the wooden pounder. There should be about an inch of space between the top of carrots and the top of the jar. Cover tightly. Leave at room temperature about 2–3 days before transferring to cold storage. **MAKES 1 QUART.**

From *Nourishing Traditions* by Sally Fallon. Used by permission.

RAW SAUERKRAUT

4 cups shredded cabbage, loosely packed	2 tsp. Celtic sea salt
½ tsp. cumin seeds	2 Tbsp. homemade whey
½ tsp. mustard seeds	1 cup filtered water

In a bowl, mix cabbage with cumin and mustard seeds. Mash or pound with a wooden pounder for several minutes to release juices. Place in a quart-sized, wide-mouthed Mason jar and pack down with the pounder. Mix water with sea salt and whey, and pour into jar. Add more water if needed to bring liquid to top of cabbage. There should be about one inch of space between the top of cabbage and the top of the jar. Cover tightly, and keep at room temperature for about 3 days. Transfer to cold storage. The sauerkraut can be eaten immediately, but it improves with age. **MAKES 1 QUART.**

From *Nourishing Traditions* by Sally Fallon. Used by permission.

Sauces, Dressings, Dips

BASIC SALAD DRESSING

½ cup extra-virgin olive oil	1 tsp. Dijon-type mustard
1 Tbsp. unrefined flaxseed oil	Herbamare seasoning to taste
2 Tbsp. apple cider vinegar or lemon juice	

Combine all ingredients and blend slowly. **MAKES ABOUT ¾ CUP.**

Adapted from *Nourishing Traditions* by Sally Fallon. Used by permission.

BALSAMIC DRESSING

1 tsp. Dijon-type dressing, smooth or grainy	½ cup extra-virgin olive oil
2 Tbsp. plus 1 tsp. balsamic vinegar	1 Tbsp. unrefined flaxseed oil

Balsamic vinegar is a red wine vinegar that has been aged in wooden casks. It has a delicious, pungent flavor that goes well with dark greens such as watercress or mache. Prepare as in Basic Salad Dressing recipe. **MAKES ABOUT ¾ CUP.**

From *Nourishing Traditions* by Sally Fallon. Used by permission.

BARBECUE SAUCE

¾ cup teriyaki sauce	¾ cup naturally sweetened ketchup

Mix ketchup into teriyaki sauce with a whisk. **MAKES 1½ CUPS.**

From *Nourishing Traditions* by Sally Fallon. Used by permission.

BETTER BUTTER

½ cup raw or organic butter (unsalted)	½ cup flaxseed or hempseed oil
½ cup extra-virgin coconut oil	¼ tsp. fine Celtic sea salt

Allow butter and coconut oil to soften at room temperature. Combine with flaxseed or hempseed oil, and add salt. Refrigerate and use as a spread. Note: Never use Better Butter for cooking. The essential fatty acids contained in the oil will be damaged by the heat. **MAKES 1½ CUPS.**

By Jordan Rubin

CREAMY AVOCADO DIP

1 ripe avocado, peeled and cut into pieces	Juice of 1 lemon
3 anchovy fillets (optional)	2 tsp. unrefined flaxseed oil
½ cup sour cream or creme fraiche	1 clove garlic, mashed

Place all ingredients in food processor and blend until smooth. Chill well before serving. Serve with vegetable sticks or baked tortillas, broken into chips. **MAKES 1½ CUPS.**

From *Nourishing Traditions* by Sally Fallon. Used by permission.

CREAMY DRESSING

¾ cup Basic Salad Dressing (page 237)	• ¼ cup sour cream, yogurt, or kefir

This is a traditional recipe of the Auvergne region of France. Prepare Basic Salad Dressing. Blend in cream with a fork. **MAKES ABOUT 1 CUP.**

From *Nourishing Traditions* by Sally Fallon. Used by permission.

EASY AVOCADO DRESSING

1 ripe avocado	• 2 Tbsp. extra-virgin olive oil
1 stalk of celery	• Herbamare seasoning to taste
1 small red pepper, seeded	•

Blend avocado together with oil, celery, and pepper slices in blender until smooth.

From *The Lazy Person's Whole Food Cookbook* by Stephen Byrnes. Used by permission.

EASY FRENCH DRESSING

½ cup high-oleic safflower, sunflower, or	• ¼ tsp. Herbamare seasoning
walnut oil (*Substitute extra-virgin olive oil)	• ¼ tsp. paprika
4 Tbsp. raw apple cider vinegar or lemon juice	• Few grains of cayenne pepper
2 tsp. raw, unheated honey	•

Combine dry ingredients and apple cider vinegar or lemon juice. Add oil slowly, beating constantly until thick.

From *The Lazy Person's Whole Food Cookbook* by Stephen Byrnes. Used by permission.

GUACAMOLE

2 ripe avocados	• 2 Tbsp. cilantro, finely chopped (optional)
Juice of 1 lemon	• Pinch Celtic sea salt or Herbamare

Peel avocados. Place flesh in a bowl and squeeze lemon juice over it. Use a fork to mash (do not use a food processor). Guacamole should be slightly lumpy. Stir in the cilantro. Guacamole should be made just before serving as it will turn dark in an hour or two. Serve with vegetable sticks or baked tortillas, broken into chips. **MAKES 1½ CUPS.**

From *Nourishing Traditions* by Sally Fallon. Used by permission.

HERB DRESSING

¾ cup Basic Salad Dressing (page 237)	• 1 tsp. very finely chopped fresh herbs such as
	parsley, tarragon, thyme, basil, or oregano

Prepare Basic Salad Dressing and stir in herbs. **MAKES ABOUT ¾ CUP.**

From *Nourishing Traditions* by Sally Fallon. Used by permission.

ORIENTAL DRESSING

2 Tbsp. rice vinegar	• 1 clove garlic, peeled and mashed (optional)
1 Tbsp. soy sauce	• ½ tsp. raw honey
1 tsp. grated ginger	• ½ cup extra-virgin olive oil
1 tsp. toasted sesame oil	• 1 tsp. unrefined flaxseed oil
1 tsp. finely chopped green onion or chives	•

Place all ingredients in a jar and shake vigorously. **MAKES ABOUT ½ CUP.**

From *Nourishing Traditions* by Sally Fallon. Used by permission.

SALSA

4 medium tomatoes, peeled, seeded, and diced	Juice of 2 lemons
2 small onions, finely diced	2 tsp. Celtic sea salt
¼ cup diced chili pepper, hot or mild	2 Tbsp. whey (if not available, use an additional
1 bunch cilantro, chopped	1 tsp. salt)
1 tsp. dried oregano	½–1 cup filtered water

Mix all ingredients except water, and place in a quart-sized, wide-mouth Mason jar. Press down lightly with a wooden pounder. Add enough water to cover vegetables. Cover tightly and keep at room temperature for 2 days before transferring to cold storage. **MAKES 1 QUART.**

From *Nourishing Traditions* by Sally Fallon. Used by permission.

TERIYAKI SAUCE

1 Tbsp. grated fresh ginger	1 Tbsp. rice vinegar
3 garlic cloves, mashed	1 Tbsp. raw honey
1 Tbsp. toasted sesame oil	½ cup soy sauce

Use as a marinade for chicken or duck. Mix all ingredients together with a whisk. **MAKES ¾ CUP.**

From *Nourishing Traditions* by Sally Fallon. Used by permission.

YOGURT TAHINI INBETWEENI

4 oz. Probiogurt	Juice of one freshly squeezed lemon
1 Tbsp. Dijon-style mustard	1 Tbsp. raw tahini (sesame butter)
1 Tbsp. yellow or brown mustard	½ tsp. of fine Celtic sea salt

Combine all ingredients together and mix thoroughly.

By Jason Dewberry. Used by permission.

Eggs

EASY SCRAMBLED EGGS

6 eggs	3 Tbsp. melted butter or extra virgin coconut oil
Celtic sea salt, pepper	Few grains of cayenne pepper (optional)
¼ cup heavy cream	

Beat eggs well. Add cream. Heat butter in skillet or pan; add egg mixture, cooking slowly, until of a creamy texture. If desired, 1 cup of chopped turkey bacon, chicken, beef, or peppers may be added for variations in taste. **SERVES 3–4.**

From *The Lazy Person's Whole Food Cookbook* by Stephen Byrnes. Used by permission.

EASY SOFT-BOILED/HARD-BOILED EGGS

Wash eggs and cover with boiling water. Simmer for 4 minutes if you're making soft-boiled eggs, and 12 minutes if you're making hard-boiled eggs. Hard-boiled eggs may be plunged into cold water if you will be using them in another recipe, such as sliced additions or garnishes. Hard-boiled eggs may also be made several at a time and then refrigerated for convenient snacking later.

From *The Lazy Person's Whole Food Cookbook* by Stephen Byrnes. Used by permission.

BASIC OMELET

4 fresh eggs, at room temperature	Pinch sea salt
3 Tbsp. extra-virgin coconut oil or butter	

Crack eggs into a bowl. Add water and sea salt, and blend with a wire whisk. (Do not over-whisk or the omelet will be tough). Melt coconut oil or butter in a well-seasoned cast iron skillet or frying pan. When foam subsides, add egg mixture. Tip pan to allow egg to cover the entire pan. Cook several minutes over medium heat until underside is lightly browned. Lift up one side with a spatula and fold omelet in half. Reduce heat and cook another 30 seconds or so—this will allow the egg on the inside to cook. Slide omelet onto a heated platter and serve. **SERVES 2.**

VARIATION: ONION, PEPPER, AND GOAT CHEESE OMELET
Sauté 1 small onion, thinly sliced, and ½ red pepper, cut into julienne strips, in a little extra-virgin coconut oil or butter until tender. Strew this evenly over the egg mixture as it begins to cook, along with 2 ounces of goat's milk cheddar or feta cheese.

VARIATION: GARDEN HERB OMELET
Scatter 1 tablespoon parsley, finely chopped, 1 tablespoon chives, finely chopped, and 1 tablespoon thyme or other garden herb, finely chopped, over omelet as it begins to cook.

VARIATION: MUSHROOM SWISS OMELET
Sauté ½ pound fresh mushrooms, washed, well dried, and thinly sliced, in extra-virgin coconut oil or butter and olive oil. Scatter mushrooms and grated Swiss cheese over the omelet as it begins to cook.

VARIATION: SAUSAGE AND PEPPER OMELET
Sauté ¼ cup turkey or buffalo sausage and red or yellow peppers in a little extra-virgin coconut oil or butter until crumbly. Scatter over the omelet as it begins to cook.

VARIATION: SPINACH AND FETA OMELET
Add chopped onion to beaten eggs. Add more onions, spinach, tomatoes, and feta cheese as it begins to cook.

VARIATION: TOMATO BASIL OMELET
Scatter ¼ cup diced tomato and chopped fresh basil over omelet as it begins to cook.

From *Nourishing Traditions* by Sally Fallon. Used by permission.

VEGETABLE FRITTATA

1 cup broccoli flowerets, steamed until tender and broken into small pieces	⅓ cup sour cream or creme fraiche
	1 tsp. finely grated lemon rind
1 red pepper; seeded and cut into a julienne	Pinch dried oregano
1 medium onion, peeled and finely chopped	Pinch dried rosemary
Butter and extra-virgin olive oil	Sea salt and freshly ground pepper
6 eggs	1 cup grated raw Monterey jack cheese

In a cast iron skillet, sauté the pepper and onion in butter and olive oil until soft. Remove with a slotted spoon. Beat eggs with cream and seasonings. Stir in broccoli, peppers, and onion. Melt more butter and olive oil in the pan and pour in egg mixture. Cook over medium heat about 5 minutes until underside is golden. Sprinkle cheese on top and place under the broiler for a few minutes until the frittata puffs and browns. Cut into wedges and serve.
SERVES 4.

From *Nourishing Traditions* by Sally Fallon. Used by permission. For variations of this recipe, order a copy of *Nourishing Traditions*. (See Appendix B.)

FISH

SIMPLE BAKED FISH

1½ lb. filet of white fish such as sole, whiting, or turbot	1 Tbsp. fish sauce (optional)
	Dash cayenne pepper
Juice of 1 lemon	1 Tbsp. snipped fresh herbs

Place fish in buttered baking dish. Sprinkle with lemon juice, cayenne, fish sauce, herbs, and salt. Cover baking dish with foil (but don't let foil touch the fish). Bake at 300 degrees for about 15 minutes. **SERVES 4.**

From *Nourishing Traditions* by Sally Fallon. Used by permission.

EASY BROILED HALIBUT

1–2 lb. halibut	Sea salt or Herbamare
Lemon juice	Pepper
Butter or extra-virgin coconut oil	

Wipe halibut slices with damp cloth and sprinkle with salt, pepper, and lemon juice. Dot with oil or butter. Broil under high heat, turning frequently till brown. **SERVES 6–8.**

From *The Lazy Person's Whole Food Cookbook* by Stephen Byrnes. Used by permission.

EASY SMOTHERED SALMON

2 cups canned salmon	2 Tbsp. melted extra-virgin coconut oil or butter
¾ cup diced celery	¾ cup onion, chopped
2 slices turkey bacon, chopped	1 tsp. sea salt
½ cup boiling water	2 thin slices lemon (optional)

Combine oil or butter, turkey bacon, celery, onion, and salt; fry until light brown. Place salmon in center of greased baking pan. Arrange vegetables and turkey bacon around salmon. Add water and cover. Bake at 375 degrees for 30 minutes. Remove cover and cook another 10 minutes. **SERVES 6.**

From *The Lazy Person's Whole Food Cookbook* by Stephen Byrnes. Used by permission. For more salmon recipes, order a copy of this cookbook.

SALMON SALAD

1 can water-packed salmon	Chopped onions
1 Tbsp. omega-3 mayonnaise	Chopped peppers
1 Tbsp. flaxseed oil or garlic-chili flax	Chopped celery

Combine all ingredients and serve over lettuce or toasted sprouted bread. **SERVES 1–2.**

By Jordan Rubin

WILD ALASKAN SALMON WITH PECAN PESTO

4 wild Alaskan salmon fillets (about 1.25–1.5 lb.)	• 1 3-inch sprig of rosemary
	• Olive oil
⅓ lb. shelled pecans	• Celtic sea salt
3 oz. butter, cold	• Pepper
2–3 fresh jalapeños	•
1 small lemon or orange	•

Heat oven to 300 degrees and toast pecans on a cookie sheet until you can smell the aroma of toasted pecans, about 20–30 minutes. Transfer to a cool cookie sheet. Rinse salmon and pat dry. Butterfly fillets with a sharp knife if desired. Rub salmon with olive oil; salt and pepper both sides. Heat iron skillet or other heavy skillet over medium heat. Sauté fillets until firm to the touch.

Prepare jalapeños by removing the tops and splitting lengthwise. De-rib and remove the seeds with a sharp knife. Chop coarsely. Cut the cold butter into ½ Tbsp. pats. Prepare the zest of ½ small lemon (or orange) and chop finely. Chop the rosemary into very fine pieces. Add the butter, chopped jalapeños, pecans, rosemary, and lemon zest to a food processor. Process for 5–8 seconds and scrape the bowl. Repeat 2–3 times until a paste has formed. Do not overprocess. Spread the pesto over the cooked salmon. **SERVES 4.**

By Keith Tindall from White Egret Farm. Used by permission.

FILLET OF SOLE WITH GREEN GRAPES

1 lb. sole or flounder fillets	• ¾ cup white wine
Celtic sea salt	• ¼ lb. seedless green grapes
1 Tbsp. lime juice	• 1 ½ Tbsp. butter
1 tsp. parsley, finely minced	• 1 Tbsp. whole-grain flour (soaked)
½ tsp. tarragon, finely minced	• 2 Tbsp. orange juice
½ clove garlic, minced	•

Rinse the fillets and pat dry. Sprinkle fillets with salt and lime juice. Place in a lightly greased skillet. Sprinkle the fillets with the parsley, tarragon, and garlic. Add the wine and simmer for 12–15 minutes until the fish flake easily and look milky white but not transparent. Add the grapes the last 5 minutes. Remove fish from the heat and keep warm on a platter. In the original skillet, melt the butter with the remaining juices. Blend in the flour until smooth. Add the orange juice and cook, stirring until the mixture thickens. Add more wine to adjust the consistency. Pour this sauce over the fillets. **SERVES 3–4.**

By Keith Tindall from White Egret Farm. Used by permission.

RED SNAPPER MEXICAN STYLE

4 red snapper fillets	• 1 bunch cilantro, chopped
2 Tbsp. lime juice	• 1 tsp. fresh chili pepper, diced
Extra-virgin olive oil	• 2 cloves garlic, peeled and mashed
1 medium onion, thinly sliced	• Pinch of cinnamon
2 ripe tomatoes, peeled, seeded, and chopped	• Sea salt

Rub fillets with lime juice; let stand, covered, in refrigerator for several hours.

Using a heavy skillet, sauté the fillets in a little olive oil briefly, on both sides. Transfer to an oiled Pyrex baking dish. Add more olive oil to the skillet. Sauté onion until soft. Add remaining ingredients and simmer for about 30 minutes or more until most of liquid is absorbed. Season to taste with sea salt. Strew the sauce over fish and bake at 350 degrees until tender, about 25 minutes. **SERVES 4.**

From *Nourishing Traditions* by Sally Fallon. Used by permission.

TUNA STEAKS, ORIENTAL STYLE

2 lb. tuna steak, about 1 inch thick	1 Tbsp. raw, unheated honey
Extra-virgin olive oil	½ cup rice vinegar
Sea salt and freshly ground pepper	2 Tbsp. fish sauce (optional)
3 cloves garlic, peeled	1 Tbsp. toasted sesame oil
¼ cup fresh ginger, peeled and coarsely chopped	⅓ cup extra-virgin coconut oil
	1 bunch green onions, chopped
2 Tbsp. Dijon-type mustard	3 Tbsp. sesame seeds, toasted in oven
¼ cup soy sauce	

Brush tuna steaks with coconut oil and sprinkle with salt and pepper. Grill about 5 minutes per side on a barbecue or under a broiler. Transfer to a heated platter and keep warm until ready to serve. Meanwhile, place garlic, ginger, mustard, fish sauce, and soy sauce in food processor; process until blended. Add honey and vinegar and process again. With motor running, add oil gradually so that sauce emulsifies and becomes thick.

Place tuna steak servings on warmed plates. Spoon sauce over and garnish with green onions and sesame seeds. This dish goes well with spinach, chard, Chinese peas, or steamed Chinese cabbage. **SERVES 6.**

From *Nourishing Traditions* by Sally Fallon. Used by permission. For more tuna recipes, order a copy of *Nourishing Traditions*. (See Appendix B.)

TUNA SALAD

1 can water-packed tuna	Chopped onions
1 Tbsp. omega-3 mayonnaise	Chopped peppers
1 Tbsp. flaxseed oil or garlic-chili flax	Chopped celery

Combine all ingredients and serve over lettuce or on toasted sprouted bread. **SERVES 1–2.**

By Jordan Rubin

Fowl

CHICKEN SALAD

6 oz. chopped chicken	Chopped onions
1 Tbsp. omega-3 mayonnaise	Chopped peppers
1 Tbsp. flaxseed oil or garlic-chili flax	Chopped celery

Combine all ingredients and serve over lettuce or on toasted sprouted bread. **SERVES 1–2.**

By Jordan Rubin

CHICKEN WITH OREGANO AND MUSHROOMS

1 broiler, cut in pieces (pasture fed)	1 clove garlic, minced
¼ cup olive oil	2 tomatoes, peeled and quartered
½ cup onion, chopped	½ cup dry white wine
1 tsp. salt	8 oz. fresh mushrooms, sliced
⅛ tsp. pepper	¼ cup parsley, chopped for garnish
¼ tsp. oregano, dried, or ½ tsp. fresh oregano, finely chopped	

Brown the chicken pieces slowly in hot olive oil. Add onion, and cook until soft. Drain the oil, and season chicken with salt and pepper. Add oregano, garlic, wine, and mushrooms. Scrape the bottom of the pan to loosen browned bits. Cover and cook over low heat until the chicken is tender, about 35 minutes. Add tomatoes. Continue cooking for 5 more minutes. Garnish with parsley. **SERVES 4.**

By Keith Tindall from White Egret Farm. Used by permission.

CILANTRO LIME CHICKEN CACCIATORE

2 lb. chicken breast sliced into 1-oz. cubes	• 2 Tbsp. extra-virgin olive oil
1 Tbsp. minced garlic	• 5 medium-sized Roma tomatoes
½ cup freshly squeezed lime juice	• Celtic sea salt to taste
3 Tbsp. chopped cilantro	• Cayenne pepper to taste

Heat sauté pan to medium. Add olive oil, garlic, cilantro, and ¼ cup of lime juice. Simmer for 4–6 minutes. While simmering, pour ¼ cup of lime juice over chicken; let stand for 1–2 minutes. Season chicken with salt and cayenne pepper. After 4–6 minutes, add seasoned chicken to the pan and cook for 8–10 minutes over medium to medium-high heat. **SERVES 4.**

By Jason Dewberry. Used by permission.

EASY CURRIED CHICKEN

2 cups diced cooked chicken	• 1 Tbsp. curry powder
2 cups coconut milk/cream	• 1 tsp. chopped onion
4 Tbsp. butter	• ½ cup lemon juice
3 Tbsp. whole-grain flour (soaked)	• Sea salt and pepper to taste

Melt butter, then add flour and curry powder; cook for 5 minutes. Pour in coconut milk/cream and stir well until boiling. Add the onion, then put in the chicken seasonings and heat. Add lemon juice when ready to serve. Goes great with brown rice and vegetables. **SERVES 6.**

From *The Lazy Person's Whole Food Cookbook* by Stephen Byrnes. Used by permission. For more chicken recipes, order a copy of this cookbook (www.powerhealth.net).

CHICKEN FAJITAS

2 lb. chicken breast cut into strips, about ¼ to ½ inch thick	• 1 green pepper, seeded and cut into julienne strips
6 Tbsp. extra-virgin olive oil	• 2 medium onions, thinly sliced
½ cup lemon or lime juice	• Extra-virgin olive oil
¼ cup pineapple juice (optional)	• 12 sprouted whole-wheat tortillas
4 garlic cloves, peeled and mashed	• Melted butter
½ tsp. chili powder	• Crème fraiche or sour cream for garnish
1 tsp. dried oregano	• Chismole for garnish
½ tsp. dried thyme	• Guacamole for garnish
1 red pepper, seeded and cut into julienne strips	•

Make a mixture of oil, lemon or lime juice, pineapple juice, and spices; mix well with the meat. Marinate for several hours. Remove with a slotted spoon to paper towels and pat dry. Using a heavy skillet, sauté the meat, a batch at a time, in olive oil, transferring to a heated platter and keeping warm in the oven. Meanwhile, mix vegetables in marinade. Sauté vegetables in batches in olive oil and strew over meat. Heat tortillas briefly in a heavy cast-iron skillet and brush with melted butter. Serve meat mixture with tortillas and garnishes. **SERVES 4–6.**

From *Nourishing Traditions* by Sally Fallon. Used by permission. For more chicken recipes, order a copy of this cookbook.

SPICY CHICKEN STUFFED PEPPERS

2 free-range chicken breasts	• ½ cup sharp cheddar cheese, shredded
2 Tbsp. stick of butter	• 2–4 red or yellow bell peppers (either whole
1 cup organic brown rice	• or halves)
½ cup diced jalapeños (optional)	• 1 slice sprouted or sourdough whole-grain
2 cups or cans organic black beans	• bread
2 Tbsp. soy sauce	•

Bake chicken breasts at 450 degrees for 30 minutes. After 15 minutes of cooking, baste with butter. Bring 2½ cups of water and 1 cup of brown rice to a boil (if brown rice was soaked overnight, add additional water to make approximately 2½ cups). Stir once, and then let simmer for 45 minutes. Add diced jalapeño peppers and shredded cheese to black beans; and cook on low heat. Add soy sauce to bean mixture, stirring occasionally. Take chicken out of oven and slice. Add to the bean mixture and simmer for 15 minutes. Mix brown rice into bean mixture and chicken and mix well. Cut the tops off of the peppers or cut in halves; place desired amount of stuffing into them. Slice the bread and place on top of stuffed peppers. Bake in oven at 450 degrees for 15 minutes. Serve warm. **SERVES 2–4.**
By Sherry Dewberry. Used by permission.

ROASTED PASTURED CHICKEN

1 pastured chicken, whole, 4–5 lb. (a broiler)	• 1 3-inch sprig rosemary
1 apple, small	• Olive oil
1 onion, small	• Celtic sea salt
1 stalk celery, plus leaves	• Pepper, freshly ground

Rinse and drain the chicken. If you are starting with a frozen chicken, be certain it is completely thawed. Preheat the oven to 350 degrees. Quarter and core the apple. Peel and quarter onion. Slice celery into 2- to 3-inch pieces. Add about 2 Tbsp. olive oil to the cavity of the bird. Stuff bird with apple, celery, onion, and rosemary. Rub the outside of the bird with olive oil. Sprinkle bird with salt and freshly ground pepper, and rub them into the skin. Place chicken in a baking dish with 2" sides. Bake approximately 1½ hours or until a meat thermometer reads 180 degrees when pushed into the thigh. Remove the chicken from the oven and allow to rest for approximately 20 minutes before carving. The rest period allows the juices to redistribute and results in more tender meat. **SERVES 4.**
By Keith Tindall from White Egret Farm. Used by permission.

WILD DUCK

4–6 ducks, preferably wild, or 2 domestic ducks	• 4–6 sprigs of celery leaves
may be used	• 4–6 pats of extra-virgin coconut butter
1 small onion	• 1–2 cups dry wine, such as a Chardonnay
1 apple, small to medium in size	•

Preheat the oven to 325 degrees. Rinse and drain the ducks. Quarter the apple and onion and cut each quarter into thirds. Place one pat of butter into the cavity of each duck. Add a sprig of celery leaves, and then one or two of the apple and onion slices to fill the cavity. Place the stuffed duck breast down on a large piece of foil (the size of a cookie sheet for a small wild duck). Fold the foil to make a tight packet, leaving one end open. Add ¼ to ½ cup wine to the packet, depending on the size of the duck. Close the packet. Place each packet in the Dutch oven (breast down). Cover with the lid and place into the preheated oven. The ducks should bake for 2–3 hours depending on size. DO NOT open the lid or the packets until done. The ducks are done when they feel soft. The ducks must steam inside the packets in an airtight pan to become tender. Opening the lid or the packets will allow the steam to escape. For ideal results, ducks must bake long and slow under relatively low heat. **SERVES 4.**
By Keith Tindall from White Egret Farm. Used by permission.

Red Meat and Game

ALL-DAY BEEF STEW

3 lb. stew beef, cut into 1-inch pieces
1 cup red wine
3–4 cups beef stock
4 tomatoes, peeled, seeded, and chopped (or 1 can tomatoes)
2 Tbsp. tomato puree
½ tsp. black peppercorns

- Several sprigs fresh thyme, tied together
- 2 cloves garlic, peeled and crushed
- 2–3 small pieces orange peel
- 8 small red potatoes
- 1 pound carrots, peeled and cut into sticks
- Celtic sea salt and freshly ground pepper

This recipe is ideal for working mothers. The ingredients can be assembled in about 15 minutes in the morning—or even the night before. Marinate meat in red wine overnight. (This step is optional.) Place all ingredients except potatoes and carrots in an oven-proof casserole, and cook at 250 degrees for 12 hours. Add carrots and potatoes during the last hour. Season to taste. **SERVES 6–8.**

From *Nourishing Traditions* by Sally Fallon. Used by permission.

CHEVON MEAT LOAF

1 lb. ground chevon (goat, preferably grass fed)
1 lb. ground beef (preferably grass fed)
½ onion, finely chopped
1 small green pepper, finely chopped
⅔ cup bread crumbs (from sprouted or sour dough whole-grain bread)

- 2 eggs
- 1 tsp. ground thyme
- ¼ tsp. Celtic sea salt
- ⅛ tsp. black pepper
- 1 cup tomato ketchup

Preheat oven to 325 degrees. Add all the ingredients to a large bowl. Mix with your hands until all the ingredients are thoroughly combined. The mixture should feel slightly sticky. Add the mixture to a baking pan with 2-inch sides, and form it into a loaf. Make an indentation longitudinally along the top of the loaf. Fill this with additional tomato ketchup. Bake at 325 degrees for approximately 1¼ hours until the loaf appears slightly brown on top. Test for doneness by checking for an internal temperature of 160 degrees. Allow the loaf to rest before slicing in order to avoid crumbling. **SERVES 4–6.**

By Keith Tindall from White Egret Farm. Used by permission.

EASY BROILED STEAK

1 sirloin or porterhouse steak

- Butter

Broil steak under hot flame or in hot frying pan, turning frequently, until well browned. Place on serving dish and season as you like. You may add a pat of butter on top of the steak before serving. **SERVES 1.**

From *The Lazy Person's Whole Food Cookbook* by Stephen Byrnes. Used by permission.

EASY LAMB STEW

1½ lb. lamb stew meat
1½ cups diced carrots
1 cup diced celery
¼ cup canned tomatoes

- 1½ cups diced potatoes
- ¼ cup chopped onion
- 1 tsp. Celtic sea salt

Brown the lamb in extra-virgin coconut oil. Cover with water and add salt. Simmer until meat is tender. Add vegetables and cover. Simmer for 30 minutes or until vegetables are cooked.

This recipe can be made in a Crock-Pot and left to cook for the whole day. Simply add all your ingredients to the pot, cover, and switch on. **SERVES 6.**

From *The Lazy Person's Whole Food Cookbook* by Stephen Byrnes. Used by permission.

LAMB CHOPS

8 lamb chops	½ cup dry red wine
Freshly ground pepper	2–3 cups beef or lamb stock

You will need a very well-seasoned cast-iron skillet for this recipe. Season the lamb chops with pepper and cut off any excess fat. Place the skillet over a moderately high fire. When it is hot, set four chops in the pan. (No fat is required. The lamb chops will render their own fat, enough to keep the chops from sticking.) Cook about 5 minutes until they are rare or medium rare. Keep in a warm oven while you are cooking the second batch and preparing the sauce.

Pour the grease out of the pan and deglaze with the red wine and the beef stock. Boil rapidly, skimming off any dirty foam that rises to the top. Reduce to about ¾ cup. The sauce should be consistency of maple syrup.

Place the lamb chops on heated plates, with their accompanying vegetables, and spoon on the sauce. **SERVES 4.**

From *Nourishing Traditions* by Sally Fallon. Used by permission.

LEG OF LAMB OR CHEVON

1 6–8 lb. leg of lamb or chevon (goat), pasture fed preferred	1 clove garlic, slivered
½ cup Dijon mustard	1-inch piece of ginger, skinned and minced
1 Tbsp. rosemary, fresh and finely minced	2 Tbsp. olive oil

Preheat the oven to 350 degrees. Blend mustard, soy sauce, herbs, and ginger in a bowl. Beat in oil to make a creamy mixture. Make 4 shallow slashes in the meat with a sharp knife; tuck a sliver of garlic into each. Brush the lamb or goat liberally with the sauce and let stand for 1–2 hours. Roast on a rack for 1 ¼ to 1 ½ hours, or until a meat thermometer reads 150 degrees. This will produce a medium degree of doneness. Allow to rest before carving. The temperature will climb to about 160 degrees as the meat rests. **SERVES 4–6.**

By Keith Tindall from White Egret Farm. Used by permission.

EASY PEPPER STEAK

4 equal-sized pieces of steak (sirloin or top round), about 1 inch thick	1 large red onion, chopped into 4 slices
1 egg, beaten and diluted with a little water	Olive oil
1 red or yellow pepper, seeded and chopped into 4 slices	Sea salt and pepper to taste
	Soy sauce

Place steak in a large bowl and add the egg. Sprinkle with salt and pepper and let sit for 15 minutes. Match up the onion and pepper slices. In a shallow baking pan, place enough olive oil to cover the bottom. Place the four steaks in the pan and sprinkle a little soy sauce on top of each. Then place one onion and pepper slice on each. Place under the broiler for 3–4 minutes. When you turn the steaks, be sure to replace the pepper and onion slices back on the tops of the steaks. Cook for another 3–4 minutes. **SERVES 4.**

From *The Lazy Person's Whole Food Cookbook* by Stephen Byrnes. Used by permission.

SIMPLE BEEF BURGUNDY

2 lb. lean beef stew meat in small cubes (preferably from pasture-fed beef)	1 cup burgundy wine
	1 medium onion, chopped
2 Tbsp. whole-grain flour (soaked overnight)	2 carrots, sliced
2 Tbsp. butter	8 oz. Crimini mushrooms, sliced
1 Tbsp. olive oil	1 clove garlic, minced
1 tsp. sea salt or Herbamare	1 bay leaf
¼ tsp. pepper	¼ tsp. ground thyme
2 cups brown beef stock (page 231)	1 Tbsp. parsley, snipped

Toss the meat in the flour, salt, and pepper in a brown paper bag. Remove. Brown in the butter/olive oil combination. Add the beef stock, wine, mushrooms, onion, carrots, garlic, bay leaf, and thyme. Simmer 2½–3 hours, until the meat is tender. Turn the burner off and add the parsley to the hot mixture. If more liquid is needed during cooking, add more stock and wine in proportions of 2 parts stock to 1 part wine. **SERVES 4–6.**

By Keith Tindall from White Egret Farm. Used by permission.

FAMILY ROAST BEEF

4–5 lb. chuck roast, preferably from grass-fed beef	½ cup Worcestershire sauce
	Celtic sea salt
¼ pound butter	Black pepper, freshly ground

Preheat oven to 325 degrees. Rub the roast with salt and pepper and place in a baking dish with 2-inch sides. In a saucepan, melt the butter and add an equal volume of Worcestershire sauce. Pour the sauce over the roast. Bake slowly at 325 degrees until a meat thermometer reads 150–155 degrees (for medium). Remove the roast from the oven and allow it to rest and redistribute the juices before carving. The temperature will climb to 160 degrees. It is particularly important that grass-fed beef be cooked more slowly at a lower temperature than commercial beef. Grass-fed beef should also be allowed to "coast in" to the desired level of doneness by removing it from the oven several minutes before you think it is done. This preserves the juiciness and produces meat that is tenderer.
NOTE: Worcestershire sauce was originally based on lacto-fermented green English walnut catsup (in addition to the fish pastes).

By Keith Tindall from White Egret Farm. Used by permission.

FRENCH-STYLE LONDON BROIL

1 or 2 flank steaks (preferably from pasture-fed beef)	2 Tbsp. onion, minced
	1 clove garlic, minced
½ cup olive oil	1½ tsp. salt
½ cup burgundy wine	5 drops of Tabasco sauce

Score both sides of the steaks in a diamond pattern about ⅛ inch deep. Combine all the ingredients in a large shallow baking dish. Coat the steaks with the marinade, and turn four times during a 2-hour period of marinating in the refrigerator. (You may also marinate overnight.) Remove the steaks from the marinade and broil for 3–5 minutes on each side. To serve, cut diagonally into thin slices. **SERVES 3–4.**

By Keith Tindall from White Egret Farm. Used by permission.

KOREAN BEEF

1 flank steak	6 cloves garlic, peeled and mashed
½ cup soy sauce	2 Tbsp. sesame seeds
2 Tbsp. toasted sesame oil	¼ tsp. cayenne pepper
1 bunch green onions, finely chopped	

Using a very sharp and heavy knife, slice the flank steak as thinly as possible across the grain and on the diagonal. (This will be easier if the meat is partially frozen.) Mix other ingredients and marinate beef in the mixture, refrigerated, for several hours or overnight.

Fold or "ribbon" the strips and stick them on skewers, making 4–6 brochettes. Cook on barbecue or under grill, about 5–7 minutes per side. Meat should still be rare or medium rare inside. This is delicious with any fermented vegetables, especially ginger carrots. The lactic-acid-producing bacteria in the fermented vegetables are the perfect antidote to carcinogens that may have formed in the meat, especially if it has been barbecued. **SERVES 4.** From *Nourishing Traditions* by Sally Fallon. Used by permission.

VENISON STEAKS WITH MARINADE

4–6 venison steaks, ½ inch thick	3 or 4 juniper berries
1 Tbsp. butter	1 sprig parsley
2 Tbsp. sesame oil	1 sprig thyme
	2 bay leaves
MARINADE:	1–2 cloves garlic, crushed
1 cup red wine	1 pinch of nutmeg
¼ cup lemon juice	1 tsp. sea salt or Herbamare
½ cup olive oil	1 dash hot pepper sauce

Combine the ingredients in the marinade. Marinate the steaks for 24 hours in the refrigerator. To keep the steaks juicy on the inside but brown on the outside, sauté 5–6 minutes on a side in the butter/sesame oil combination. **SERVES 4–6.**

By Keith Tindall from White Egret Farm. Used by permission.

Organ Meats

Preparation Tip: Try to marinate organ meats for about 2 hours prior to cooking as it will significantly improve the taste. Place meat in container, cover with water, and then add 1–2 Tbsp. of fresh lemon juice, plain yogurt, or raw apple cider vinegar. Cover and place in refrigerator. When ready to cook, pour off water and rinse meat under cold water.

LIVER WITH TURKEY BACON AND ONIONS

1–2 lb. organic beef liver	1 egg, beaten
8 pieces of turkey bacon	½ cup whole-grain flour (soaked overnight)
1 onion, chopped	

Marinate the liver before cooking. Wash and dry the liver slices and set aside on a plate. Fry the bacon till crisp in a large skillet or frying pan. Remove bacon from the pan. Dredge the liver slices first in the egg, then in the flour. Place in a skillet, and cook in extra-virgin coconut oil or butter.

The pieces will cook quickly, so be sure to turn after 2–3 minutes. (Don't overcook liver; it tastes terrible.) Melt some butter in another skillet, and sauté onions in it. Strew the onions over the liver on a large platter and top with crumbled turkey bacon. **SERVES 4–6.**

Note: You can prepare this recipe without the turkey bacon, sautéing the liver in butter or extra-virgin coconut oil instead and serve with onions only.

From *The Lazy Person's Whole Food Cookbook* by Stephen Byrnes. Used by permission.

LIVER, RICE CASSEROLE

1 lb. chopped cooked liver	1 cup boiling water
3 Tbsp. melted butter	1 onion, chopped and sautéed in butter
2 cups cooked brown rice	Herbamare seasoning to taste
2 cups chopped tomatoes (you may use canned)	

Grease your casserole dish. Place onions on the bottom, then liver, then the rice. Add tomatoes, water, and seasoning. Bake at 400 degrees for 20 minutes. **SERVES 6.**

From *The Lazy Person's Whole Food Cookbook* by Stephen Byrnes. Used by permission.

Grains, Nuts, Seeds, and Legumes

PREPARATION TIPS

FOR WHOLE GRAINS: For millet, brown rice, oatmeal, amaranth, etc., soak desired amount of grain in an equal amount of water to which you've added 1 Tbsp. raw vinegar, fresh lemon juice, or plain yogurt. (Use 2–3 Tbsp. if you're cooking a large amount of grain.) Cover and let sit at room temperature for at least 7 hours, preferably longer. When ready to cook, add remaining required amount of water or stock and cook. NOTE: To soak whole-grain flours or pancake mixes, follow the same procedure as above but make sure the flour is mixed well with the soaking water.

FOR RAW BEANS AND LENTILS: Soak desired amount of beans in an equal amount of water to which you've added 1 Tbsp. raw vinegar, fresh lemon juice, or plain yogurt. (Use 2–3 Tbsp. if you're cooking a large amount of beans or lentils.) Cover and let sit at room temperature for at least 7 hours, preferably longer. When ready to cook, discard soaking water; add remaining required amount of water or stock and cook.

FOR RAW NUTS AND SEEDS: Place raw nuts or seeds in a bowl, add 1 Tbsp. sea salt, and cover with water. Leave at room temperature for 6–8 hours. Drain the water. Place nuts on a cookie sheet, and dry on low heat in the oven. You can also air-dry the nuts on a towel, but it takes much longer to dry them this way.

SPROUTED ALMONDS

Sprouted almonds are much more digestible than untreated ones. Rinse 3 times per day. Ready in 3 days. Sprout is merely a tiny white appendage, about ⅛-inch long.

From *Nourishing Traditions* by Sally Fallon. Used by permission.

BREAKFAST PORRIDGE

1 cup oats, steel cut or rolled, or coarsely ground in your own grinder	½ tsp. Celtic sea salt
1 cup water plus 2 Tbsp. fermented whey, yogurt, or buttermilk	1 cup water
	1 Tbsp. flaxseeds (optional)

For highest benefits and best assimilation, porridge should be soaked overnight or even longer. (Ancient recipes from Wales and Brittany called for a 24-hour soaking.) Once soaked, oatmeal cooks up in less than 5 minutes—truly a fast food.

Mix oats and salt with water mixture; cover and let stand at room temperature for at least 7 hours and as long as 24 hours. Bring additional 1 cup of water to boil. Add soaked oats. Reduce heat, cover, and simmer several minutes.

Meanwhile, grind flaxseeds in a mini-grinder. Off heat, stir in flaxseeds and let stand for a few minutes. Serve with butter or cream thinned with a little water, and a natural sweetener like Sucanat, date sugar, maple syrup, or raw honey. **SERVES 4.**

From *Nourishing Traditions* by Sally Fallon. Used by permission.

CRISPY PECANS

4 cups pecan halves	Filtered water
1 tsp. sea salt or Herbamare	

The buttery flavor of pecans is enhanced by soaking and slow-oven drying. Soak pecans in salt and filtered water for at least 7 hours or overnight. Drain in a colander. Spread pecans on two stainless steel baking pans and place in a warm oven (no more than 150 degrees) for 12 to 24 hours, stirring occasionally, until completely dry and crisp. Store in an airtight container. Great for school lunches. **MAKES 4 CUPS.**

VARIATION: TAMARI PECANS
In place of salt, add ¼ cup tamari sauce to soaking water.

From *Nourishing Traditions* by Sally Fallon. Used by permission.

EASY BROWN RICE

2 cups brown rice	1 Tbsp. apple cider vinegar or yogurt
4 cups water or 2 cups water mixed with 2 cups chicken stock	

Soak rice in 2 cups of water with the vinegar or yogurt for at least 7 hours. Transfer to your pot or rice cooker. Add the remaining water or water/broth, and cook till tender. If you're cooking the rice on a stovetop, bring to a boil then lower heat to a simmer and cook covered, stirring occasionally. **SERVES 6–8.**

NOTE: This recipe can be used for ANY whole grain you wish to serve by itself—millet, quinoa, buckwheat, amaranth, etc.

From *The Lazy Person's Whole Food Cookbook* by Stephen Byrnes. Used by permission.

EASY FRENCH TOAST

1 cup plain yogurt	½ tsp. sea salt
½ tsp. honey	8 slices sprouted or sourdough whole-grain bread
2 eggs, slightly beaten	

Combine eggs, yogurt, honey, and salt in a mixing bowl. Dip each slice of bread quickly into the mixture. Brown in extra-virgin coconut oil. Serve with butter and unheated honey or maple syrup or fresh fruit. **SERVES 4.**

From *The Lazy Person's Whole Food Cookbook* by Stephen Byrnes. Used by permission.

EASY WHOLE-GRAIN WAFFLES

1⅓ cups whole-grain flour (spelt, kamut)	1 cup water
¾ tsp. sea salt	2 Tbsp. plain yogurt
2 tsp. nonaluminum baking powder	4 Tbsp. extra-virgin coconut oil
2 Tbsp. unheated honey	2 eggs, separated

Soak the flour in water with 2 Tbsp. yogurt for at least 7 hours. Separate the eggs. Beat the yolks and add the yogurt and butter. Combine salt, honey, and flour; add this to the first mixture. Beat the egg whites until they form stiff peaks; fold them into the mix. Mix in the baking powder quickly. Cook in your waffle iron. **SERVES 6.**

From *The Lazy Person's Whole Food Cookbook* by Stephen Byrnes. Used by permission.

FIVE-GRAIN CEREAL MIX

2 cups wheat or spelt	2 cups barley or oats
2 cups millet	2 cups split peas or lentils
2 cups short-grain rice	

This combination of grains conforms to the five grains recommended in the *Yellow Emperor's Classic of Internal Medicine*. Mix together and grind coarsely. Store in refrigerator. **MAKES 10 CUPS.**

From *Nourishing Traditions* by Sally Fallon. Used by permission.

FIVE-GRAIN PORRIDGE

1 cup Five-Grain Cereal	½ tsp. Celtic sea salt
1 cup water plus 2 Tbsp. fermented whey or yogurt	1 cup water
	1 Tbsp. flaxseeds (optional)

Mix Five-Grain Cereal and salt with water plus whey or yogurt. Cover and let stand at room temperature for at least 7 hours and as long as 24 hours. Bring additional 1 cup of water to boil. Add soaked cereal. Reduce heat, cover, and simmer several minutes. Meanwhile, grind flaxseed in a mini-grinder. Remove cereal from heat, and stir in flaxseed. Serve with butter or cream, thinned with a little water, and a natural sweetener like Sucanat, date sugar, maple syrup, or raw honey. **SERVES 4.**

From *Nourishing Traditions* by Sally Fallon. Used by permission.

MUFFINS

1¼ cups freshly ground and/or soaked spelt, kamut, or whole-wheat flour	½ cup extra-virgin coconut oil
¾ cup water mixed with 1 Tbsp. yogurt	⅓ cup honey
1 egg, lightly beaten	2 tsp. baking powder
¼ tsp. fine Celtic sea salt	1 tsp. vanilla

Preheat oven to 400 degrees. Mix flour with water and yogurt, and let stand overnight. Mix in remaining ingredients. Pour into well-buttered muffin tin about three-quarters full. Bake for 15–20 minutes. These muffins will puff up and then fall back a bit to form flat tops. Note: 1 cup buckwheat flour or cornmeal may be used in place of 1 cup spelt, kamut, or wheat flour. **MAKES ABOUT 12.**

Adapted from *Nourishing Traditions* by Sally Fallon. Used by permission.

VARIATION: RAISIN MUFFINS
Add ½ cup raisins and ½ tsp. cinnamon to batter.

VARIATION: BLUEBERRY MUFFINS
Pour batter into muffin tins. Place 5–7 blueberries, fresh or frozen, on each muffin. Berries will fall into the muffins. (If they are added to the batter, they sink to the bottom of the muffin.)

VARIATION: DRIED CHERRY MUFFINS
Add 4 oz. dried cherries (available at health food stores and gourmet markets) and ½ cup chopped crispy pecans to batter.

VARIATION: FRUIT SPICE MUFFINS
Add 2 ripe pears or peaches, peeled and cut into small pieces, and ½ tsp. cinnamon, ⅛ tsp. cloves, and ⅛ tsp. nutmeg to batter.

VARIATION: LEMON MUFFINS
Add grated rind of 2 lemons and ½ cup chopped crispy pecans to batter. Omit vanilla.

VARIATION: GINGER MUFFINS
Add 1 Tbsp. freshly grated ginger and 1 tsp. ground ginger to batter. Omit vanilla.

BLUEBERRY PECAN PANCAKES

1½ cups freshly ground or soaked spelt, kamut, or whole-wheat flour	½ cup crispy pecans
¾ cup water mixed with 1 Tbsp. yogurt	¼ tsp. fine Celtic sea salt
1 egg, lightly beaten	½ cup extra-virgin coconut oil
½ cup blueberries (fresh or frozen)	2 tsp. baking powder
	1 tsp. vanilla

Mix flour with water and yogurt and let stand overnight. Defrost blueberries in refrigerator if frozen. Mix ingredients into a bowl. Heat extra-virgin coconut oil in a skillet or pan over low heat. Increase temperature to moderate heat. Use about 3 Tbsp. of batter for each pancake. Serve with honey, maple syrup, or butter. **MAKES ABOUT 12.**

VARIATIONS: Use different kinds of fruit.

From *Nourishing Traditions* by Sally Fallon. Used by permission.

PEPITAS

4 cups raw, hulled pumpkinseeds	1 tsp. cayenne pepper (optional)
1 Tbsp. sea salt or Herbamare	Filtered water

This recipe imitates Aztec practices of soaking seeds in brine, then letting them dry in the hot sun. They ate pepitas whole or ground into meal.

Dissolve salt in water and add pumpkinseeds and optional cayenne. Soak for at least 7 hours or overnight. Drain in a colander, then spread on 2 stainless steel baking pans. Place in a warm oven (no more than 150 degrees) for about 12 hours or overnight, stirring occasionally, until thoroughly dry and crisp. Store in an airtight container. **MAKES 4 CUPS.**

VARIATION: TAMARI PEPITAS Use 2 Tbsp. tamari sauce in place of sea salt and cayenne.

From *Nourishing Traditions* by Sally Fallon. Used by permission.

SIMPLE BEANS

2 cups black beans, kidney beans, pinto beans, black-eyed beans, or white beans	2 Tbsp. whey
	1 tsp. sea salt
Filtered water	4 cloves garlic, peeled and mashed (optional)

Soak beans in filtered water, salt, and whey for 12–24 hours, depending on the size of the bean. Drain, rinse, place in a large pot, and add water to cover beans. Bring to a boil, skimming off foam. Reduce heat and add optional garlic. Simmer, covered, for 4–8 hours. Check occasionally and add more water as necessary. **SERVES 8.**

From *Nourishing Traditions* by Sally Fallon. Used by permission.

SIMPLE LENTILS

2 cups lentils, preferably green lentils	2 cloves garlic, peeled and mashed
Filtered water	Several sprigs fresh thyme, tied together
2 Tbsp. homemade whey or yogurt	1 tsp. dried peppercorns, crushed
1 tsp. Celtic sea salt	Pinch dried chili flakes (optional)
2 cups beef or chicken stock	Juice of 1–2 lemons

Soak lentils in filtered water, salt, and whey for several hours. Drain and rinse. Place in a pot and add stock to cover. Bring to a boil and skim. Add remaining ingredients except lemon and simmer, uncovered, for about 1 hour, or until liquid has completely reduced. Add lemon juice and season to taste. Serve with a slotted spoon. Excellent with sauerkraut and strongly flavored meats such as duck, game, or lamb. **SERVES 6–8.**

From *Nourishing Traditions* by Sally Fallon. Used by permission.

SPROUTED SUNFLOWER SEEDS

These are among the most satisfactory seeds for sprouting. Sunflower sprouts are just delicious in salads, but they must be eaten very soon after sprouting is accomplished, as they soon go black. Try to find hulled sunflower seeds packed in nitrogen packs. Rinse 2 times per day. Ready in 12–18 hours, when sprout is just barely showing.

From *Nourishing Traditions* by Sally Fallon. Used by permission.

Beverages

APPLE "CIDER"

1 gallon unfiltered, unpasteurized apple juice	½ cup homemade whey
1 Tbsp. sea salt	

Place all ingredients in a large bowl. Cover and leave at room temperature for 2 days. Skim foam that rises to the top. Line a strainer with several layers of cheesecloth; strain juice into jars or jugs. Cover tightly and refrigerate. Flavors will develop slowly over several weeks. The "cider" will eventually develop a rich buttery taste.

If you wish to further clarify the cider, add lightly beaten egg whites to the jugs (1 egg white per quart). Set aside a few hours, and then filter again through several layers of cheesecloth. **MAKES 4 QUARTS.**

From *Nourishing Traditions* by Sally Fallon. Used by permission.

BALANCED VEGETABLE JUICE

Vegetable juices can be a great source of essential nutrients. Here is a staple vegetable juice blend:

50 percent carrot juice	1 tsp. cream, goat's milk yogurt, coconut milk
10 percent beet juice	1–2 Tbsp. of Green Superfood Powder with
30 percent celery juice	HSOs (optional)
10 percent parsley or other green juice	

By Jordan Rubin

CULTURED VEGETABLE JUICE

3 red beets	1 oz. grated ginger
1 carrot	1 tsp. fine Celtic sea salt
2–4 Tbsp. fermented whey or 1 packet cultured	Purified water
vegetable starter (see Appendix B)	

Peel and chop beets and carrot; combine with peeled and grated ginger. Place in a 1–2 quart glass container with a seal. Cover with water, and add whey and salt. Stir well and cover. Leave at room temperature for 2–3 days, then transfer to the refrigerator.

By Jordan Rubin

GINGER ALE

¾ cup ginger, peeled and finely chopped or	2 tsp. Celtic sea salt
grated	¼ cup homemade whey
½ cup fresh lime juice	2 quarts filtered water
¼–½ cup Rapadura or dehydrated cane juice	

Place all ingredients in a 2-quart jug and fill with water. Stir well and cover tightly. Keep at room temperature for two days before transferring to the refrigerator. This will keep several months well chilled. To serve, strain and mix

half ginger ale with half purified water or naturally sparkling water. Best consumed at room temperature, not cold.
MAKES 2 QUARTS.

From *Nourishing Traditions* by Sally Fallon. Used by permission.

HOMEMADE KEFIR

1 qt. raw goat's or cow's milk	1 packet kefir starter (see Appendix B)

Pour into quart-size Mason jar. Add kefir starter. Set in a room temperature area for 12–48 hours, then transfer to refrigerator. A cupboard is an ideal place to ferment. The temperature range should be between 70–75 degrees. Kefir can last several months in the refrigerator and will become sourer over time.

By Jordan Rubin

NEW WINE

1 case organic concord, black, or red grapes, about 16 lb.	½ cup Probiogurt or continental acidophilus 1 Tbsp. Celtic sea salt

This beverage is best made with a vegetable juicer, although a high-speed blender or food processor will do. It takes a bit of time, but the results are worth it. This delicious and refreshing drink is an excellent substitute for wine, containing all the nutrients of grapes found in wine, including many enzymes, but none of the alcohol. In fact, a drink similar to this may have been what the Bible referred to as "new wine."

Remove grapes from stems, wash well, and pass through the juicer. Place liquid in a large bowl with salt and Probiogurt, and stir well. Cover and leave at room temperature for 2 days. If you don't use a juicer, you may want to scoop off the skins and strain juice through a strainer lined with several layers of cheesecloth. It is best to store new wine in airtight containers in refrigerator. Delicious flavors will develop over time. May be served diluted with half water. **MAKES 5–6 QUARTS.**

By Jordan Rubin

RASPBERRY DRINK

2 12-oz. packages frozen raspberries, or 24 oz. fresh raspberries Juice of 12 oranges ¼–½ cup Rapadura or dehydrated cane juice	¼ cup homemade whey 2 tsp. Celtic sea salt 2 quarts filtered water

Place raspberries in food processor and blend until smooth. Mix in a large bowl with remaining ingredients. Cover and let sit at room temperature for 2 days. Skim foam that may rise to top. Strain through a strainer lined with cheesecloth. Pour into jugs or jars. Cover tightly and store in refrigerator. If you wish to further clarify the raspberry drink, add lightly beaten egg whites to the jugs (1 egg white per quart). Set aside a few hours, and then filter again through several layers of cheesecloth. To serve, dilute with sparkling mineral water. **MAKES 2 QUARTS.**

From *Nourishing Traditions* by Sally Fallon. Used by permission.

Smoothies

Author's note: During my healing process, I consumed this smoothie one to two times per day with raw eggs. Contrary to popular belief, eggs from healthy, free-range, pastured chickens are almost always free of dangerous germs. If the egg has an odor, obviously it should not be eaten. Since most of the salmonella infections are caused by germs on the shell, for added protection it is best to wash the eggs in the shell with a mild alcohol or hydrogen peroxide solution or a fruit and vegetable wash.

BERRY SMOOTHIE

10 oz. plain whole-milk yogurt, kefir, or coconut milk/cream	1 Tbsp. flaxseed or hempseed oil
	1–2 Tbsp. unheated honey
1–2 raw high omega-3 whole eggs (optional)	1 Tbsp. goat's milk protein powder (optional)
1 Tbsp. extra-virgin coconut oil	1–2 cups fresh or frozen berries

Combine ingredients in a high-speed blender.

Properly prepared, this smoothie is an extraordinary source of easy-to-absorb nutrition. It contains large amounts of "live" enzymes, probiotics, vitally important "live" proteins, and a full spectrum of essential fatty acids. Smoothies should be consumed immediately or refrigerated for up to 24 hours. If frozen in ice cube trays with a toothpick inserted into each cube, smoothies can make for a great frozen dessert. **MAKES TWO 8-OZ. SERVINGS.**

By Jordan Rubin

VARIATIONS FOR SMOOTHIES

To enjoy the same life giving nutrients with different flavors, add the following ingredients to the "basic" ingredients used in the smoothie listed above:

BANANA COCONUT CREAM SMOOTHIE—10 oz. coconut milk/cream (instead of whole-milk yogurt or kefir); 1–2 fresh or frozen bananas (instead of berries); ½ tsp. vanilla extract

BLACKBERRY BANANA SMOOTHIE—½–1 cup fresh or frozen blackberries (instead of berries); 1 fresh or frozen banana

CHERRY VANILLA SMOOTHIE—½–1 cup fresh or frozen cherries (instead of berries); 1 fresh or frozen banana

CHOCOLATE MOUSSE SMOOTHIE—2 Tbsp. cocoa or carob powder or Healthy Chocolate Spread (instead of berries) (See Appendix B.)

CREAMSICLE SMOOTHIE—6 oz. (not 10) of plain whole-milk yogurt or kefir; 4 oz. freshly squeezed orange juice; 1–2 fresh or frozen bananas (instead of berries)

MOCHA SWISS ALMOND SMOOTHIE—2 Tbsp. cocoa or carob powder (instead of berries); 2 Tbsp. raw almond butter (or 4 Tbsp. Chocolate Almond Spread—see Appendix B)

MOCHACCINO SMOOTHIE—2 Tbsp. cocoa or carob powder; 1 Tbsp. organic-roasted coffee beans; 1–2 fresh or frozen bananas (instead of berries)

PEACHES 'N CREAM SMOOTHIE—½–1 cup fresh or frozen peaches (instead of berries); 1 fresh or frozen banana

PINA COLADA SMOOTHIE—10 oz. coconut milk/cream (no whole-milk yogurt or kefir); 1 cup fresh or frozen pineapple (instead of berries); 1 fresh or frozen banana

By Jordan Rubin

Snacks and Desserts

BANANA BREAD

3 cups freshly ground spelt or wheat flour	¼ to ½ cup maple syrup
2 cups cultured buttermilk, water mixed with 2 Tbsp. whey or yogurt	2 tsp. baking soda
	¼ cup melted butter
3 eggs, lightly beaten	2 ripe bananas, mashed
1 tsp. sea salt	½ cup chopped crispy pecans

Mix flour with buttermilk or water mixture and let stand overnight. Beat in remaining ingredients. Pour into a well-buttered and floured loaf pan. Bake at 350 degrees for 1 hour or more, until a toothpick comes out clean. **MAKES ONE 9 X 13 LOAF.**

For variations of this recipe, order a copy of *Nourishing Traditions* by Sally Fallon. (See Appendix B.)

COCONUT ALMOND FUDGE

1 cup extra-virgin coconut oil	¼ cup unheated honey
¾ cup carob powder	1 Tbsp. vanilla
¼ cup raw almond butter	

Place all ingredients in a glass container and set in simmering water until melted if needed. Mix together well. Spread thick paste mixture on a piece of buttered parchment paper; allow to cool in refrigerator or freezer. Remove and serve immediately. **MAKES 1¼ CUP.**

By Jordan Rubin

PINEAPPLE CREAMY TREAT

1 cup organic ricotta cheese	½ tsp. vanilla extract
1 Tbsp. unheated honey	1 cup pineapple or fruit of choice

Mix ricotta, honey, and vanilla extract. Top with fruit of choice. **SERVES 2–3.**

By Jordan Rubin

CREAMY HIGH-ENZYME DESSERT

4 oz. Probiogurt, plain yogurt, or cultured cream	1 tsp. flaxseed oil
1 Tbsp. raw, unheated honey	½ cup fresh or frozen organic berries

Mix yogurt, honey, and flaxseed oil. Top with berries.

By Jordan Rubin

SUPER SEED BAR

¾ cup and 3 Tbsp. SuperSeed Whole Food Fiber Powder (See Appendix B.)	6 Tbsp. cocoa or carob powder
½ cup tahini (sesame butter)	¼ tsp. salt
½ cup almond butter	⅓ cup honey
¼ cup and 1 Tbsp. Goatein goat's milk protein powder (See Appendix B.)	2½ Tbsp. extra-virgin coconut oil
	1 tsp. vanilla extract
	1 tsp. orange or almond extract

Combine wet and dry ingredients and form into bars. Freeze or refrigerate. **MAKES 4–6 3-OZ. BARS.**

By Phyllis Rubin. Used by permission.

VARIATIONS Add organic chocolate or carob chips, shredded coconut, dried fruit, or chopped almonds.

TRAIL MIX

1 cup crispy pecans	1 cup raisins
1 cup crispy cashews	1 cup dried sweetened coconut meat
1 cup unsulphured dried apricots, apples, pears, or pineapple cut into pieces	1 cup carob chips (optional)

Mix all ingredients together. Store in an airtight container. **MAKES 5–6 CUPS.**

From *Nourishing Traditions* by Sally Fallon. Used by permission.

ZESTY POPCORN

⅓ cup popcorn	2 Tbsp. melted butter
3 Tbsp. extra-virgin coconut oil	Herbamare to taste
2 Tbsp. garlic-chili flax	

Melt coconut oil in pan over medium heat. Pour popcorn into pan. Cover pan with lid. While popping, melt butter. Cook until popped. Pour into large bowl. Pour melted butter and garlic chili-flax and seasoning and mix thoroughly.

By Nicki Rubin. Used by permission.

Appendix B

Garden of Life Companion Guide
to Healthy Living

••

Health Organizations

GARDEN OF LIFE, INC.
770 Northpoint Parkway, Suite 100, West Palm Beach, FL 33407
Toll Free: (866) 465-0094, Telephone: (561) 472-9277, Fax: (561) 472-9297
Web site: www.gardenoflife.com

Garden of Life is a health and wellness company empowering millions of people to attain extraordinary health through a timeless, historically correct, and scientifically proven approach. Garden of Life is redefining "healthy" by providing revolutionary products, education, and service. Garden of Life manufactures many of the products used in The Maker's Diet 40-Day Health Experience, including Perfect Food, a super green food packed with antioxidant green grasses, micro-algae, sea vegetables, whole vegetables and their juices, sprouted grains, seeds, legumes, and acerola cherries; Living Multi, a complete whole-food vitamin and mineral supplement; Olde World Icelandic Cod Liver Oil, an excellent source of vitamins A and D, and that plays an important role in supporting cardiovascular health; SuperSeed, whole-food fiber blend of seeds, sprouted grains, and legumes; Extra-Virgin Coconut Oil, one of the healthiest and most versatile unprocessed dietary oils in the world; Goatein, pure protein powder from goat's milk; Clenzology Advanced Hygiene kit; AlphaTherapy and OmegaTherapy, biblical aromatherapy morning and evening products; AlphaCleanse and OmegaCleanse, purification morning and evening products; and many other fine whole-food nutritional products.

Garden of Life set out to create a new standard in nutrition and health, bringing a new awareness to the concept of whole-food nutrition by reeducating the public about the fundamental ability of whole food in its natural state to function in a balanced, symbiotic relationship with the body.

Garden of Life believes in offering only the highest-quality, most viable, nutrient-rich whole-food ingredients; therefore, whenever possible, many of their raw materials are certified organic or pesticide/herbicide free and are never genetically modified or artificially preserved.

GARDEN OF LIFE COMMUNICATIONS
770 Northpoint Parkway, Suite 100, West Palm Beach, FL 33407
Toll Free: (800) 365-7709, Telephone: (561) 472-9277, Fax: (561) 472-9297
Web site: www.makersdiet.com

Garden of Life Communications is a premier provider of educational products and services imparting lifestyle knowledge for everyone to achieve extraordinary health. Garden of Life Communications offers innovative educational tools, including books, DVDs, CDs, journals, and guides that are motivational and easy-to-understand. Garden of Life Communications' line of products and services include: The Maker's Diet Success Kit, everything you need to maximize your 40-day experience with The Maker's Diet; *Shopping for Optimal Health* DVD, your step-by-step resource for understanding product labels and making healthier purchasing decisions—the only video guide of its kind; *Functional Fitness* DVD, which improves the normal actions you perform each and every day while helping your body become more agile, flexible, and injury-resistant; small groups, education programs for churches, corporations, clubs, health food stores, and other organizations; live events, providing consumers with the information they need to attain optimal health; and a free monthly HTML e-newsletter that focuses on optimal health of the body, mind, and spirit.

MAKERSDIET.COM

MakersDiet.com is an incredible resource for those who desire optimal health of the body, mind, and spirit. Detailed information about the philosophy, diet, and recommended products is just the surface of this fully interactive site. Subscribe to a free monthly e-newsletter, become a member of the Maker's Diet Street Team, sign up to win in a health and wellness sweepstakes, and find out about live events, recent news appearances, and free small group resources.

REJUVENATIVE FOODS
(Deer Garden Foods)
P. O. Box 8464, Santa Cruz, CA 95061
Telephone: (800) 805-7957
Web site: www.rejuvenative.com

Rejuvenative Foods offers the highest-quality raw fermented and cultured vegetables, including sauerkraut and kim-chi, as well as raw nut and seed butters to promote and support optimal health. These foods are available in some grocery and health food stores, and via Internet or mail order.

These delicious, raw, organic, cultured vegetables are one of the richest sources of enzymes and lactobacillus (including acidophilus) available. Other sauerkrauts have been heated, eliminating life-producing enzymes from which our bodies, our health, and our immune systems function. In addition, their Web site includes valuable information about raw foods and fermentation.

Their fresh-dated, raw, refrigerated nut and seed butters are special because they're unheated (not roasted) and still contain their life energy, vitamins, and minerals, which are further retained as a result of immediate refrigeration. An important aspect of retention of life energy is to monitor the temperature during grinding so that heat friction doesn't cook the nuts and seeds.

BARLEAN'S ORGANIC OILS
4936 Lake Terrell Road, Ferndale, WA 98248
Telephone: (800) 445-3529
Web site: www.barleans.com

Transform your health with flax oil. Fresh, unfiltered, unrefined, organic flax oil—chock-full of beneficial omega-3 fatty acids—is simply one of the most important whole-food, nutritional products that you can consume to transform your health, beauty, and vitality.

Many people report enhanced energy, endurance, glowing skin, and radiant hair from regular Barlean's consumption. Dietary essential fatty acids in flax oil permeate every cell of your body, nurturing and nourishing your vital organs and tissues. Relief from PMS and menopause, as well as from pain, swelling and arthritic conditions, and heart health are also areas of high interest concerning omega-3 supplementation.

Family owned and operated, Barlean's Organic Oils produces the absolute highest-quality, purest, freshest, and most pristine flax oil in the world. Barlean's claim to fame is same-day, fresh-pressed flax oil, shipped manufacture direct, next day air to health food stores and loyalists across the country.

Unlike competing flax oil manufacturers, Barlean's does not refine or filter their flax oil. The result is beautiful, rich amber-colored flax oil that tastes great and is abundant in naturally occurring essential fatty acids, accessory and antioxidant nutrients, and lignans. Barlean's is the undisputed, best-selling flax oil and omega-3 supplement in the country according to SPINS/AC Neilson and is the five-time consecutive winner of the Health and Nutrition Industries coveted VITY Award.

Flax oil has a nutty flavor and can be used straight off the spoon, in salad dressings, stirred in yogurt or oatmeal, or in blended beverages and protein drinks.

Barlean's offers a 100 percent satisfaction, money-back guarantee.

FREE OFFER: Receive a FREE 12-oz. sample of Barlean's Organic Flax Oil, a $12.99 retail value for only $4.95 to cover the cost of shipping and handling. Visit www.barleans .com/sample. Enter promotion code "Makers Diet." Or call (800) 445-3529.

ORGANIC PASTURES DAIRY CO.
7221 S. Jameson Avenue, Fresno, CA 93706
Telephone: (559) 846-9732
Web site: www.organicpastures.com

Organic Pastures Dairy Co. is California's first certified organic pasture-grazed raw milk dairy. This family-owned and operated dairy was founded in 2000 as an extension of an organic farming operation located near Fresno, California, in the heart of the fertile San Joaquin Valley.

The dairy produces Grade A raw milk using an innovative mobile milking parlor, which moves to where the cows are grazing. The decentralized milking system was invented by Organic Pastures' founder, Mark McAfee. This unique design eliminates the need for cows to walk long distances on concrete and through manure-filled pens to be milked. The company has been recognized repeatedly in independent NFO (National Farmers Organization) tests as having the best milk taste of all the organic dairies surveyed.

Organic Pastures produces certified organic and pasture-fed milk in harmony with nature. Their Jersey, Ayreshire, and Holstein cows produce fresh delicious milk alive with flavor. The milk is high in antioxidants (CLA), vitamins (including B_{12}), all twenty-two amino acids, live enzymes (including lactase), naturally occurring probiotics, and essential fatty acids. The organic raw butter produced by Organic Pastures is rich in Activator X, the fat-soluble activator that was discovered by Dr. Weston Price and believed to be an incredible health-promoting substance virtually absent from today's modern diet. All their milk products are as our Maker intended, without changes or damages done through pasteurization, homogenization, or other processing. None of their individually named cows are ever given antibiotics, hormones, or GMOs (genetically modified organisms). Only pasture, organic brown rice bran, and approved homeopathic methods are used to feed and care for the cows.

Organic Pastures produces the finest quality raw butter and cream. It is available in many health food stores in California and via mail order.

FOOD FOR LIFE BAKING COMPANY
2991 East Doherty Street Corona, CA 92879
Telephone: (909) 279-5090
Web site: www.foodforlife.com

Food For Life is a family owned and operated bakery producing some of the industry's finest certified organic, certified kosher, sprouted grain loaves, tortillas, buns, and cereals. We also produce a variety of wheat- and gluten-free breads and tortillas.

Food For Life Bakery makes breads of unmatched nutritional value and flavor using America's finest certified organically grown Montana spring wheat. Different from most breads today, Food For Life sprouted grain breads are made from freshly sprouted, certified organically grown live grains and contain absolutely no flour. Food For Life breads are better for you because they are made with live grains. Live grains make the difference because they have more nutrients and taste better.

Food For Life breads, made from sprouted grains, are richer in protein and vitamins than bread baked from dry grains ground into flour. Their exclusive sprouting process not only significantly increases valuable nutrients but also causes a natural change that makes the protein and carbohydrates easier for the body to use. In fact, sprouts are lower in carbohydrates and calories than the grains from which they were sprouted.

Their mission is to produce only the highest-quality baked goods from the finest natural ingredients for optimum health and nutrition.

EAT WILD
Web site: www.eatwild.com

Eat Wild explains the benefits of eating meat and dairy products from grass-fed, not grain-fed, animals. On their suppliers' page, you can find out how to purchase grass-fed meat and dairy products in your area.

EatWild.com is a Web site that provides a comprehensive, state-by-state listing of farms that supply certified organic and pasture-fed meat, poultry, and dairy products. Animals that are fed nothing but pasture grasses live healthy, stress-free lives. They are rarely sick, so they never require the use of pharmaceutical drugs. As in nature, their rate of growth is determined by their health and the quality of the forage, not hormonal implants or growth-promoting additives. For all these reasons and more, the meat and dairy products are healthy, wholesome, and natural in every sense of the word.

Finishing meat and dairy animals on pasture alone requires far more knowledge and skill than sending them to a feedlot or confinement dairy. For example, in order for grass-fed beef to be succulent and tender, the animals need high-quality forage, especially in the months prior to slaughter. This requires healthy soil and careful management so that the pastures remain lush and the growth is spread as evenly as possible over the growing season. Also, the animals' grazing patterns must be carefully managed on a daily basis to keep the pasture from being grazed too little or too much, which would compromise its quality and availability.

WESTON A. PRICE FOUNDATION
PMB 106-380, Washington, DC 20016
Telephone: (202) 333-4325
Web site: www.westonaprice.org

The Weston A. Price Foundation is one of the finest health and wellness organizations in the world. The teachings of this organization are based on the principles of one of my nutritional heroes, Dr. Weston Price. I would encourage anyone interested in health and human nutrition to become a member of this great organization. For a nominal membership fee, you can receive some of the best health information in the business.

The Weston A. Price Foundation is a nonprofit, tax-exempt charity founded in 1999 to disseminate the research of nutrition pioneer Dr. Weston Price, whose studies of isolated cultures established parameters for human health and determined optimum characteristics for human diets. Dr. Price's research demonstrated that humans achieve perfect physical form and perfect health, generation after generation, only when they consume nutrient-dense whole foods and vital fat-soluble activators found exclusively in animal fats.

The Foundation is dedicated to restoring these nutrient-dense foods to the human diet through education, research, and activism. It supports accurate nutrition instruction, organic and biodynamic farming, pasture feeding of livestock, community-supported farms, honest and informative labeling, nutritionally prepared parenting, and nurturing therapies. Specific goals include the establishment of universal access to clean, certified raw milk and a ban on the use of soy formula for infants.

The Foundation seeks to establish a laboratory to test nutrient content of foods, particularly butter produced under various conditions; to conduct research into the "X" Factor, discovered by Dr. Price; and to determine the effects of traditional preparation methods on nutrient content and availability in whole foods.

The Foundation's quarterly journal, *Wise Traditions in Food, Farming, and the Healing Arts,* is dedicated to exploring the scientific validation of dietary, agricultural, and medical traditions throughout the world. It features illuminating and thought-provoking articles on current scientific research, human diets, nontoxic agriculture, and holistic therapies. The journal also serves as a reference for sources of foods that have been conscientiously grown and processed.

DR. MERCOLA'S OPTIMAL WELLNESS NEWSLETTER
Web site: www.mercola.com

Dr. Mercola provides cutting-edge information in the areas of health and fitness. His free biweekly e-newsletter is received by over 150,000 people. Dr. Mercola's Web site, www .mercola.com, is one of the most popular alternative health Web sites in the world.

This resource section contains contact information and distributors for many of the products that I have recommended you make a part of your regimen as you follow the Maker's Diet. To the best of my ability, I have included only reputable information from well-established resources. However, while I recommend the supplements and products listed, neither the author nor the publisher has any association with or makes any representations regarding any of the companies or groups listed. I cannot guarantee that these resources subscribe to the same belief system to which I subscribe. Please refer also to the general disclaimer included on the copyright page for this health-related book.

Foreword

Ingesting healthy foods from organically grown sources whenever possible is one of the primary keys to a successful nutritional program. With the endless array of food choices lining the shelves of our local health food and grocery stores—all displaying colorful, eye-catching labels with marketing buzzwords like *pure, natural, healthy,* and *organic*—it is important to look closely at the ingredient listing in very small print. You may soon discover that it may only contain one or two of the desired "clean" ingredients among a multitude of questionable, often unpronounceable "other" ingredients.

To that end, the following products have successfully been used or observed by the author of *The Maker's Diet,* Jordan S. Rubin, personally in clinical practice and in scientific research. Undoubtedly, many more products than are listed here meet the criteria of this list. Wherever possible, addresses, telephone numbers, fax numbers, and Web sites have been included to help you obtain these foods. Many of the companies and products listed in this section are available at health food and grocery stores nationwide. Others are available by mail order only. To find a health food store or mail order company that carries these and other fine products, log on to www.makersdiet.com.

Dairy Products (Goat's Milk)

AMALTHEIA DAIRY LLC
3380 Penwell Bridge Road
Belgrade, MT 59714
Telephone: (406) 388-0569
Fax: (406) 388-4030
E-mail: mbamaltheia@aol.com
Web site: www.amaltheiadairy.com

Grade A goat's dairy and cheeses, fresh chevre, flavored chevre, ricotta, and feta

REDWOOD HILL FARM
5480 Thomas Road
Sebastopol, CA 95472
Telephone: (707) 823-8250
Fax: (707) 823-6976
Web site: www.redwoodhill.com

Pasteurized goat's milk yogurt and cheeses

MT. STERLING CHEESE COOPERATIVE
P. O. Box 103
Sterling, WI 54645
Telephone: (608) 734-3151 or (866) 289-4628 (toll free)
Fax: (608) 734-3810
Web site: www.buygoatcheese.com

Goat's cheese and goat's milk butter

GOLDEN FLEECE
1500 West Sunturf Street
Lecanto, FL 34461
Web site: www.goldenfleece.net

Raw goat's cheeses; available in some health food and grocery stores

VERMONT BUTTER AND CHEESE COMPANY
40 Pitman Road
Westerville, VT 05678
Telephone: (802) 479-9371
Fax: (802) 479-3674
Web site: www.vtbutterandcheeseco.com

Offers goat's milk butter and cheeses

PEACEFUL PASTURES
69 Cowan Valley Lane
Hickman, TN 38567
Telephone: (615) 683-4291
Web site: www.peacefulpastures.com

Dairy products including milk, cream, butter, buttermilk, whey, kefir, colostrum, and a "Pro-Yo-Gurt." Raw dairy also available. Ships nationwide.

GRACE HARBOR FARMS, INC.
5157 Drayton Harbor Road
Blaine, WA 98230
Telephone: (360) 371-9060 or (866) 371-9060 (toll free)
Web site: www.graceharborfarms.com

Bottles goat milk as well as makes yogurt and cheese

Dairy Products (Cow's Milk)

ORGANIC PASTURES
7221 South Jameson Avenue
Fresno, CA 93706
Telephone: (559) 846-9732
Web site: www.organicpastures.com

Organic raw dairy products from grass-fed cows. Products include cream, butter, colostrum, and cheeses. Butter and cream can be purchased via mail order and are shipped frozen. These products are more expensive than commercially available dairy products, but are truly worth their weight in gold.

REAL FOODS MARKET
743 West 1200 North, Suite 200
Springville, UT 84663
Telephone: (866) 284-7325
Web site: www.realfoodsmarket.com

Organic raw dairy products from grass-fed cows. Products include cream, butter, yogurt, kefir, and cheeses. Available via mail order and shipped frozen.

WWW.MERCOLA.COM

Supplies raw cheeses from grass-fed cows. Available online for mail order delivery.

NATURAL BY NATURE
P. O. Box 464
West Grove, PA 19390
Telephone: (610) 268-6962
Web site: www.natural-by-nature.com

Grass-fed, organic cream, soft cheeses, hard cheeses, butter, and whipped cream

ORGANIC VALLEY
507 West Main Street
LaFarge, WI 54639
Telephone: (608) 625-2602
Web site: www.organicvalley.com

Certified organic raw-milk hard cheeses as well as organic soft cheeses, cream cheese, sour cream, and butter

HORIZON ORGANIC
6311 Horizon Lane
Longmont, CO 80503
Telephone: (303) 530-2711
Web site: www.horizonorganic.com

Certified organic raw-milk hard cheeses and butter

TREE OF LIFE
P. O. Box 9000
St. Augustine, FL 32085
Telephone: (904) 940-2100
Web site: www.treeoflife.com

Certified organic raw-milk hard cheeses

HELIOS NUTRITION
214 Main Street South
Sauk Centre, MN 56378
Telephone: (888) 3-HELIOS
Web site: www.heliosnutrition.com

Certified organic plain low-fat kefir

LIFEWAY FOODS
6431 West Oakton
Morton Grove, IL 60053
Telephone: (847) 967-1010
Web site: www.lifeway.net

Plain whole-milk kefir and soft cheeses

STONYFIELD FARM
Ten Burton Drive
Londonderry, NH 03053
Telephone: (603) 437-5050
Web site: www.stonyfield.com

Certified organic whole-milk plain yogurt

BROWN COW FARM
3810 Delta Fair Boulevard
Antioch, CA 94509
Telephone: (925) 757-9209
Web site: www.browncowfarm.com

Whole-milk plain yogurt

SEVEN STARS FARM
Phoenixville, PA
Telephone: (610) 935-1949

Organic yogurt, soft and hard cheeses

SPRINGFIELD CREAMERY/NANCY'S YOGURT
29440 Airport Road
Eugene, OR 97402
Telephone: (541) 689-2911
Web site: www.nancysyogurt.com

Whole-milk plain yogurt

STRAUS FAMILY CREAMERY
P. O. Box 768
Marshall, CA 94940
Telephone: (213) 481-0745
Web site: www.strausmilk.com

Organic cream, soft and hard cheeses, and butter

ALTA DENA DAIRY
17637 E. Valley Boulevard
City of Industry, CA 91744
Telephone: (800) MILK 123
Web site: www.altadenadairy.com

Organic yogurt, cheeses, sour cream, etc.

PEACEFUL PASTURES
69 Cowan Valley Lane
Hickman, TN 38567
Telephone: (615) 683-4291
Web site: www.peacefulpastures.com

Dairy products including milk, cream, butter, buttermilk, whey, kefir, colostrum, and a "Pro-Yo-Gurt." Raw dairy also available. Ships nationwide.

Dairy Products (Sheep's Milk)

OLD CHATHAM
SHEEPHERDING COMPANY
155 Shaker Museum Road
Old Chatham, New York 12136
Telephone: (518) 794-7733

Web site: www.blacksheepcheese.com

Delicious full-fat sheep's milk yogurt and several varieties of cheeses

Kefir Starter

BODY ECOLOGY
2103 North Decatur Road, Suite 224
Decatur, GA 30033
Telephone: (800) 511-2660
Web site: www.bodyecologydiet.com

Body Ecology's kefir starter can be used to make your own kefir from healthy goat's or cow's milk. Directions for use are included.

Fermented Whey

CONTINENTAL ACIDOPHILUS
2100 Smithtown Avenue
Ronkonkoma, NY 11779
Telephone: (631) 244-2021
Web site: www.continentalyogurt.com

Red Meat

EAT WILD
Web site: www.eatwild.com

Explains the benefits of eating meat and dairy products from grass-fed, not grain-fed, animals. Visit their suppliers' page to find out how to purchase grass-fed meat and dairy products in your area.

WWW.MERCOLA.COM

Supplies grass-fed beef. Available online for mail order delivery.

REAL FOODS MARKET
743 West 1200 North, Suite 200
Springville, UT 84663
Telephone: (866) 284-7325
Web site: www.realfoodsmarket.com

Organic grass-fed beef available frozen by mail order

GREEN CIRCLE ORGANIC BEEF
360 Main Street
Washington, VA 22747
Telephone: (540) 675-2627
Web site: www.greencircle.com

Pasture-fed organic beef

BRADY AXIS VENISON
P. O. Box 536
Okeechobee, FL
Telephone: (800) 291-9555

Web site: www.bradyranchmeats.com

Pasture-fed venison

HOMESTEAD HEALTHY FOODS
1313 West Live Oak Street
Fredricksburg, TX 78624
Telephone: (888) 861-5670
Web site: www.homesteadhealthyfoods.com

Certified organic, grass-fed beef

WYOMING NATURAL
P. O. Box 962
New Castle, WY 82701
Telephone: (800) 969-9946
Web site: www.wyomingnatural.com

Grass-fed beef

ORGANIC VALLEY
507 West Main Street
LaFarge, WI 54639
Telephone: (608) 625-2602
Web site: www.organicvalley.com

Packaged organic steaks, hot dogs, etc.

ZOOKS ORGANIC POULTRY
Christiana, PA
Telephone: (717) 442-8745

Organic beef, chicken, eggs, and dairy

APPLEGATE FARMS
10 County Line Road, Suite 22
Branchburg, NJ 08876
Telephone: (800) 587-8289
Web site: www.applegatefarms.com

Packaged meats and deli slices

MEYER FOODS
4611 W. Adams Street
Lincoln, NE 68524
Telephone: (402) 470-4362
Web site: www.meyerbeef.com

Natural Angus beef (hormone- and antibiotic-free)

MAVERICK RANCH NATURAL MEATS
5360 North Franklin Street
Denver, CO 80216
Telephone: (303) 294-0146
Web site: www.maverickranch.com

Natural beef, chicken, lamb, and buffalo

COLEMAN NATURAL MEATS
1767 Denver West Marriott Road, Suite 200
Golden, CO 80401
Telephone: (800) 442-8666

Web site: www.colemannatural.com

Naturally raised, hormone- and antibiotic-free beef products.

LIBERTY FAMILY FARMS
Hart, MI
Telephone: (231) 873-3737
E-mail: adwright@netpenny.net

Organic, grass-fed beef and lamb. Available in select regions only.

PEACEFUL PASTURES
69 Cowan Valley Lane
Hickman, TN 38567
Telephone: (615) 683-4291
Web site: www.peacefulpastures.com

Providers of grass-fed and grass-finished beef, lamb, and goat that are all natural and hormone- and antibiotic-free. Ships nationwide.

BALDWIN FAMILY FARMS
5341 Highway 86 South
Yanceyville, NC 27379
Telephone: (800) 896-4857
E-mail: vmac@baldwincharolais.com
Web site: www.baldwinfamilyfarms.com

Grass-fed, all-natural beef

U.S. WELLNESS MEATS
17260 State Highway A
Monticello, MO 63457-9704
Telephone: (877) 383-0051
Fax: (573) 767-8837
Web site: www.uswellnessmeats.com

Grass-fed beef and lamb; free-range chicken; butter and cheese. All products are hormone free, antibiotic free, non-irradiated, and free of any preservatives or additives. Ships overnight nationwide every Monday, Tuesday, and Wednesday.

Poultry

EAT WILD
Web site: www.eatwild.com

Visit their suppliers' page to find out how to purchase free-range, pastured poultry in your area.

OAKLYN PLANTATION
1312 Oaklyn Road
Darlington, SC 29532
Telephone: (843) 395-0793
Fax: (843) 395-0794
Web site: www.freerangechicken.com

Free-range chickens (hormone- and antibiotic-free)

ROSIE'S ORGANIC CHICKEN
2700 Lakeville Highway
Petaluma, CA 94955
Telephone: (800) 556-6789
Web site: www.healthychickenchoices.com

ZOOKS ORGANIC POULTRY
Christiana, PA
Telephone: (717) 442-8745

Organic chicken, eggs, beef, and dairy

SHELTON'S POULTRY, INC.
204 Loranne Avenue
Pomona, CA 91767
Telephone: (909) 623-4361
Web site: www.sheltons.com

Free-range turkey and chicken (hormone- and antibiotic-free)

EBERLY POULTRY
1095 Mount Airy Road
Stevens, PA 17578
Telephone: (717) 336-6440

Free-range and organic poultry

RAISED RIGHT
College Hill Poultry
220 North Center Street
Fredericksburg, PA 17026
Telephone: (800) 767-4537
Web site: www.raisedright.com

Certified organic, free-range poultry

BELL & EVANS
P. O. Box 39
Fredericksburg, PA
Telephone: (717) 865-1176
Web site: www.bellandevans.com

Fresh and frozen natural poultry products

APPLEGATE FARMS
10 County Line Road, Suite 22
Branchburg, NJ 08876
Telephone: (800) 587-8289
Web site: www.applegatefarms.com

Packaged chicken and turkey deli slices

LIBERTY FAMILY FARMS
Hart, MI
Telephone: (231) 873-3737
E-mail: adwright@netpenney.net

Organic free-range chicken and eggs without antibiotics or hormones.

Available in select regions only.

PEACEFUL PASTURES
69 Cowan Valley Lane
Hickman, TN 38567
Telephone: (615) 683-7291
Web site: www.peacefulpastures.com

Providers of free-roaming chicken and turkey that are all natural and hormone- and antibiotic-free. Ships nationwide.

U.S. WELLNESS MEATS
17260 State Highway A
Monticello, MO 63457-9704
Telephone: (877) 383-0051
Fax: (573) 767-8837
Web site: www.uswellnessmeats.com

Grass-fed beef and lamb; free-range chicken; butter and cheese. All products are hormone free, antibiotic free, non-irradiated, and free of any preservatives or additives. Ships overnight nationwide every Monday, Tuesday, and Wednesday.

Deli Meat

APPLEGATE FARMS
10 County Line Road, Suite 22
Branchburg, NJ 08876
Telephone: (800) 587-8289
Web site: www.applegatefarms.com

Packaged meats and deli slices (nitrate- and nitrite-free)

Chicken Feet

OAKLYN PLANTATION
1312 Oaklyn Road
Darlington, SC 29532
Telephone: (843) 395-0793
Fax: (843) 395-0794
Web site: www.freerangechicken.com

Free-range chickens (hormone- and antibiotic-free). Use chicken feet in broth recipes.

Eggs

GOLD CIRCLE FARMS
Boulder, CO
Web site: www.goldcirclefarms.com

DHA omega-3 eggs

ORGANIC VALLEY
507 West Main Street
LaFarge, WI 54639
Telephone: (608) 625-2602
Web site: www.organicvalley.com

Certified organic high omega-3 eggs

CHINO VALLEY RANCHERS
5611 Peck Road
Arcadia, CA 91006
Telephone: (800) 354-4503
Web site: www.chinovalleyranchers.com

High omega-3 eggs

EGG INNOVATIONS
3420 Highway W
Port Washington, WI 53074
Telephone: (262) 284-1619
Web site: www.egginnovations.com

High omega-3 eggs

HAPPY HEN EGGS
Pleasant View Farms
Winfield, PA 17889

Certified organic eggs

POLYFACE EGGS
15488 Barnrock Road
Mendota, VA 24270
Telephone: (540) 466-8689
Web site: www.ecofriendly.com

Organic eggs

ZOOKS ORGANIC POULTRY
Christiana, PA
Telephone: (717) 442-874

Organic eggs, chicken, beef, and dairy

PETE AND GERRY'S ORGANIC EGGS
140 Buffman Road
Monroe, NH 03771
Telephone: (800) 438-3447
Web site: www.peteandgerrys.com

Organic omega-3 eggs

Locally produced, farm-fresh eggs from free-range chickens are also very beneficial.

Fish

BARLEAN'S FISHERY
4936 Lake Terrell Road
Ferndale, WA 98248
Telephone: (360) 384-0485
Web site: www.barleans.com

Ecologically wild harvested salmon, a rich source of omega-3 fatty acids

ECOFISH, INC.
78 Market Street
Portsmouth, NH 03801
Telephone: (603) 430-0101

Fax: (603) 430-9929
Web site: www.ecofish.com
  Ocean-caught salmon, halibut, tuna, and other fish

WWW.MERCOLA.COM
  Wild-caught salmon. Available online for mail order delivery.

REAL FOODS MARKET
743 West 1200 North, Suite 200
Springville, UT 84663
Telephone: (866) 284-7325
Web site: www.realfoodsmarket.com
  Wild salmon and salmon jerky. Available via mail order and shipped frozen

AVALON
201 SW Second Street
Corvallis, OR 97333
Telephone: (541) 752-7418
Web site: www.oregongourmet.com
  An assortment of smoked wild northwest salmon

VITAL SEAFOOD
605 30th Street
Anacortes, WA 98221
Telephone: (800) 608-4825
Web site: www.vitalchoice.com

ECHO FALLS
1100 West Ewing Street
Seattle, WA 98119
Telephone: (206) 285-6800
Web site: www.oceanbeauty.com
  Smoked salmon

CROWN PRINCE NATURAL
18581 Railroad Street
City of Industry, CA 91748
Telephone: (626) 912-5850
Web site: www.crownprince.com
  Canned salmon and other fish

ROLAND FOOD COMPANY
71 West 23rd Street
New York, NY 10010
Telephone: (800) 221-4030
Web site: www.rolandfood.com
  Canned sardines and other fish

BRISTOL BAY WILD SALMON
Telephone: (207) 233-4353
Web site: www.bristolbaywildsalmon.com
  Wild sockeye salmon

RAINCOAST
Telephone: (604) 582-8268
  Smoked wild sockeye salmon

ILIAMNA FISH COMPANY
844 SW Vista Avenue
Portland, OR 97205
Telephone: (503) 224-8844
Web site: www.redsalmon.com
  Wild Alaskan sockeye salmon

BLUE GALLEON
260 Boston Post Road, Suite 1
Wayland, MA 01778
Telephone: (866) 4MyBela
Web site: www.mybela.com
  Tuna and sardines from Portugal. Sardines are canned within two hours of catch.

Cultured/Fermented Vegetables

**REJUVENATIVE FOODS
(DEER GARDEN FOODS)**
P. O. Box 8464
Santa Cruz, CA 95061
Telephone: (800) 805-7957
Web site: www.rejuvenative.com
  The highest-quality raw fermented vegetables, including sauerkraut and kimchi. Available in some grocery and health food stores, and online for mail order.

DEEP ROOT GRAIN & SALT SOCIETY
273 Fairway Drive
Asheville, NC 28805
Telephone: (800) 867-7258
Web site: www.celtic-seasalt.com

Cultured Vegetable Starter

BODY ECOLOGY
273 Fairway Drive
Asheville, NC 28805
Telephone: (800) 511-2660
Web site: www.bodyecologydiet.com
  This starter can be used to make your own cultured vegetables at home.

Nuts and Seeds

LIVING NUTZ
P. O. Box 11413
Portland, ME 04104
Telephone: (207) 780-1101
Web site: www.organicglobal.com

WOODSTOCK ORGANICS
250 West Nyack Road
W. Nyack, NY 10994
Telephone: (914) 623-7649
Web site: www.woodstockorganics.com

LIVING TREE COMMUNITY CO-OP
P. O. Box 10082
Berkeley, CA 94709
Telephone: (510) 526-7106
Web site: www.livingtreecommunity.com
   Extensive supply of organic raw nuts and seeds. Available by mail order only.

GLASER ORGANIC FARMS
19100 SW 137th Avenue
Miami, FL 33012
Telephone: (305) 238-7747
Web site: www.glaserorganicfarms.com
   Extensive supply of organic raw nuts and seeds. Available by mail order only.

DEEP ROOT GRAIN & SALT SOCIETY
273 Fairway Drive
Asheville, NC 28805
Telephone: (800) 867-7258
Fax: (828) 299-1640
Web site: www.celtic-seasalt.com
   Extensive supply of organic raw nuts and seeds. Available by mail order only.

SILVER SPRING SUPPLEMENTS
2915 29th Avenue SW, Suite E
Tumwater, WA 98512
Telephone: (800) 520-1791
Web site: www.silverspringsupplements.com
   Extensive supply of organic raw nuts and seeds. Available by mail order only.

TIERRA FARMS
71 Oliver Street
Cohoes, NY 12047
Telephone: (888) 674-6887
Fax: (518) 237-4671
Web site: www.tierrafarm.com
   Nuts and seeds. Available in health food stores.

AUSTRIA'S FINEST NATURALLY
Box 69
Mt. Vernon, VA 22121
Telephone: (703) 360-5766
Fax: (703) 780-8393
Web site: www.austrianpumpkinoil.com
   Austrian pumpkinseeds high in nutrients, including zinc

THE RAW WORLD
P.O. Box 16156
West Palm Beach, FL 33416
Telephone: (866) RAW DIET
Web site: www.therawworld.com
   Supplier of raw foods, live food supplements, juicers, blenders, and many other excellent products

Nut and Seed Butters

REJUVENATIVE FOODS
(Deer Garden Foods)
P. O. Box 8464
Santa Cruz, CA 95061
Telephone: (800) 805-7957
Web site: www.rejuvenative.com
   The highest-quality raw organic nut and seed butters, including those made from almond, sesame, pumpkin, cashew, and sunflower seeds. Available in some grocery and health food stores, online, or by mail order.

LIVING TREE COMMUNITY CO-OP
P. O. Box 10082
Berkeley, CA 94709
Telephone: (510) 526-7106
Web site: www.livingtreecommunity.com
   Organic raw nut and seed butters. Available by mail order only.

GLASER ORGANIC FARMS
19100 SW 137th Avenue
Miami, FL 33012
Telephone: (305) 238-7747
Web site: www.glaserorganicfarms.com
   Organic raw nut and seed butters. Available by mail order only.

MARANATHA
P. O. Box 1046
Ashland, OR 97520
Web site: www.nspiredfoods.com
   Nut and seed butters. Available in health food stores.

ARROWHEAD MILLS
P. O. Box 2059
Hereford, TX 79045
Telephone: (800) 749-0730
Web site: www.arrowheadmills.com
   Nuts and seeds. Available in health food stores.

ONCE AGAIN NUT BUTTER
P. O. Box 429
Nunda, NY 14517
Telephone: (800) 804-8520
Web site: www.onceagainnutbutter.com

Nuts and seeds. Available in health food stores.

Healthy Fats and Oils

GARDEN OF LIFE
Visit Garden of Life's Web site,
www.gardenoflife.com,
or call (866) 465-0094 for product
information or for the retailer nearest you.

Once thought to be a "bad" fat, coconut oil has been shown to be a stable, healthy saturated fat. In fact, extra-virgin coconut oil is one of the healthiest and most versatile unprocessed dietary oils in the world. Garden of Life Extra-Virgin Coconut Oil is unprocessed culinary oil full of natural coconut flavor and aroma.

BARLEAN'S ORGANIC OILS
4936 Lake Terrell Road
Ferndale, WA 98248
Telephone: (360) 384-0485
Web site: www.barleans.com

Organic high-lignan flaxseed oil and borage seed oil. Available at health food stores.

OMEGA NUTRITION
6515 Aldrich Road
Bellingham, WA 98226
Telephone: (800) 661-3529
Fax: (360) 384-0700
Web site: www.omeganutrition.com

Organic flax oil, olive oil, and garlic-chili flax oil.

PURITY FARMS
14635 Westcreek Road
Sedalia, CO 80135
Telephone: (303) 647-2368
Fax: (303) 647-9875
Web site: www.purityfarms.com

Organic ghee, the traditional Indian clarified butter

MANITOBA HARVEST
15-2166 Notre Dame Avenue
Winnipeg, MB, Canada R3H 0K2
Telephone: (204) 953-0233
Web site: www.manitobaharvest.com

Organic hempseed oil

FLORA, INC.
805 East Badger Road
Lynden, WA 98264
Telephone: (800) 498-3610
Web site: www.florahealth.com

Organic oils in glass bottles, including hard-to-find oils, such as pumpkin, borage, flax, etc.

OLIO BEATO
Bitetto, Italy
Web site: www.organicoil.com

Organic extra-virgin olive oil

BIONATURAE
5 Tyler Drive
North Franklin, CT 06254
Telephone: (860) 642-6996
Web site: www.bionaturae.com

Organic extra-virgin olive oil

SPECTRUM NATURALS
1304 South Point Boulevard
Petaluma, CA 94954
Telephone: (707) 778-8900
Web site: www.spectrumorganic.com

Organic extra-virgin olive oil

AUSTRIA'S FINEST NATURALLY
Box 69
Mt. Vernon, VA 22121
Telephone: (703) 360-5766
Fax: (703) 780-8393
Web site: www.austrianpumpkinoil.com

Austrian pumpkinseed oil

CATANIA-SPAGNA CORPORATION
Telephone: (800) 343-5522
Web site: www.cataniausa.com

Organic extra-virgin olive oil

Water

WAIWERA INFINITY
7-11 Waiwera Road
P.O. Box 70, Waiwera, 1240
Auckland, New Zealand
Telephone (USA): (480) 767-7782
Web site: www.waiwera.co.nz

Available in health food stores nationwide.

MOUNTAIN VALLEY SPRING WATER COMPANY
150 Central Avenue
Hot Springs, AR 71901

Telephone: (800) 643-1501
Web site: www.mountainvalleyspring.com
   Only U.S. water still bottled in glass

TRINITY SPRINGS
P. O. Box 8810
Ketchum, ID 83340
Telephone: (800) 390-5693
Web site: www.trinitysprings.com

NARIWA, INC.
35104 Euclid Avenue, Suite 302
Willoughby, OH 44094
Telephone: (866) 4-NARIWA
E- mail: ask@nariwa.com
   Naturally bio-energized water from
Japan's magnetic mountain has been
found to increase cell hydration, detox,
and pH balance; visit www.ohno.org for
studies and evidence.

Organic Produce, Fresh and Frozen

CASCADIAN FARMS
719 Metcalf Street
Sedro-Wooley, WA 98284
Telephone: (360) 855- 2730
Web site: www.cfarm.com
   Frozen, packaged organic fruits and
vegetables, including berries. Available
in health food and grocery stores
nationwide.

EARTHBOUND FARMS
1721 San Juan Highway
San Juan Bautista, CA 95045
Telephone: (800) 690-3200
Web site: www.earthboundfarm.com
   Fresh, packaged organic produce

CHAMPLAIN VALLEY FARMS
5105 Fisher
St-Laurent, Quebec H4T 1J8, Canada
Telephone: (613) 674-2444
   Frozen, packaged organic fruits and
vegetables

Produce Wash

VEGGIE WASH
1560 Big Shanty Drive
Kennesaw, GA 30144
Telephone: (800) 451-7096
Web site: www.citrusmagic.com
   100 percent natural vegetable-based

ingredients taken from citrus fruit, corn,
and coconut

Vegetables, Canned or in Glass Jars

NATIVE FOREST
Edward and Sons Trading Co.
P. O. Box 1326
Carpenteria, CA 93014
Telephone: (805) 684-8500
Web site: www.edwardandsons.com
   Organic hearts of palm and asparagus
spears

BIONATURAE
5 Tyler Drive
North Franklin, CT 06254
Telephone: (860) 642-6996
Web site: www.bionaturae.com
   Whole tomatoes (peeled, crushed,
stewed, and tomato paste) in glass jars

MEDITERRANEAN ORGANICS
215 Katonah Avenue
Katonah, NY 10536
Telephone: (914) 232-3102
Web site: www.mediterraneanorganic.com
   Organic red peppers; rehydrated
organic sun-dried tomatoes in organic
olive oil and spices; and capers—all
packaged in glass jars

MUIR GLEN
719 Metcalf Street
Sedro Woolley, WA 98284
Telephone: (800) 832-6345
Web site: www.muirglen.com
   Canned tomato products, tomato
sauces, and salsas

Cultured/Fermented Soy Products (Miso, Tamari, Tempeh)

Fermented/cultured soy is the only
form of soy that is recommended.

OHSAWA
San Diego, CA 92126
Telephone: (800) 475-3663
   Unpasteurized organic miso and
soy sauce. Also, the best, least salty
umeboshi plums.

SOUTH RIVER MISO COMPANY
Conway, MA 01341
Telephone: (413) 369-4057
 A wide variety of refrigerated,
unpasteurized organic miso

WHITE WAVE
1990 North 57th Court
Boulder, CO 80301
Telephone: (800) 488-9283
Web site: www.whitewave.com
 Certified organic tempeh

LIGHTLIFE
153 Industrial Boulevard
Turners Falls, MA 01376
Telephone: (413) 863-8500
Web site: www.lightlife.com
 Certified organic tempeh

TURTLE ISLAND FOODS
P. O. Box 176
Hood River, OR 97031
Telephone: (800) 508-8100
Web site: www.tofurky.com
 Certified organic tempeh

Dried Fruit

LIVING TREE COMMUNITY CO-OP
P. O. Box 10082
Berkeley, CA 94709
Telephone: (510) 526-7106
Web site: www.livingtreecommunity.com
 Organic dried fruits. Available by mail
order only.

SILVER SPRING SUPPLEMENTS
2915 29th Avenue SW, Suite E
Tumwater, WA 98512
Telephone: (800) 520-1791
Web site: www.silverspringsupplements.com
 Organic dried fruits. Available by mail
order only.

WOODSTOCK ORGANICS
250 West Nyack Road
W. Nyack, NY 10994
Telephone: (914) 623-7649
Web site: www.woodstockorganics.com

PAVICH FAMILY FARMS
3651 Pegasus Drive, Suite 101
Bakersfield, CA 93308
Telephone: (661) 391-6354
Web site: www.pavich.com

GLASER ORGANIC FARMS
19100 SW 137th Avenue
Miami, FL 33012
Telephone: (305) 238-7747
Web site: www.glaserorganicfarms.com
 Organic dried fruits. Available by mail
order only.

TIERRA FARM
71 Oliver Street
Cohoes, NY 12047
Telephone: (888) 674-6887
Fax: (518) 237-4671

INTERNATIONAL HARVEST INC.
71-40 242nd Street
Douglaston, New York 11362
Telephone: (800) 277-4268
 Organic dried fruit, nuts, seeds, and
nut butters under the GO! brand

FINE DRIED FOODS
INTERNATIONAL
2553 A Mission Street
Santa Cruz, CA 95060
Telephone: (831) 426-1413
E-mail: awesomefruit@yahoo.com

Apple Sauce and Fruit Spreads

SOLANA GOLD ORGANICS
Appleseed Orchards
P. O. Box 1340
Sebastopol, CA 95473
Telephone: (707) 829-1121
Web site: www.solanagold.com
 Organic "Gravenstein" apple sauce

EDEN FOODS
701 Tecumseh Road
Clinton, MI 49236
Telephone: (800) 248-0320
Web site: www.edenfoods.com
 Organic apple sauce

SANTA CRUZ ORGANIC
P. O. Box 369
Chico, CA 95927
Telephone: (530) 899-5000
Web site: www.knudsenjuices.com
 Organic apple sauce

HARVEST MOON
Tree of Life
P. O. Box 410
St. Augustine, FL 32085

Telephone: (904) 825-2026
Web site: www.treeoflife.com
　　Organic fruit-juice-sweetened fruit spreads

CASCADIAN FARMS
719 Metcalf Street
Sedro-Wooley, WA 98284
Telephone: (360) 855-2730
Web site: www.cfarm.com
　　Organic fruit spreads (look for fruit-juice-sweetened; some have sugar)

BIONATURAE
5 Tyler Drive
North Franklin, CT 06254
Telephone: (860) 642-6996
Web site: www.bionaturae.com
　　Organic fruit spreads of the highest quality

Coconut Milk

THAI KITCHEN
229 Castro Street
Oakland, CA 94607
Telephone: (800) 967-8424 or (510) 268-0209
Web site: www.thaikitchen.com
　　Thai Kitchen Pure Coconut Milk and other coconut milk and coconut cream products

NATIVE FOREST
Edward & Sons Trading Co.
P. O. Box 1326
Carpenteria, CA 93014
Telephone: (805) 684-8500
Web site: www.edwardandsons.com
　　Certified organic coconut milk

Grains and Flour

ARROWHEAD MILLS
P. O. Box 2059
Hereford, TX 79045
Telephone: (800) 749-0730
Web site: www.arrowheadmills.com
　　Packaged and bulk organic grains and flour

LUNDBERG FAMILY FARMS
P. O. Box 369
Richvale, CA 95974
Telephone: (530) 882-4551
Web site: www.lundberg.com
　　Packaged and bulk organic grains

and flour

WOODSTOCK ORGANICS
250 West Nyack Road
West Nyack, NY 10994
Telephone: (914) 623-7649
Web site: www.woodstockorganics.com

Breads

FRENCH MEADOW BAKERY
2610 Lyndale Avenue
South Minneapolis, MN 55408
Telephone: (612) 870-4740
Web site: www.frenchmeadow.com
　　Organic yeast-free breads

FOOD FOR LIFE
2991 East Doherty Street
Corona, CA 92879
Telephone: (909) 279-5090
Web site: www.food-for-life.com
　　Sprouted breads, including Ezekiel 4:9 bread, sprouted bagels, and sprouted tortillas

ALVARADO STREET BAKERY
500 Martin Avenue
Rohnert Park, CA 94928
Telephone: (707) 585-3293
Web site: www.alvaradostbakery.com
　　Sprouted breads, tortillas, and bagels

SUNNYVALE BAKERY
2410 Santa Clara
Richmond, CA 94804
Telephone: (510) 527-7066
　　Sprouted breads

NATURE'S PATH
7453 Progress Way
Richmond, BC V4G 1E, Canada
Telephone: (604) 940-0505
Web site: www.naturespath.com
　　Producers of manna-sprouted grain bread

Pastas

EDEN FOODS
701 Tecumseh Road
Clinton, MI 49236
Telephone: (800) 248-0320
Web site: www.edenfoods.com

EDDIE'S PASTAS
Mrs. Leepers
12455 Kerran Street, Suite 200

Poway, CA 92064
Telephone: (858) 486-1101
Web site: www.mrsleeperspasta.com

TINKYADA PASTAS
120 Melford Drive, Suite 8
Scarborough, ON M1B 2X5, Canada
Telephone: (416) 609-0016
Web site: www.tinkyada.com

Wheat-free/gluten-free

RIZOPIA
4490 Sheppard Avenue, Suite 13
Toronto, ON M1S 4J9, Canada
Telephone: (416) 609-8820
Web site: www.rizopia.com

Organic wild rice and organic corn pasta

ANNIE'S HOMEGROWN
P. O. Box 554
Wakefield, MA 01880
Telephone: (781) 224-9639
Web site: www.annies.com

BIONATURAE
5 Tyler Drive
North Franklin, CT 06254
Telephone: (860) 642-6996
Web site: www.bionaturae.com

Organic whole-grain pasta from Italy

Cereals

FOOD FOR LIFE
2991 East Doherty Street
Corona, CA 92879
Telephone: (909) 279-5090
Web site: www.food-for-life.com

Producers of the highest-quality sprouted cereals, including Ezekiel 4:9 cereal

KASHI COMPANY
P. O. Box 8557
La Jolla, CA 92038
Telephone: (858) 274-8870
Web site: www.kashi.com

SAVE THE FOREST
New England Natural Bakers
74 Fairview Street East
Greenfield, MA 01301
Telephone: (800) 910-2884
Web site: www.nenb.com

Packaged organic granolas

NATURE'S PATH
7453 Progress Way
Richmond, BC V4G 1E8, Canada
Telephone: (604) 940-0505
Web site: www.naturespath.com

BREADSHOP
Hain-Celestial Group
50 Charles Lindbergh Boulevard
Uniondale, NY 11553
Telephone: (516) 237-6200
Web site: www.hain-celestial.com

Popcorn

LITTLE BEAR ORGANICS
(BEARITOS BRAND)
Hain-Celestial Group
Melville, NY
Telephone: (800) 434-4246

Packaged organic popcorn

NATURE'S POPCORN
RASTAPOP
491 Seminole Avenue
Atlanta, GA 30307
Telephone: (404) 688-6193
Web site: www.rastapop.com

Prepackaged popcorn using corn, non-irradiated herbs, and 100 percent vegan ingredients. Four flavors available.

Packaged Organic Popcorn

We highly recommend that you pop your own corn from dried, organic popping corn found in the bulk department of your local health food store. If a hot air popper is not available, try using extra-virgin coconut oil, and then season generously with nutritional yeast (for a "cheesy" flavor), Celtic sea salt, or Herbamare seasoning.

Beans (Canned and Dried)

SHARIANN'S ORGANIC
3245 Broad Street
Dexter, MI 48130
Telephone: (734) 426-0989
Web site: www.shariannsorganic.com

Full line of organic canned beans/legumes

EDEN FOODS
701 Tecumseh Road

Clinton, MI 49236
Telephone: (800) 248-0320
Web site: www.edenfoods.com
    Full line of organic dried and canned
beans/legumes

AMY'S KITCHEN
2330 Northpoint Parkway
Santa Rosa, CA 95407
Telephone: (707) 578-7188
Web site: www.amys.com
    Full line of organic canned beans/
legumes

WALNUT ACRES/ACIRCA INC.
4120 Douglas Boulevard, Suite 306-377
Granite Bay, CA 95746
Telephone: (916) 791-7334
Web site: www.walnutacres.com
    Full line of organic canned beans/
legumes

DEEP ROOT GRAIN & SALT
SOCIETY
273 Fairway Drive
Asheville, NC 28805
Telephone: (800) 867-7258
Fax: (828) 299-1640
Web site: www.celtic-seasalt.com

Soups (Canned and Dried)

AMY'S KITCHEN
2330 Northpoint Parkway
Santa Rosa, CA 95407
Telephone: (707) 578-7188
Web site: www.amys.com

WALNUT ACRES/ACIRCA INC.
4120 Douglas Boulevard, Suite 306-377
Granite Bay, CA 95746
Telephone: (916) 791-7334
Web site: www.walnutacres.com

SHARIANN'S ORGANIC
3245 Broad Street
Dexter, MI 48130
Telephone: (800) 434-4246
Web site: www.shariannsorganic.com

ANKE KRUSE ORGANICS INC.
14191 Crewson's Line
Acton, ON, Canada L7J2L7
Telephone: (519) 853-3899
Web site: www.ankekruseorganics.ca
    Harvest Sun organic dried soups

Canned/Dried Soup Stock (Chicken, Beef, Fish)

PACIFIC FOODS
19480 SW 97th Avenue
Tualatin, OR 97062
Telephone: (503) 692-9666
Web site: www.pacificfoods.com
    Certified organic free-range chicken
stock

IMAGINE FOODS
1245 San Carlos Avenue
San Carlos, CA 94070
Telephone: (800) 333-6339
Web site: www.imaginefoods.com
    Certified organic free-range chicken
stock

HEALTH VALLEY
Hain-Celestial Group
50 Charles Lindbergh Boulevard
Uniondale, NY 11553
Telephone: (516) 237-6200
Web site: www.hain-celestial.com
    Beef and chicken stock in cans

ANKE KRUSE ORGANICS INC.
14191 Crewson's Line
Acton, ON, Canada L7J2L7
Telephone: (519) 853-3899
Web site: www.ankekruseorganics.ca
    Harvest Sun organic chicken bouillon
cubes

KITCHEN BASICS
P. O. Box 41022
Brecksville, OH 44141
Telephone: (440) 838-1344
    All-natural chicken, beef, and seafood
stock

Seaweed

ISLAND HERBS & KELP
P. O. Box 25
Waldron Island, WA 98297
E-mail: ryandrum2020@yahoo.com
    The finest hand-harvested bull-
whip kelp and bladderwrack seaweed
from moving cold water in the Pacific
Northwest

MAINE COAST
3 Georges Pond Road
Franklin, ME 04634
Telephone: (207) 565-2907

Web site: www.seaveg.com

EDEN FOODS
701 Tecumseh Road
Clinton, MI 49236
Telephone: (800) 248-0320
Web site: www.edenfoods.com

Marinades

GLASER ORGANIC FARMS
19100 SW 137th Avenue
Miami, FL 33012
Telephone: (305) 238-7747
Web site: www.glaserorganicfarms.com

DYMO-ZEST
P. O. Box 822
Laguna Beach, CA 92652
    Sea palm marinades

SPECTRUM NATURALS
1304 South Point Boulevard
Petaluma, CA 94954
Telephone: (707) 778-8900
Web site: www.spectrumorganic.com

CHELTEN HOUSE PRODUCTS
607 Heron Drive
Bridgeport, NJ 08014
Telephone: (856) 467-1600
Web site: www.cheltenhouse.com
    Organic sauces, dressings, and
marinades

Sauces

WIZARD ORGANIC SAUCES
Edwards & Sons Trading Co.
P. O. Box 1326
Carpenteria, CA 93014
Telephone: (805) 684-8500
Web site: www.edwardandsons.com
    Organic vegetarian Worcestershire
sauce and hot sauce

SEEDS OF CHANGE
P. O. Box 15700
Santa Fe, NM 87506
Telephone: (888) 762-4240
Web site: www.seedsofchange.com
    Organic tomato sauces and salsas

MUIR GLEN
719 Metcalf Street
Sedro-Woolley, WA 98284
Telephone: (800) 832-6345
Web site: www.muirglen.com

    Organic tomato sauces and salsas

WALNUT ACRES/ACIRCA INC.
4120 Douglas Boulevard, Suite 306-377
Granite Bay, CA 95746
Telephone: (916) 791-7334
Web site: www.walnutacres.com
    Organic salsas

Honey

SILVER SPRING SUPPLEMENTS
2915 29th Avenue SW, Suite E
Tumwater, WA 98512
Telephone: (800) 520-1791
Web site: www.silverspringsupplements.com
    The highest quality organic, raw,
unheated honey

REALLY RAW HONEY COMPANY
3500 Boston Street, Suite 32
Baltimore, MD 21224
Telephone: (800) 732-5729 or (410) 675-7233
Fax: (410) 675-7411
Web site: www.ReallyRawHoney.com
    The finest enzyme-rich raw honey.
Available in some health food and gro-
cery stores.

NORTHWOODS APIARIES
P. O. Box 94
Lowell, VT 05847
Telephone: (802) 744-2007
E-mail: jwhite@surfglobal.net
    Certified organic raw honey, pollen,
propolis, and beeswax

FARM STYLE RAW APITHERAPY
HONEY
Honey Gardens Apiaries
P. O. Box 189
Hinesburg, VT 05461
Telephone: (802) 985-5852
Fax: (802) 985-9039
Web site: www.honeygardens.com/contact.htm
    Raw honey, propolis, and other bee
products. Available in some health food
and grocery stores.

MANUKA HONEY USA
88878 Highway 101 North
P. O. Box 2474
Florence, OR 97439
Telephone: (541) 902-0979
Fax: (541) 902-8825
Web site: www.manukahoneyusa.com
    A variety of raw honey products.

Available in some health food and grocery stores.

SACKEL CORPORATION USA-BRAZIL
Telephone: (800) 336-8470
Fax: (954) 784-6232
Telephone: (201) 420-0718
Fax: (201) 420-1775
Web site: www.sackel.com
Varieties of natural honey

Sweeteners

SHADY MAPLE
2585 Skymark Avenue, Suite 305
Mississauga, ON L4W 4L5, Canada
Telephone: (905) 206-1455
Web site: www.shadymaple.ca
Organic maple syrup

UP COUNTRY NATURALS
1052 Portland Street
St. Johnsbury, VT 05819
Telephone: (800) 525- 2540
Web site: www.upcountrynaturals.com
Organic maple syrup

RAPUNZEL PURE ORGANICS
2424 Route 203
Valatie, NY 12184
Telephone: (518) 392-8620
Web site: www.rapunzel.com
Rapadura organic unrefined sugar

EQUAL EXCHANGE
251 Revere Street
Canton, MA 02021
Telephone: (781) 830-0303
Web site: www.equalexchange.com
Certified organic unrefined sugar

WHOLESOME FOODS
8016 Highway 90-A
Sugar Land, TX 77478
Telephone: (281) 490-9582
Web site: www.wholesomesweeteners.com
Sucanat organic unrefined sugar

SWEETLEAF
2546 West Birchwood Avenue, Suite 104
Mesa, AZ 85202
Telephone: (800) 899-9908
Web site: www.sweetleaf.com
Stevia products (safe for diabetics)

Salt and Seasonings

DEEP ROOT GRAIN & SALT SOCIETY
273 Fairway Drive
Asheville, NC 28805
Telephone: (800) 867-7258
Fax: (828) 299-1640
Web site: www.celtic-seasalt.com
Celtic sea salt (course and fine) and other health food products. Available in some health food and grocery stores.

REALSALT
(Redmond RealSalt)
P. O. Box 219
Redmond, UT 84652
Telephone: (800) 367-7258
Fax: (435) 529-7486
Web site: www.realsalt.com
RealSalt is mined in central Utah. Available in health food and grocery stores.

RAPUNZEL PURE ORGANICS
2424 State Route 203
Valatie, NY 12184
Telephone: (518) 392-8620
Web site: www.rapunzel.com
A good selection of seasonings, including Herbamare and Trocomare seasonings made with sea salt and organic herbs. Available online or in health food and grocery stores.

LE TRESOR
20623 SE 24th Street
Sammamish, WA 98075
Telephone: (415) 761-7122
Web site: www.saltworks.us
Certified organic sea salt

SPICE HUNTER
184 Suburban Road
San Luis Obispo, CA 93401
Telephone: (800) 444-3096
Web site: www.spicehunter.com
Packaged organic spices in glass jars

FRONTIER HERBS
P. O. Box 299
Norway, IA 52318
Telephone: (800) 669-3275
Web site: www.frontiernaturalbrands.com
Packaged organic spices in glass jars

COCINA DE VEGA
8014 Olson Memorial Highway
Golden Valley, MN 55427
Telephone: (877) 321-5703
Web site: www.cocinadevega.com
   Mesquite meal and hot chiltepin peppers

Apple Cider and Other Vinegars

BRAGG APPLE CIDER VINEGAR
Bragg Live Foods
P. O. Box 7
Santa Barbara, CA 93102
Telephone: (800) 446-1990
   Apple cider vinegar made from organically grown apples, as well as other natural products. Available in some health food and grocery stores.

SPECTRUM NATURALS
1304 South Point Boulevard
Petaluma, CA 94954
Telephone: (707) 778-8900
Web site: www.spectrumorganic.com
   Organic balsamic, cider, brown rice, and wine vinegars

BIONATURAE
5 Tyler Drive
North Franklin, CT 06254
Telephone: (860) 642-6996
Web site: www.bionaturae.com
   Organic balsamic vinegar

SOLANA GOLD ORGANICS
APPLESEED ORCHARDS
P. O. Box 1340
Sebastopol, CA 95473
Telephone: (707) 829-1121
Web site: www.solanagold.com

CATANIA-SPAGNA CORPORATION
Telephone: (800) 343-5522
Web site: www.cataniausa.com
   Organic balsamic vinegar

Condiments

SPECTRUM ORGANIC PRODUCTS
1304 South Point Boulevard, Suite 280
Petaluma, CA 94954
Telephone: (707) 778-8900
Fax: (707) 765-8470
Web site: www.spectrumorganic.com
   Healthy, organic omega-3 mayonnaise using expeller-pressed soy and flaxseed

oils. Available in some health food and grocery stores.

WESTBRAE NATURAL FOODS
(Distributed by Novelco Distribution)
264 South La Cienega Boulevard, Suite 1193
Beverly Hills, CA 90211
Telephone: (562) 948-2872
Fax: (707) 202-7129
Web site: www.novelco.com/westbrae/index.htm
   Natural catsup and mustard. Available in some health food and grocery stores.

ROLAND FOODS
71 West 23rd Street
New York, NY 10010
Telephone: (800) 221-4030
Web site: www.rolandfood.com

Organic Mustards

HEINZ FOODS
P. O. Box 57
Pittsburgh, PA 15230
Telephone: (800) 255-5750
Web site: www.heinz.com

Organic Ketchup

DREAM FOODS INTERNATIONAL
1223 Wilshire Boulevard
Santa Monica, CA 90403
Telephone: (310) 392-6324
Web site: www.dreamfoods.com
   Organic volcano lemon burst, lemon juice with lemon oil

Bottled Fruit Beverages

APPLE & EVE ORGANICS
P.O. Box K
Roslyn, NY 11576
Telephone: (800) 969-8018
Fax: (516) 621-2164
Web site: www.appleandeve.com
   A variety of quality juice products

GTS KOMBUCHA AND SYNERGY DRINKS
Millennium Products Inc.
P. O. Box 2352
Beverly Hills, CA 90213
Telephone: (877) RE-JUICE
Web site: www.naturezone.net
   Fermented beverage. Available in select regions; call for availability.

BIONATURAE
5 Tyler Drive
North Franklin, CT 06254
Telephone: (860) 642-6996
Web site: www.bionaturae.com
   The highest-quality organic bottled juices from Italy

DREAM FOODS INTERNATIONAL
1223 Wilshire Boulevard
Santa Monica, CA 90403
Telephone: (310) 392-6324
Web site: www.dreamfoods.com
   Italian volcano orange juice, organic blood orange juice high in antioxidants

POM WONDERFUL
11444 W. Olympic Boulevard, Suite 210
Los Angeles, CA 90064
Telephone: (310) 966-5800
Web site: www.pomwonderful.com
   Pomegranate juice

AUSTRIA'S FINEST NATURALLY
Box 69
Mt. Vernon, VA 22121
Telephone: (703) 360-5766
Fax: (703) 780-8393
Web site: www.austrianpumpkinoil.com
   Austrian black currant juice a rich source of antioxidants

STEAZ GREEN TEA SODAS
Telephone: (800) 295-1388
Web site: www.steaz.com
   Organic green tea sodas

SACKEL CORPORATION
Trop Coco, Kero Coco, and H₂ Coco
29 SW 5th Street
Pompano Beach, FL 33060-7901
Telephone: (800) 336-8470
Fax: (954) 784-6232
Web site: www.sackel.com
   Coconut water beverages

Tea and Coffee

GUAYAKI
P. O. Box 14730
San Luis Obispo, CA 93406
Telephone: (888) 482-9254
Web site: www.guayaki.com
   Organic Yerba Mate

CHOICE TEAS
Granum Inc.

Seattle, WA 98106
Telephone: (800) 882-8943
   Organic herbal teas

SELECT TEAS
1145 Shelly Court
Orange, CA 92868
Telephone: (714) 771-3317
   Organic herbal teas

ONE WORLD TEAS
Great Eastern Sun
Asheville, NC 28806
Telephone: (828) 665-7790
Web site: www.great-eastern-sun.com
   Organic Japanese teas

YOGI TEAS
Golden Temple Inc.
2545 Prairie Road
Eugene, OR 97402
Telephone: (800) 964-4832
Web site: www.yogitea.com
   Organic herbal teas

LONG LIFE TEAS
180 Vanderbilt Motor Parkway
Hauppauge, NY 11788
Telephone: (800) 645-5768
Web site: www.long-life.com
   Organic herbal teas

REPUBLIC OF TEA
8 Digital Drive, Suite 100
Novato, CA 94949
Telephone: (415) 382-3400
Web site: www.republicoftea.com
   Organic herbal teas

ORGANIC COFFEE COMPANY
1933 Davis Street, Suite 308
San Leandro, CA 94577
Telephone: (800) 829-1300
Web site: www.o-coffee.com

ANKE KRUSE ORGANICS INC.
14191 Crewson's Line
Acton, ON Canada L7J2L7
Telephone: (519) 853-3899
Web site: www.ankekruseorganics.ca
   Wild country organic coffee and coffee substitutes, as well as loose teas

GREEN MOUNTAIN COFFEE ROASTERS
33 Coffee Lane
Waterbury, VT
Telephone: (800) 545-2326

Web site: www.greenmountaincoffee.com

Certified organic coffees produced worldwide using sustainable agricultural practices

NUMI TEA
P. O. Box 20420
Oakland, CA 94620
Telephone: (510) 567-8903
Web site: www.numitea.com

Certified organic full-leaf teas and fresh herbs

AVALON ORGANIC COFFEE
P. O. Box 92830
Albuquerque, NM 87199
Telephone: (505) 856-5282
Web site: www.avaloncoffee.com

Certified organic coffees

ECOTEAS
P. O. Box 1192
Ashland, OR 97520
Telephone: (541) 482-7745
Web site: www.yerbamate.com

Certified organic Yerba Mate from Argentina

GROWERS FIRST
16191 Construction Circle West
Irvine, CA 92606
Telephone: (949) 551-1085
Web site: www.growersfirst.org

A nonprofit organization providing organic coffee, while helping those in need.

Snacks

ORGANIC CHOCOLATE SPREADS
Rejuvenate Foods
P.O. Box 8464
Santa Cruz, CA 95061
Telephone: (800) 805-7957
Web site: www.rejuvenative.com

JENNIE'S MACAROONS
2905 5th Street
Brooklyn, NY 11211
Telephone: (718) 384-2150
Web site: www.zerocarbsjenniesmacaroons.com

These snacks are made with only three ingredients: coconut, honey, and egg whites with a high amount of lauric acid. Available in many health food and grocery stores.

THE RAW WORLD
P. O. Box 116156
West Palm Beach, FL 33416
Telephone: (866) RAW DIET
Web site: www.therawworld.com

Raw food snacks. Available by mail order only.

GOVINDA'S RAW POWER
Raw Power Food
2651 Ariane Drive
San Diego, CA 92117
Telephone: (800) 900-0108
Fax: (619) 270-0696

A healthy snack made from germinated seeds and dried fruit. Available in some health food and grocery stores.

NUTIVA BARS
P. O. Box 1716
Sebastopol, CA 95473
Telephone: (800) 993-4367
Web site: www.nutiva.com

SILVER SPRING SUPPLEMENTS
2915 29th Avenue SW, Suite E
Tumwater, WA 98512
Telephone: (800) 520-1791
Web site: www.silverspringsupplements.com

GOPAL'S POWER STIX
P. O. Box 2160
Valley Center, CA 92082
Telephone: (866) 646-7257

Raw organic food sticks

REAL GREEN & REAL BERRY
395 Glen Ellyn Road
Bloomingdale, IL 60108
Web site: www.puresource.ca

High-energy food bars

BIO INTERNATIONAL
215 East Orangethorpe Avenue
Fullerton, CA 92832
Telephone: (800) 246-4685
Web site: www.organicfoodbar.com

ANKE KRUSE ORGANICS INC.
14191 Crewson's Line
Acton, ON, Canada L7J2L7
Telephone: (519) 853-3899
Web site: www.ankekruseorganics.ca

Wild Country organic honey and nut bars

Ice Cream

JULIE'S ORGANIC ICE CREAM
885 Grant Street
Eugene, OR 97402
Telephone: (480) 857-0865
Web site: www.oregonicecream.com
  Certified organic ice creams

Flavoring Extracts

FRONTIER HERBS
P. O. Box 299
Norway, IA 52318
Telephone: (800) 669-3275
Web site: www.frontiernaturalbrands.com

FLAVORGANICS
268 Doremus Avenue
Newark, NJ 07105
Telephone: (973) 344-8014
Web site: www.flavorganics.com

SIMPLY ORGANIC
P. O. Box 229
Norway, IA 52318
Telephone: (800) 669-3275
Web site: www.frontiernaturalbrands.com

Baking Products

RAPUNZEL PURE ORGANICS
2424 State Route 203
Valatie, NY 12184
Telephone: (518) 392-8620
Web site: www.rapunzel.com
  Organic dried baking yeast and organic cocoa powder

RUMFORD BAKING POWDER
Web site: www.clabbergirl.com/history_rumford.htm
  Aluminum-free baking powder

OETKER LTD.
2229 Drew Road
Mississauga, ON L5S 1E5, Canada
Telephone: (905) 678-1311
Web site: www.oetker.ca
  Certified organic baking powder and baking mixes

AH!LASKA
14855 Wicks Boulevard
San Leandro, CA 94577
Telephone: (510) 686-0110
Web site: www.nspiredfoods.com
  Certified organic cocoa powder and baker's chocolate

EQUAL EXCHANGE
251 Revere Street
Canton, MA 02021
Telephone: (781) 830-0303
Web site: www.equalexchange.com
  Certified organic cocoa powder

SUN ORGANIC
P. O. Box 409
San Marcos, CA 92079
Telephone: (888) 269-9888
Web site: www.sunorganicfarm.com
  Carob powder

WHOLESOME FOODS
8016 Highway 90-A
Sugar Land, TX 77478
Telephone: (281) 490-9582
Web site: www.wholesomesweeteners.com
  Certified organic confectioners sugar

Paper Products

BEYOND GOURMET
Olsson Trading Company
Stamford, CT 06902
  Unbleached coffee filters, parchment paper, and muffin holders

NATURAL VALUE
14 Waterthrush Court
Sacramento, CA 95831
Telephone: (916) 427-3784
Web site: www.naturalvalue.com
  Unbleached waxed paper

SEVENTH GENERATION
212 Battery Street
Burlington, VT 05401
Telephone: (800) 456-1191
Web site: www.seventhgeneration.com
  Unbleached paper towels, napkins, toilet paper, tissue

ENVISION
Ft. James Corporation
Deerfield, IL 60015
Telephone: (414) 435-8821
  Paper towels, toilet paper, tissue

Organic Spirits

ORGANIC WINE WORKS
Web site: www.organicwineworks.com
  The finest certified organic wines from around the world.

ALL ORGANIC LINKS
Web site: www.allorganiclinks.com/foods/
  wineandbeer/more2/.shtml
  Offers a complete listing of certified
organic beer and wine companies.

FREY VINEYARDS
14000 Tomki Road
Redwood Valley, CA 95470
Telephone: (800) 760-3739
Web site: www.freywine.com
  Certified organic, biodynamic, and
sulfite-free wines

FETZER VINEYARDS
Hopland, CA
Telephone: (800) 846-8637

Web site: www.fetzer.com
  Certified organic and sulfite-free
wines

OTTER CREEK BREWERY
793 Exchange Street
Middlebury, VT 05753
Telephone: (800) 473-0727
Web site: www.wolavers.com
  Certified organic beer

EEL RIVER BREWERY
1777 Alamar Way
Fortuna, CA 95540
Telephone: (707) 725-2739
Web site: www.climaxbeer.com
  Certified organic beer

Nutritional Supplements

Why are supplements so important? At no time in recorded history has the human body been exposed to such an extreme high level of toxins from our environment. Daily we are barraged with harmful, potentially carcinogenic pollutants through the air we breathe, the water we drink, and the foods we consume. From fifty to one hundred years ago, the nutrients derived from the foods we ate were significantly higher and more diverse, because the mineral-rich soil they were grown in had not yet been depleted by the commercial agro-chemical industry. Vital nutrient content in the foods consumed today can be as much as 30–90 percent less than what it once was.

So, it has become increasingly important that in addition to eating a healthy diet of organically produced foods, we supplement with the highest-quality nutritional formulas made from whole-food ingredient sources and lacto-fermented with active beneficial microorganisms and live enzymes. The following formulas meet and exceed these criteria. Many of these products are recommended in The Maker's Diet 40-Day Health Experience program.

Many of the companies and products listed in this section are available from health food stores, health practitioners, and physicians nationwide.

Living Multivitamin/Mineral With Homeostatic Nutrients

LIVING MULTI OPTIMAL
FORMULA BY GARDEN OF LIFE
Visit Garden of Life's Web site,
www.gardenoflife.com, or call (866) 465-0094 for
product information or for the retailer nearest you.
  Living Multi Optimal Formula is a
complete vitamin and mineral supplement that delivers superfoods to support your demanding nutritional needs.

This comprehensive whole food multi-nutrient formula contains fruits, vegetables, ocean plants, tonic mushrooms, botanicals, and ionic minerals including enzymes, antioxidants, amino acids, and Homeostatic Nutrient Complexes.

Cod Liver Oil

OLDE WORLD ICELANDIC COD
LIVER OIL BY GARDEN OF LIFE
Visit Garden of Life's Web site,
www.gardenoflife.com, or call (866) 465-0094 for

product information or for the retailer nearest you.

Olde World Icelandic Cod Liver Oil is one of nature's richest sources of vitamins A and D, which can play an important role in supporting cardiovascular health. To ensure that its naturally occurring ingredients remain intact, Olde World Icelandic Cod Liver Oil is always harvested from the pure cold waters of Iceland and is cold-processed using traditional methods.

Green Super Food

PERFECT FOOD BY GARDEN OF LIFE
Visit Garden of Life's Web site, www.gardenoflife.com, or call (866) 465-0094 for product information or for the retailer nearest you.

Perfect Food is the #1 selling green food in the Natural Products Industry, according to SPINS, and is a complete whole-food supplement that provides the essential vitamins and minerals your body needs. The Perfect Food formula is packed with antioxidant green grasses, micro-algae, sea vegetables, whole vegetables and their juices, sprouted grains, seeds, legumes, and acerola cherries. Perfect Food is ideal for those on low-carbohydrate diets who are unable to eat enough dark green leafy vegetables.

CORE FOOD BY SAGEANT
611 North Wallace Street
Bozeman, MT 59715
Web site: www.sageant.com

High-quality green super food providing a wide array of vegetable nutrients

FOODS FOR LIFE BY LIFE SCIENCE PRODUCTS
Web site: www.lifescienceproducts.com

High-quality green super food powder

Super Food Meal Replacements

LIVING FUEL RX
Telephone: (866) 580-3835 or (813) 254-5150
Web site: www.livingfuel.com
E-mail: info@livingfuel.com

Living Fuel Rx is a whole, raw, complete super-food meal replacement. It is a blend of organic, wild-crafted, and all natural foods that have been optimized with the most bio-available and usable nutrients available. It is a low-glycemic, nutrient dense, high-ORAC (antioxidant) foundational food for all blood and metabolic types. Living Fuel Rx is available in two formulas: Super Berry and Super Greens.

Whole-Food Fiber Blend

SUPER SEED BY GARDEN OF LIFE
Visit Garden of Life's Web site, www.gardenoflife.com, or call (866) 465-0094 for product information or for the retailer nearest you.

Super Seed is a vegetarian source of soluble and insoluble dietary fiber containing a whole-food blend of seeds, sprouted grains, and legumes. Every Super Seed ingredient is specifically chosen for its exceptional ability to enhance bowel health.

CORE FIBER BY SAGEANT
611 North Wallace Street
Bozeman, MT 59715
Web site: www.sageant.com

Core Fiber is a blend of whole-food fiber sources.

Morning and Evening Purification

ALPHA AM CLEANSE AND OMEGA PM CLEANSE BY GARDEN OF LIFE
Visit Garden of Life's Web site, www.gardenoflife.com, or call (866) 465-0094 for product information or for the retailer nearest you.

"Tune up the body" in support of overall health and vitality with these personal care products. Alpha AM Cleanse is a unique essential oil blend designed to refresh the body in the morning. Omega PM Cleanse is a unique essential oil blend designed to be used at night to prepare the body for rest.

Probiotic With Soil-Based Organisms

PRIMAL DEFENSE BY GARDEN OF LIFE
Visit Garden of Life's Web site, www.gardenoflife.com, or call (866) 465-0094 for

product information or for the retailer nearest you.

Primal Defense is the #1 selling probiotic in the Natural Products Industry according to SPINS. It is the only whole-food probiotic containing Homeostatic Soil Organism blends (HSOs). Unlike other probiotics, the key bacteria in Primal Defense can thrive in the toughest digestive environments and are undeterred by stomach acid.

Immune System Support

RM-10 BY GARDEN OF LIFE
Visit Garden of Life's Web site, www.gardenoflife.com, or call (866) 465-0094 for product information or for the retailer nearest you.

RM-10 is the #1 selling immune product in the Natural Products Industry according to SPINS. RM-10 is a combination of ten tonic mushrooms, balanced with aloe vera and the herb *Uncaria tomentosa* (cat's claw). Tonic mushrooms have been used for thousands of years, and now science has confirmed their tremendous value to health.

Antioxidant Formulas

FRUITS OF LIFE AND RADICAL FRUITS BY GARDEN OF LIFE
Visit Garden of Life's Web site, www.gardenoflife.com, or call (866) 465-0094 for product information or for the retailer nearest you.

Fruits of Life is a great-tasting, 100 percent natural blend of more than 21 nutrients, including antioxidant food concentrates of blueberries, raspberries, strawberries, and blackberries. Fruits of Life provides a unique blend of minerals and enzymes from goat's milk that support beneficial flora in the gastrointestinal tract.

Radical Fruits is a comprehensive blend of antioxidant-rich fruit extracts and alkalinizing minerals that provide a wide range of health benefits, such as neutralizing free radicals and protecting against oxidative stress in the body.

Fruits of Life and Radical Fruits are whole-food antioxidant blends rich in nutrients from berries and other fruits.

CORE PROTECT BY SAGEANT
611 North Wallace Street
Bozeman, MT 59715
Web site: www.sageant.com

Core Protect is a liquid antioxidant beverage with high-potency food source antioxidants.

Digestive Enzymes

Ω-ZYME BY GARDEN OF LIFE
Visit Garden of Life's Web site, www.gardenoflife.com, or call (866) 465-0094 for product information or for the retailer nearest you.

Ω-Zyme is the #1 selling digestive enzyme in the Natural Products Industry according to SPINS. The best way to get the enzymes you need is to consume a diet high in "live" raw and fermented foods, and to consume a digestive enzyme supplement such as Ω-Zyme. The more than 20 different digestive enzymes in Ω-Zyme help process proteins, carbohydrates, fats, and dairy.

Goat's Milk Protein Powder

GOATEIN BY GARDEN OF LIFE
Visit Garden of Life's Web site, www.gardenoflife.com, or call (866) 465-0094 for product information or for the retailer nearest you.

Goatein is an exceptional goat's milk protein powder. A source of eight essential amino acids (protein building blocks crucial to good health), Goatein is easy to digest and is well tolerated by those who cannot digest cow's milk.

Lifestyle Products (Hygiene and Essential Oils)

Essential oils are substances extracted from the petals, fruits, twigs, leaves, bark, root, herbs, and seeds of plants. They are used in a variety of ways to promote healing and to restore body, mind, and spirit to a state of balance and well-being.

More than 180 verses in the Bible refer to essential oils. The wise men brought frankincense and myrrh to the Christ child, Moses instructed that hyssop was to be mixed with lamb's blood prior to applying it to the doorpost, and spikenard was used to anoint the feet of Jesus. In biblical times, oils extracted from herbs and spices were used as a currency and considered to be as valuable or even more valuable than gold and precious jewels.

Modern-day therapeutic uses for aromatherapy include inhalation, compresses, massage, footbaths, saunas, insect repellents, perfumes, room fragrances, aromatic candles, and hair and skin care products. Babies and children can greatly benefit from the use of essential oils, but care should be taken to use the oils in greater dilution.

Caution should be taken to avoid using undiluted oils on your skin or in conjunction with homeopathic remedies, as they may compete with or neutralize the effects of these remedies.

Many of the products listed in this section are available at health food stores nationwide. To find a health food store near you that carries these and other fine products, visit www.gardenoflife.com/retail_locator.

Morning (a.m.) and Evening (p.m.) Biblical Aromatherapy

ALPHA AROMATHERAPY & OMEGA AROMATHERAPY BY GARDEN OF LIFE
Visit Garden of Life's Web site, www.gardenoflife.com, or call (866) 465-0094 for product information or for the retailer nearest you.

Garden of Life aromatherapy products feature all-natural, multi-beneficial essential oils to elicit a positive, healthy response. Alpha Aromatherapy is an invigorating morning blend to energize your mood, stimulate your mind, and boost your spirit. Omega Aromatherapy is a soothing blend that provides a pleasing, relaxing calm as you wind down for the night.

OSHADHI
1340-G Industrial Avenue
Petaluma, CA 94952
Telephone: (888) 674-2344
Web site: www.oshadhiusa.com
    Undiluted organic essential oils

TISSERAND
1105 Industrial Avenue
Petaluma, CA 94952
Telephone: (800) 227- 5120
Web site: www.avalonnaturalproducts.com
    Undiluted organic essential oils

WYNDMERE NATURALS
5417 Opportunity Court
Minnetonka, MN 55343
Telephone: (800) 207-8538

Advanced Hygiene Products

CLENZOLOGY ADVANCED HYGIENE SYSTEM BY GARDEN OF LIFE
Visit Garden of Life's Web site, www.gardenoflife.com, or call (866) 465-0094 for product information or for the retailer nearest you.

Clenzology is a revolutionary system of advanced hygiene products that help you support vibrant health by thoroughly cleansing the areas of your body most vulnerable to germs: hands, eyes, mouth, ears, and nose. Regular use of the Clenzology Advanced Hygiene System reinforces overall health and well-being, promotes vibrant, clear skin, and refreshes teeth and gums. Clenzology is available as a complete system or as individual products.

Exercise and Fitness

Eating healthy foods is only half the equation when embarking on the path of total physical health. Historically, the longest-lived, most robust cultures led very active lives. Today, modern civilization is oriented around office settings and more sedentary leisure time. As a result, functional fitness programs are required to help maintain physically fit, healthy bodies.

FUNCTIONAL FITNESS DVD BY GARDEN OF LIFE COMMUNICATIONS
770 Northpoint Parkway, Suite 100
West Palm Beach, FL 33407
Telephone: (800) 365-7709, (561) 472-9277
Fax: (561) 472-9296

Experience the energizing, enjoyable world of functional fitness exercise. Functional exercise teaches you to train whole body movements, not just isolated muscles. Increase fitness, coordination, flexibility, and agility. Decrease your chances of injury during daily activity. Featuring fun and easy routines that can be performed anywhere and anytime, functional fitness is great for people of any age or skill level. Presented by Garden of Life Communications, a premier provider of educational tools and services imparting lifestyle knowledge for everyone to achieve extraordinary health.

OPTIMUM PERFORMANCE SYSTEMS
438 NW 13 Street
Telephone: (561) 393-3881
Fax: (561) 417-8809
Web site: www.opsfit.com

Exercise videos, books, and programs for recreational, amateur, and professional athletes

REBOUND AIR
520 South Commerce Drive
Orem, UT 84058
Telephone: (888) 464-5867
Web site: www.reboundair.com

Supplies rebounders—great for low impact exercise.

LYMPHOLINE BY LIFE SOURCE INTERNATIONAL, LLC
1112 Montana Avenue, Suite 125
Santa Monica, CA 90403
Telephone: (310) 284-3565
Web site: www.lympholine.com

The LYMPHOLINE rebounder, while great for exercise, is also designed to act like the missing lymphatic pump in order to support detoxification.

HOLISTIC PERSONAL TRAINING SERVICES
1854 Hendersonville Road, PMB 171
Asheville, NC 28803
Telephone: (828) 231-7305
Fax: (828) 667-8001

Cellular exercise through rebounding. Call for special Maker's Diet discount.

Mental and Emotional Health

Physical health is dependent on mental and emotional health. Historically, the longest-lived, most robust cultures maintained excellent mental and emotional health. In today's fast-paced society, it is imperative that we "get a grip" on our emotions and learn to use stress as an ally, not an enemy.

TERRY LYLES, INC.
Telephone: (800) DR LYLES [(800) 375-9537]
Web site: www.terrylyles.com

Life coach, author, and psychologist Dr. Terry Lyles is a foremost expert in mental and emotional health. He is the author of *The Secret to Navigating Life's Storms.*

Spiritual Health

Spirituality is the fourth pillar of health. Each human being is on a quest for purpose. Connecting with God can provide true purpose in our lives.

IN TOUCH MINISTRIES
P. O. Box 7900
Atlanta, GA 30357
Telephone: (800) 789-1473
Web site: www.intouch.org

A worldwide ministry led by visionary pastor Dr. Charles Stanley that publishes a monthly magazine and devotional that helps lead us on a journey to find true purpose

Nontoxic Body Care Products

Your skin is your largest, most absorbent organ. Your choice of healthy body care products is as important as your choice of healthy foods. When determining whether or not to purchase a skin care product for use, ask yourself one basic question: "Would I feel safe if I ate these ingredients?" In effect, that is precisely what your skin is doing. Skin, much the same as your internal organs, doesn't always exhibit an immediate or obvious toxic reaction to a particular product or food. Toxicity in the body has a subtle, cumulative effect over time that unfortunately doesn't make itself known until it reaches critical mass and overburdens the system. So, the best insurance policy you can give your skin (which also feeds your whole body) is to choose the cleanest, most nontoxic skin and body care products on the market. Many of the companies and products listed in this section are available at health food stores nationwide. To find a health food store near you that carries these and other fine products, visit www.gardenoflife.com/retail_locator.

Skin and Body Care

AUBREY ORGANICS
4419 North Manhattan Avenue
Tampa, FL 33614
Telephone: (813) 877-4186
Web site: www.aubrey-organics.com

Aubrey Organics is the leading supplier of organic skin and body care products. The founder of Aubrey Organics, Aubrey Hampton, has been formulating and manufacturing skin and body care products for the last thirty years. Aubrey Organics is a voice for truth in the skin and body care industry. They produce hundreds of products—including skin care, hair care, soaps and cleansers, toothpaste, natural hair color, perfumes and colognes, and many more.

TROPICAL TRADITIONS
P.O. Box 333
Springville, CA 93265
Telephone: (866) 311-COCO (2626)
Web site: www.tropicaltraditions.com

Tropical Traditions supplies the highest-quality skin and body care products made from virgin coconut oil and other high-quality ingredients. Available by mail order and in select health food stores.

MYCHELLE DERMACEUTICALS
P. O. Box 1
Frisco, CO 80443
Telephone: (800) 447-2076
Web site: www.mychelleusa.com

MyChelle Dermaceuticals provides high-quality effective skin and body care products. MyChelle Dermaceuticals utilizes innovative fruit and vegetables and their enzymes to deliver outstanding results for both men and women.

COMMON SENSE FARM
41 North Union Street
Cambridge, NY 12816
Telephone: (518) 677-0224
Web site: www.commonsensefarm.com

LUMINA HEALTH PRODUCTS
3696 Walden Pond Drive
Sarasota, FL 34240
Telephone: (800) 749-9196
Fax: (941) 379-2572
Web site: www.luminahealth.com

Lumina Health Products is the supplier of Cellfood Oxygen Gel—a cell-oxygenating formula we recommend for its therapeutic skin benefits. The Cellfood product line takes an internal/topical approach to oxygenating and feeding the skin.

MIRACLE DISTRIBUTORS
P.O. Box 2455
Matthews, NC 28106
Telephone: (866) 567-2326
Web site: www.miracledistributors.com

Nontoxic soaps and cleansers great for hair, skin, and home.

WELEDA INC.
175 North Route 9
West Congers, NY 10920

Telephone: (845) 268-8599
Web site: www.weleda.com
  Spray deodorants

TERRESSENTIALS
2650 Old National Pike
Middletown, MD 21769
Telephone: (301) 371-7333
Web site: www.terressentials.com

SUKI'S NATURALS
740 Gulf Road
Northfield, MA
Telephone: (413) 498-5063
Web site: www.sukisnaturals.com

NATURE'S GATE/LEVLAD INC.
9200 Mason Avenue
Chatsworth, CA 91311
Telephone: (800) 327-2012
Web site: www.levlad.com

KISS MY FACE
P. O. Box 224
Gardiner, NY 12525
Telephone: (845) 255-0884
Web site: www.kissmyface.com
  We recommend their organic product line and olive oil bar soaps.

DR. BRONNERS
P. O. Box 28
Escondido, CA 92033
Telephone: (760) 743-2211
  Liquid soaps

JASON NATURALS
5500 West 83rd Street
Los Angeles, CA 90045
Telephone: (877) 527-6601
Web site: www.jason-natural.com

MEADOW STONE FARM
199 Hartford Road
Brooklyn, CT 06234
Telephone: (860) 617-2982
Web site: www.MeadowStoneFarm.com
  Fresh from the farm raw goat milk soaps, cremes, and salves. Organic pet cleaners/shampoos.

GRACE HARBOR FARMS, INC.
5157 Drayton Harbor Road
Blaine, WA 98230
Telephone: (360) 371-9060 or (866) 371-9060 (toll free)
Web site: www.graceharborfarms.com
  Goat milk soaps and lotions.

Bath Salts and Oils

COMMON SENSE FARM
41 North Union Street
Cambridge, NY 12816
Telephone: (518) 677-0224
Web site: www.commonsensefarm.com
  Excellent bath salts

DEAD SEA BATH SALTS
Masada
21133 Superior
Chatsworth, CA 91311
Telephone: (818) 717-8300
Web site: www.masada.spa.com

Skin Scrub Brushes

EARTH THERAPEUTICS
163 East Bethpage Road
Plainview, NY 11803
Telephone: (516) 777-7770
Web site: www.earththerapeutics.com

Nontoxic Hair Color

AUBREY ORGANICS
4419 North Manhattan Avenue
Tampa, FL 33614
Telephone: (813) 877-4186
Web site: www.aubrey-organics.com

LIGHT MOUNTAIN
P. O. Box 1008
Silver Lake, WI 53170
Telephone: (800) 548-3824
Web site: www.lotuslight.com

Sunscreens

GARDEN OF LIFE
Visit Garden of Life's Web site, www.gardenoflife.com, or call (866) 465-0094 for product information or for the retailer nearest you.
  Coconut oil has been traditionally used by tropical cultures to condition skin during and after sun exposure, and is widely incorporated into modern-day skin-care products for outdoor activities.

AUBREY ORGANICS
4419 North Manhattan Avenue
Tampa, FL 33614
Telephone: (813) 877-4186
Web site: www.aubrey-organics.com
  As mentioned earlier, your skin is your largest, most absorbent organ.

Would you eat or drink the ingredients in your sunscreens? Many commercial sunscreen ingredients are not only toxic, but also potentially carcinogenic. This is also true of many lotions, deodorants, and facial products.

Feminine Products

ORGANIC ESSENTIALS
822 Baldridge Street
O'Donnell, TX 79351
Telephone: (800) 765-6491
Web site: www.organicessentials.com
   Also producers of organic cotton balls and cotton swabs

NATRACARE
191 University Boulevard, Suite 294
Denver, CO 80206
Telephone: (303) 617-3476
Web site: www.natracare.com

LIFE-FLO
8126 North 23rd Avenue, Suite A
Phoenix, AZ 85021
Telephone: (602) 995-8715
Web site: www.life-flo.com
   Natural care for women and men

Dental and Gum Products

DENTIZYME
Natura Botanicals
Scottsdale, AZ 85260
Telephone: (800) 284-8880

WELEDA
175 North Route 9
West Congers, NY 10920
Telephone: (845) 268-8599
Web site: www.weleda.com

UNCLE HARRY'S
704 228th Avenue, N.E.
Redmond, WA 98053
Telephone: (425) 643-4664
Web site: www.uncleharrys.com

HERBS FOR KIDS
1441 West Smith Road
Ferndale, WA 98248
Telephone: (800) 232-4005
Web site: www.herbsforkids.com
   We recommend their Gumomile for inflamed gums.

ECO-DENT
3130 Spring Street
Redwood City, CA 94063
Telephone: (888) 326-3368
Web site: www.eco-dent.com

JASON NATURALS
5500 West 83rd Street
Los Angeles, CA 90045
Telephone: (877) 527-6601
Web site: www.jason-natural.com

SUSTAINABLE COMMUNITY DEVELOPMENT, LLC
P. O. Box 15155
Kansas City, MO 64106
Telephone: (913) 541-9299
Web site: www.scdworld.com
   All-natural products for human health and environmental sustainability

Organic Clothing

MAGGIE'S ORGANICS
1955 Pauline Boulevard, Suite 100-A
Ann Arbor, MI 48103
Telephone: (800) 609-8593
Web site: www.organicclothes.com

UNDER THE CANOPY
1141 South Rogers Circle, Suite 7
Boca Raton, FL 33487
Telephone: (888) 226-6799
Web site: www.underthecanopy.com
   World's largest source of modern and sophisticated organic fiber fashions for women, men, children, and home

HARMONY CATALOG
360 Interlocken Boulevard
Broomfield, CO 80021
Telephone: (800) 869-3446
   Mail order catalog containing a wide range of organic and alternative products for the home and body

MAMA'S EARTH
Telephone: (800) 620-7388
Web site: www.mamasearth.com
   Organic cotton and hemp clothing

TOMORROW'S WORLD
Telephone: (800) 229-7571
Web site: www.tomorrowsworld.com
   Organic cotton and hemp cloth

WILD AND WOOLY WEAR
Telephone: (303) 642-3144

Web site: www.wildandwoolywear.com
    Organic cotton clothing
GARDEN KIDS
Telephone: (541) 465-4544

Web site: www.gardenkids.com
    Children's organic cotton clothing

The Nontoxic Home

Making headlines in the news today are stories of people suffering from multiple chemical sensitivities (MCS) and a myriad of other workplace and home-related maladies. Children and pets are also at grave risk from the unseen toxins that permeate our school, work, and living spaces. Municipal water treatment, toxic cleaning fluids, improper lighting, chemically laden carpets and floor finishes, artificially scented room fresheners, perfumes and colognes, chemically treated bedding—as well as the misunderstood effects of electromagnetic influences from appliances, TVs, computers, hairdryers, and so on—pose hazards to which we expose ourselves every day. Cleaning up our personal environments should be of primary importance as part of an overall health program. Once you explore some of the resources in this section, you will be pleased to discover that there are many options offered by those who have traveled this road before you.

Many of the companies and products listed in this section are available at health food stores nationwide. To find a health food store near you that carries these and other fine products, visit www.gardenoflife.com/retail_locator.

Water Purification Systems

NATURALIZING WATER SYSTEM
P. O. Box 270
Ardmore, PA 19003
Telephone: (866) 663-8888
Web site: www.waterforwellness.us
    The highest-quality water purification options for your home, including countertop and whole-house filtration systems.

HARMONY CATALOG
360 Interlocken Boulevard
Broomfield, CO 80021
Telephone: (800) 869-3446
    Mail order catalog containing a wide range of organic and alternative products for the home and body

N.E.E.D.S
P. O. Box 580
E. Syracuse, NY 13057
Telephone: (800) 634-1380
Web site: www.needs.com
    Mail-order catalog containing a wide range of organic and alternative products for the home and body

NIKKEN INC.
52 Discovery

Irving, CA 92618
Telephone: (949) 789-2000
Web site: www.nikken.com
    Filters, plus exclusive PIMAG mineral restoration process creating living water

Shower Filters

NEW WAVE ENVIRO PRODUCTS
Web site: www.newwaveenviro.com

CARE FREE TECHNOLOGIES
2110-G McFadden Avenue
Santa Ana, CA 92705
Telephone: (714) 545-4500
Web site: www.carefreewater.com
    Catalytic water conditioner system

N.E.E.D.S
P. O. Box 580
E. Syracuse, NY 13057
Telephone: (800) 634-1380
Web site: www.needs.com
    Mail-order catalog containing a wide range of organic and alternative products for the home and body

SILVER SPRING SUPPLEMENTS
2915 29th Avenue SW, Suite E
Tumwater, WA 98512

Telephone: (800) 520-1791
Web site: www.silverspringsupplements.com

Mail-order catalog containing a wide range of organic and alternative products for the home and body

HARMONY CATALOG
360 Interlocken Boulevard
Broomfield, CO 80021
Telephone: (800) 869-3446

Mail order catalog containing a wide range of organic and alternative products for the home and body

---

Air Purifiers

PIONAIR AIR PURIFIERS
Telephone: (866) PIONAIR
Web site: www.pionair.net

The Pionair air purification system enhances the quality of air in the home and reduces harmful toxins such as yeasts, molds, bacteria, and debris.

AUSTIN AIR SYSTEMS
500 Elk Street
Buffalo, NY 14210
Telephone: (800) 724-8403
Web site: www.austinair.com

Removes both gases and odors. Medical HEPA and granulated carbon filters.

VENTA AIR WASH
180 Stanley Street
Elk Grove Village, IL 60007
Telephone: (847) 758-9598
Web site: www.venta-airwash.com

LIFE KIND CATALOG
P. O. Box 1774
Grass Valley, CA 95945
Telephone: (800) 284-4983
Web site: www.lifekind.com

HEALTH MORE
3631 Perkins Avenue
Cleveland, OH 44114
Telephone: (216) 432-1990
Web site: www.filterclean.com

SILVER SPRING SUPPLEMENTS
2915 29th Avenue SW, Suite E
Tumwater, WA 98512
Telephone: (800) 520-1791
Web site: www.silverspringsupplements.com

Mail-order catalog containing a wide range of organic and alternative products for the home and body

N.E.E.D.S.
P. O. Box 580
E. Syracuse, NY 13057
Telephone: (800) 634-1380
Web site: www.needs.com

Mail-order catalog containing a wide range of organic and alternative products for the home and body

HARMONY CATALOG
360 Interlocken Boulevard
Broomfield, CO 80021
Telephone: (800) 869-3446

Mail order catalog containing a wide range of organic and alternative products for the home and body

NIKKEN INC.
52 Discovery
Irving, CA 92618
Telephone: (949) 789-2000
Web site: www.nikken.com

Patented 5 filter systems, including HEPA 3 filter (the same as those used in operating rooms)

Dish and Laundry Detergents

SEVENTH GENERATION
212 Battery Street, Suite A
Burlington, VT 05401
Telephone: (802) 658-3773
Web site: www.seventhgeneration.com

BI-O-KLEEN
P. O. Box 2679
Clackamas, OR 97015
Telephone: (503) 557-0216
Web site: www.bi-o-kleen.com

SAL SUDS
Dr. Bronners
P. O. Box 28
Escondido, CA 92033
Telephone: (760) 743-2211

All-purpose cleaner; great for laundry, dishes, and general household cleaning

FLORA, INC.
805 East Badger Road
Lynden, WA 98264
Telephone: (800) 498-3610
Web site: www.florahealth.com

Turbo Plus Ceramic Laundry Discs

and Flora Brite papaya enzyme laundry additive and whitener

Cleaning Fluids

EARTH FRIENDLY PRODUCTS
44 Green Bay Road
Winnetka, IL 60093
Telephone: (800) 335-3267
Web site: www.ecos.com

LIFE TREE PRODUCTS
P. O. Box 40339
Santa Barbara, CA 93140
Telephone: (800) 347-5211
Web site: www.goturtle.com

HEATHER'S OXYGEN BLEACH
Jason Naturals
3515 Eastham Drive
Culver City, CA 90232
Telephone: (310) 838-7543
Web site: www.jason-natural.com
   Nontoxic alternative to cleansers

TKO ORANGE
Calgary, AL T2E 6T3, Canada
Telephone: (800) 995-2463
Web site: www.tkoorange.com
   All-purpose cleaner, stain remover, and odor remover made only from organic orange oil

SUSTAINABLE COMMUNITY DEVELOPMENT, LLC
P. O. Box 15155
Kansas City, MO 64106
Telephone: (913) 541-9299
Web site: www.scdworld.com
   All-natural, microbial-based products for human health and environmental sustainability

Natural Odor Removers

ZEOLITE DEPOT
P. O. Box 711
Montclair, NJ 07042
Telephone: (973) 979-3876
Web site: www.zeolitedepot.com
   Zeolites are lightweight volcanic stones, known to be the most odor-absorbent substance on earth! Scent-free and completely nontoxic, Zeolite products range from room deodorizers and carpet deodorizers to pet odor removers.

Organic Bedding

NATURA BED SYSTEMS
Nirvana Safe Haven
3441 Golden Rain Road, Suite 3
Walnut Creek, CA 94595
Telephone: (800) 968-9355
Web site: www.nontoxic.com/natura
   Wide selection of organic mattresses and futons

HEART OF VERMONT
P. O. Box 612
Barre, VT 05641
Telephone: (800) 639-4123
Web site: www.heartofvermont.com
   Great selection of handmade organic futons, blankets, sheets, and other organic bedding

HARMONY CATALOG
360 Interlocken Boulevard
Broomfield, CO 80021
Telephone: (800) 869-3446
   Mail-order catalog containing a wide range of organic and alternative products for the home and body

NIKKEN INC.
52 Discovery
Irving, CA 92618
Telephone: (949) 789-2000
Web site: www.nikken.com
   Bedding with magnetic and far infrared technologies

EMF Reducers

CUTTING EDGE CATALOG
P. O. Box 5034
Southampton, NY 11969
Telephone: (800) 497-9516
Web site: www.cutcat.com

REAL GOODS CATALOG
360 Interlocken Boulevard
Broomfield, CO 80021
Telephone: (800) 762-7325
   Mail-order catalog containing a wide range of organic and alternative products for the home and body

LESS EMF CATALOG
26 Valley View Lane
Ghent, NY 12075
Telephone: (888) 537-7363
Web site: www.lessemf.com

Full-Spectrum Lighting

SEVENTH GENERATION
212 Battery Street, Suite A
Burlington, VT 05401
Telephone: (802) 658-3773
Web site: www.seventhgeneration.com

CHROMALUX
Lumiram Electric Corp.
179 Westmoreland Avenue
White Plains, NY 10606
Telephone: (800) 354-5596
Web site: www.lumiram.com

Cookware and Household Appliances

GREEN MOUNTAIN SOAPSTONE
680 East Hubbardton Road
Castleton, VT 05735
Telephone: (802) 468-5636
Web site: www.greenmountainsoapstone.com/cookware

Soapstone cookware heats very quickly and has remarkable heat retention properties, which creates a more even cooking surface. Because soapstone is nonporous, it also has a natural nonstick surface.

VITA-MIX BLENDER
8615 Usher Road
Cleveland, OH 44138
Telephone: (800) 848-2649
Web site: www.vita-mix.com

High-quality durable blender excellent for smoothies and soups

LEHMAN'S GRAIN MILL
1 Lehman Circle
P. O. Box 321
Kidron, OH 44636
Telephone: (888) 438-5346
Web site: www.grainmills.com

COUNTRY LIVING GRAIN MILL
Telephone: (800) 321-2900
Web site: www.zyz.com/survivalcenter/mills

CF RESOURCES FERMENTING CROCKS
P. O. Box 405
Kit Carson, CO 80825
Telephone: (719) 962-3228
Web site: www.cfamilyresources.com/fermenting_crock

SALTON YOGURT MAKER
81-A Brunswick
Dollard-des-Ormeaux, QC H9B 2J5, Canada
Web site: www.salton.com

RONCO YOGURT MAKER & FOOD DEHYDRATOR
Telephone: (800) 486-1806
Web site: www.ronco.com

Nontoxic Paint

OSHADI
1340-G Industrial Avenue
Petaluma, CA 94952
Telephone: (707) 763-0662
Web site: www.oshadiusa.com

N.E.E.D.S.
P. O. Box 580
E. Syracuse, NY 13057
Telephone: (800) 634-1380
Web site: www.needs.com

Nontoxic Carpeting

NATURLICH FLOORING AND INTERIORS
7120 Keating Avenue
Sebastopol, CA 95472
Telephone: (707) 829-3959
Web site: www.floorguy411.com

Nontoxic wool carpets and other flooring

BUILDING FOR HEALTH
P. O. Box 113
Carbondale, CO 81623
Telephone: (800) 292-4838
Web site: www.buildingforhealth.com

Nontoxic carpets and other nontoxic building materials

HARMONY CATALOG
360 Interlocken Boulevard
Broomfield, CO 80021
Telephone: (800) 869-3446

Mail-order catalog containing a wide range of organic and alternative products for the home and body

Small Group Study

GARDEN OF LIFE COMMUNICATIONS SMALL GROUP STUDY
Garden of Life Communications
770 Northpoint Parkway, Suite 100

West Palm Beach, FL 33407
Telephone: (800) 365-7709, (561) 472-9277
Fax: (561) 472-9296
Web site: www.makersdiet.com

Educational Resources

MAKERSDIET.COM
Finally, a Diet You Can Have Faith In

Makersdiet.com is the complete online companion to the revolutionary new book *The Maker's Diet* from *New York Times* best-selling author Jordan S. Rubin.

Based on scriptural wisdom and scientific resources, The Maker's Diet is the only complete wellness program that helps you achieve your optimum level of personal health—physically, mentally, spiritually, and emotionally.

So much more than just a diet, The Maker's Diet also focuses on prayer, advanced hygiene, functional exercise, nutrition and supplements, and more. Makersdiet.com sheds light on these and other differences between The Maker's Diet and the countless fad diets we encounter almost daily.

Makersdiet.com also gives you access to the tools you need to maximize the results of your own individual 40-day health journey with The Maker's Diet. These tools include sample menus and suggested daily regimens, as well as tips for dining out and grocery shopping that support your Maker's Diet experience.

Makersdiet.com is also the place to go to learn more about best-selling author Jordan S. Rubin, his perspectives and writings on health and wellness, and current events or upcoming speaking engagements featuring the author.

WESTON A. PRICE FOUNDATION
4200 Wisconsin Avenue, NW
Washington, DC 20016
Telephone: (202) 333-4325
Web site: www.westonaprice.org

OPTIMAL WELLNESS CENTER
Web site: www.mercola.com

A health Web site by Dr. Joseph Mercola that includes an archive of Dr. Mercola's weekly health newsletters

THE WELLNESS JOURNAL
The Wellness Journal is a monthly e-newsletter empowering consumers with information on how to achieve extraordinary health of the body, mind, and spirit. Learn more about latest health trends, new products, delicious healthy recipes, and health tips. Subscribe at www.makersdiet.com.

Cookbooks

Nourishing Traditions (1999)
Sally Fallon and Mary Enig, Ph.D.
New Trends Publishing
Washington, DC

This well-researched and thought-provoking guide to traditional foods contains a startling message: animal fats and cholesterol are not villains but vital factors in the diet necessary for normal growth, proper function of the brain and nervous system, protection from disease, and optimum energy levels. Sally Fallon dispels the myths of the current low-fat fad in this practical, entertaining guide to a can-do diet that is both nutritious and delicious.

Topics include the health benefits of traditional fats and oils (including butter and coconut oil); dangers of vegetarianism; problems with modern soy foods; health benefits of sauces and gravies; proper preparation of whole grain products; pros and cons of milk consumption; easy-to-prepare enzyme-rich condiments and beverages; and appropriate diets for babies and children.

Lazy Person's Whole Food Cookbook
Web site: www.powerhealth.net

Educational Web Sites

www.westonaprice.org
www.makersdiet.com
www.eatwild.com
www.gardenoflife.com
www.mercola.com
www.terrylyles.com

Notes

Introduction

1. Statistics Related to Overweight and Obesity, NIDDK Weight-Control Information Network, http://www.niddk.nih.gov/health/nutrit/pubs/statobes.htm#other (accessed November 5, 2003).

Chapter 1: From Tragedy to Triumph: My Personal Journey From Sickness to Health

1. The premise of the Specific Carbohydrate Diet is that bacterial/fungal overgrowth causes damage to the intestinal walls in a vicious cycle that breaks down our health and immune systems. The goal of the diet is to eliminate certain carbohydrates containing sugars known as disaccharides (such as grains, sugar, dairy products, corn, and potatoes) that tend to nourish certain harmful bacteria and fungal species.

2. Digestive Disease Statistics, National Digestive Diseases Information Clearinghouse (NDDIC), a service of the National Institute of Diabetes and Digestive and Kidney Diseases, http://digestive.niddk.nih.gov/statistics/statistics.htm (accessed November 12, 2003).

3. Morton Walker, DPM, "Homeostatic Soil Organisms for One's Primal Defense," Medical Journalist Report of Innovative Biologics, *Townsend Letter for Doctors and Patients* (February/March 2001).

Chapter 2: The World's Healthiest People

1. Elmer A. Josephson, *God's Key to Health and Happiness* (Old Tappan, NJ: Fleming H. Revell Company, 1976), 160.

2. Rex Russell, M.D., *What the Bible Says About Healthy Living* (Ventura, CA: Regal Books, 1996), 68.

3. Peter Rothschild, M.D., Ph.D., unpublished book entitled *The Art of Health*.

4. "Strong's Electronic Concordance (KJV)," *PC Study Bible* software program, s.v. "*tame*." Copyright © 1989, TriStar Publishing. All rights reserved.

5. Josephson, *God's Key to Health and Happiness*, 47.

6. Ibid., 46.

7. Ibid., 49.

8. Rothschild, *The Art of Health*.

9. Dr. Michael D. Jacobson, *The Word on Health: A Biblical and Medical Overview of How to Care For Your Body and Mind* (Chicago: Moody Press, 2000), 11.

10. S. Lindeberg and B. Lundh, "Apparent Absence of Stroke and Ischaemic Heart Disease in a Traditional Melanesian Island: A Clinical Study of Kitava," *J Intern Med* 233 (1993): 269–275.

11. S. Lindeberg, et al., "Cardiovascular Risk Factors in a Melanesian Population Apparently Free From Stroke and Ischaemic Disease—the Kitava study," *J Intern Med* 236 (1994): 331–340.

12. M. Murray and J. Pizzorno, *Encyclopedia of Natural Medicine* (Rocklin, CA: Prima Publishing, 1998).

13. Albert Schweitzer, in his Preface to A. Berglas, *Cancer: Cause and Cure*, as quoted in James South, MA, "Laetrile—the Answer to Cancer," IAS Bulletin, http://www.antiaging-systems.com/extract/laetrile.htm (accessed November 17, 2003).

14. Vilhjalmur Stefanson, *Cancer: Disease of Civilization* (New York: Hill and Wang, 1960).

15. E. Dewailly, et al., "High Organochlorine Body Burden in Women With Estrogen Receptor-Positive Breast Cancer," *Journal of the National Cancer Institute* 86 (February 2, 1994): 232–234.

16. K. O'Dea, "Marked Improvement in Carbohydrate and Lipid Metabolism in Diabetic Australian Aborigines After Temporary Reversion to Traditional Lifestyle," *Lipids* 33 (1984): 596–603.

17. K. O'Dea, "Traditional Diet and Food Preferences of Australian Aboriginal Hunter-Gatherers," *Philosophical Transactions of the Royal Society of London, Series B* 334 (1991): 233–241.

18. Weston Price, *Nutrition and Physical Degeneration*, sixth ed. (Los Angeles: Price-Pottenger Foundation, 1939, 1997).

19. Ibid.

20. Ibid.

21. J. E. Buikstra, "The Lower Illinois River Region: A Prehistoric Context for the Study of Ancient Diet and Health," in M. N. Cohen and G. J. Armelagos, eds. *Paleopathology at the Origins of Agriculture* (Orlando, FL: Academic Press), 217–230.

22. A. H. Goodman, et al., "Health Changes at Dickson Mounds, Illinois," in Cohen and Armelagos, *Paleopathology at the Origins of Agriculture*, 271–305.

23. Michael Browning, "China's Taste for Critters May Have Aided SARS," *Palm Beach Post*, May 25, 2003.

24. Ibid.

Chapter 3: Life and Death in a Long Hollow Tube: The Importance of the GI Tract

1. *The Surgeon General's Report on Nutrition and Health*, U.S. Dept. of Health and Human Services (Public Health Service), 1988.

2. *Merriam-Webster's Collegiate Dictionary, Tenth Ed.* (Springfield, MA: Merriam-Webster, Incorporated, 1994), s.v. "gut."

3. Sandra Blakeslee, "Complex and Hidden Brain in Gut Makes Stomachaches and Butterflies," *New York Times*, January 23, 1996, emphasis mine.

4. Dr. Michael Gershon, *The Second Brain* (New York: HarperCollins, 1998), emphasis mine.

5. Ibid.

6. Michael Loes, M.D., M.D.(H.), *The Healing Response* (N.p.: Freedom Press, 2002).

7. *The Surgeon General's Report on Nutrition and Health*.

8. Ibid.

9. H. H. Boeker, "Autointoxication," *Medical Journal and Record* 128 (September 19, 1928): 293.

10. Ibid.

Chapter 4: Hygiene: The Double-edged Sword

1. S. I. McMillen, M.D. and David E. Stern, M.D., *None of These Diseases* (Grand Rapids, MI: Fleming H. Revell, 2000), 9–11, 13–14; citing excerpts from *The Edwin Smith Surgical Papyrus,* trans. James H. Breasted (Chicago: University of Chicago Press, 1930), 473–475.

2. Ibid., 25.

3. Unpublished literature from Kenneth Seaton, Ph.D., "Why the Need for Better Hygiene," www.advancedhygieneproducts.com/why_the_need_for_better_hygiene.shtml (accessed November 17, 2003).

4. Ibid.

5. Ibid.

6. P. Raeburn. "Down in the Dirt, Wonders Beckon: Soil and Sea Yield Unknown Lodes of Useful Microbes," *Business Week,* December 3, 2001.

7. Ibid.

8. Ibid.

9. Ibid.

10. M. Downey, "Let Them Eat Dirt," *Toronto Star,* January 10, 1999, F1.

11. Ibid.

12. William Campbell Douglass, M.D., *The Milk Book,* revised ed. (N.p.: Second Opinion Publishing, 1997.)

13. C. Pignata, et al., "Jejunal Bacterial Overgrowth and Intestinal Permeability in Children With Immunodeficiency Syndromes," *Gut* 31 (1990): 879–882.

14. A. Csordas, *Toxicology of Butyrate and Short-Chain Fatty Acids in Role of Gut Bacteria in Human Toxicology and Pharmacology,* M. Hill, ed. (Bristol: Taylor & Francis Inc., 1995), 286.

15. A. Hunnisett, et al., "Gut Fermentation (or the "Autobrewery") Syndrome: A New Clinical Test With Initial Observations and Discussion of Clinical and Biochemical Implications," *J Nut Med* 1 (1990):33–38.

16. V. M. Melfikova, et al., "Problems in Drug Prevention and Treatment of Endogenous Infection and Dysbacteriosis," *Vestn Ross Akad Med Nauk* 3 (1997): 26–29.

17. Joseph Mercola with Rachael Droege, "100 Trillion Bacteria in Your Gut: Learn How to Keep the Good Kind There," http://www.mercola.com/2003/oct/18/bacteria_gut/htm.

18. M. Walter, "Medical Innovative Biologics: Homoestatic Soil Organisms Support Immune System Functions From the Ground Up," *Townsend Letter for Doctors and Patients* (February/March 2001).

Chapter 5: How to Get Sick: A Modern Prescription for Illness

1. Russell, *What the Bible Says About Healthy Living,* 241.

2. Joseph Mercola, "Don't Let Sleep Pass You By," http://www.mercola.com/nograindiet/bottomline/sleep.htm (accessed November 18, 2003).

3. *Lancet* 354 (October 23, 1999): 1435–1439, as referenced in Joseph Mercola, "Too Little Sleep May Accelerate Aging," http://www.mercola.com/1999/archive/

sleep_and_aging.htm (accessed November 18, 2003).

4. Josephson, *God's Key to Health and Happiness*, 197.

5. David Steinman and Samuel S. Epstein, M.D., *The Safe Shopper's Bible: A Consumer's Guide to Nontoxic Household Products, Cosmetics, and Food* (New York: Hungry Minds, Inc., 1995), 265–266, 355, 427, 434; citing C. N. Martyn, et al, "Geographical Relation Between Alzheimer's Disease and Aluminum in Drinking Water," *Lancet* (January 14, 1989):59-62; H. D. Foster, "Aluminum and Health," *Journal of Orthomolecular Medicine* 7 (1992): 206–208; A. B. Graves, et al, "The Association Between Aluminum-Containing Products and Alzheimer's Disease," *Journal of Clinical Epidemiology* 43 (1990): 35–44; "OTC Topical Antimicrobial Products," *Federal Register* (January 6, 1978):1231–1232.

6. David Steinman, *Diet for a Poisoned Planet: How to Choose Safe Foods for You and Your Family* (New York: Harmony Books, a division of Crown Publishers, 1990), 225–226.

7. See Dr. H. J. Roberts, *Aspartame (NutraSweet): Is It Safe?* (Philadelphia: The Charles Press, Publishers, September, 1992).

8. Brian Bretsch, "Winter Brings Cold & Dry Itchy Skin," Barnes Jewish Hospital, http://www.barnesjewish.org/groups/default.asp?NavID+1014 (accessed January 5, 2004).

9. Steinman, *Diet for a Poisoned Planet*, 208–209.

10. Russell, *What the Bible Says About Healthy Living*, 215–216.

11. Dr. Vijendra Singh, Ph.D., reprinted from *AAPN, The Autism Autoimmunity Project Newsletter*, vol. 1, number 2, December 1999.

12. A. J. Wakefield, et al., "Ileal-Lymphoid-Nodular Hyperplasia, Non-Specific Colitis, and Pervasive Developmental Disorder in Children," *Lancet* 351 (February 28, 1998): http://www.thelancet.com/search/search.isa (accessed November 18, 2003).

13. "New Changes for Airline Medical Safety," http://www.mercola.com/2002/apr/20/airline_safety.htm.

14. Steinman and Epstein, *The Safe Shopper's Bible*, 159.

15. Ibid. Information summarized from detailed information presented on pages 181–192, 230.

16. "More Drug Company Conflict of Interest," http://www.mercola.com/2003/apr/2/drug_companies.htm.

17. BioProbe Frequently Asked Questions, http://www.bioprobe.com/faq.asp#top (accessed June 4, 2003).

18. Vivian Bradshaw Black, "Diet and Nutrition Principles," *Townsend Letter for Doctors and Patients*, December 2002, 106.

19. "Wearing Contacts Overnight Boosts Infection Risk," http://www.mercola.com/1999/archive/contacts_overnight_increase_infection.htm.

20. Steinman and Epstein, *The Safe Shopper's Bible*, 157–159, 384.

21. Ibid., 373–374.

22. Don Colbert, M.D., *Toxic Relief* (Lake Mary, FL: Siloam, 2001), 16.

23. Barbara Starfield, "Is US Health Really the Best in the World," *Journal of the American Medical Association* 284 (July 26, 2000): 483–485.

24. Ibid.

Chapter 6: The Desperate Search for Health

1. D. M. Eisenburg, et al., "Unconventional Medicine in the United States," *N Engl J Med* 328 (1993): 246–252, cited in "Report 12 of the Council on Scientific Affairs (A-97) Full Text," American Medical Association, June 1997, http://www.ama-assn.org/ama/pub/article/2036-2523.html (accessed June 5, 2003).

2. *"Fiscal Year 2001 President's Budget Request for the NCCAM,"* Stephen E. Straus, M.D., Director, National Center for Complementary and Alternative Medicine before the House Appropriations Subcommittee on Labor, HHS, Education and Related Agencies, Thursday, March 2, 2000, http://www.nccam.nih.gov (accessed June 5, 2003).

3. Ibid.

4. Stephen Byrnes, Ph.D., RNCP, "The Myths of Vegetarianism," *Townsend Letter for Doctors and Patients,* July 2000, revised January 2002.

5. Russell L. Smith, Diet, *Blood Cholesterol and Coronary Heart Disease: A Critical Review of the Literature,* vol. 2 (N.p.: Vector Enterprises, 1991).

6. Byrnes, "The Myths of Vegetarianism."

7. Robert Atkins, *Dr. Atkins' New Diet Revolution* (New York: Avon Books, 1992), 280–281.

Chapter 7: Seven Victims Find Victory

1. For more information on this subject, visit the Web site for PBS Healthcare Crisis: Who's at Risk? Managed Care, http://www.pbs.org/healthcarecrisis/managedcare.html (accessed November 20, 2003).

2. S. Konno, "Maitake D-fraction: Apoptosis Inducer and Immune Inhancer," *Alternative and Complementary Therapies* (April 2001): 102–107.

3. R. Chang, "Functional Properties of Edible Mushrooms," *Nutr Rev* 54 (1996): S91–93.

Chapter 8: Return to the Maker's Diet

1. Protein and Amino Acids, Origin of the Word "Protein," National Academy Press, http://books.nap.edu/books/0309063469/html/109.html (accessed August 19, 2003).

2. Sally Fallon with Mary G. Enig, Ph.D., *Nourishing Traditions: The Cookbook That Challenges Politically Correct Nutrition and the Diet Dictocrats,* second ed. (Washington, DC: New Trends Publishing, Inc., 1999), 26.

3. Ibid., 27, citing J. G. Webb, et al., *Canadian Medical Association Journal* 135 (October 1, 1986): 753–758.

4. Ibid., 29, citing J. J. Rackis, et al., *Qual Plant Foods Hum Nutri* 35 (1985): 232; Sally Fallon and Mary Enig, Ph.D., "Soy Products for Dairy Products—Not So Fast," *Health Freedom News,* September 1995; Sally Fallon and Mary Enig, Ph.D., *The Ploy of Soy* (San Diego, CA: Price-Pottenger Nutrition Foundation).

5. Ibid., citing M. DeBakey, et al., *JAMA* 189 (1964): 655–659; *Nutr Week* 21 (March 22, 1991): 2–3; A. Cohen, *Am Heart J* 65 (1963): 291.

6. Ibid., 11.

7. Ibid., citing U. Ravnskov, *J Clin Epidemiol* 51 (June 1998): 443–460; C. V. Felton, et al., *Lancet* 344 (1994): 1195.

8. Uffe Ravnskov, M.D., Ph.D., *The Cholesterol Myths* (Washington, DC: New Trends Publishing, Inc., 2000), from an excerpt citing A. G. Shaper, "Cardiovascular Studies in the Samburu Tribe of Northern Kenya," *American Heart Journal* 63 (1962):

437–442, http://www.ravnskov.nu/myth3.htm (accessed June 19, 2003).

9. Sally Fallon with Mary G. Enig, Ph.D., "Diet and Heart Disease—Not What You Think," *Consumer's Research*, July 1996, 15–19.

10. Russell, *What the Bible Says About Healthy Living*, 148, citing Udo Erasmus, *Fats That Heal, Fats That Kill* (Burnaby, B.C., Canada: Alive Books, 1994), 232–233.

11. Alfred J. Merrill, et al., *Ann Rev Nutr* 13 (1993): 539–559; as cited by Fallon and Enig, 29.

12. Mary G. Enig, Ph.D., *Trans Fatty Acids in the Food Supply: A Comprehensive Report Covering 60 Years of Research*, second ed. (Silver Spring, MD: Enig Associates, Inc., 1995); B. A. Watkins, et al., *Br Pouli Sci* 32 (December 1991): 1109–1119.

13. Fallon *Nourishing Traditions*, 23, citing Joseph D. Beasly, M.D., and Jerry J. Swift, M.A., *The Kellogg Report* (Annandale-on-Hudson, NY: The Institute of Health Policy and Practice, 1989), 144–145.

14. CNN.com: "Global Health Group: Slash Sugar Intake—Experts Want No More Than 10 Percent of Calories From Sugar," March 3, 2003, http://edition.cnn.com/2003/HEALTH/diet.fitness/03/03/fat.world.ap (accessed June 19, 2003).

15. Sugar Association Continues Disapproval of Release of Misguided Who Diet and Nutrition Report," Washington, DC—April 21, 2003, by The Sugar Association, http://www.sugar.org/ (accessed June 19, 2003).

16. "Choose a Diet Moderate in Sugars," National Agricultural Library, USDA, http://www.nalusda.gov/fnic/dga/dga95/sugars.html (accessed June 19, 2003).

17. Charlene Laino, WebMD Medical News; and Michael Smith, M.D., reviewer, "One in Three Kids Will Develop Diabetes," citing "American Diabetes Association 63rd Scientific Sessions, New Orleans, June 13–17, 2003; K. M. Venkat Narayan, M.D., chief of the diabetes epidemiology section, CDC; Judith Fradkin, M.D., director of diabetes, endocrinology and metabolic diseases, NIDDK," http://my.webmd.com/content/Article/66/79851.htm (accessed June 19, 2003).

18. See note 14.

19. Fallon, *Nourishing Traditions*, 25, citing David A. Jenkins, et al., *Am J Clin Nutr* 34 (March 1981): 362–366.

20. For more information, see Dr. Edward Howell, *Enzyme Nutrition* (Wayne, NJ: Avery Publishing Group, 1985.)

21. D. Burkitt, "Varicose Veins Among the Masai?" *Lancet* 1 (April 1973): 890.

22. Annelies Schoneck from *Des Crudites Toute L'Annee*, as cited in Fallon, *Nourishing Traditions*, 93.

23. Howell, *Enzyme Nutrition*.

24. "Consumer Research on Dietary Supplements," U.S. Food and Drug Administration, Center for Food Safety and Applied Nutrition, Consumer Studies Branch, http://vm.cfsan.fda.gov/~lrd/ab-suppl.html (accessed November 24, 2003).

25. Soon to be published research currently being conducted at Southwest College of Naturopathic Medicine and Arizona State University in Tempe, Arizona.

26. Weston A. Price, "Ancient Dietary Wisdom for Tomorrow's Children," The Weston A. Price Foundation, http://www.westonaprice.org/traditional_diets/ancient_dietary_wisdom.html (accessed November 24, 2003).

27. G. V. Skuladottir, et al., "Influence of Dietary Cod Liver Oil on Fatty Acid Composition of Plasma Lipids in Human Male Subjects After Myocardial Infarction," *J*

Intern. Med 228 (1990): 563–568.

28. Mary N. Megson, M.D. "Is Autism a G-Alpha Protein Defect Reversible With Natural Vitamin A?", http://www.whale.to/vaccines/autism35.html (accessed September 10, 2003).

29. Attaie, et al., *Journal of Dairy Science* 83 (2000): 940–944; Jensen, *Goat Milk Magic: One of Life's Greatest Healing Foods* (Escondido, CA:, n.p., 1994).

30. Park, *Journal of Dairy Science* 74 (1991): 3326–3333; J. A. Gamble, et al., "Composition and Properties of Goat's Milk as Compared with Cow's Milk," Technical Bulletin No. 671, United States Department of Agriculture, 209280 (1939): 40–41.

31. M. A. Mehaia, "Studies on Camel and Goat Milk Proteins: Nitrogen Distribution and Amino Acid Composition," *Nutrition Reports International* 39 (1989): 351–357.

32. G. F. W. Haenlein, "Goat Management: Lipids and Proteins in Milk, Particularly Goat Milk," Delaware Cooperative Extension, http://bluehen.ags.udel.edu/deces/goatmgt/gm-08.htm; L. S. Hinckley, "Quality Standards for Goat Milk," *Dairy, Food and Environmental Sanitation* 11(1991): 511–512.

33. Baum, et al., *Journal of Infectious Diseases* (2000); Patrick, et al., *Alternative Medicine Review* (1999).

34. Weston A. Price, "Nasty, Brutish, and Short?", Weston A. Price Foundation, http://www.westonaprice.org/traditional_diets/nasty_brutish_short.html (accessed November 24, 2003).

Chapter 9: You Are What You Think

1. Kevin Lehman, *Keeping Your Family Together When the World Is Falling Apart* (New York: Delacorte Press, Bantam Doubleday Dell Publishing Group, Inc., 1992), 273, citing David Elkind, *The Hurried Child*, rev. ed. (Reading, MA: Addison-Wesley, 1988), 42.

2. Ibid, 274.

3. Jacobson, *The Word on Health*, 166.

4. Ibid., 190, citing Research Update, Institute of HeartMath (Boulder Creek, CO: Institute of HeartMath, 1995).

5. J. Muller-Nordhorn and S. N. Willich, "Triggering of Acute Coronary Syndromes," *J Clin Cardiol* 3 (2000): 73, citing J. Leor, et al., "Sudden Cardiac Deaths Triggered by an Earthquake," *N Engl J Med* 334 (1996): 413–419; S. R. Meisel, et al., "Effect of Iraqi Missile War on Incidence of Acute Myocardial Infarction and Sudden Death in Israeli Civilians," *Lancet* 338 (1991): 660–661; J. D. Kark, et al., "Iraqi Missile Attacks on Israel: The Association of Mortality with a Life-Threatening Stressor," *Journal of the American Medical Association* 273 (19 April 1995): 1208–1210.

6. Jacobson, *The Word on Health*, 161, citing Rollin McCraty, "Stress and Emotional Health" (paper read at Steroid Hormones Clinical Correlates: Therapeutic and Nutritional Considerations, Chicago: February 25, 1996).

7. *The Merck Manual of Diagnosis and Therapy*, Section 16: Cardiovascular Disorders, Chapter 201—Arteriosclerosis, http://www.merck.com/pubs/mmanual/section16/chapter201/201a.htm (accessed June 13, 2003).

8. "Laughter 'Protects the Heart'," BBC News Online: Health, Wednesday, 15 November 2000, 16:23 GMT, http://news.bbc.co.uk/1/low/health/1024713.stm (accessed June 13, 2003).

9. McMillen and Stern, *None of These Diseases*, 175–177.

10. Ibid., 196.

11. Don Colbert, M.D., *What You Don't Know May Be Killing You!* (Lake Mary, FL: Siloam, 2000), 94–95; citing George Ritchey and Elizabeth Sherrill, *Return From Tomorrow* (Grand Rapids, MI: Baker Book House, 1979).

12. Ibid., 95.

13. Ibid., emphasis mine.

14. Dan Baker, *What Happy People Know* (Rodale Press, 2003).

15. WebMD Feature: "Make Room for Happiness," by Richard Trubo (reviewed by Brunilda Nazario, M.D., http://my.webmd.com/content/article/61/71452.htm (accessed November 24, 2003).

16. Jacobson, *The Word on Health*.

17. Andrea Braslavsky, WebMD Medical News Archive, reviewed by Dr. Jacqueline Brooks, May 23, 2001.

18. Ibid.

19. McMillen and Stern, *None of These Diseases*, 200.

20. Colbert, *What You Don't Know May Be Killing You!*, 92.

21. See note 8.

Chapter 10: Stop, Drop, and Roll

1. Mark and Patti Virkler, *Eden's Health Plan—Go Natural!* (Shippensburg, PA: Destiny Image Publishers, 1994), 64; citing Max Gerson, *A Cancer Therapy* (Bonita, CA: The Gerson Institute, 1990), 176–181.

2. Josephson, *God's Key to Health and Happiness*, 163.

3. Virkler, *Eden's Health Plan—Go Natural!*, 186, citing Lee Bueno, *Fast Your Way to Health* (Springdale, PA: Whitaker House, 1991), 94.

4. Arthur Wallis, *God's Chosen Fast: A Spiritual and Practical Guide to Fasting* (Fort Washington, PA: Christian Literature Crusade, 1968), 103–104.

5. Ibid., 104.

6. Fallon, *Nourishing Traditions*, 13, citing J. B. Ubbink, *Nutr Rev 52* (November 1994): 383–393.

7. Paul Chek, "The Power of Walking," C.H.E.K. Institute, http://www.chekinstitute .com/articles.cfm?select=38 (accessed June 14, 2003).

8. Juan Carlos Santana, M.Ed., CSCS, "The 4 Pillars of Human Movement: A Movement Approach to Exercise Design and Implementation," http://www.canfitpro.com/html/ documents/Santana-The4PillarsofHumanMovement.doc (accessed November 30, 2003).

9. For detailed information about the benefits and methods to instill deep breathing patterns, see Davis, Eshelman, and McKay, *The Relaxation and Stress Reduction Notebook*, 2nd ed. (New Harbringer Publications, 1982).

10. Morton Walker, D.P.M., "Jumping for Health," *Townsend Letter for Doctors* (n.d.).

11. Virkler, *Eden's Health Plan—Go Natural!*, 132, citing "Exercise: A Little Helps a Lot," *Consumer Reports on Health*, volume 6, number 8 (August 1994), 89.

Chapter 11: Biblical Medicine: Herbs, Essential Oils, Hydrotherapy, and Music Therapy

1. *Merriam-Webster's Collegiate Dictionary*, tenth ed. (Springfield, MA: Merriam-Webster, Incorporated, 1994), s.v. "herb."

2. Russell, *What the Bible Says About Healthy Living*, 198, citing David Darom, Ph.D., *Beautiful Plants of the Bible* (Herzlfia, Israel: Palphot, Ltd., n.d.).

3. Ibid., 201–202.

4. Ibid., 202; citing James R. Balch, M.D. and A. Phyllis Balch, C.N.C., *Prescription for Nutritional Healing* (Garden City, NY: Avery Publishing, 1990), 46.

5. James A. Duke, Ph.D., *Herbs of the Bible: 2000 Years of Plant Medicine* (Loveland, CO: Interweave Press, 1999), 8.

6. Ibid., 33–36.

7. Ibid., 47–49.

8. Ibid., 54–55.

9. Ibid., 77–80.

10. Ibid., 85–87.

11. Ibid., 93–95.

12. Ibid., 97–99.

13. Ibid., 109–111.

14. Ibid., 144–146.

15. Ibid., 119–121.

16. Ibid., 132.

17. Russell, *What the Bible Says About Healthy Living*, 198, citing Darom, *Beautiful Plants of the Bible*, 196.

18. Ibid., 152.

19. Ibid., 154–155.

20. Ibid., 163–165.

21. Ibid., 149–151.

22. Ibid., 170–172.

23. Gannet News Service, "Discovery Finds Myrrh Kills Cancer," *The Des Moines Register DM*, December 17, 2001.

24. Duke, *Herbs of the Bible: 2000 Years of Plant Medicine*, 179.

25. Ibid., 203

26. Ruth F. Rosevear, *Nutrition in Biblical Times* (Cincinnati, OH: Clifton Hills Press, Inc., 2000), 49, citing Diane Ward, *Smithsonian*, August, 1988, 106–107.

27. Duke, *Herbs of the Bible: 2000 Years of Plant Medicine*, 203–205.

28. Ibid., 210–212.

29. Ibid., 218–220.

30. David Stewart, Ph.D., *Healing Oils of the Bible* (Marble Hill, MO: Center for Aromatherapy Research & Education, 2002), xvi–xix, 96–113.

31. Ibid., 18.

32. Ibid., 287.

33. Ibid., 297.

34. Ibid., 291.

35. Joseph L. Garlington, *Worship: The Pattern of Things in Heaven* (Shippensburg, PA: Destiny Image Publishers, 1997), 9.

Chapter 12: The Maker's Diet:
Your 40-Day Health Experience

1. The Purpose Factor, taken from www.terrylyles.com. Used by permission.

Index